Liisa H. Malkki

# PURITY AND EXILE:

VIOLENCE, MEMORY, AND NATIONAL COSMOLOGY
AMONG HUTU REFUGEES IN TANZANIA

The University of Chicago Press
*Chicago & London*

The University of Chicago Press, Chicago 60637
The University of Chicago Press, Ltd., London
© 1995 by The University of Chicago
All rights reserved. Published 1995
Printed in the United States of America
15 14 13 12 11 10 09 08 07 06    6 7 8 9 10

ISBN: 0-226-50271-6 (cloth)
0-226-50272-4 (paper)

Library of Congress Cataloging-in-Publication Data

Malkki, Liisa Helena.
   Purity and exile : violence, memory, and national cosmology among
Hutu refugees in Tanzania / Liisa H. Malkki.
      p.  cm.
   Includes bibliographical references and index.
   1. Hutu (African people)—Tanzania—Ethnic identity.  2. Refugees,
Political—Burundi.  3. Refugees, Political—Tanzania.  I. Title.
DT499.3.H88M35  1995
305.896′39461—dc20                                94-37099
                                                  CIP

In memory of
**Marja-Liisa Malkki**
and
**Eino Jokinen**

and

**for**
**Aila, Elias, and Hélène**

# Contents

# Narrative Panels

## Acknowledgments

This book has grown out of a dissertation submitted to the Department of Anthropology, Harvard University, in June 1989. It is based on one year (October 1985–October 1986) of anthropological fieldwork in Rukwa and Kigoma Regions in western Tanzania, funded by the Academy of Finland. The Academy of Finland has made this study possible by providing many years of financial support, not only for the field research, but also for much of my graduate study at Harvard University and for a short archival research trip to Belgium in the summer of 1987. The Department of Anthropology at Harvard University enabled a preliminary research trip to Tanzania in January of 1984 through a Travel Grant, and also supported the writing up of the study through the Social Science Dissertation Fellowship. During two crucial years of revising, I was supported by a postdoctoral Grant for Advanced Area Research from the Africa Program of the Social Science Research Council (1990–91), and by a postdoctoral fellowship at the Michigan Society of Fellows, University of Michigan, Ann Arbor (1990–91).

The arch of thanks and gratitude encompassing all those who have offered help, advice, and kindness during the many stages of this study is so great that it could not fit in the space of a few pages.

My most profound debt is to all those people in Mishamo and Kigoma whose words and actions gave form to this study. I want to thank them for the generosity and good faith with which they created a space for me in their midst, and for the thoughtfulness and interest they showed toward my study. They let me see forms of courage and kindness which continue to impress upon me how privileged I was in having walked into their lives. I would also like to give special thanks to the many people there who have corresponded with me and kept me abreast of events through the past seven years.

In Dar-es-Salaam, Dr. Benson Nindi, Chairman of the Department of Sociology at the University of Dar-es-Salaam, provided invaluable help in the application for research clearance and in acting as the local academic supervisor of my research project. The Ministry of Home

Affairs of the United Republic of Tanzania made it possible for me to gain permission to work in Mishamo and Kigoma and also generously gave me the use of one of the staff houses in Mishamo. The National Scientific Research Council of Tanzania (Utafiti) allowed me to take the first step by granting me research clearance. Also in the capital, Tellervo and Rauno Ekholm kindly supplemented my assortment of provisions before the departure for western Tanzania.

Mr. J. Lyimo, Settlement Commandant and chief representative of the Ministry of Home Affairs in Mishamo, extended his kind cooperation, for which I am grateful. Mr. Lyimo's entire family were always ready with help and advice. The staff of the Ministry of Home Affairs in Mishamo, as well as in Kigoma, facilitated the progress of the research and helped to make my stay enjoyable.

At the Tanganyika Christian Refugee Service (TCRS), Egil Nilssen, Vijay Gaikwad, Catherine Rotte-Murray and Jan Rotte, Nasim Sayed, Gibson Mwakambonja, Edwin Ramathal, Ruth Hombach, Tony Waters, Carolus and Wilma Poldervaart, Ricky and Willem van Gogh, Monique Gautier, and numerous other people extended hospitality and advice. They also provided valuable assistance in offering me the use of the TCRS wireless radio and other facilities, in relaying mail, in locating documents, and in many other ways. I learned a great deal from conversations with the TCRS staff in Dar-es-Salaam as in western Tanzania. I also thank TCRS for furnishing the maps, and Rosemary Boyd for redrawing them for reproduction in this book.

At the office of the United Nations High Commissioner for Refugees (UNHCR), Emmanuel Owusu, Mukda and Daniel Bellamy, Cornelius and Yvonne van Laarhoven, Oluseyi Bajulaye, Evelyn Warioba, Robert G. White, Arafa Rajabu, Eadie Moran, and many others extended further assistance in matters of practical importance and offered companionship which was much appreciated.

The Norwegian Agency for International Development (NORAD) in Kigoma kindly allowed me to rent one of its houses for the duration of the research in Kigoma. At the "NORAD compound," I want to thank, especially, Helge Høve and Joëlle Rouget.

I first learned of Mishamo from Nicholas van Praag, who, at the time, worked at the office of the United Nations High Commissioner for Refugees in Washington.

For encouragement and support, critical insights, and helpful suggestions during the formulation of this study I would like to thank many friends and colleagues, among them Peter Nobel, Emily Martin, Allen Armstrong, Sven Hamrell, Jane Guyer, Marcel D'Hertefelt, Marja-Liisa Swantz, and Sharon Stephens. Here I would also like to take the opportunity to thank those who first created a nurturing, exciting academic environment in which to discover anthropology: A. Thomas Kirsch, Carol Greenhouse, and James Boon.

Sections and preliminary versions of this study were commented on with care and great thoughtfulness by the late F. M. Rodegem, the late Hilda Kuper, Jennifer Robertson, Karen Leonard, Jean Lave, Maria Teresa Koreck, Monique Djokič, and Frederick Bailey. I have profited greatly from my discussions with all of them. But, most of all, I have benefited from the abiding generosity and always kind critical eye that René Lemarchand has brought to his readings of this manuscript.

I am grateful to the members of my dissertation committee—Sally Falk Moore, Stanley Tambiah, Nur Yalman, and Charles Lindholm—for their encouragement, insight, and friendship over many years. My debts to them can never be repaid or forgotten. To Sally Falk Moore I would like to express my appreciation and respect for her always principled guidance, her fine ways of thinking and questioning, and, above all, her loyalty. Her influence on my work has been profound.

Much of the rethinking and rewriting that went into this book happened during one wonderful year at the Michigan Society of Fellows and the Department of Anthropology, University of Michigan, Ann Arbor. I would like to thank all my colleagues at Michigan, but most especially Ann Stoler, Roy Rappaport, John Pemberton, Fernando Coronil, Uzoma Esonwanne, Geoff Eley, Sherry Ortner, Roger Rouse, Valentine Daniel, Frederick Cooper, and Jane Burbank. At a late rewriting stage at the University of California, Irvine, Deborah Mindry's assistance in library research, as well as her intellectual companionship, were also much appreciated.

I would like to thank the following for their generous assistance in locating documentation for the Postscript, written in April 1994: Christine Nieuwenkamp, René Lemarchand, Michael Burton, Akhil Gupta, Armi Malkki, Timo A. Malkki, Eric Kaldor, Jane Ferguson, Erica Bornstein, Tony Waters, Catherine Rotte-Murray, Jan Rotte, Lloyd Dakin, Jeff Sharlet, Curt Goering, Bernhard Staub, and Paddy McGuinness.

Deep-running intellectual and personal debts of gratitude are due to Jim Ferguson, Jean Comaroff, John Comaroff, Olli Alho, John Borneman, George Bisharat, Roberto Kant de Lima, Melchior Mbonimpa,

Purnima Mankekar, Akhil Gupta, and Laurie Kain Hart. Jim Ferguson read every chapter of this study, and his insights were crucial in shaping it. The curiosity and seriousness which he brings to anthropology and to his life have enriched my life immeasurably.

Map 1. Burundi, showing place names mentioned by informants.

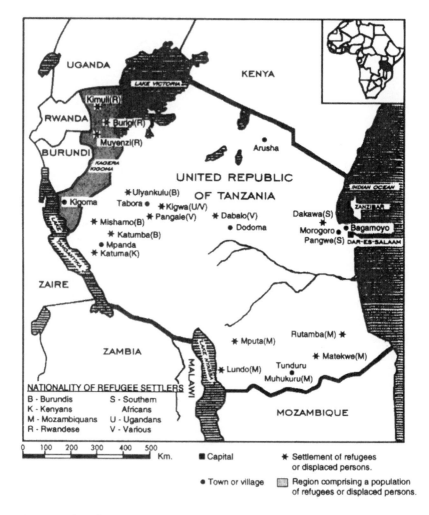

Map 2. Main refugee settlements / transit camps in Tanzania. Source: Armstrong (1987) for the Tanganyika Christian Refugee Service.

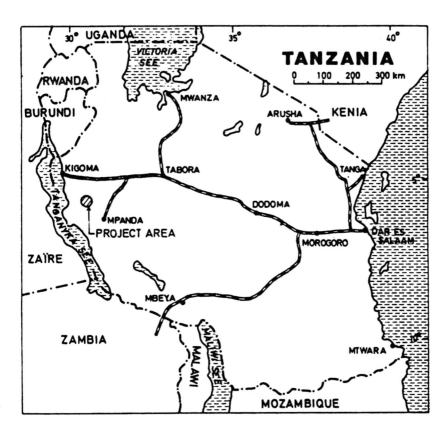

Map 3. Tanzania railway lines in relation to Mishamo. Source: Agrar-
und Hydrotechnik GMBH (1978:3).

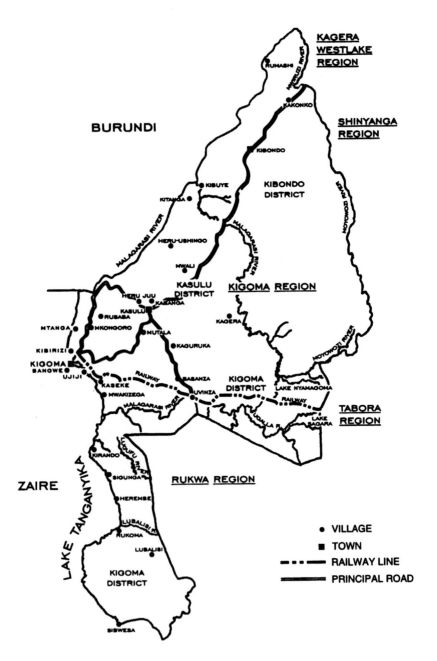

Map 4. Kigoma Township and Region.

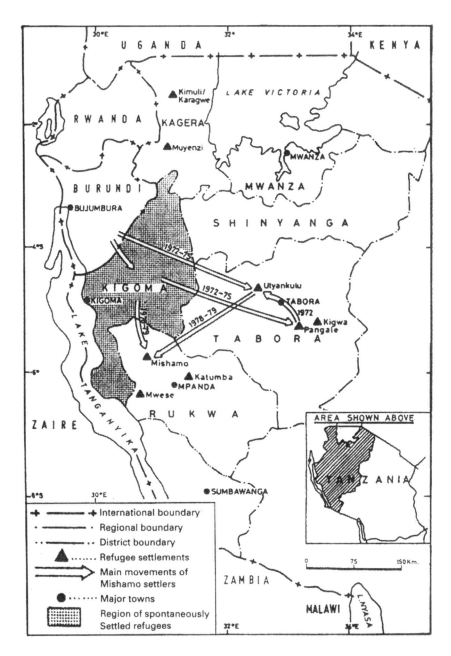

Map 5. Movements of Hutu refugees in Tanzania (1972–79). Source: Armstrong (1985) for the Tanganyika Christian Refugee Service.

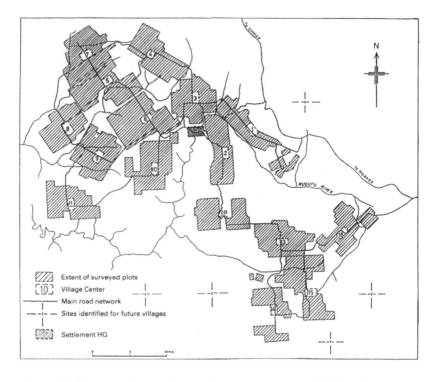

Map 6. Mishamo, settlement layout. Source: Armstrong (1985:1) for
the Tanganyika Christian Refugee Service.

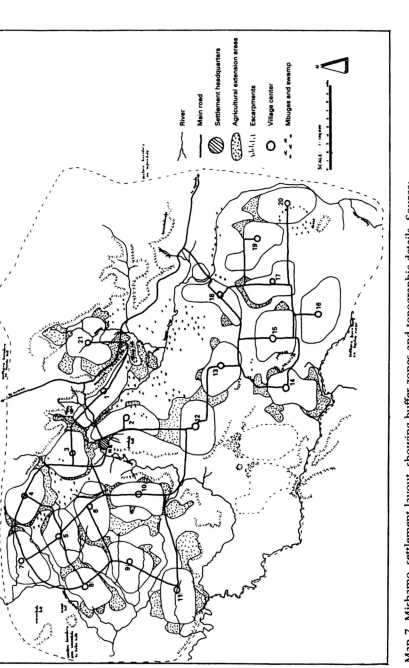

Map 7. Mishamo, settlement layout, showing buffer zones and topographic details. Source: UNHCR/TCRS (1982:77).

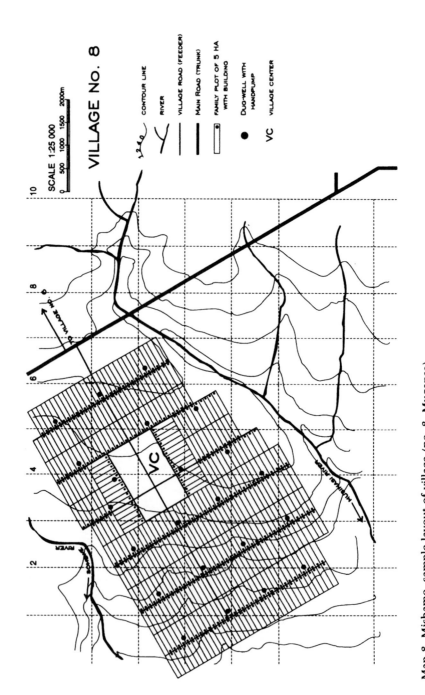

Map 8. Mishamo, sample layout of village (no. 8, Mugansa).

# AN ETHNOGRAPHY OF DISPLACEMENT IN THE NATIONAL ORDER OF THINGS

Depending on one's vantage point, this study can be read in a number of different ways. It is, first of all, an ethnography. But it is not an ethnography of any eternal place or "its people," nor is its aim to give a comprehensive account of the social life of "a community." Instead, and in quite a different spirit, this book trains its ethnographic lens on a much more specific set of processes and relationships. In particular, it is concerned to explore how displacement and deterritorialization—conditions which are "normal" for increasingly large numbers of people today—may shape the social construction of "nationness" and history, identity and enmity. The construction of a national past is a construction of history of a particular kind; it is one that claims moral attachments to specific territories, motherlands or homelands, and posits time-honored links between people, polity, and territory.[1] How such collective histories come to challenge one another, or to engage in struggles over history and truth, can become a particularly challenging question among refugees and other displaced people. It is precisely the interstitial position of refugees in the system of nation-states that makes their lives uniquely clarifying and enabling for the anthropological rethinking of nationness, of statelessness, and of the interconnections between historical memory and national consciousness. This book, then, is *an ethnography of processes and interconnections.*

Exploring questions of identity and history among people who by virtue of their "refugeeness" occupy a problematic, liminal position in the national order of things—an order which, despite its historical recency, presents itself as ancient and natural (Anderson 1991 [1983]: 14; Renan 1990; Balibar and Wallerstein 1991)—opens up new theoretical spaces for anthropological inquiry. Working in social settings of displacement invites in a very direct way the further questioning of the anthropological concepts of culture, society, and community as bounded, territorialized units. Similarly, one is led to question the notion of identity as a historical essence rooted in particular places, or as a fixed and identifiable position in a universalizing taxonomic order (e.g., in a world order of nationalities). Work in such sites also generates new, urgent ways of asking old questions about the relations between history and culture, violence and dehumanization, and, finally, even between culture and humanity.

## THE HUTU IN EXILE

The people who appear as refugees in this book lived until the spring of 1972 in the central African state of Burundi. In 1972, the Burundi army, controlled by members of the minority Tutsi ethnic group, initiated mass killings of the majority ethnic group, the Hutu, in response to an attempted Hutu rebellion on 29 April. An estimated 100,000, or 3.5 percent of the country's population at the time, were killed within a few weeks (Lemarchand and Martin 1974:5). These massacres were part of a long history of oppression and inequality between Hutu and Tutsi in Burundi. The historical background to this, one of the most appalling episodes of political violence in Africa or anywhere, is outlined in the following chapter. More recent conflicts in the region—particularly the mass violence of 1993 in Burundi and 1994 in Rwanda—are discussed in the Postscript.

I did one year of anthropological field research (1985–86) in rural, western Tanzania, with two groups of Hutu refugees who had fled the mass killings of 1972 in Burundi. One group was settled in a carefully planned, physically isolated refugee camp named Mishamo Refugee Settlement, while the other lived in the less regimented setting of Kigoma township on Lake Tanganyika (see map 3). Living outside of any camp context, these "town refugees" tended to be dispersed in nonrefugee neighborhoods. Comparison of the camp and township settings revealed radical differences in the meanings that people ascribed to national identity and history, to notions of home and homeland, and to exile as a collectively experienced condition.

The most unusual and prominent social fact about the camp was that its inhabitants were continually engaged in an impassioned construction and reconstruction of their history as "a people." The narrative production of this history ranged from descriptions of the "autochthonous" origins of Burundi as a "nation" and of the primordial social harmony that prevailed among the originary inhabitants (the Twa and the Hutu), to the coming of the pastoral Tutsi "foreigners from the north," to the Tutsi theft of power from the "natives" (Hutu and Twa) by ruse and trickery, and, finally, to the culminating mass killings of Hutu by Tutsi in 1972. These narratives, ubiquitous in the camp, formed an overarching historical trajectory that was fundamentally also a national story about the "rightful natives" of Burundi. The camp refugees saw themselves as a nation in exile, and defined exile, in turn, as a moral trajectory of trials and tribulations that would ultimately empower them to reclaim (or create anew) the "homeland" in Burundi.

In contrast, the town refugees had not constructed such a categorically distinct, collective identity. Rather than defining themselves collectively as "the Hutu refugees" (or even just as "the Hutu"), they tended to seek ways of assimilating and of inhabiting multiple, shifting identities—identities derived or "borrowed" from the social context of the township. Here, identities were like "porous sieves" (Tambiah 1986:6) to move in and out of, and assimilation was always intricately situational. In the course of the everyday, those in town were creating not a heroized national identity, but rather a lively cosmopolitanism—a worldliness that led the camp refugees to see them as an impure, problematic element in the "total community" of the Hutu refugees heroized as a people in exile.

The opposition between the historical-national thought of the camp refugees and the cosmopolitan ways of the town refugees made it possible to discern how the social, imaginative processes of constructing nationness and identity can come to be influenced by the local, everyday circumstances of life in exile, and how the spatial and social isolation of refugees can figure in these processes.[2] For the camp had become a central means of asserting separateness from "other" categories, of resisting any form of "nationalization," and was in this sense a locus of categorical purity. Never intended as such by its architects, the camp had become the most central place from which to imagine a "pure" Hutu national identity.[3] The irony of this was, as I will

3

argue below, that in the national order of things, refugeeness is itself an aberration of categories, a zone of pollution.

Identifying themselves as a people in exile, the camp refugees responded to their own displacement from the national order by creating another nation. The town refugees' response to displacement was radically different and in the end perhaps more subversive: they dissolved national categories in the course of everyday life and produced more cosmopolitan forms of identity instead.

Displacement and deterritorialization in the contemporary order of nations always present at least two logical possibilities. The first is that a liminal collectivity tries to make itself "fit" into the overarching national order, to become a "nation" like others. This was the case in the camp (although, ironically, people there deployed their very refugeeness in an effort to achieve this). The second possibility entails an insistence on, and a creative exploitation of, another order of liminality. This constitutes a sweeping refusal to be categorized, a refusal to be fixed within one and only one national or categorical identity, and one and only one historical trajectory. This is, precisely, a subversion of *identification*, of the implicit taxonomic process that makes it appear that the most natural and authentic identities people can have are those most resembling species identities—and that we have only to learn the appropriate signs, characteristic markings, or traits in order to correctly identify this or that person or group as a representative of a type or kind.

What emerges in this case is a study, not just of liminality or marginality in general, but of two quite specific, locally situated liminalities that were intimately related to each other and yet irreconcilably opposed. For the camp refugees perpetuated and reified that very categorical order in terms of which they were displaced, while the town refugees' lives seemed to have the effect of challenging and dissolving totalizing, essentializing categories.

CLASSIFICATION AND LIMINALITY: ON BEING OUT OF CATEGORY IN
ANTHROPOLOGY AND IN THE NATIONAL ORDER OF THINGS

Refugee camps are not, of course, a routine site for ethnographic fieldwork, and displaced people are not the usual "native informants" of anthropologists. And yet, as this study will show, fieldwork among refugees almost necessarily speaks to profound riddles and questions that live at the very heart of the discipline. One classic analytic arena, the anthropological study of classification and categories, has—as it turns out—much to say about some key dynamics in the social construction of refugeeness in the contemporary world order (not only in Africa but all over the world).

The ways in which the contemporary system of nation-states composes a hegemonic topography,[4] an "ultimate verity" (Herzfeld 1987:13), has been explored from diverse angles by Balibar and Wallerstein (1991), Anderson (1991:3), Arendt (1973:294), Appadurai (1990, 1991), Chatterjee (1986), Gilroy (1991), Wright (1985), Spencer (1990), Kapferer (1988), Handler (1988), and others. All of these theorists have in one way or another suggested that the modern system of nation-states requires study, not just as a political system narrowly understood, but as a powerful regime of order and knowledge that is at once politico-economic, historical, cultural, aesthetic, and cosmological. Anderson's appeal to anthropology reflects this reality: "nationalism has to be understood by aligning it, not with self-consciously held political ideologies, but with the large cultural systems that preceded it, out of which—as well as against which—it came into being" (Anderson 1991 [1983]:19). Bhabha's introduction to *Nation and Narration* (1990:1) refers to the nation as "a system of cultural signification." (I would suggest that the "system" is to be found less at the level of the single nation than that of "relations among relations"—the whole relational constellation of imagined national communities.) Balibar's analysis of what he calls "the nation form" is likewise empowering for rethinking the nation as a transnational cultural form (Balibar and Wallerstein 1991: 86–106; cf. Appadurai 1990). Jonathan Spencer's (1990) analysis of the unsettling similarities between nationalist and scholarly constructions of culture in Sri Lanka, in turn, suggests how profoundly influential the nation form has been as a generative order of knowledge. Elsewhere (Malkki 1989:13ff.; 1992a:37; 1994), I have attempted to indicate in what sense exactly the modern system of nation-states has come to be a natural order of things in many dimensions of human lives. It is in this spirit that I have suggested that we think not just of national*ism*, but of *a national order of things*. The phrase is intended to describe "a class of phenomena that is deeply cultural and yet global in its significance" (Malkki 1992a:37)—to underscore that the nation is always associated with particular places and times, yet simultaneously constitutes a supralocal, transnational cultural form (Appadurai and Breckenridge 1988:1ff.).

One of the generalized, global aspects of the nation is its social life as a powerful regime of classification, an apparently commonsensical system of ordering and sorting people into national kinds and types. The national order of things obviously does not just involve making order in a trivially aesthetic or folklorically ritual sense. Making national order implies aesthetics and ritual, certainly, but it is also a continual, taken-for-granted exercise of power (Watts 1992:117)—or, as one might say, adapting Foucault (1972b), a naturalizing physics of power that is at once micro-political and monumental in scale.

The intent here is to map out some of the analytical advantages of seeing the national order of things as a categorical order, as a matter of "the fundamental operation of classification" (Balibar 1990:290); and of politicizing the anthropological study of classification—following theorists such as Foucault (1972), Balibar and Wallerstein (1991), Anderson (1991:163–185), Mitchell (1992:289ff.), Dirks (1992: 5–6), and others. This project seeks to make a specifically anthropological contribution to the study of nationness, then, through exploring the status of nations as a *categorical order*, and the effects of that kind of classification on the essentialization, aestheticization, policing, and historical transformation of our social and political identities.

One of the most illuminating ways of getting at the categorical quality of the national order of things is to examine what happens when this order is challenged or subverted. Refugees can represent precisely such a subversion. They are an "abomination" (Douglas 1966) produced and made meaningful by the categorical order itself, even as they are excluded from it.

The question of categories and their aberrations has, of course, a long history in anthropology. The work done on classification and rites of passage, liminality and pollution, by van Gennep (1960), Douglas (1966), Turner (1967), Tambiah (1985), and others is remarkably applicable to the study of the ways in which order and liminality are constituted in the national order of things.[5]

In his pioneering work, van Gennep defines rites of passage as "rites which accompany every change of place, state, social position and age" (van Gennep 1960, cited in Turner 1967:94),[6] and demonstrates that all such rites are composed of three phases: rites of separation (*séparation*), rites of transition (*marge* or *limen*),[7] and rites of incorporation (*agrégation*) (1960:11,vii).[8] Turner's essay "Betwixt and Between: The Liminal Period in *Rites de Passage*" (1967:582ff.) further develops some of van Gennep's key formulations. It also provides a particularly apt comment on the problem of what Turner (1967:95–96) conceptualizes as "structural invisibility":

The subject of the ritual passage is, in the liminal period, structurally, if not physically, "invisible." As members of society, most of us see only what we expect to see, and what we expect to see is what we are conditioned to see when we have learned the definitions and classifications of our culture. [. . .] The structural "invisibility" of liminal *personae* has a twofold character. They are at once no longer classified and not yet classified.

This is, in fact, a concise statement of some key reasons for the systematic invisibility of refugees in the literature on nations and nationalism, as in the familiar old anthropology of "peoples and cultures": refugees are at once no longer classified and not yet classified. They are no longer unproblematically citizens or native informants. They can no longer satisfy as "representatives" of a particular local culture. One might say they have lost a kind of imagined cultural authority to stand for "their kind" or for the imagined "whole" of which they are or were a part.

The structural invisibility of refugees in anthropology and political theory is transformed into a particular kind of markedness in the domain of policy—in the discursive and other practices of the states and nongovernmental agencies that manage or administer programs for refugees, and for which refugees are a focal object of intervention and knowledge. It is from this point that anthropological analysis of the refugee category as unclassified/unclassifiable can be initiated, in a direction that Turner's analysis (1967:97) already suggests: "transitional beings are particularly polluting, since they are neither one thing nor another; or may be both; or neither here nor there; or may even be nowhere (in terms of any recognized cultural topography), and are at the very least 'betwixt and between' all the recognized fixed points in the space-time of cultural classification."

The danger or pollution posed by statelessness or refugeeness to the categorical order of nation-states corresponds quite neatly to the processes studied by Mary Douglas in *Purity and Danger* (1966). Refugees are seen to hemorrhage or weaken national boundaries and to pose a threat to "national security,"as is time and again asserted in the discourse of refugee policy.[9] Here, symbolic and political danger cannot be kept entirely distinct. Refugees are constituted, in Douglas's sense

(1966), as a dangerous category because they blur national (read: natural) boundaries, and challenge "time-honoured distinctions between nationals and foreigners" (Arendt 1973:286).[10] At this level, they represent an attack on the categorical order of nations which so often ends up being perceived as natural and, therefore, as inherently legitimate.

But there is a big difference between "matter out of place" in the classification of plants and animals and "matter out of place" when people are in question. For people categorize back. The social and political significance of refugee status for the Hutu exiled in Tanzania attests to this. As this book will show, the Hutu refugees lived at some level within categories that were not of their own making, but they also subverted these categories, to create new ones. The possibility of such creative subversion and aberration is, of course, already written into the classificatory processes themselves. "The encoding and enactment of classifications and cosmologies as performative blueprints and exemplars inevitably generates puzzles, anomalies, liminal categories, vacant and fuzzy spaces which may be seen as requiring correctives and avoidances or as enabling creative constructions and transformations" (Tambiah 1985:4).

REFUGEES, HUMANISM, AND HISTORY

Asylum states and international agencies dealing with refugees, as well as much of the policy-oriented, therapeutic literature on refugees, tend to share the premise that refugees are necessarily "a problem." Not just "ordinary people," they are constituted, rather, as an anomaly requiring specialized correctives and therapeutic interventions. It is striking how often the abundant literature claiming refugees as its object of study locates "the problem" not first in the political oppression or violence that produces massive territorial displacements of people, but within the bodies and minds of people classified as refugees.

This interiorization—making it appear that there are specific empirical features or personal traits that render this or that person recognizable as a refugee—is related to another aspect of the literature: the universalization of the figure of "the refugee." "The refugee" has come to be an almost generic, ideal-typical figure—so that it is not uncommon to see references to "the refugee," "the refugee experience" (Benard 1986; Stein 1981b:64, 1981a:320, Benthall 1980), "the refugee mentality" (Benard 1986:629), "refugee psychology" (Norwood 1969, vol. 2:468), and so on. Thus, for example, we are told by one refugee specialist that "despite the diversity among refugees," "refugees should be seen as a *social-psychological type*" (Stein 1981a:64). And as the refugee has become idealized and generalized as a type of person, he or she has also become an object of *specialization*. A whole internationally standardized way of discussing people who have been displaced across national frontiers has emerged in the course of the last several decades, as I have tried to show in previous work (Malkki 1985, 1992b).

The generalization and problematization of "the refugee" may be linked to yet another process, that of the discursive *externalization* of the refugee from the national (and, one might say, cosmological) order of things. Some examples may clarify this process. In a study of post–World War II refugees, Stoessinger (1956:189) notes the importance of studying "the peculiar psychological effects arising from prolonged refugee status," and stresses that "such psychological probings constitute an excursion into what is still largely *terra incognita*." The title of a more recent article reflects a comparable perception of the strangeness and unfamiliarity of the world peopled by refugees: "A Tourist in the Refugee World" (Shawcross 1989:28–30). The latter is a commentary in a photographic essay on refugees around the world, entitled *Forced Out: The Agony of the Refugee in Our Time* (Kismaric 1989). Finally, Michael Walzer, in a study of disobedience, war, and citizenship (1970: 146), writes, "Just beyond the state there is a kind of limbo, a strange world this side the hell of war, [. . .] prisoners [of war] and refugees belong alike to the limbo world." Excursions into terra incognita, guided tours in "the refugee world," the image of being "forced out," and the limbo world: all these point to the externality of "the refugee" in the national order of things.[11] Refugees live—not here, in this (national) world, this functionalist dream of a Family of Nations—but somewhere "on the outside" (cf. van Gennep 1960; Turner 1967; Arendt 1973).

The tendency to universalize "the refugee" as a special "kind" of person occurs not only in the textual representation of refugees, but also in their photographic representation. This is not the setting for a lengthy exploration of the visual representation of displacement by scholars, journalists, humanitarian organizations, fund raisers, international agencies, or others, but it is relevant to indicate some of the themes and questions that might be explored here. The first observation that can be made is that photographic portrayals of refugees are, in our day, extremely abundant. Most readers have probably seen such photographs, and most of us have a strong visual sense of what "a refugee" looks like. At the very mention of the word, we may be transported in our mind's eye to the Somalia of 1993, or to the fractured ruins of what was Yugoslavia, and find there "the refugee," captured by the journalist's camera as a singularly expressive emissary of horror and powerlessness.[12]

Such photographs—even while displaying differences and "cultural diversity" among refugees—tend toward documenting experiences and activities that are understood to be universally human. In a recent book entitled *Refugee Women*, for example, most of the photographs chosen by the author portray women engaged in some kind of productive, nurturing, or virtuous activity (Forbes Martin 1992). Captions under the pictures include the following:

Palestinian woman with child (p. 6)
Ethiopian women carrying firewood (p. 8)
Vietnamese woman with a rice cup (p. 18)
Central American woman with an identity card (p. 25)
Central American woman with two children (p. 32)
Iraqi woman making bread (p. 34)
Afghan woman with child seeing a doctor (p. 39)
African woman spinning (p. 41)
African children with school books (p. 46)
Central American women making fishing nets (p. 48)
Southeast Asian woman in a vegetable garden (p. 53)
Palestinian woman sewing (p. 55)
African woman with sewing machine (p. 57)
Beneficiary of loan to open small shop (p. 59)
Mexican Guatemalan refugees [cooking] (p. 73)
Integration. African women tilling land (p. 75)
Southeast Asian children watching TV (p. 84)
Iraqi women learning German with a teacher (p. 86)

A similar array of pictorial themes appears in a 1985 wall calendar entitled "Refugee Women" put out by the United Nations High Commissioner for Refugees (UNHCR). There is one beautiful, glossy color photograph for each month. All of the pictures depict one of three things: close-up portraits of individual women; women cradling babies or children; and women sewing, weaving, cooking, etc.

While it is a commonly agreed-upon fact that most refugees are women and children, it is nevertheless quite remarkable how pervasive

is the portraiture of women and children in the overall visual representation of displacement.[13] Having looked at photographs of refugees over
several years, one becomes aware of the perennial resonance of the
woman with her child. This is not just any woman; she is composed
as an almost madonnalike figure.

Perhaps it is that women and children embody a special kind of
powerlessness; perhaps they do not tend to look as if they could be
"dangerous aliens"; perhaps their images are more effective in fund-
raising efforts than those of men. One thing does seem to be certain:
children are a crucial element in the representation of refugees. Review
of contemporary photographs of refugees would seem to suggest that
children have come to embody, more easily than adults, the universalism of a bare humanity. The intent here is not to make a definitive
statement about what these photographs might mean to different people, or how they get used; it is, rather, to signal the operation of a
humanistic, universalizing representational practice that should be
studied further.

The discursive constitution of the refugee as bare humanity is
associated with a widespread a priori expectation that, in crossing an
international border, he or she has lost connection with his or her culture and identity. One refugee specialist, for example, states categorically, "All refugees will confront the loss of their culture, their identity,
their habits" (Stein 1981a:67). Another writes: "the culture of the refugees and displaced persons has already been tampered with" (Forbes
Martin 1992:12). This image of the loss or distortion of culture is also
reflected in an article entitled "Involuntary International Migration,"
which claims that there is a "remarkable similarity between the needs
of the new immigrant and those of the newborn human being" (David
1969:78). The image of the infant as *tabula rasa* is only one in an
extensive repertory of references to a basic humanity in the contemporary policy-oriented and humanitarian literature on refugees. An infant—a powerless being with no consciousness of history, traditions,
culture, or nationality—embodies this elementary humanity.

Here, of course, we return once more to Turner's famous characterization of liminal personae as "naked unaccommodated man," "un-
differentiated raw material" (1967:98–9). Refugees, liminal in the categorical order of nation-states, fit this description. Arendt also saw this
political and cosmological fact about displacement in the national order
of things when she wrote of the refugees of the Second World War that

"the abstract nakedness of being nothing but human was their greatest danger" (Arendt 1973:300).

One vital underpinning of the generalization and universalization of the refugee in contemporary therapeutic discourses on refugees is to be found, then, in the common assumption that "the refugee"—apparently *stripped of the specificity of culture, place, and history*—is human in the most basic, elementary sense. The refugee as bare humanity stands, we imagine, for all of us at our most naked and basic level. This imagined loss of specificity is one more refraction of the liminality of the refugee in the national order of things—an order premised precisely on a vision of "culture in neat and tidy national formations" (Gilroy 1990b:268); on the wholeness and boundedness of nation, culture, people, and society; on the possibility of a "play of substitutions between race, people, culture, and nation" (Balibar in Balibar and Wallerstein 1991:26); and, finally, on the territorial rooting of histories and political loyalties (cf. Walzer 1970:147). Refugees confront this order as a symptom of its own fragility and endangerment.

This humanistic universalization of "the refugee" as an embodiment of pure humanity (and as a pure victim) is suggested in the following words by the Refugee Secretary of the All-Africa Council of Churches, Melaku Kifle: "It is the refugee who reveals to us the defective society in which we live. He is a kind of mirror through whose suffering we can see the injustice, the oppression and the maltreatment of the powerless by the powerful" (cited in Oxfam America 1984:1).

The "defective society" to which Kifle refers would seem to be an imagined universal human society: the family of man, not a specific historical location. References to a common humanity such as Kifle's are numerous in the therapeutic discourse on displacement. One point of entry into the wider meaning of such discursive invocations of, or appeals to, a common humanity can be found in Barthes's (1992[1957]) review of the famous exhibition of photographs, "The Family of Man".[14]

A big exhibition of photographs has been held in Paris, the aim of which was to show the universality of human actions [. . .]. We are at the outset directed to this ambiguous myth of the human "community," which serves as an alibi to a large part of our humanism. This myth functions in two stages: first the difference between human morphologies is asserted, exoticism is insistently stressed, the infinite variations of the species, the diversity in skins, skulls, and customs are made manifest, the image of Babel is complacently projected over that of the world. Then, from this pluralism, a type of unity is magically produced: man is born, works, laughs and dies everywhere in the same way; and if there still remains in these actions some ethnic peculiarity, at least one hints that there is underlying each one an identical "nature," that their diversity is only formal and does not belie the existence of a common mould. Of course this means postulating a human essence, and here is God reintroduced into our Exhibition (Barthes 1992[1957]:100).

Everything in the exhibit, Barthes observes, *"aims to suppress the determining weight of History: we are held back at the surface of an identity, prevented precisely by sentimentality from penetrating into this ulterior zone of human behaviour where historical alienation introduces some 'differences' which we shall here quite simply call 'injustices'"* (1992[1957]:101; emphasis added). Barthes might just as well have been writing about the humanistic (textual and photographic) representation of "the refugee." The universalism of the "Family of Man" depoliticizes fundamental inequalities and injustices in the same manner that the homogenizing, humanitarian images of refugees work to obscure their actual sociopolitical circumstances—erasing the specific, historical, local politics of particular refugeees, and retreating instead to the depoliticizing, dehistoricizing register of a more abstract and universal suffering.

*This myth of the human "condition" rests on a very old mystification, which always consists in placing Nature at the bottom of History.* Any classic humanism postulates that in scratching the history of men a little [. . .], one very quickly reaches the solid rock of a universal human nature. Progressive humanism, on the contrary, must always remember to reverse the terms of this very old imposture, constantly to scour nature, its "laws" and its "limits" in order to discover History there, at last to establish Nature itself as historical (Barthes 1992[1957]:101; emphasis added).

Just as there are good reasons for seeing humanity in historical terms, so, too, is it necessary to radically historicize our visions of culture and identity, and to cease digging down toward imagined sources of deep, originary essence.

Barthes's observations, made in Europe of the 1950s, find a contemporary counterpart in Balibar's seminal essay "Paradoxes of Universality," where he contrasts "a secular wisdom that subordinates the idea of human beings to that of nature" to an "analysis of social conflict and liberation movements that substitutes *specific social relations* for the generality of human beings and the human species" (1990:289, emph. added). Where Barthes wrote about the naturalization of history, Balibar analyzes the essentialization of culture. Balibar—in the context of characterizing the new "racism without races" that he and others have recently observed in Europe[15]—identifies a contemporary tendency to essentialism that he terms "anthropological culturalism" (Balibar and Wallerstein 1991:21). This is a perspective "entirely orientated towards the recognition of the diversity and equality of cultures—with only the polyphonic ensemble constituting human civilization [. . .]" (Balibar and Wallerstein 1991:21).[16] He recognizes that this vision "provided the humanist and cosmopolitan anti-racism" of the post-Second World War period "with most of its arguments" (Balibar and Wallerstein 1991:21). (And this recognition is, perhaps, also of relevance to the "Family of Man" exhibition.) Nevertheless, in the present historical moment, Balibar is right: constituting cultural differences as insurmountable and positing essential properties for pregiven "peoples"—as the anthropological vision of "peoples and cultures" and "culture gardens" (Fabian 1983) is wont to do—readily gets appropriated by new racisms that center upon immigration, alienness, and the objectifying and policing of difference. Similar critiques have been made by Rushdie (1991), Ghosh (1989), Anzaldua (1987), and others.

In fact, the consequences of the vision of ethnic differences as rooted in essential differences between species-like "types" or "peoples" is a vital and tragic part of the story that this book will tell. As will be shown, there is a chilling traffic back and forth between the essentialist constructions of historians, anthropologists, and colonial administrators, and those of Hutu and Tutsi ethnic nationalists. "Types" and "traits" incautiously and sometimes fancifully ascribed by social scientists and bureaucrats have often taken on a terrible social reality as the reification and essentialization of cultural difference have been harnessed to deadly political visions. The links between what I will call the mythico-historical knowledges of the antagonists in the struggle for Burundi and the essentialization of cultural/racial constructions of social science recur as an unsettling motif in the ethnography to follow.[17]

Paul Gilroy's concept of "ethnic absolutism" is a profoundly helpful way of reconceptualizing issues of culture and identity in this context. Ethnic absolutism, Gilroy explains, is "a reductive, essentialist understanding of ethnic and national difference which operates through *an absolute sense of culture so powerful* that it is capable of separating people off from each other and diverting them into social and historical locations that are understood to be mutually impermeable and incommensurable" (Gilroy 1990a:115).[18]

The urgency of Gilroy's argument derives from his effort to understand the current historical moment in Britain where the "confluence of 'race,' nationality, and culture" acts continually to vitalize and empower a "contemporary politics of racial exclusion" (1990a:114) so that black British citizens are fundamentally externalized from the "national body."[19]

For the present purposes, his argument performs other work, as well. It enables one to see, through the lens of displacement, how problematic the nationalizing or ethnicizing of identity and culture can be, and it punctures "the related notion that unchanging essences of ethnic and national distinctiveness are automatically, though mysteriously, produced from their own guts" (Gilroy 1990a:116). "These ideas can be effectively counterposed," Gilroy continues, "to forms of identity and struggle developed—of necessity—by dispersed peoples for whom nationality, ethnicity and the nation-state are perhaps not so tightly associated and for whom the condition of exile becomes a privilege rather than a handicap" (1990a:116). Certainly, not all displaced people are led to challenge ethnic absolutism—on the contrary, I will argue that *some* circumstances of exile may positively *produce* it. And the Hutu refugees in Tanzania could hardly be described as "privileged." But the central idea, that displacement may enable a different and sometimes subversive reshuffling of nationalist verities, is well supported in what follows.

If territorially "uprooted" people are so easily seen as "torn loose from their culture" (Marrus 1985:8),[20] as I have argued elsewhere (1992a), this is only because culture is itself a profoundly territorialized (and even a quasi-ecological[21]) concept in so many settings. As Clifford (1988:338) observes: "Common notions of culture" are biased "toward rooting rather than travel." Violated, broken roots signal an ailing cultural identity and a damaged nationality. In this logic, the ideal-typical refugee is like a native gone amok. (Cf. Arendt 1973:302.)[22] And in uprooting, a metamorphosis occurs: The territorializing metaphors of identity—roots, soils, trees, seeds—are washed away in human floodtides, waves, flows, streams, and rivers. These liquid names for the uprooted reflect the sedentarist bias in dominant modes of imagining homes and homelands, identities and nationalities.[23]

Insofar as *"culture can also function like a nature"* (Balibar 1991: 22) that fixes people in native places and pure points of origin (Hebdige 1987:10, cited in Malkki 1992a:37), "uprootedness" becomes profoundly unnatural, and perhaps the ultimate human tragedy. In the words of Albert Schweitzer: "This is *the worst violation* of historic truths and of the rights of man: when the right to their homeland is denied to certain human beings so that they are forced to leave their homesteads" (Norwood 1969, vol. 2:468; emphasis added).

But as the pages to follow will show, understanding displacement as a human tragedy and looking no further can mean that one gains no insight at all into the lived meanings that displacement and exile can have for specific people, in this case the Hutu refugees from Burundi. In addition to the differing experiences and thoughts that individual persons might have of their own refugeeness, there were also marked divergences between the camp refugees and the town refugees in the broader social significance attributed to refugeeness. Exile did not erode collective identity among the Hutu refugees in Mishamo refugee camp. Far from "losing" their collective identity—and far from living in an absence of culture or history—the Hutu refugees in the camp located their identities within their very displacement, extracting meaning and power from the interstitial social location they inhabited. Instead of losing their collective identity, this is where and how they made it. The refugee camp had become both the spatial and the politico-symbolic site for imagining a moral and political community. Among the town refugees in Kigoma, on the other hand, relationships between roots and identity were very differently constituted. There, as we shall see, the very ability to "lose" one's identity and to move *through* categories was for many a form of social freedom and even security. There, the whole logic of uprootedness and exile was differently constituted— one might even say that it was sometimes meaningless. For there, creolization[24] and cosmopolitanism tended to be celebrated, and categorical loyalties to be regarded with caution, sometimes disdain.

This ethnography of displacement will trace such local differences in the construction of identity and nationness, exile and refugeeness, among the two groups of Hutu in Tanzania. In the course of the study, it will become evident that this is neither an ethnography of a pregiven "people" nor a holistic description of an ethnologically conceived "total way of life." It is, rather, an ethnography of the contingent sociohistorical *processes* of making and unmaking categorical identities and moral communities in two specific sites. It is in order to see such processes clearly that we must let go of both anthropological culturalism, with its subtly dehistoricizing, dehumanizing effects, and that variety of humanism that will acknowledge people's tragedies and longings only within a framework of universal timelessness.

# one

# HISTORICAL
# CONTEXTS, SOCIAL
# LOCATIONS:
# A ROAD MAP

In order to understand the meanings that the Hutu refugees gave to their predicament in Tanzania, it is necessary to understand something of how they arrived at it. A brief review of some aspects of the recent political history, and of the events leading up to the 1972 genocide, is therefore required. What follows is offered, not as an original contribution to the historical or ethnographic study of Burundi, but as a skeletal summary of research done by others—most notably, Jan Vansina, René Lemarchand, F. M. Rodegem, Warren Weinstein, Marcel d'Hertefelt, Jacques Maquet, and Albert Trouwborst. It is meant as an abridged "Baedeker guide" which will make subsequent chapters more meaningful to the reader. It is followed by a brief sketch of the two fieldwork sites, Mishamo and Kigoma, and some remarks on the conditions under which fieldwork was conducted.

## BACKGROUND TO GENOCIDE
Often called the "Switzerland of Africa," Burundi has been described as a country commanding a "bucolic charm as well as a touch of grandiose beauty" (Lemarchand 1970:13). Situated in one of the highest-lying areas of the continent in the central African rift valley, and bounded by Lake Tanganyika, Rwanda, Tanzania, and Zaire, Burundi covers an area of 27,834 square kilometers (11,000 square miles) (d'Hertefelt, Trouwborst, and Scherer 1962:119; Vansina 1972:3–4; Lemarchand and Martin 1974:5). Along with Rwanda, it supports one of Africa's highest popula-

tion densities, with 202 persons per square kilometer (Economist Intelligence Unit 1993:58).[1] Burundi's population was estimated at 3.5 million in 1972, and at 5.62 million in 1991.[2] However, as F. Rodegem has pointed out (personal communication), there has never been a full population census in Burundi.

The World Bank has estimated that 93 percent of the work force worked in agriculture in 1980; that figure has remained relatively stable for decades (Economist Intelligence Unit 1993:61). The bulk of the economy consists of subsistence agriculture. The main subsistence crops are bananas, sweet potatoes, cassava, beans, maize, and rice (ibid.: 63). Coffee is the main cash crop, and "accounted for 75 percent of Burundi's merchandise export earnings in 1990" (ibid.). Less important cash crops are tea, cotton, rice, palm oil, pyrethrum, and tobacco (Lemarchand and Martin 1974:5).[3] All these crops are mostly grown by peasant farmers on little, privately owned plots. Cattle are of "exceptional prestige" and play an "important role in the political structure of the country" (Vansina 1972:4).[4] About 60 percent of the country's total land area is devoted to pasture (Economist Intelligence Unit 1993: 62). Despite its lush, fertile appearance, Burundi is one of the poorest countries in Africa; this has been attributed to the absence of any significant mineral resources and to a lack of "incentives for development" (Lemarchand and Martin 1974:50, 1970:14).[5]

Rural people in Burundi do not generally live in villages.[6] As Lemarchand (1970:15) and others have described it, "today, as in the more distant past, the hill remains the primary focus of political activity in the countryside. Beyond the hill there is relatively little sense of unity among the rural communities. [. . .] And in the absence of adequate communications, the forbidding nature of the topography raises further obstacles in the way of any large-scale political mobilization." Sociopolitical action appears to be structured by regional affiliations and membership in patrilineal clans (umuryango) and lineages, as well as three main ethnic groups, sometimes styled "castes": the Tutsi, the Hutu, and the Twa (Vansina 1972:4–5).

Most scholars of Burundi and of the other interlacustrine kingdoms now agree that any history of the settlement of the region must remain largely hypothetical due to paucity of reliable evidence.[7] However, as Vansina (1972:192) notes, it is generally thought that the Twa were the first inhabitants, followed by the Hutu and later, the Hima and the Tutsi (cf. Weinstein 1976:ix; Lemarchand 1970:19; Melady 1974:40–1).[8]

One should, of course, be wary of projections of contemporary ethnic categories backward in time to describe population movements doubtless more complex than such formulations imply. For the present, I summarize the scholarly consensus in its own terms. But the idea that the history of Burundi is to be narrated as a story featuring fixed categorical actors ("the Hutu," "the Tutsi," "the Twa") conceived as separate and self-perpetuating collectivities is a problematic one— notwithstanding the prominent place it occupies both in the scholarly literature and (as I will show) the historical consciousness of the Hutu refugees in Mishamo, Tanzania.

The Twa (Batwa, Abatwa) are usually described as a "group of pygmoid forest dwellers" (Lemarchand 1970:19) who are regarded as lowly and inferior by the two other categories of the society, the Hutu and the Tutsi (Melady 1974:41).[9] Constituting less than 1 percent of the country's population, people of the Twa category are now politically marginal (Weinstein 1976:ix; Maquet 1961:10–11; Lemarchand 1970). Maquet (1961:10) describes the politico-economic position of the Twa in Rwanda as follows: "The Twa are hunters, potters and ironworkers. [. . .] Some of them make a living as singers, dancers and buffoons. [. . .] The Twa are said, half jokingly, [. . .] to be more akin to monkeys than to human beings."[10] (If the following discussion makes frequent reference to sources on Rwanda, it is because Rwanda and Burundi historically bear many similarities. Parallels and contrasts between the two societies have been charted by Lemarchand [1970:2ff.], Vansina [1972], Richards [1960] and others.)

The Hutu (Bahutu, Abahutu, sing. Muhutu, Umuhutu) have long constituted the bulk of Burundi's population and are supposed to have begun settling in Burundi between the fifth century B.C. and the tenth or eleventh century A.D. (Weinstein 1976:ix, 1). Prior to the arrival of the Tutsi, the Hutu are thought to have constituted relatively decentralized, "minor polities" (Weinstein 1976:ix; Lemarchand 1970:18; Vansina 1972:193). Trouwborst notes that, according to some oral traditions, the earliest kings were of Hutu origins (d'Hertefelt, Trouwborst, and Scherer 1962:120). The Hutu are always described as the agriculturalists. In addition to being cultivators, they are often artisans, and many have cattle (d'Hertefelt, Trouwborst, and Scherer 1962:120).

According to Vansina (1972:192), archeological evidence suggests that the region was already settled before 250 A.D. by agriculturalists who knew metal and who raised at least small livestock. They succeeded "Stone Age," nonagricultural populations. Based on variations in pottery styles, Vansina notes that it is not prudent to identify these agriculturalists with the contemporary "agricultural civilization" of the Hutu.

The "gradual infiltration" of pastoralists, from the east and from the north, began before 1520 (Vansina 1972:192). These immigrants are thought to have been the ancestors of the Tutsi (*Batutsi, Abatutsi* ["*Watusi*"], sing. *Mututsi, Umututsi*). The composition of the Tutsi category is somewhat more complex in Burundi than in neighboring Rwanda (Trouwborst 1962:120). According to Trouwborst (1962:120), two subcategories of Tutsi are distinguished in Burundi: the Tutsi-Abanyaruguru and the Tutsi-Hima. The Hima are an impure caste from the point of view of other Tutsi; they are pastoralists, but there are also impoverished Hima who are cultivators (Trouwborst 1962:120). The Tutsi-Banyaruguru are also preeminently pastoralists, but they constitute a "noble caste" whose members can marry members of the royal families (Trouwborst 1962:120).

Finally, the Abaganwa (*ganwa*), "princes of the blood," are members of the royal family and the source of the kings (*bami*, sing. *mwami*) and chiefs; and they, as Trouwborst (1962:120) notes, are not generally considered to be Tutsi. However, it should be underscored that, in the narratives of the Hutu refugees that will be explored in following chapters, even the Abaganwa are classed under the totalized category, the Tutsi. It seems that prior to independence in 1962, the Abaganwa were the principal fund of political authority in the country and were considered to be the "ruling caste" (d'Hertefelt, Trouwborst, and Scherer 1962:120). Since the early sixties and the end of the monarchy, however, the Hima have come to command political authority (Lemarchand and Martin 1974:6). As Lemarchand (1992:3) has recently observed, during the years after independence, "the Hima emerged as the dominant group within the army, and thus bear much of the responsibility for the 1972 massacre. To this day they stand as the social axis around which much of the country's power structure seems to revolve."

Weinstein (1976:ix) for his part suggests that the people now grouped together as Tutsi came to Burundi in successive waves and in different manners. The first major wave consisted of the Ganwa who, either through conquest by force or through absorption by means of political alliances with the Hutu polities already in place, "infiltrated" into Burundi in the fourteenth and fifteenth centuries (Weinstein 1976:ix,1). They are presumed to be the ancestors of the Tutsi-Banyaruguru (i.e., "those who came from the North") (Weinstein 1976:ix,1; Lemarchand 1970). "The exact origin of these Ganwa is a matter of historical debate, but it is clear that they were closely affiliated with Burundi's Tutsi, who arrived centuries after the Hutu" (Weinstein 1976:ix). The second "wave of Tutsi infiltration from the east" is estimated to have occurred in the seventeenth and eighteenth centuries, and these latter are presumed to be ancestors of the Tutsi-Bahima (Hima) (Weinstein 1976:ix, 1). The Tutsi-Hima are considered "lower caste" in relation to the Tutsi-Banyaruguru, but they are politically dominant. While the latter are represented in the government, they have little power (Lemarchand and Martin 1974:6). The Tutsi today (apparently including Ganwa, Abanyaruguru, and Hima) are usually said to make up 14 percent of Burundi's population, though truly reliable population statistics do not exist.

Speaking of both Rwanda and Burundi, Lemarchand (1970:18) says: "In both kingdoms, the invading tribes were Tutsi or Hima pastoralists. Although their origins are not firmly established, their physical features suggest obvious ethnic affinities with the Galla tribes of southern Ethiopia." The "origins" of the Tutsi have been a focus of much speculation, particularly during the colonial period.[11]

It should be noted that this history of the "origins" of Burundi is subject, not only to scholarly debate and paucity of firm evidence, but to bitter political struggle. The stakes involved in the political struggles over origins and over the ethnic composition of the "nation" will be discussed at length in subsequent chapters. Here, it need be noted only that the present Tutsi-dominated government of Burundi, and the research it appears to condone, present a version of history that is quite starkly different from the Hutu refugees' version. (See, e.g., Ndoricimpa and Guillet 1984; Acquier 1986; Chrétien 1983; Gahama 1983: 297ff.; Mworoha 1987.)[12]

The beginnings of the Burundi kingdom have been placed at ca. 1550 (Weinstein 1976:1).[13] In his comparative study of Rwanda and Burundi, Lemarchand (1970:22) says: "There was no parallel in Burundi for the centralized, hierarchical pattern of authority found in Rwanda. Instead, power was fragmented among relatively autonomous political units, each under the authority of a prince." The prominent status of the princes of the blood (ganwa) was associated with violent rivalries (Lemarchand 1970:23). "Because of the special eminence conferred upon them by the accidents of history, they became identified as a separate ethnic group, whose prestige in society ranked far above that of the ordinary Tutsi. If, in addition, one remembers that there are in Burundi two distinctive categories of Tutsi—the 'low-caste' Tutsi-Hima and the 'upper-caste' Tutsi-Banyaruguru—the total picture of society appears decidedly more variegated than in Rwanda."[14] Lemarchand (1970:28) also notes: "[A] remarkable feature of the traditional system was the comparatively high proportion of Hutu chiefs who held office in the royal domains (the so-called *ivyivare*). [. . .] That the king relied so heavily upon Hutu elements for administering the crown lands helps to explain the long-standing attachment of the Hutu peasantry to the cause of the Burundi monarchy."

That Burundian society has been, and continues to be, extremely hierarchical is not disputed among scholars. The exact nature of socio-political stratification and inequality in Burundi, however, has been characterized in diverse manners. "Feudalism" is one characterization that appears often (Lemarchand 1970:1; Coquery-Vidrovitch and Moniot 1974:145).[15] Vansina (1972:7) is one of many who have concluded that Burundi has all the political characteristics of a feudal system.[16] Coquery-Vidrovitch and others have also emphasized the relative coincidence of ethnic divisions with class stratification. But perhaps the most frequent designation has been that of "caste".[17] Lemarchand (1970:4–5ff.) considers the concepts of caste, class, and elites in his characterization of social stratification in Burundi (and Rwanda), and references to each are threaded throughout his study. All of these characterizations seem to express, with varying degrees of accuracy, something of the social hierarchy in Burundi—which has undergone profound transformations from precolonial to colonial days and from the end of the monarchy to the present.[18] These transformations will be further discussed below. For the moment, it is necessary to examine the historical and anthropological texts focussed on the social, symbolic, and political stratification of Burundian society. Vansina (1972:5) explains his usage of the caste analogy thus:

La structure sociale est caractérisée par un régime de castes. Les Ganwa ou les princes de sang royal gouvernent le royaume. On les distingue des éleveurs

Tutsi à qui on confie les commandements politiques aux échelons inférieurs. Les Tutsi méprisent les Hima, qui sont leurs semblables, également pasteurs, mais considérés comme de 'mauvaise famille'. La masse de la population, 80% environ, est composée d'agriculteurs Hutu et, enfin, on trouve un pour-cent environ de chasseurs et de pottiers Twa. L'esprit d'inégalité est si prononcé qu'on classe tous les clans et sous-clans en une hiérarchie de supériorité et d'infériorité relative.

A question that occupies a prominent place in the historiography of Burundi (as of Rwanda) is how the castelike hierarchy of categories came to be formed—and how it was possible for a minority to establish such hegemonic control over the mass of the population in each region. Vansina (1972:193–4), for example, characterizes the "evolution of the general political situation" of Burundi as being necessarily concerned with the process of the "installation of the Tutsi and Hima and with the fashion in which they ended by dominating the Hutu." He goes on to question how it was that the Hutu lost their autonomy. "One explanation would be that the Hima and the Tutsi had developed the *ubugabire* clientage contract with the transfer of cattle"; the recipient of the cattle would then "lose his sovereign rights" (Vansina 1972: 195).[19] Vansina also suggests that the evolution of the sociopolitical hierarchy may have been due to a military advantage on the part of the Tutsi (1972:195). (Cf. Codere 1962).

Maquet's work (1961), *The Premise of Inequality in Rwanda*, also privileges cattle clientship (called *buhake* in Rwanda) as a central constitutive feature of the hierarchy.[20] In concord with both Vansina and Maquet, Lemarchand (1970:19) likewise focuses on clientship in Burundi (*ubugabire*):

How the Tutsi managed to extend their hegemony over the mass of the Hutu peasants is a question to which different people have given different answers. For Hans Meyer, the German authority on Burundi, the secret of Tutsi domination lay in their innate superiority—in "their superior intelligence, calmness, smartness, racial pride, solidarity and political talent." A more widely accepted explanation is that the Tutsi used their cattle as a lever of economic power to subdue the indigenous tribes; according to this view, the key to the whole situation was a special form of cattle clientship, or cattle-contract, through which the Tutsi oligarchy acquired sovereign political rights over their Hutu clients. Historically, however, the situation appears to have been much more complex. At some time in the remote past wandering tribes of Tutsi and Hima pastoralists infiltrated among the indigenous tribes, with whom they established a symbiotic relationship. In some places these intruders set themselves up as minor chiefs controlling a few hills; elsewhere, relations between the two communities were essentially of a commercial nature, involving the exchange of cattle for agricultural products.

The concept of a symbiosis, as described by Lemarchand above, seems to be central in conceptualizing Burundian society as feudal or "parafeudal" (Vansina 1972:4). In Lemarchand's words (1970:36):

In each kingdom the ties of clientship ran like a seamless web, linking men in a relationship of mutual dependence. At the core of this relationship lay an institution called *buhake* in Rwanda and *bugabire* in Burundi, translated alternatively as "cattle contract" or "contract of pastoral servitude." [. . .] But clientship involved more than just economic transaction between an inferior and a superior. It also involved a close personal relationship, in some ways reminiscent of the ties of fealty which linked the medieval lord to his vassal. The reciprocal bonds of loyalty between client and patron meant that one became the other's "man," just as in feudal Europe the lord was the "man" of the king, and the serf the "man" of his lord.

Lemarchand also sees this feudal symbiosis as a source of the social "cohesion" in Burundi, along with the "unifying effects" of the monarchy. Noting that the "roles of client and patron were not mutually exclusive" in Burundi (1970:37), Lemarchand concludes that, while the clientship institution reinforced caste differences in Rwanda, it blurred them in Burundi (1970:40). Describing Burundi as a cohesive "pyramidal system," Lemarchand and Martin (1974:7) say: "Through the institution of clientship (*bugabire*) Hutu and Tutsi were caught in a web of interlocking relationships extending from the very top of the social pyramid to its lowest echelons, with the Mwami acting as the supreme Patron—which in turn underscores the unifying aspects of the monarchy, both as a symbol and an institution."

The image of precolonial, dynastic Burundi emerging from these descriptions is one of "cohesive" hierarchy in which "caste," ethnic, and racial differences were crosscut and modulated by numerous other levels of segmentation and relations.[21] Vansina (1972:219) notes, however, that the oral traditions that are such an important source for the historiography of Burundi operate in a selective manner, and may not have recorded ethnically or racially defined divisions or conflicts where they existed.[22] Vansina (1972:219) argues: "As the oral traditions of Burundi are abundant, particularly in the political domain, one might suppose that they have registered everything. This is not true. It is like this that the oral tradition does not note the antagonisms between the Hutu and the Tutsi" (Vansina 1972:219).[23]

Catholic missionaries (White Fathers) and German soldier-explorers formed the first European presence in Burundi in the late nineteenth century, when the country was a decentralized kingdom ruled by a *mwami* (king or paramount chief) (Weinstein 1976:ix). The Berlin Conference of 1885 designated Burundi and Rwanda as a German sphere of influence, and German control was established in the first decade of the twentieth century (Weinstein 1976:ix, 2). Belgium occupied the region that is now Burundi in 1916 and was given the region as a mandate. The mandate included not only Burundi but Rwanda, and the region was administered as Rwanda-Urundi (Weinstein 1976: ix,4–5). In 1946, the mandate was transformed into a United Nations trusteeship, and Rwanda-Urundi was henceforth a Belgian trust territory (Weinstein 1976:4–5).

Both German and Belgian colonial rulers exercised "indirect rule" through giving and consolidating political office in the hands of the Tutsi and Ganwa elite, and both enforced highly extractive labor policies and taxation measures (Weinstein 1976:ix,4–5). In this period, trade and migration linked Burundi with the neighboring region of Buha in what was then Tanganyika (today, Tanzania), despite the efforts of the Belgian government, in particular, to suppress such border crossings.[24] A compulsory cultivation system was emplaced by the Belgian colonialists in 1932, largely for the exploitation of coffee as a cash crop (Lemarchand 1970:14).

Both colonial administrations made efficient use of preexisting political hierarchies in Burundi for the purposes of administration and production, and both were implicated in the ever greater hierarchizing of the three-tiered ethnic or "caste" pyramid of Tutsi, Hutu, and Twa (Codere 1962; Richards 1960). The Tutsi/Ganwa political supremacy that had existed before colonialism was reinforced and inscribed with new significations during both periods of colonial administration.

Examining colonial texts describing Burundian society forces the realization that the colonialists not only governed by means of the "caste" hierarchy; they were fascinated by it. The social categories observed were inscribed with essentialized "traits" and personalities like taxa, and the sociopolitical hierarchy became also a symbolic one, a natural order, one might say. It is, of course, not uncommon to find these preoccupations in the colonial literature on Africa, but it might be ventured that they were strikingly elaborate and powerful in the case of Burundi and Rwanda (at that time jointly administered as Rwanda-Urundi). This is suggested by the wealth, not only of colonial literature, but also of postcolonial anthropological and historical literature on the meaning of the hegemonic social hierarchy in Burundi. As Lemarchand and Martin (1974:6) have written:

The standard image of Burundi society conveyed by much of the colonial literature is that of an ethnic pyramid in which the cattle-herding Tutsi, representing 14 per cent of the population, held the commanding heights of power and influence; next in rank came the Hutu agriculturalists, forming the bulk of the population (85 per cent); at the bottom of the heap stood the pygmoid Twa, a group of relatively little significance numerically (1 per cent) and otherwise. Presumably reinforcing this hierarchy of rank and privilege were the physical characteristics commonly attributed to each group: Proverbially tall and wiry, the Tutsi have been said to "possess the same graceful indolence in gait which is peculiar to Oriental people"; the Hutu, on the other hand, were seen as "a medium-sized type of people, whose ungainly figures betoken hard toil, and who patiently bow themselves in abject bondage to the later arrived yet ruling race, the Tutsi."[25]

Such essentialist accounts are of special importance in the context of this study because they served not only to describe Burundi's social configuration but also to construct it. For, as will become evident in the chapter to follow, such constructions (even long after being discredited in academic circles) continue to shape the imaginative landscape of many contemporary Burundians, Hutu and Tutsi alike. (And they also still flourish in the media coverage of political violence in this region of central Africa.)

Lemarchand (1970:45) argues that in both Rwanda and Burundi, "certain physical and moral stereotypes" were already attached to the castes before the colonial era. Thus, both were "elitist, hierarchically-organized societies, in which power was concentrated at the top in the hands of a small oligarchy"; and both "tended to associate qualities of intelligence and resourcefulness to the upper strata." He emphasizes, however, that it was the colonial era that served to transform a complex status hierarchy into a simplified ethnic antagonism—a hierarchy in which, apparently, the subdivision among the Tutsi became less significant. In this way, the more intricate, multilayered hierarchies of the precolonial era were reduced to the more essentialized ethnic pyramid of Tutsi, Hutu, and Twa.

The colonial literature not only attributed moral characteristics to the three categories; physical "traits" also played a major part. These physical and moral ascriptions became conflated in a kind of Lamarckian evolutionary order. Such orders speak perhaps more loudly about the European observers of Burundian society than they ever did about Burundi itself.

It seems that the colonial visions and fantasies focused particularly on the Tutsi, and on their supposed origins in the "Orient"—or, at any rate, beyond the heart of the "Dark Continent" itself. An early missionary, Menard, wrote: "La race des Batutsi est sans contredit l'une des plus belles et des plus intéressantes de l'Afrique équatoriale. Au physique, le Mututsi est parfaitement constitué. Sa conformation le rapproche du blanc plus que du nègre, si bien que l'on pourrait dire sans beaucoup exagérer qu'il est un Européen sous une peau noire" (F. Ménard, cited in Gahama 1983:275).[26]

The colonial focus on racial "traits" led many to hypothesize that the ancestors of the Tutsi must have been ancient Egyptians (Jamoule, cited in Gahama 1983:276; Richards 1960:29).[27] Indeed, one report stated that the Tutsi remind one in a "troubling fashion" of the "type" of the mummy of Ramses II.[28] The compilation of physical "traits" was accompanied by treatises on the Tutsi character or temperament. Thus, Meyer, for example, wrote:

The Tutsi never or only seldom says what he thinks; one has to guess it. Lying is not only customary with strangers but a permanent and deeply rooted defect. [. . .] The Tutsi consider themselves as the top of the creation from the standpoint of intelligence and political genius. [. . .] To be rich and powerful and to enjoy life by doing nothing is the symbol of all wisdom for the Tutsi, the ideal for which he strives with utmost shrewdness and unscrupulousness. (Meyer 1916:14, cited in Lemarchand 1970:42)

Of the Hutu, Meyer wrote: "Due to four centuries of terroristic rule, they have become slaves in thinking and acting, though not so slave-like in character as the Banyarwanda under their Hamitic despots" (Meyer 1916, cited in Lemarchand 1970:42).[29] The Hutu were considered as "negroes properly speaking" (Jamoulle, cited in Gahama 1983:276), and were catalogued as "short and stocky." The Twa, finally, were profoundly animalized and sometimes considered "half-monkeys" (Gahama 1983:276, 279).

These colonial conceptualizations of the social categories in Burundi have been considered briefly here because they still have contemporary relevance: they seem, on the one hand, to creep into much writing on Burundi and Rwanda in the form of natural, primordial fact,[30] and, on the other, to impart familiar, repeating shapes to discursive historical memory among the Hutu refugees in Tanzania. As the chapters to follow will show, the old academic and administrative constructions of ethnic difference are like chilling echoes in Burundi's (and Rwanda's) appalling recent histories of mass violence and ethnic polarization.

Colonial rule lasted from 1900 to 1962. Independence was declared on July 1, 1962,[31] when Rwanda-Urundi became two states, the Republic of Rwanda and the Kingdom of Burundi. The monarchy in Burundi was overthrown in November 1966 (Kay 1987:3). Michel Micombero was the President of the First Republic. In 1976, he was overthrown in a bloodless coup by his cousin, Colonel Bagaza, who inaugurated the Second Republic. Bagaza, in turn, was overthrown by Pierre Buyoya in 1987.[32] All three of these presidents have been Tutsi-Hima.

Weinstein (1976:x) notes that

as a result of changes brought about during colonial rule [. . .] relations between the ethnic groups in Burundi worsened. Even before European penetration, the Hutu had rebelled against Ganwa and Tutsi authority, but this was localized and it never attained proportions which qualified the violence as conscious ethnic civil war. Burundians tended to identify according to their native region first, and then the genetico-status distinctions amongst them. By the end of colonial rule the regional distinctions were still important but the ethnic cleavage was the primary social division. [. . .] In the competition for power which accompanied independence, Ganwa and Tutsi tended to align as one ethnic bloc, and Hutu as the opposing bloc. The Twa most often aligned themselves according to their locality and in a very pragmatic way. It is only later that they threw their lot in with the Hutu.

In neighboring Rwanda, independence (1 July 1962) was accompanied by a Hutu-led revolution (1959–62), a Tutsi counterattack, and mass killings in which tens of thousands of people, most of them Tutsi, died (Newbury 1988:197–8; Reyntjens 1985; Clay 1984). These events put the Hutu majority in power, and produced tens of thousands of Tutsi refugees.[33] "Some 150,000 [Tutsi from Rwanda] were driven into exile during the turbulent years of the Hutu revolution, from 1959–1962 [. . .]. The size of the Rwanda refugee community has increased about threefold since the early 1960's (though born in exile their offspring are legally treated as refugees by the host governments). Approximately 200,000 live in Uganda, perhaps half as many in Burundi, with Zaire and Tanzania each claiming 30,000. (Lemarchand n.d.[a]:1)[34]

Sayinzoga (1982), Lemarchand (n.d.[a]), Kabera (1987), Clay (1984), Watson (1992) and others have written at length about these movements of people.[35] The historical route of escape to Uganda seems to have been in use in the colonial era due to harsh labor policies, and even earlier (e.g., Kabera 1987).

Writing against all those who saw "ruin" in the end of colonial domination in Africa, Lemarchand (1970:47) argued that "despite the brevity of the colonial interlude, its impact was overwhelming. In Rwanda it unleashed one of the most violent upheavals ever witnessed by an African state at a similar stage of its evolution; in Burundi it sowed the seeds of a racial conflict that may well prove equally devastating." When these words were published, the 1972 massacre in Burundi was still two years away. In more recent work, Lemarchand (1992:4) also suggests that the revolution in Rwanda played a decisively important role in consolidating the political significance of a Hutu-Tutsi split in Burundi—the violence and fear in Rwanda propelling the political imagination of irretrievably opposed categorical actors beyond its southern border.[36]

Competition for political power—and not "the old African problem of tribalism" (Lemarchand and Martin 1974:8)[37]—served to bifurcate the populations in Rwanda and Burundi into two opposing categories, Hutu and Tutsi, and to render other social divisions less meaningful and less powerful. The exclusive predominance of the ethnic bifurcation was at this level a markedly recent political phenomenon.[38]

The decade following independence in Burundi saw several efforts by the Hutu to challenge the political supremacy of the Tutsi minority.[39] Attempted Hutu uprisings in 1965, 1968, and 1969 led to purges in which thousands of Hutu were killed (Weinstein 1976:x–xi). Concerning the 1965 uprising, Weinstein (1976:x) writes:

In 1965 the Hutu attempted to seize power by force and to put an end to the *mwamidom.* They failed, and the Tutsi expanded their control over Burundi's government and its repressive mechanisms. Captain Michel Micombero, then head of Burundi's armed forces, led an armed repression against the Hutu leadership and masses. Most Hutu intellectuals were executed, they were purged from the army with a few exceptions, and as many as 5000 Hutu were killed in the hillsides. The Hutu attempt to seize power and its aftermath left Burundi under almost total Tutsi control.

The violence of these years produced Hutu refugees who fled mainly into Tanzania, Rwanda, and Zaire. These years in some sense provided a precedent for the most massive, large-scale killings in Burundi's history, the massacres beginning in April 1972. It was these massacres that produced the refugees who are the key informants in this study.

The events of 1972 are not fully documented anywhere, but Weinstein provides a competent chronology of events in the *Historical Dictionary of Burundi* (1976). He writes (1976:xi):

The exact causes of the civil war are still being analyzed. [. . .] The event which triggered it was the unexpected return of former king Ntare V, whom Micombero had dethroned in 1966. [. . .] During the first two weeks it was Hutu in southern Burundi who initiated the fighting and had to be overcome. But within one week of the outbreak, Burundi armed forces and government were purged of almost all Hutu. [. . .] The regime launched an unprecedented slaughter of the country's educated and socially prominent Hutu. [. . .] The killings continued through the fall [1972], and then abated until the spring of 1973 when a new outbreak followed incursions into Burundi by armed Hutu guerillas. Over 100 000 Hutu fled the country and between 150 000 and 250 000 were killed. In the fighting some 2000–3000 Tutsi died as well.

It is perhaps well to mention some of the events immediately preceding the Hutu uprising of April 29, 1972. Weinstein (1976:34) reports that in March 1972, Burundi security and military personnel visited Tanzania to organize surveillance of the Hutu refugees who had lived there in exile since the sixties, and that road blocks were set up throughout the east, south, and capital regions of Burundi. In March also, the former King Ntare was arrested in Bujumbura, and accused of "trying to invade Burundi with a force of white mercenaries" (Weinstein 1976:34). On April 16, there were "mass arrests of young and old peasants (Hutu) in the Nyanza-Lac region of southwestern Burundi," and Hutu primary-school teachers fled schools in the area, seeking refuge in Tanzania (Weinstein 1976:35). On April 27, the minister of the interior visited Nyanza-Lac "for a secret meeting of local Tutsi leaders. Hutu allege[d] he announced a government plan to exterminate all but the uneducated Hutu peasants. The Hutu allege[d] that arms were distributed to the local Tutsi officials and government workers" (Weinstein 1976:35). On the following day, Hutu in southern Burundi, being aware of the meeting at Nyanza-Lac, organized the peasants into defense groups (Weinstein 1976:35). On April 29, the former king, Ntare, was executed at Gitega, and fighting broke out at Bujumbura in the south. The groups of attackers were Hutu (Weinstein 1976:36). On the same night, "festivities were organized at all major military centers in Burundi" (Weinstein 1976:36), and the rebels appear to have attacked these. Reprisals by the government began on the following day.

The death toll has been variously estimated. No authoritative figure exists. A former United States ambassador to Burundi gives two estimates: 90,000 and 250,000 (Melady, cited in Chomsky and Herman 1979:109).[40] Another estimate, considered reliable by Kuper (1982:164) ranges from 80,000 to 200,000.[41]

In the weeks following the initial events of April 29–30, 1972, it started to appear to many observers that the so-called reprisals for the Hutu uprising had become systematic, genocidal killing. The United States ambassador to Burundi reported (Melady 1974:15):

By mid-May the Western diplomatic corps, plus the ambassadors of Zaire and Rwanda, felt that the Burundi government had completed its mop-up of the remaining rebels and that the killings now occurring were part of an effort to eliminate increasing numbers of Hutus. We had reports that every morning trucks would leave the army camp and other installations for the outskirts of Bujumbura. Hundreds of bodies would consequently be placed in newly dug mass graves. We later learned that the pattern was being repeated throughout the country. [. . .] In mid-May there was a body of evidence that Tutsi leaders were arresting and executing (all without trial) Hutu intellectuals, teachers, and secondary-school students. We feared that few, if any, educated professionals among the Hutus would survive. In my report to the State Department on May 10, I indicated for the first time that the embassy felt the period of civil strife was clearly past and the actions now were approaching selective genocide. This opinion was shared by most diplomats.

Chomsky and Herman (1979:106) note that, according to an American Universities Field Staff report on Burundi, "which U.S. officials judged accurate, the extermination toll included 'the four Hutu members of the cabinet, all the Hutu officers and virtually all the Hutu soldiers in the armed forces; half of Burundi's primary school teachers;

and thousands of civil servants, bank clerks, small businessmen, and domestic servants. At present (August [1972]) there is only one Hutu nurse left in the entire country, and only a thousand secondary school students survive'."[42] Priests were also killed in great numbers. Greenland (1973) reports that "more Burundi priests were killed during the summer of 1972 than have died of natural causes since the first ordination in 1925" (Greenland 1973:443–51).

Lemarchand and Martin (1974:15) have called the massacres a "selective genocide" because they were "directed at all the educated or semi-educated strata of Hutu society." "The aim was to decapitate not only the rebellion but Hutu society as well, and in the process lay the foundation for an entirely new social order. [. . .] [W]hat is left of Hutu society is now systematically excluded from the army, the civil service, the university and secondary schools. [. . .] Hutu status has become synonymous with an inferior category of beings; only Tutsi are fit to rule, and among them none are presumably better qualified than the Banyabururi" (Lemarchand and Martin 1974:18; Lemarchand 1992; Greenland 1976).

The term *genocide* began to appear with some regularity in international coverage of the killings, and already in May of 1972, the Prime Minister of Belgium informed his cabinet that a "veritable genocide" was happening in Burundi (Chomsky and Herman 1979:107; Kuper 1982:163).

The government of Burundi issued several different announcements defining the events that were taking place. On the night when the uprising began, April 29, Radio Bujumbura announced that a "monarchist and imperialist plot" had been uncovered, and that curfew had been imposed throughout Burundi (Weinstein 1976:36). On May 1, Radio Bujumbura announced that the uprising was organized by Mulelist guerillas from Zaire, Rwandan Tutsi refugees, and Burundians (Weinstein 1976:36). On May 4, it was announced that the uprising was organized by "tribalists," a term that, according to Weinstein (1976:36) was a euphemism for Hutu. On May 19, the embassy of Burundi in Brussels alleged that the instigators of violence were Hutu and Mulelist rebels whose "goal was to kill the Tutsi" (Weinstein 1976:37). On June 15, the government of Burundi termed the violence "external aggression," not a revolt, and claimed that the "masses had nothing to do with it" (Weinstein 1976:39). Finally, a fuller "official version" was presented by the government of Burundi in the form of a white paper to the United Nations, which claimed that the genocide was in fact a genocide of Tutsi by Hutu. This paper is discussed in detail in chapter 6.[43] In opposition to these state-sanctioned views, there have been allegations that "the Micombero government started to plan the massacres through carefully calculated provocations and misinformation as soon as it overthrew the monarchy in November 1966" (Kay 1987:3).

In the international media, the massacres in Burundi received astonishingly little coverage. In an analysis of the processes and mechanisms which render some atrocities invisible in the international arena while emphasizing others, Chomsky and Herman (1979:105) note that the case of Burundi was one of extreme invisibility: "In surveying the selective concern with terror, bloodbaths and human rights, we will focus on instances where attitudes in the United States have been characterized mainly by sheer indifference. The terror and violence in these cases we designate as 'benign'. [. . .] The Burundi case is perhaps closest to purely benign."

One frequent response, when it was not silence, was to express shock at what was happening while noting that it would be "improper" to interfere in the internal affairs of a sovereign state.[44] As Kuper (1982:161) points out, the sovereignty of territorial states guarantees them the right even to genocide.[45]

It appears that when the massacres were covered in international papers as "tribal bloodshed," this very term contained within it an explanation of what was happening: "the old African problem of tribalism." Other terms used were "civil war" (as in Weinstein cited above) and "peasant uprising." It hardly seems appropriate to term the massacres a civil war since only one side had a monopoly on the real instruments of destruction.[46]

In October of 1972, Prime Minister Nyamoya of Burundi announced that "all refugees who have not returned by November 12 will be considered foreigners, and lose their belongings and property" (Weinstein 1976:44). It seems that many of the relatively few refugees who did return were jailed by the National Army of Burundi (ibid.).

Several major consequences of the killings have been identified by observers. Lemarchand and Martin (1974:5) write:

What the long-term consequences will be for Burundi society as a whole is impossible to determine. That the country has undergone something of a metamorphosis as a result of these events is nonetheless undeniable. It has become the only state in independent black Africa to claim the appurtenances of a genuine caste society; a country in which power is the monopoly of a dominant ethnic minority (Tutsi) representing less than 15 per cent of the total population. [. . .] Racial differences aside, the nearest parallel to this situation is provided by South Africa, Rhodesia and the Portuguese territories of Angola and Mozambique. The pattern of dominance extends to virtually all sectors of life, restricting access to material wealth, education, status and power to representatives of the dominant minority. For anyone even remotely familiar with the relatively open and flexible system of stratification that once characterized Burundi society the transformation is little short of astonishing.

The government of Burundi has since 1972 insisted on the denial of ethnic differences while concentrating all political authority among those in the Tutsi-Hima category (Kay 1987:6).[47] In his report, *Burundi Since the Genocide*, Kay (ibid.) states:

The conclusion that the few Hutu in prominent positions have served only as window dressing for the outside world has been inescapable. It is an especially unfortunate irony that the rulers of Burundi, while denying the existence of ethnic differences, clearly felt those very divisions had to be exhibited as a public relations exercise. The surviving educated people in Hutu society were almost entirely excluded from influence in the armed forces, civil service, public sector companies and institutions of higher education.

Kay (1987:7) goes on to observe that "the government does not acknowledge ethnic distinctions and the mere mention of the country's glaring divided loyalties could well prompt a charge of incitement to racial hatred." He then lays out the principal domains of ethnic discrimination in contemporary Burundi, noting that discrimination in the educational system has become "a hallmark of the Second Republic" (Kay 1987:7). A partial explanation for the consistent and marked underrepresentation of Hutu students may be found in "the reluctance of many Hutu parents, mindful of the pattern of the killings in 1972, to allow their children to submit themselves for the higher level" (ibid.).[48]

Churches have also come under increasing restrictions since 1972. A large proportion of the priesthood, both Catholic and Protestant, used to be composed of foreigners, but the 1980s have seen a "policy of non-renewal of visas and expulsions" (Kay 1987:8). In 1985, the minister of the interior issued a circular to provincial governors stating the following points:

No public meeting for whatever purpose may take place without previous permission from the appropriate authority which, in turn, must inform its superiors. All religious activities must be confined to Saturday afternoons and Sundays

[. . .]. Masses which are celebrated at a residence on the occasion of "lifting of mourning" or similar circumstances are forbidden. Home visits to the sick are forbidden unless the patient requests the presence of a priest for the administration of the sacraments of extreme unction and confession. Any church which wishes to introduce a new service whose practice will distract the faithful from their usual occupations must announce it to the Minister of the Interior. (Kay 1987:9)

These measures were justified by the argument that "regulations covering the hours of work (and therefore of prayer) for the population are essential if a poor country, such as Burundi, is to maximize its production" (Kay 1987:9). The churches have since the colonial days played an extremely important role in schooling (see Greenland 1980). It is apparently considered in government that the churches are too closely involved in social and political affairs (Kay 1987:10).

As for the possibility of future uprisings, Lemarchand and Martin write in 1974: "Internally, the ruling elites have no reason to anticipate further challenges from the Hutu community: lacking all potential sources of leadership, decimated and deeply traumatized by the terrible vengeance visited upon them, the Hutu living in Burundi are neither willing nor able to instigate further revolts. Entirely different, however, is the attitude of the Hutu refugee community in exile" (1974:19).[49]

The refugees beyond its borders are by no means ignored by Burundi. It is reported that the "police authorities follow the movements of exiles abroad even when they have renounced their Burundian citizenship" (Kay 1987:8). It further appears that intimidation techniques continue to be used to some degree within the country. Kay (1987:8) writes, for example, that "a favourite ruse of the police is to send a parcel of compromising leaflets from Rwanda or Tanzania to an unsuspecting Burundian who is arrested on presenting himself/herself at the post office to collect." This technique is premised on the existence of Hutu refugees in exile.

The foregoing review of history in Burundi, once again, has been compiled entirely through published sources, and does not in any sense represent an original contribution to, or an exhaustive study of, the history of the region. It has been provided only as a guide to the reader; authoritative sources have been indicated in the footnotes to this section. More recent historical and political transformations in both Burundi and Tanzania—and especially events that have taken place after the completion of this study—will be discussed in the postscript.

THE HUTU IN TANZANIA: TWO FIELDWORK SITES

Starting in May of 1972, Hutu began to arrive by land and by water into the Kigoma region of western Tanzania. They came by the tens of thousands in movements that continued for months. An immediate emergency relief program was set up by several international agencies as well as regional and national authorities. Among the first measures was to establish "reception centers" and "holding" or "transit" camps in which the Hutu could be given emergency assistance and registered as refugees.[50] Kibirizi on Lake Tanganyika and Pangale in Tabora region, 500 kilometers inland from the lake, were such temporary camps. Shortly thereafter, plans for more permanent settlements or camps for the Hutu refugees were implemented by three agencies. The government of Tanzania (Ministry of Home Affairs), the United Nations High Commissioner for Refugees (UNHCR), and the Tanganyika Christian Refugee Service (TCRS), which is a local arm of the Lutheran World Federation (LWF), entered into a "Tripartite Agreement" to settle the refugees. The overriding concerns seem to have been to remove the refugees from the Tanzania-Burundi border zone to inland sites and to prevent them from permanently settling in or around Kigoma-Ujiji township.[51]

Already in mid-1972, only a few months after the massacres began in Burundi, a more permanent settlement, Ulyankulu, was established in Tabora Region. Ulyankulu covers an area of 1,000 square kilometers about 75 kilometers northeast of the town of Tabora in Urambo District, and currently accommodates about 34,000 Hutu refugees (TCRS 1975:6; TCRS 1984b, n.p.).[52] Between May 1972 and 1975, however, some 54,000 Hutu refugees had been brought in several large groups to Ulyankulu. (This number included thousands who had already been living for two to three years in the Tanzania-Burundi border zone (TCRS 1984b, n.p.).

In 1973, less than a year later, a second settlement, Katumba, was established in western Rukwa Region. Among the three settlements for the Hutu, Katumba is the largest in population with an estimated 60,000 people on an area of 1,000 square kilometers, situated on the Tabora-Mpanda railway line, in Mpanda District (TCRS 1975:7). These are considered to be three of the world's largest refugee settlements, presumably in terms of both area and population (Armstrong 1988: 58).[53]

MISHAMO

After a 1977 survey of land and water resources in Ulyankulu, the first camp, it was decided that half of Ulyankulu's population which had risen to 60,000 would be moved to an entirely new site by mid-1978. (See map 5.) The government of Tanzania offered three potential sites, all located in the country's remote western periphery (Armstrong 1987). Mishamo district was selected. (See map 3.) Mishamo was designed for the excess population of Ulyankulu and for the resettlement of the "spontaneously settling" or "self-settled" Hutu refugees in Kigoma Region. By the end of 1979, exactly 27,205 refugees had been brought to Mishamo, by one account "very much against their will" (Gasarasi 1984). Only 2,169 of these were Hutu refugees from Kigoma, however (TCRS 1984b, n.p.). The Kigoma refugees had been living in local villages and towns for six or seven years by 1979, and most of them resisted and circumvented the efforts to resettle them. (Map 6 indicates the sites in Mishamo that were designated for villages that would house the town refugees.) Thus, the bulk of the refugees in Mishamo already had experience of the Ulyankulu camp, and many had also passed through the transit camps of Kibirizi or Pangale. (See map 2.) The 1985–86 population of Mishamo was estimated at 35,000.

Mishamo is located in an isolated area of northern Mpanda District in Rukwa Region about 50 kilometers east of the shore of Lake Tanganyika, 105 kilometers north of the district capital of Mpanda, and 70–80 kilometers south of Uvinza, a small station on the central railway line (Armstrong 1987:3). It is spatially the most isolated of the three settlements (maps 2, 3, 5). While Ulyankulu offers relatively convenient access to the town of Tabora and the central railway line and Katumba is near the district capital of Mpanda and another segment of the railway line, Mishamo is buffered by virtually uninhabited forest zones in all directions and is accessible by only one north-south motorable dirt road which is seasonally damaged by rains, occasionally to the point of impassability. Driving to the nearest village or town, whether north or south, takes several hours. (Driving through Mishamo itself can take between one and two hours.)[54]

The physical appearance of Mishamo and the surrounding area is of relevance because it was capable of so directly constraining (and sustaining) people's lives there. It was also an extraordinary place for an outsider like myself to see for the first time. Thick forest, and stretches of bush and swampland, surrounded Mishamo on all sides. Clouds of tsetse flies and occasional groups of wary monkeys were the only living things one could depend on encountering in the forest on the way to Mishamo. To the visitor's senses, this forest was frightening because of the near total absence of human habitation, the scarcity of other traffic, and the overpowering expanse of the forest itself, which was sometimes noisy with insects and at other times eerily silent. Every now and then, one might catch a glimpse, swaying high up on a tree branch, of a dark, elongated bundle. It emerged later that these bundles were hung up on branches for the benefit of bees by Wabende hunters. Prior to the establishment of the camp, this "tsetse-infested miombo bushland" had served as the "extensive hunting and honey and beeswax collection grounds" for Wabende, "most of whom [had] been moved away from the area and settled in villages to the south during the 1970's villagization programme" (Armstrong 1987:3–4).

The landscape quite suddenly lost some of its forbidding quality as the road improved at the points of entry into Mishamo, where road barriers were attended by armed gatekeepers. Here, documents authorizing entry into the camp were officially required.

Mishamo did not answer to any common images of what a refugee camp "ought to" look like. No crowds of people or any sudden burst of closely clustered makeshift houses, barracks, or white UN tents met the eye. The greatest presence was always that of the trees and the bushland through which well-graded, reddish dirt roads had been cut. Occasionally one might see an orderly arrangement of common buildings in a village center or, away from the village centers, shielded by banana trees and other domestic greenery, a small house or two. This quiet, forested atmosphere was due, in large part, to the stunningly large expanse of land that the boundaries of the camp marked off from the surrounding wilderness. Equal in size to the island of Zanzibar, Mishamo covered an area of 2,050 square kilometers, of which 1,200 were settled (Armstrong 1987:3). Its sixteen villages, identical in basic infrastructural layout, were separated by forested buffer zones and connected by an extensive network of "main roads." The large buffer zones had been included in the layout of the settlement as forest reserves and sites for future agricultural expansion (Agrar- und Hydrotechnik 1978). Household plots of five hectares each were arranged in neat rows along "feeder roads" connecting to main roads. The feeder roads within the villages were placed at approximately thousand-meter intervals

(UNHCR/TCRS 1985:1).[55] The average number of plots per village was four hundred (UNHCR/TCRS 1985:1). The plots and roads formed an orderly, geometric pattern. (Map 8 gives a sample layout of a village in Mishamo, and map 7 shows the buffer zones.) The plots, the roads, and the villages had all been assigned numbers. The considerable distances between the sixteen villages did not seem to hinder social interaction greatly, although only one quarter of the refugee households owned bicycles in the mid-eighties (Armstrong 1988:62–3),[56] and almost nobody owned a car.[57]

Much of the labor power that went into the establishment of this infrastructure was supplied by the refugees through organized "self-help" projects (Doheny 1982:4; TCRS n.d.[a]; TCRS n.d.[b]).[58] The building of wells, roads, schools, dispensaries, offices, homes for staff and refugees, godowns, a stadium, an airstrip, and cultivation were all heavily reliant on "self-help," a practice also much used elsewhere in Tanzania (cf., e.g., Lomoy 1981:19).

When the camp was first established, the refugees relied on food rations provided by the Tri-Partite partners, but relatively soon they were self-sufficient: "With each family cultivating their own substantial (five-hectare) plot, Mishamo was virtually self-sufficient in food after only two farming seasons. And with the cultivated area increasing by 2,000 hectares each year, the settlement raked in an impressive 4,500,000 shillings from surplus crop sales and 3,000,000 shillings in tobacco sales, the main cash crop, [in 1985]" (Armstrong 1986c:33).[59]

All of Mishamo's sixteen villages were formally registered cooperative entities, and together they formed a larger cooperative union, the Mishamo Primary Cooperative (Armstrong 1985).[60] However, the cash and other crops sold through the cooperative to the National Milling Corporation (NMC) and the Tobacco Authority of Tanzania (TAT) do not reflect the total agricultural output of the camp. There appeared to be some illegal marketing of crops, but good statistical figures could not be fixed on these. It was widely agreed, at any rate, both by the refugees themselves and by the agencies involved, that the refugees had substantially boosted the agricultural output of the whole of Rukwa Region.[61] The Hutu refugees of Mishamo, then, were successful, small-scale peasant farmers who were self-supporting and capable of marketing a surplus.

The main food crops cultivated in Mishamo were maize, beans, and cassava. Rice and sorghum were also cultivated and marketed as surplus. In addition, people produced bananas, tomatoes, onions, and groundnuts mainly for household consumption. In the weekly village markets, these latter items were sold in token amounts. Livestock keeping was minimal, mainly because of the tsetse fly infestation.

There had been resistance to growing cash crops such as tobacco and sunflower seeds. Many refugees refused to cultivate tobacco on the grounds that they were Pentecostals and forbidden to smoke (Armstrong 1985). The more recent program to persuade the refugees to grow sunflower seeds for the new factory producing cooking oil in the district capital of Mpanda also met with resistance. Informants pointed out that they had their hands full with their other crops and could not even clear, plant, weed, and harvest their full five hectare plots. Most people reported cultivating between two and three hectares out of the five, noting that the number of unmarried children in their households was an important factor in productivity.

The camp had been since its establishment an object of abundant surveying and documentation, and this was particularly evident in regard to its agricultural production. Noting that "animal projects" had moved slowly because Mishamo was "an area infected with tse-tse flies," one project report nevertheless gave a precise accounting of the number of animals in the settlement; thus, at the "end of 1982, the settlement had 179 goats, 64 cattle, 43 pigs, 32 rabbits, 443 ducks, 17 oxen, 1 donkey, and 17,886 poultry" (TCRS 1984b:n.p.). Inventories akin to this one were also available for the camp's fruit trees, crops, plots, households, people, dispensaries, schools, and so on (Armstrong 1985, 1987; UNHCR/TCRS 1985).[62] These figures and lists told of Mishamo's accessibility as an object of surveying and documentary accumulation. They also reflected the degree to which it had been possible to create an uncommon level of spatial and social order in the camp.

This sense of order and control was also to be seen at the political level. Each village within the camp had been systematically formed as an *ujamaa* village in accordance with Tanzania's Villages Act of 1975 (Coulson 1975, 1979, 1982; Mwansasu and Pratt 1979:13; McHenry 1979).[63] Refugee villages therefore took on the political structure of other Tanzanian villages, with "ten-house cells" and "village councils" providing the basic formal organizational structures of governance. Village councils were comprised of elected Ten-cell Leaders and Road Chairmen as well as religious leaders, and it was from the ranks of the council that the Village Chairman and Village Secretary were elected (Armstrong 1987:67).[64]

In addition to this village-level structure, however, the camp as a whole was presided over by a Tanzanian Settlement Commandant, who exercised supreme command over the camp and directly represented the Ministry of Home Affairs. The Commandant and his staff—representing what one UNHCR report characterized as "an almost military leadership structure" (Armstrong 1988:67)—were charged with administering rural development, cooperatives, health care, family planning, education, law enforcement, and other sectors.[65] The Commandant also enforced a rule that required refugees to be granted a "Leave Pass" before being allowed to leave the camp. This pass was valid for fourteen days. It could be applied for in the office of the Village Chairman, who forwarded refugees' applications to the office of the Commandant. If an applicant had unpaid levies or other problems or infractions according to the records of the Village Chairman or of the Commandant, his or her application might be denied. The Commandant and his staff, along with most of the other Tanzanian government personnel, lived in the Settlement Headquarters, also known as "Village Two" or "*Ifumbula*". (See maps 6 and 7.) Most of these staff, as well as many primary-school teachers and headmasters resident in the villages, were nonrefugees.

Mishamo was widely regarded as a successful example, a model, of refugee settlement. One report called it the "most highly developed refugee settlement established in Tanzania" (Armstrong 1987:1, 19) and "a prototype of a new generation of refugee settlements" (Armstrong 1987:5). Another stated that Mishamo was not only an "encouraging example" of what a "programme for the installation of refugees can be," but equally, "an ambitious project of the colonization of virgin lands, creating an enclave in the heart of the bush" (Armstrong 1986a: 33).[66] In the eight-year period from its initial planning stage to 1985, when the camp was handed over to the Government of Tanzania, it was estimated to have cost in excess of US$30 million.[67]

In many respects, Mishamo could be seen as a special case of the general Tanzanian policy of promoting "pioneer" settlements in sparsely settled areas. As a result of the establishment of the refugee camp, the area had seen infrastructural development which had made the whole region an object of attention and rendered it more accessible.

An article about the camp entitled "Mishamo: Taming the Wilderness" notes: "Tanzania has also benefited from her hospitality. By directing major refugee settlements like Mishamo to its thinly populated and most inaccessible western regions, it has found a way, both generous and ingenious, to promote regional development and expand food production. In doing so, it was able to mobilize international aid to meet the bulk of the sizeable investment involved" (Armstrong 1986c:33–4).

In August of 1985, Mishamo was officially "handed over" to the Government of Tanzania by UNHCR and TCRS. This ceremonialized event marked the substantive end of the programs and financial assistance invested in the camp by UNHCR and TCRS under the Tri-Partite Agreement. The staff of the international agencies was largely replaced by new staff employed by the Ministry of Home Affairs. Fieldwork for this project was begun in October of 1985, two months after the "Hand-over."

KIGOMA

A sizable group of Hutu refugees in Tanzania also lived outside of the camps, largely in Kigoma Region, and it was here that the second half of the field research was conducted. The Kigoma Region encompasses Kasulu, Kibondo, and Kigoma Districts in western Tanzania. (See maps 1, 2, and 4.) The region corresponds in large part to the area historically known as Buha (Scherer 1962; Richards 1960:212–28.)[68] Buha is one of a cluster of precolonial interlacustrine kingdoms studied by Mafeje (1991); Beattie (1964); Vansina (1966,1972); d'Hertefelt, Trouwborst, and Scherer (1962); De Heusch (1966); Richards (1960); Mair (1977); and others. Its name derives from the name of the Ha (Waha) people who have lived there for centuries (Richards 1960:212; Scherer 1962). The township of Kigoma-Ujiji is located on the northern shores of Lake Tanganyika, a few hours' drive from the Burundi-Tanzania border. (See map 4.)

According to the 1978 census, the population of the Kigoma Region was 648,950.[69] This figure included nearly 16,000 Zairean refugees and over 20,000 Hutu refugees (Nindi and Mbago 1983:37).[70] The population of Kigoma also includes Waha and Hutu (and, to a lesser extent, Tutsi) from Burundi who fled forced cultivation and other repressive practices during the Belgian colonization of Burundi. The latter are now considered to be immigrants. A large group of Tanzanian citizens coming from all over Tanzania are also employed in Kigoma in government service.

Kigoma is a major port on Lake Tanganyika and thus has water links with Burundi, Zaire, and Zambia. It also lies at one end of a major, cross-country rail line connecting the lake with Dar-es-Salaam on the Indian Ocean. It is thus a major trading hub and a crossroads of various streams of people and commodities. As a key node in the old Arab trade network in central Africa, Kigoma/Ujiji was for centuries a regional trading center and a site for the mixing of goods and peoples (Wagner 1991: 10-4,489–91,499–506; Sheriff 1987:155–200; Northrup 1988:13–36). Today, Kigoma's reputation as *"capitale de tous les trafics"* remains intact (de Barrin 1986). The town always seems to host traders and other travellers who do not permanently reside there, and one often has the sense that everyone there is in one way or another involved in some kind of trade. Kigoma's twin city of Ujiji is perhaps even more of a crossroads for trafficking.[71] While research clearance for Ujiji was given in Dar-es-Salaam, in practice this was rendered impossible by local authorities.

Research was concentrated principally in Kigoma town and its immediately surrounding villages. Principal informants came, however, from a number of areas around the town. They included farmers, fishermen, petty traders, domestic servants, tailors, students, construction workers, lorry drivers, hospital employees, and unemployed people. While reliable figures on occupations and wages in Kigoma do not exist, it seems that, generally, most Hutu refugees combined petty trade with fishing and/or farming. Occupations were defined by opportunity and social networks to a much greater extent than in the camps, and they were much more shifting. Among informants and people whom it was possible to observe at length, continual planning, strategizing, and searching for new opportunities seemed to be a routine aspect of securing one's livelihood.

Residential patterns were likewise more shifting than in Mishamo. The Hutu refugees lived interspersed with Tanzanian, Zairean, and other residents, and there were no clearly bounded, observable refugee communities in town, although some areas were informally known to have more refugees than others.[72] Many young men, in particular, lived in rented quarters, often sharing rooms with friends, but families also rented. Most informants told of kinship, friendship, employment, and informal patronage relationships which had allowed them to secure housing.

The Hutu refugees in town relied on networks of their own making and had little to do with TCRS, UNHCR, or the government agencies in Kigoma. Thus, while the Tri-Partite partners established a project in 1982 to assist the "spontaneously settling" refugees in Kigoma, these organizations have had little impact on the social and economic lives of the Hutu refugees.

The minimal role of the international and governmental agencies in the everyday lives of the Hutu refugees here will become clearer in chapter 4, but it is of interest to observe that, just as the abundance of documentation and statistical knowledge produced by the project in Mishamo was an important aspect of the setting there, so the absence of documentation was a social fact about the setting in Kigoma. The town refugees were not a visible or self-defining "community". The inaccessibility of the refugees is reflected in the rather impressionistic characterizations usually given of their socioeconomic circumstances, as in the following excerpt from a UN survey of Hutu refugees in Kigoma: "Socially, as part of the local community, the refugees in Kigoma Region seem to be fully integrated. However, the general economic condition of refugees is poor. [. . .] Chances for education, training and employment are very limited. However, if one compares the refugees' situation with that of the indigenous people, no difference arises. In some cases the refugees are better off than the nationals!" (Lugusha 1981:49).

"Integration" is often described as a goal in refugee projects, but this very process makes the keeping of statistics and the running of the projects difficult. The assimilation of the Hutu refugees in town was reflected, not only in their inaccessibility to formal interventions, their residential patterns, and their diverse occupational practices, as described above, but also in other domains. There was a great deal of intermarriage with nonrefugees, and social relationships in general crosscut ethnic and national identities. The substantial commonalities of language between the Ha and the Hutu did much to facilitate these relationships. The Hutu refugees were also very mobile, travelling for economic and social reasons around the whole of Kigoma Region and beyond and gaining familiarity with the area in the process. That these processes took place in large measure beyond the reach of the governmental and international agencies is reflected in the fact that the refugees had arranged very little in the way of personal identity documentation for themselves. As one survey (Lugusha 1981:51) notes: "The majority do not have residence permits nor any passports. Not even Burundi passports! This makes their living here uncertain and vulnerable to corrupt or hostile elements among the nationals. In this situation they cannot take up longterm plans in improving their standard of living as they are not assured of the continued stay here."

The town refugees did not appear to have any plans of leaving Kigoma or town life, however. The survey cited above (Lugusha 1981: 53) discusses this fact as well: "In 1979 attempt was made to get all the self-settled refugees in Kigoma Region to shift to Mishamo Settlement. However, shifting was voluntary. The number that finally joined Mishamo was very small[,] hardly a quarter of the expected refugee population. It seems the refugees did not like to join Mishamo."

Ever since 1979, the town refugees seem to have been suspicious of any effort to resettle them in camps. And not only do they resist removal to the camps; they are also generally unwilling to consider repatriation to Burundi (Lugusha 1981:54): "What emerged from the survey was [. . .] that they have no plans whatever of going back. Afterall [sic] they have land here and they are at least not threatened with possible civil war in which they would directly be involved as is the possibility in Burundi at any time. [. . .] [I]t is clear that the Hutu refugees are here to stay unless they are forcibly repatriated. [. . .] All refugees preferred to remain where they are."

FIELDWORK CONDITIONS

In ethnographic fieldwork, *"methodology"* rarely means a set of standard tools and techniques applicable independently of context. The settings in which the anthropologist finds him- or herself shape the day-to-day practices and the "tool kit" of field research. Such was certainly the case with this project. Since "refugees" is a category often seen as politically sensitive—even an issue of national security—obtaining research permission and doing research in this area can be an unusually complex process. For this reason, a brief description of the circumstances of this project seems appropriate.

In order to conduct research among the Hutu refugees, it was necessary to secure, not only a general research permit, but a special permit for entry into the Mishamo camp from the Ministry of Home Affairs in Dar-es-Salaam. Clearance was also given for clearly delimited areas of Kigoma District. In Mishamo, the question of residence had been determined prior to my arrival. I was given a house free of rent in the Settlement Headquarters or Village Two, immediately next to the house of the Settlement Commandant and his family. My initial request to live in one of the other villages was not granted for reasons, I was told, of my own safety and comfort.

While numerous survey and project evaluation teams, as well as researchers connected with one of the international agencies, had become a routine sight in Mishamo, it seemed that my position and activities were less usual. Initially, a guide from the office of the Commandant was assigned to me, and he accompanied all visits to the villages. These more formal tours seemed to be greeted with suspicion and sometimes even fear on the part of the refugees. Gradually, as the camp became more familiar, it was possible to start visiting the villages alone and to invite informants to my house.

Later on, refugees with whom I had become familiar recalled that, while they were familiar with survey takers interested in their birthrates, their agricultural productivity, and the state of the buildings, wells, and roads in the villages, they feared talking with an independent researcher not sent by any of the organizations involved with the project. It was rumored that I was a spy cleverly sent by the government of Burundi, to gather "knowledge" which would bring harm to them. As one old woman remembered with some amusement, I had been nicknamed "the Tutsi woman" because I was "long and narrow like a Tutsi" and, presumably, because my business in the camp was not understood. It seems that only the most detailed and frequent explanation of my nationality and my academic and personal life dispelled suspicions. A "university student" was what I was, and, in the end, it was one of the best things I could have been because—for reasons to be examined later—the refugees in Mishamo tended to value scholarship and the opportunity for advanced studies very highly.

Several factors shaped the social spaces available for "participant observation." My leaving the villages at sunset to return to the Headquarters area was one such factor; my absence from my house after dark would have been considered noteworthy. Another was a marked concern among the refugees not to be conspicuous. These concerns are justifiably seen as one refraction of a more generalized anticipation of some kind of surveillance. People also hesitated to gather in larger groups to talk or to spend time together, explaining that unauthorized group meetings were not permitted. One-to-one conversations were common, as were small groups when these gathered in the homes or gardens of particular informants along the smaller "feeder roads" or in my house. I worked without an interpreter, interviewing in French or Swahili.

The historical narratives with which this project is concerned were told in a wide variety of contexts, sometimes by familiar informants and at other times by more casual acquaintances and even strangers. Narratives emerged, not only in homes, but also on lorry drives, during walks along forest paths, in the fields while people were working, in courtyards during the cooking of food or the preparation of tobacco leaves, after Sunday services, at wakes, at the markets, and in numerous other circumstances. Conversations in these diverse settings about everyday topics, personal circumstances, and immediate concerns often (indeed, usually) led to broader, historicizing reflections.

Among the town refugees of Kigoma, in contrast, the whole notion of participant observation was challenged by the fact that the setting did not readily produce informants. Embarrassingly, it provided no ready context to participate in or to observe. As was noted earlier, the Hutu refugees did not form a single, distinct community in town and had assimilated to the point of invisibility. Moreover, most Hutu refugees did not wish to be singled out as refugees, or as informants in any study. More will be said about this context in chapter 4. However, here it is necessary to note that the avoidance of conspicuousness was a problem not only in the camp but also in town, if for different reasons.

The gradual creation of relationships with informants in and around the township happened through processes that have been described as culminating in "snowball samples." Relationships with an initially small group of informants produced larger groups through introductions to friends, neighbors, business associates, and kin.

In Kigoma, I was accompanied by a research assistant, a young farmer from Mishamo whom I had only just met as I was preparing to leave for Kigoma. (I have judged it prudent not to publish his name here; I unfortunately cannot now reach him to ask his own preference.) He came to live in Ujiji for the duration of my fieldwork period in town (six months), and he was soon doing interviews on his own. His informants also seemed to constitute "snowball samples." He spoke Kirundi, Kiha, Swahili, and French.[73] His assistance was invaluable.

Housing was extremely scarce in town, but I was able to rent a house on a month-to-month basis in the compound of a water-development project. This turned out to be a fortunate arrangement because the compound was considered neutral and private ground by informants, who readily visited me when I was not visiting them. Indeed, many preferred the compound, coming there regularly. However, restaurants, hotels, markets, my car, streets, shops, visits to the tree under which Stanley met Livingstone in Ujiji, the beach, and workshops owned by informants were also contexts which generated the conversations and information that will appear in chapter 4.

A significant difference between camp and town was that the historical narratives that had begun to emerge so spontaneously and continually in Mishamo did not emerge in town. Indeed, when asked about history, the town refugees frequently enquired why this should be of any interest to anyone. My research assistant also made similar observations, and added, "Some were asking for a salary before they would start telling stories."

In Mishamo, as in Kigoma, more refugees spoke French than had been anticipated. People who reported having had only primary school education in Burundi often spoke French with considerable ease, particularly if they were of an older generation. When possible, French was used in preference to Swahili or Kirundi. Informants usually selected French over Swahili when this was within their power to do, and my knowledge of Kirundi was so rudimentary as to be of limited use. Familiar informants in Mishamo often stopped to repeat proverbs, points, and other fragments of conversation that they considered especially important in Kirundi and in some other translation. Some people, particularly in town, spoke English. And finally, many informants mixed languages in order to better express themselves, often to powerful performative effect.

In town, as in the camp, almost all principal informants were men. Efforts to work with women were frustrated for a number of reasons.[74] The most significant of these was that women seemed to be less accustomed, and to feel less of an entitlement, to assume authorship of narrative expression—perhaps particularly in the presence of an outsider like myself. Women were visibly frightened by my presence in the beginning of the research, and even when more familiar with me, they readily referred me to their husbands, fathers, brothers, or other men. When women did speak, they did so timidly, in short sentences, in the give and take of dialogue, and not in longer, more sustained narrative form. One is not justified, I believe, in concluding from this difference of vocality and narrative style that women did not share the forms of historical consciousness that found narrative expression in the discourse of the men. Indeed, there were a number of indications that women did share in the historical vision to which the men so much more readily gave voice. But it would, of course, be difficult to draw sweeping conclusions about the convictions of persons who were so reluctant to be informants.

I would emphasize that in all of this, the success of the fieldwork hinged not so much on a determination to ferret out "the facts" as on a willingness to leave some stones unturned, to listen to what my informants deemed important, and to demonstrate my trustworthiness by not prying where I was not wanted. The difficult and politically charged nature of the fieldwork setting made such attempts at delicacy a simple necessity; like Feldman, I found that "in order to know, I had to become expert in demonstrating that there were things, places, and people I did not want to know" (1991:12). But there may be more than simple expediency to such a procedure. Too often, the anthropologist takes on the role of police detective, discovering what is "hidden," assembling "evidence" to make a strong "case," relentlessly probing for ever more information. But sometimes what is called for is not an "investigator" at all, but an attentive listener. It may be precisely by giving up the scientific detective's urge to know "everything" that we gain access to those very partial vistas that our informants may desire or think to share with us. And as Roberto Kant de Lima has pointed out (personal communication),[75] there is no reason to suppose that pursuing "the hidden" guarantees that one is going to find out the most important things—or that one is being a good anthropologist. Against the logic of the "investigation," then, there may be a greater wisdom in refraining from the blind accumulation of "data" and the extraction of truth for its own sake.

# THE
# MYTHICO-HISTORY

I did not come to Mishamo to study history. Having previously done research on the emergence of the refugee camp as a standardized, transferable device of power in post–World War II Europe, I arrived instead with the intention of pursuing a comparative study of the actual sociopolitical effects of the refugee camp as a technology of power. What Foucault had had to say about the prison had proved enabling for the study of the operation of the postwar refugee camps in Europe. Foucault's vision of power made it possible to see prisons and refugee camps as sites of politico-spatial practices that were in some important respects of the same order.

As I have attempted to show elsewhere (Malkki 1985), the device of the refugee camp that emerged in the processes of managing people displaced by the Second World War in Europe (and that eventually became standardized) played a part in the discursive constitution of a modern figure that would acquire more and more transnational significance in the postwar decades: "the refugee." Mishamo was undeniably yet another site for the discursive and political constitution of "the African refugee," an ideal-typical figure. The processual constitution of "the refugee" (or "refugees") as an object of knowledge and control was an important effect of this refugee camp. But something else was going on, something that, to me, became crucial to try to understand. Unexpectedly, Mishamo turned out to be a site that was enabling and nurturing an elaborate and self-conscious historicity among its refugee inhabitants. This, indeed, was perhaps the single most important socio-political effect of the Mishamo camp, considered as a technology of power.

In virtually all aspects of contemporary social life in the Mishamo camp, the Hutu refugees made reference to a shared body of knowledge about their past in Burundi. Everyday events, processes, and relations in the camp were spontaneously and consistently interpreted and acted upon by evoking this collective past as a charter[1] and blueprint. I had not come to this refugee camp to study history or historical conscious-ness, but it was unmistakable that history had seized center stage in everyday thought and social action in the camp.

Talk about history in Mishamo took the form of narratives of quite specific type. One of the most immediately obvious characteris-tics of the refugees' telling of their history was its didacticism.[2] Many of the accounts and conversations recorded were characterized by the skilled use of such formal devices as rhetorical questions, repetition, repetition with variation, tonal emphasis, and familiar elements of the Socratic method. Indeed, very often discussions with people in Mishamo had a way of becoming akin to educational lectures. In this process of teaching, numbers and statistics were used for both docu-mentary and performative ends. Likewise, lists appeared very promi-nently in the narratives.[3] There were lists of traits, lists of "symptoms," lists of faults, lists of numbered points to be made, lists that were like inventories, lists of many kinds. Proverbs were likewise deployed as rhetorical devices for persuasion and "proof." (Cf. Rodegem 1960, 1973a.) These stylistic features helped to punctuate the narratives and to form them into logical progressions that had a powerful forward momentum. The didacticism was in itself a central performative de-vice, but it also reflected the refugees' urgent preoccupation with docu-menting and rendering credible to outsiders the history that had brought them to Mishamo and that they could not escape living.

Further, many of the longer narratives—regularly evolving from dialogue into extended and sometimes impassioned monologue—were crafted with considerable oratorical eloquence. Whether these narra-tives lasted only hours or required several days for completion, they clearly had a beginning, a development, a climax, and a closure or end. Once the narratives were completed, those present tended to comment on the lessons and implications contained in them. In this regard, the narratives were like Bible stories—heavily moral stories whose purpose was to educate, explain, prescribe, and proscribe. Indeed, biblical themes were often evoked directly. The persecutions waged by Herod, the Israelites' forty years of wandering in the desert, the betrayal of Samson by Delilah, and many other themes and metaphors were drawn from the Bible and set side by side with analogous themes in the refugees' own history.

Another way of describing these narratives would be to compare them to morality plays, those allegorical plays popular in fifteenth- and sixteenth-century Europe "in which some moral or spiritual lesson was inculcated, and in which the chief characters were personifications of abstract qualities."[4] Both aspects of this definition capture constitutive dimensions of the refugees' historical narratives. The narratives contained prescriptions for conduct and drew potent moral lessons by making connections where not everyone might look for them. Moreover, they continually explored, reiterated, and emphasized the boundaries between self and other, Hutu and Tutsi, and good and evil. It was clear that here were categorical distinctions of vital importance, and that the "chief characters," Hutu and Tutsi, had become identified with abstract, moral qualities. "The Tutsi" were constituted, not only as a categorical opposite and enemy, but also as the embodiment of such abstract moral qualities as evil, laziness, beauty, danger, and "malignity". "The Hutu" tended to emerge out of this, reflexively, as that which "the Tutsi" were not.

The recurring themes that emerged from the historical narratives told by the refugees in the course of their daily lives, then, represented a collective history of a particular kind. As "event history" (Comaroff 1985:17ff.), these exhaustively detailed narratives generally corresponded to records of events, processes, and relationships published in colonial and postcolonial historical texts on Burundi.[5] The Hutu history, however, went far beyond merely recording events. It represented, not only a description of the past, nor even merely an evaluation of the past, but a subversive recasting and reinterpretation of it in fundamentally moral terms. In this sense, it cannot be accurately described as either history or myth. It was what can be called a *mythico-history.*

Like the Bible stories and morality plays to which I have likened them, the refugees' historical narratives comprised a set of moral and cosmological ordering stories: stories which classify the world according to certain principles, thereby simultaneously creating it. Tambiah's characterization of classification (1985:4) goes a long way toward describing these ordering processes:

[A] classification as a system of categories in the first place *describes* the world, and [. . .] this description usually also implies and entails evaluations and moral premises and emotional attitudes, translated into taboos, preferences, prescriptions, and proscriptions. Imperatives are thus related to indicatives, and the actors who subscribe to particular classifications and cosmologies ordinarily [. . .] accept them as given in "nature," and as the "natural" way the world is ordered.

The Hutu mythico-history represented an interlinked set of ordering stories which converged to make (or remake) a world. "Worldmaking," as Nelson Goodman says (1978:7), is a process "on the one hand, of dividing wholes into parts and partitioning kinds into sub-species, analyzing complexes into component features, drawing distinctions; on the other hand, of composing wholes and kinds out of parts and members and subclasses, combining features into complexes, and making connections."[6] The mythico-history was such a process of world making because it constructed categorical schemata and thematic configurations that were relevant and meaningful in confronting both the past in Burundi and the pragmatics of everyday life in the refugee camp in Tanzania. In both cases, the mythico-historical world making was an oppositional process; it was constructed in opposition to other versions of what was ostensibly the same world, or the same past. The oppositional process of construction also implied the creation of the collective past in distinction to other pasts, thereby *heroizing* the past of the Hutu as "a people" categorically distinct from others.

It should perhaps be added that the designation of the Hutu refugees' collective narrative of their past as mythico-historical is *not meant to imply that it was mythical in the sense of being false or made up.* No doubt—as is the case with all myth, and all history—some narrative claims could be shown to be factually correct, and others not. But what made the refugees' narrative mythical, in the anthropological sense, was not its truth or falsity, but the fact that it was concerned with *order* in a fundamental, cosmological sense. That is the key. It was concerned with the ordering and reordering of social and political categories, with the defining of self in distinction to other, with good and evil. It was most centrally concerned with the reconstitution of a *moral order* of the world. It seized historical events, processes, and relationships, and reinterpreted them within a deeply moral scheme of good and evil.

## REPRESENTING A MYTHICO-HISTORY

To be told and retold such similar, almost formulaic historical accounts, and to see stories of people's own lives melt into the general themes of a collective narrative, was a compelling experience. But how can such a powerful sense be conveyed in the retelling? An ethnographic representation here needs to capture, not only the content of the refugees' conceptions of their history, but also a feel for the repetition and thematic unity that characterized the way people told their stories, and a sense of the specifically narrative construction of their historicity. This cannot be conveyed simply through scattered short quotations from informants. The challenge is to find a representational strategy that does not suppress what was the most powerful and striking quality of these narratives: the sense of a collective voice.

My strategy here has been to create "panels"—extended narrative passages clearly demarcated and set apart from the rest of the text. These panels give fragments or chapters of the standardized historical narrative that centrally characterized the camp context. They are not simply quotations, however. Sometimes the panels present a record of one person's words; at other times composites of several persons' accounts on the same theme or topic will form one panel. The particular construction of each panel will be explained in an appended footnote.

This explicitly experimental strategy seeks to address both the specific (and quite unusual) circumstances of this research setting and, at the same time, a much more general problem in ethnographic representation. Whenever the anthropologist wants to say that a collectivity holds $X$ belief or $Y$ value, it is necessary either to use statistical and survey methods (with their own well-known limitations) or to make ethnographic generalizations that convince by showing how particular or idiosyncratic observations exemplify wider patterns. The problem of representation is, at this point, tied to that of representativeness. For ethnographic generalizations are inevitably supported with citations of particular events and utterances. But which particularity is to be privileged? Which specific statement will be quoted? Does one always omit "freak utterances," comments that were heard only once, in favor of recurring statements?

The answers to such questions, of course, depend on the nature of the research in which one is engaged. In the present case, the most startling feature was precisely the recurrence and uniformity of utterances, and it was this feature that demanded attention. But how does one represent such recurrence? When confronted with fifty versions of a narrative that bear great similarities and overlaps of form and content, does one choose to present only a single informant's version? Does one try to present all versions? The panels are an attempt to improve upon the inadequacy of the first approach while avoiding the tedium of the second, trying to capture the sense of a standard version of a narrative, either through a single person's narrative or through a composite of several narratives. (These are not used to the exclusion of ordinary quotations from interviews and conversations, of course.)

There is an uncomfortable silence in anthropological theory around the question of the editing of the testimony of informants. As Feldman (1991:12) has noted, "editing is often portrayed in recent theoretical discussions as the betrayal of the 'dialogical' ethic. In this approach the dialogical is reduced to the positivist model of face-to-face encounter with the other, which is deformed by writing and editing as practices that subtract from the originary *mise-en-scène*." But of course editing is not the distortion of a pregiven object; it is an integral (though almost wholly untheorized) part of the process through which a knowable ethnographic object is constructed. As Feldman says (1991:12), editing "can be part of the construction, reconstruction, and simulation of context." Rather than be silent or apologetic about the editing process, a theoretically principled ethnography must be both self-conscious and explicit about the motives and justifications for its editing strategies. And it must face squarely the consequences of whatever conventions or devices are used to represent or evoke "what was said."

The device of constructing narrative panels has both methodological advantages and disadvantages. One advantage of the panels is that they make it possible to demonstrate and underscore the specifically *narrative* construction and expression of historical-national consciousness among the camp refugees. Second, and more important, the panels are a way of representing the process of the standardization of narratives into thematically interrelated forms in the course of their telling and retelling. The construction of the panels conveys the way that all the different, specific tellings of historical events constituted variations on a single, shared grand narrative.

The principal disadvantage of the panels, on the other hand, is that they present material as if there were total standardization. They give no indication of what variations existed, or of how different versions might have been told by different people. They have a homogenizing effect, taking the words of many informants and merging them into one. In the present case, there are specific and compelling reasons for concentrating on the phenomenon of "standard versions," as I hope will become clear in the following chapters. But clearly, the panels are a simplification. They grew out of the very particular circumstances of the refugee camp and the research issues which were raised there, but they are by no means taken as the only possible approach to the material. Just as different research problems and sites demand different fieldwork methods, so too do they call for different conventions of ethnographic representation.

Kigoma was a site from which no narrative panels emerged. Quite simply, it was not a place where people commonly arranged memories or experiences into mythico-historical configurations, or where standard versions of events routinely produced themselves. There will be a great deal of narrative evidence in the discussion of the Hutu town refugees in Kigoma and its environs, but it will take the form of ordinary quotations from individual persons.

## THE SCOPE AND PROGRESSION OF THE MYTHICO-HISTORICAL THEMES

The mythico-historical discourse of the past to be laid out here encompassed the ancient, legendary life and foundation of Burundi as an aboriginal nation; the arrival of the Tutsi from the North, their artful theft of power from the "native" Hutu and Twa, and their institution of a social hierarchy and a monarchy; the colonial period and, in particular, the role of the Belgian colonial authorities as protectors of the Hutu; the postcolonial period and the foundation of an independent republic; and, finally, the 1972 massacre and the Hutu flight from Burundi. The massacre was a cataclysmic event comparable in its effects to the Holocaust in Europe, and it represented an end or a culmination in the mythico-history insofar as "the past" that lived in Burundi stopped at the moment of flight.

In a strictly chronological sense, of course, the refugees' years of exile in Tanzania (fifteen years in 1986) were also "the past," but for them, these years lay on the opposite side of a great historical divide from the premassacre years. The divide was precisely historical and not merely temporal; the flight from the homeland marked a moment of fundamental transition, a crossing of multiple borders—spatial, social, and symbolic.

The moment of flight and exile from Burundi, however, did not by any means mark the end or closure of the mythico-historical process. The mythico-history remained open-ended, cumulative, and dynamic because in it, "the past" of Burundi was articulated with the present, that is, with the fifteen-year period of exile in Tanzania and, more specifically, with contemporary experiences being lived in 1986 in the refugee camp. The massacre represented the end of an era in time and space, but it was not the final closure of the mythico-history; quite the contrary, contemporary events and processes were one of the main catalysts of its production.

A large number of the key themes in the mythico-history were so closely interconnected and reinforced each other to such an extent that they are best presented here in their original, relational configurations, as "clusters" of themes. These thematic clusters have been arranged here in a roughly chronological order, following as closely as possible the chronology implicit in the mythico-history itself.

FIRST CLUSTER OF THEMES: FOUNDATION MYTHS AND THE GOLDEN AGE OF INNOCENCE; THE IMPORTANCE OF AUTOCHTHONY; AND THE MYTHICO-HISTORICAL LOCATION OF THE "ABORIGINAL" TWA

The first cluster of themes consists of interpenetrating themes at the center of which are accounts of the foundation of Burundi as an ancient, aboriginal nation. These were directly tied in with Hutu reconstructions of the order of the aboriginal nation as an ideal one, as a golden age of social harmony and primordial equality.[7] The idealizing construction of this golden age as a morally pure and just social order will be the second theme considered. The third theme of this cluster will raise the issue of the double-edged implications of claims to historical precedence, autochthony, and what can be called "pioneer rights."

MYTHS OF FOUNDATION AND PRECEDENCE

The issue of who were the original, primordial occupants of the land now known as Burundi was central to the Hutu claim to rightful moral and historical precedence over the Tutsi, and to the Hutu people's status as "the true members" of the primordial nation, the aboriginal homeland. This issue was not taken by people in Mishamo to be merely a matter of the past, or a question of academic or historical interest in any trivial sense. Rather, it was very much a contemporary question concerning the "true essence" of the Burundian "nation" as it *should* be, and as it was, according to the mythico-history, prior to the arrival of the Tutsi "impostors" or "race of foreigners."[8]

Several of the foundational narratives in the mythico-history centered on a mythical hero who became the founder of the nation of Burundi. Panel 1 gives one person's version of these.

Panel 1:

**THE MYTHICAL FOUNDER OF BURUNDI AND THE "FIRST BIRTH OF THE NATION"**

It was one hundred years before Jesus Christ that we [the Hutu] came to Burundi. We came from central Africa. It was the Central African Republic. We came as hunters, cultivators, and herders. The Batwa, their work was to hunt quite simply. They knew neither cultivating nor herding.

Concerning the meeting between the Twa and us? There was no war. Before leaving our country of origin in the Central African Republic, there were wars . . . We came as Bantus. We were not Hutu. But because the name Hutu is already scattered in the entire world, we accept that we are of the race Hutu.

After leaving the Central African Republic, we spread all the way to Katanga—there, to Zaire, there where there are many copper mines. [. . .] Well, there there was a war. Our ancestor whose name was Burundi had to leave Katanga in pursuing the hunt with his dogs, and he arrived in Burundi. [. . .] In his time, the country had no name. At the time of his return to Katanga after his hunting expedition, he [Burundi] lost his way. He met some Batwa who lived in the place where he had lost his way. He mixed with them. He married the woman of the Batwa. He produced children with her. It is a very big relation between the Bahutu and the Batwa. In the long run, the children whom [Burundi] had left in Katanga followed him, looking for him, and found the place that is called Burundi today. But in the end, what did he do? His children asked him to return there to Katanga. *He* sent them to bring his wife, his whole family. He had already had a wife in Katanga. He brought them to Burundi. After their return [to Burundi], he distributed his family in several regions of the country because the country was good to live in. After his death, his children named the country in the name of their father. That was the first birth of the country of Burundi. This is why the country today is called Burundi. There! The Batutsi, when they came in the sixteenth century, they kept the name Burundi because the citizens of Burundi were very numerous and their language was Kirundi . . .

and because they [the Hutu] had mixed with the Twa and spread over the surface of the country. The Batwa have lost their language because they were not numerous, and because they mixed with the Bantus. Even the Tutsi have lost their language because almost in all of Africa, there where the Tutsi have spread themselves, they have come in little groups. In order to be able to live there, they had to learn the language of the citizens of the place where they had come.

The claim to historical precedence is straightforward in this panel. Whereas the Tutsi were said to have come "only four centuries ago," the Hutu were said to have come one hundred years before Christ.[9] They came as Bantu (as "human beings" or as "the Bantu peoples") to a land that did not yet exist as a country. Before their arrival, "the country had no name." The mythico-history did not claim, as many settler myths do (Wilson 1964:3), that the land was empty. The mythical hero, Burundi, had two wives—Bantu and Twa—and hence, two sets of descendants bonded together through his blood.[10] The presence of the Twa in the land from time immemorial was never contested; indeed, it was emphasized. What *was* being claimed was that it was only the arrival of the Bantu and their peaceful mixing with the autochthons that marked the "first birth of the country." The founder of the country was "father" to both Bantu and Twa, and, therefore, the inception of the nation occurred at this moment. (The metaphor of birth is, of course, not at all unusual in the imagining of nations. In English, for instance, the words *nation* and *native* come from the Latin root for birth, *natio*.)[11]

Panel 1 and other versions not included here also make claims against the rights of the Tutsi "newcomers" by asserting precedence on another level: the early "citizens" had already "spread over the surface of the country" when the Tutsi found them there. Thus, the early inhabitants could make claims to pioneer status, to having settled and worked the land for centuries. Another story relating to Hutu precedence in Burundi was explicitly called a "legend" and so distinguished from "history" by the man who recounted it:

Panel 2:
### THE HUTU MOLE KING

[The Tutsi] chose what is called the *mwami* [king], Ntare I. Before this there was no king [in Burundi]. But there were arguments—[about whether] there had existed a Hutu sorcerer king. This so-called sorcerer king is said to have been a clairvoyant and a dream interpreter, like Joseph of Egypt. It was also said that this Hutu king was called Ntare Rufuku. *Rufuku* is an animal which lives in the savannah and passes under plants. [. . .] It is like quite a fat rat. It is called *ifuku* [mole]. They have roads in the dust. He helped men to spread. That is to say, he gave them places so that the men could multiply.

The mole king's roads in the soil mapped out a whole landscape where the early pioneers had multiplied and come to inhabit the length and the breadth of the land before the Tutsi ever set foot there. This imagery emphasized yet again the precedence of the Hutu over the Tutsi and the "native" or "indigenous" rights that were deemed to come with pioneer status. The mole king was evoked with didactic intent to reiterate these rights. This legend would appear to be a parable characteristically told by people who hold cultivation in high regard, as most Hutu do, and not by pastoralists like the Tutsi whose disdain for "digging in the ground" was similarly legendary among the Hutu refugees. In fact, for the Tutsi, ancestry was said to be traced from the sky.[12]

The parable of the mole king would seem to be an especially literal assertion of autochthony, insofar as being dug into the soil, like a mole, meant being a native and inextricable part of the land and even springing forth and multiplying from the land.[13] Consider the dictionary definition of autochthon: "one held to have sprung from the ground he inhabits" and: "fr. aut- + chthon earth—more at HUMBLE."[14]

In this case, as in many other well-known cases elsewhere (the question of Palestine/Israel being but one example), contesting the foundation and legitimacy of a nation almost necessarily implies the question of autochthony and historical precedence. In the mythico-history, these issues were interlocked as a fundament on which much of the moral force of the entire discourse rested. As has already been suggested, the role of the Twa was pivotal here because they provided an affinal link to autochthonism for the Hutu. The following comments were characteristic affirmations of the link: "[The Twa] are pygmies who are found in Zaire, in Burundi, even here [in Tanzania]. These are the first, the *true*, citizens of Burundi—like the Hutu." "The Hutu and the Twa are really the same." "The Twa are like us." People also talked about the importance of trying to maintain the "principle of authenticity" among contemporary Hutu in exile and in Burundi, and in this context the Twa were again evoked. "Authenticity" referred to the need for maintaining a "purity" as Hutu and an awareness of the collective past (cf. chapter 5 below). The Twa were distinctly ennobled by their unquestionable autochthony in the aboriginal land. In terms of national classification, they were "pure" because "native" and "original."

However, the position of the Twa in the mythico-history was more complicated and ambiguous than might at first appear; and this ambiguity derived precisely from their autochthonous status. For autochthony can be a double-edged sword.[15] By asserting that they are autochthons, people may at the same time be taking on, or acknowledging, a cultural construction of themselves as "primitives" and as inferior.[16] In other words, romantic autochthonization—be it in the form of the Noble Savage or a mole king or an "indigenous people"[17]—is likely to come attached to an evolutionary developmentalism which relegates autochthons to the bottom of the "Progress of Man" and to the beginning of the "Grand March of History." The tension evident in the mythico-history between romanticized autochthony and stigmatized primitivity broke through here, in the words of one old man:

Panel 3:

"THE TWA ARE LIKE US"

The Twa, if truth be told, are also Hutu. Between the Twa and the Hutu there is an error [i.e., a different attitude toward "progress" and education, which are valued by the Hutu]. Now, for example—the Twa do not like revolution, they do not like going to school. Me, I do not know the wherefore. A true Twa does not even like to hold a conversation with Hutu, nor to hold a conversation with the Tutsi, either. From the point of view of habitation, he does not want to live with the Hutu [or with the Tutsi]. His wife has the habit of her husband. His children have the habit of their parents. The true Twa do not cultivate. Their function is to make pottery. It is their profession. Also, the Twa love, love greatly, the hunt. They live near valleys. If, for example, you give him food on a saucer, he excuses himself for a moment, takes a leaf from a banana tree, pours the food on the leaf, and eats with his own fingers. He dares not touch the saucer. Why not? Lack of evolution, I do not know. They did not want to send their children to school. The Tutsi do not kill them because these are inferior fellows. They are used only for hunting.

They do not know how to utter even one word before the population [i.e., they are not public orators], they are not rich, they are not intellectuals. They lack civilization, how would I say? Like this. They had nothing to lose, while we, we are worthy of being pursued.

One possible interpretation of this panel's ambiguity appears to be better than other possible ones. Considering the opening sentence of the panel first—"The Twa, if truth be told, are also Hutu"—it is clear that this assertion of common identity fits with the claims to autochthony as these relate to the legitimacy derived from precedence and nativeness. When the mythico-history moved within this domain of autochthony, the Twa were idealized as natives. In this respect, the Hutu were themselves likewise "humble"; they, too, lived "without civilization" or "progress," and therefore easily fell prey to the refined "malignity" and trickery of the Tutsi "foreigners." In panel 5 below, for example, it is argued that the Tutsi accomplished the "theft" of the nation and all that was in it because "there was not anything like progress at the moment when [the Tutsi] arrived" and because "the Hutu had not even the least civilization." The Hutu and the Twa thus shared the innocence of natives in what was reconstructed as a harmonious and pristine social order in a golden age of equality, hospitality, and peaceableness. Here, of course, was one explanation for the origin of hierarchical inequality in Burundi; the adulteration of the pristine order and the end of the golden age befell the primitive nation in the wake of foreign intrusion, and the autochthons were too docile in their naïve purity to foresee or prevent it.

But even as it asserted a common identity, the mythico-history drew a substantial distinction between the Twa and the Hutu. The Twa, it was asserted, rejected progress and education. They wanted no part in any revolution to oust the Tutsi. They preferred, rather, to maintain a distance from both Hutu and Tutsi, the principal categories locked in opposition against each other in Burundi. Thus, as the narrative rather bitterly ended, the Twa stood as neither numerically nor socially "worthy enemies" of the Tutsi. (The Twa represented 1 percent of the population according to the mythico-history and according to most population estimates.) The Twa were peripheral to such an extent that they posed no threat to the rulers, and they preferred to be left alone. In the end, the real opposition was located between the elite Tutsi minority ("14 percent") and the mass of Hutu peasants ("85 percent").[18] At issue here was no longer historical precedence or idealized autochthony, but rather, the period after the golden age when the Tutsi had already settled in Burundi. Here, the relation of opposition between Hutu and Tutsi dominated the foreground of the mythico-historical vision of the past.

It is perhaps worth noting here that the Twa became, in this later stage of the mythico-history of the past, "inferior fellows" because they rejected "civilization," "education," and "progress." Yet the acceptance of these things had, in the mythico-history, its own dangers, since rising in a system defined and dominated by the Tutsi signified being corrupted or polluted by the illegitimate power condensed at the summit of the Tutsi hierarchy. In this sense, the Twa, relegated to the most powerless and least "civilized" end of the imagined social scale, were also the purest category; being dominated was in this sense a sign of moral and political virtue.

The Hutu in Mishamo, then, saw themselves as occupying the massive middle position in a hierarchy where the high/corrupt summit was occupied by the Tutsi and the lowest/purest "ground level" by the Twa. Both Twa and Tutsi were numerical minorities compared to the Hutu, but this fact obviously did not detract from their symbolic or political significance. Several persons in Mishamo conceptualized the relations between the three categories as a layered pyramid, with each layer expressed as a percentage: Tutsi : Hutu : Twa :: 14 percent : 85 percent : 1 percent.

THE USES OF A "TUTSI VERSION" OF THE FOUNDATION MYTH
What was presented in the Hutu mythico-history as the Tutsi version of the origin of ancient Burundi and its "three tribes" was also put to effective use by the refugees. As panel 4 illustrates, the "false version" was incorporated into the Hutu mythico-history as yet another, self-explanatory "symptom" of "the Tutsi character."

Panel 4:
KIGWA AND HIS THREE SONS

In primary school [in Burundi], we had a little book of readings. This book was full of lies—made by the Tutsi—[in order] to hide their native country which they had left, so that the Hutu would not know the national country of the Tutsi. [. . .] The text said: "Once, Kigwa, a man, descended from the sky. He had three sons: Rututsi, Ruhutu, Rutwa. The first son was called

Rututsi. Why? The second, Ruhutu. Why? The third who was the last was called Rutwa." At that moment, we were *obliged* to read this text, and to learn it by heart—*ip-so fac-to*! I ask myself: Kigwa, he descended from the sky, coming in what object? There were no aeroplanes at that moment. A Murundi falling from the sky . . .? This [story] was some of the malignity of the Tutsi so that the Hutu would not find out where the Tutsi came from. That they stay with their lies, these Tutsi coming from the sky, sons of Kigwa![19]

Kigwa thus represented a heavenly ancestor whose origin was outside of and beyond Burundi (in the sky and not in the ground like Ntare Rufuku, the Hutu "mole king").[20] His sons, clearly, were the three "tribes" of Burundi: Tutsi, Hutu, and Twa. The claim implied in this version was that all three groups came to the nation *simultaneously* as the sons of one father.

These claims were, as it were, ideal grist for the mill; the Hutu mythico-history seized on them and pried them apart, simultaneously denaturalizing them. First of all, instead of being accorded the status of "history," the Tutsi version of the foundation of the nation was treated as a "myth," a "mere story": "This is just a story the Tutsi told to trick us."[21] The mythico-history denied the legitimacy of this version by historicizing, in other words, by insisting on the illusoriness of "unity under one nation." Here an implicit distinction is being made between the nation and nationality on the one hand, and the nation-state and citizenship, on the other. Further, the Hutu in Mishamo emphasized the motivatedness of this "story" by stating that it signified the Tutsis' desire to "hide their origins," which lay outside of Burundi, "in the north." Thus, according to the mythico-history, the Tutsi were trying in this story to annul the importance of the historical precedence in Burundi of the Twa and the Hutu by deceitfully claiming simultaneous arrival and common ancestry.

One of the central axes of the Hutu mythico-history was to combat exactly such unifying metadiscursive maneuvers and to establish and demonstrate *difference* instead. As will become clear in the course of the panels, the primary oppositional differentiation—that between the Hutu and the Tutsi—was elaborated in the mythico-history on many levels: cultural, social, political, and physical. Each of these levels signified the others, and they all came together in establishing a fundamental and irreconcilable *categorical difference* between Hutu and Tutsi. An indispensable aspect of this assertion of irreconcilable difference in this case was to insist, against the dominant political discourse of the contemporary Burundi government, that there were indeed three distinct and distinguishable groups in Burundi, and that these did not form one unified or "true" nation. Indeed, in this view, contemporary Burundi was not a nation at all, but only a corrupt and illegitimate Tutsi state.

The distinct subgroups of Burundi were called by the refugees "tribes" and often also, in more self-conscious discourse, "races." The difference between "race" and "tribe" was frequently reflected upon by the refugees in Mishamo, and "race" was selected as more apt a description of difference—perhaps precisely because it was seen as a more irreducible difference than that implied by "tribe," and because the elaboration of *physical* ("racial") difference played such a large part in the mythico-history. It was clearly important to assert difference in and of itself, and it was equally important to show that the Tutsi regime did not operate along national lines, but on tribal ones, hence, that it was a tribalist government. Many in Mishamo echoed the spirit of this question: "The Tutsi do not like to admit that there are three tribes in Burundi, but if that is so, why are we here [in a Tanzanian refugee camp]?"

SECOND CLUSTER OF THEMES: THE ARRIVAL OF THE TUTSI BY STEALTH;
FROM THE GIFT OF COWS INTO SERVITUDE; FROM ABANTU TO HUTU

Panel 5:
THE THEFT OF THE ABORIGINAL NATION IN THE ABSENCE OF CIVILIZATION

One fault of the Tutsi, let us say that it is theft [. . .]. What have they stolen from us? First of all, our country. The Tutsi are of Nilotic provenance. They came from Somalia. And then [they stole] that which exists in a country—the livestock, cows, chicken, domestic animals, . . . let us say, the living things— even the birds, the fish, the trees, the banana fields, whatnot. . . . All the wealth of the country, you understand, was ours. Because we were the natives of the country. They came perhaps four or five hundred years ago—that is approximate. [. . .] There was not anything like progress at the moment when they arrived. They arrived pursuing [. . .] the source of the Nile [which] exists in our country, in Burundi. [. . .] Uniquely for what? To look for a place where they could find pastures for their cows. They live on nothing but cows and milk. At that moment the Hutu had not even the least civilization, whereas the land was for them, the Hutu. [. . .] There are all the things in the country—X, Y, Z. They stole all that.[22]

It is evident that the Tutsi appear in the mythico-history first of all as foreigners—historically recent arrivals "from the north," "from Somalia," or "from the Nile." It was often claimed in this connection that the Tutsi were really "Hamites," who did not belong in the land of the "Bantu" Hutu. The refugees seem to have been influenced on this point, as I suggested in chapter 1, by the old "Hamitic hypothesis," a long-discredited academic theory which saw the centralized kingdoms of central Africa as the work of an "advanced race" of invading "Hamites." As historical reconstruction, the vision of invading hordes of "Hamites" has not held up very well.[23] But the mythico-history shows that, like so many failed academic theories, "the Hamitic hypothesis" has taken on a life of its own.

Now the Tutsi were presented in the above panel, not only as foreigners, but as thieves who stole the country from the indigenous Hutu. There were several narratives explaining how the Tutsi, possessed of "innate cleverness" in the art of deception, *tricked* the original inhabitants of Burundi into servitude by the gift of cows.[24] Just about everyone in Mishamo appeared to be familiar with some version of the story elaborately charting how the ancestors of the Hutu, by accepting in good faith the gift of the Tutsi, were caught in lifelong servitude under them, and how this servitude has been reproduced from generation to generation.[25] Panel 6 is a particularly complete version of this moment in the mythico-history.

Panel 6:

**FROM THE GIFT OF COWS INTO SERVITUDE**

The Tutsi came pursuing the Nile to find pasture for their herds. They asked the Hutu, who were the natives, if they could have places [to live in for their herds and for themselves]. The Hutu, our ancient parents, said: "Me, I live here, my brother lives there, and my uncle lives over there, further. But you can install yourselves here, between us, or there." So, our ancestors gave them land, and they constructed their homes. After some time, the Tutsi said: "We, we have many cows. Why not utilize the dung for your cultivation?" They went to a Hutu woman, and gave her dung to put around her tree. She did not know what this was, but she accepted, thinking: "Why not? This cannot harm me." After a time, two weeks perhaps, she saw that the tree had become vigorous, that it grew very well, with green leaves. She was pleased. Then the Tutsi began to give dung to [all] the Hutu. After some more time, the Tutsi gave milk to the Hutu children. And then, making observations, the mama found that the child, too, had become vigorous. The people saw that the children became stronger, that they grew. Well, they started to go to the Tutsi to obtain milk. At this moment, the Tutsi asked that the Hutu women come to their houses to tend to their children, to work in their houses, and they came. Then the Tutsi gave some cows to the Hutu men. After this, they said: "Why do you not come to our enclosures to guard our herds at the same time that you guard your own cows?" The Hutu agreed to do this. Then, the Tutsi became their chiefs. [. . .] [The narrative goes on to list all the duties that then ensued for the Hutu:]

The Tutsi gave one cow to the Hutu. With this cow, the Hutu got duties following this cow that he got. First, cultivating for the Tutsi twenty-four times a year, that is, two times per month—because of the cow. Second, to bring to the Tutsi two jugs of beer—banana juice—twice a year. Third, to give a young cow when the cow given by the Tutsi [. . .] gives birth. Fourth, there were words to be utilized. The Hutu who had received the cow from the Tutsi was named his Hutu. Possessive adjective. That is to say, his worker! Well, the Tutsi who gave the cow was named shebuja. [. . .] This signifies, "he who has given the cow." [. . .] Fifth, the Hutu was never to work else-where. He was sold by this cow. Never to work elsewhere—only for his shebuja. Sixth, we arrive then at the guarding of the cows at pasture. It is the Hutu who has to guard them. He has become a shepherd, then! So, he has one single cow. Let us say that the Tutsi has 300 cows. At this moment, it is the 300 plus 1. He has to guard 301 cows because of the single cow that he got. Seventh, if at any time the Tutsi wants to go on a voyage, it is the Hutu who has to accompany him. [. . .] All the provisions [. . .] have to be transported by the same Hutu. At this moment, the Tutsi had malignities. The Hutu was not a single one. The Tutsi had to deceive ten Hutu, or fifteen Hutu, or twenty, by giving these cows [to each of them]. [This entourage carried the Tutsi and the provisions on their shoulders up to] where the merry fellow wanted to go. [. . .]

We have forgotten something: Once the Hutu receives a cow from the Tutsi, all his descendants have to work for this Tutsi. [. . .] For a single cow?! I, my son, his son, his son—a chain like that . . . Adam and Eve: do we have a relation with them? Yes. They are our ancient parents. At that time, when Adam and Eve were living, were there schools? No. Were there intellectual capacities? No. This is the wherefore that they were deceived by Satan. Our ancient parents were deceived by the Tutsi.

Presently, I am not like our ancient parents, like Adam and Eve. Be-cause I see what has come to us—us, their descendants; it is misery that we have. That is the long and the short of the history, I can say to you. It is the abbreviation. You see that the Tutsi were more intelligent than our ancient parents. It was a blunder. Lack of schools, of intellectual capacities. . . . If ever we could return to our country, we could not commit a mistake such as our ancient parents made.[26]

In this book *The Premise of Inequality in Rwanda* (1961), Jacques Maquet terms this "hutu-shebuja" relationship, "the *buhake* agreement" and describes it as a feature of traditional society in Rwanda.[27] Similar accounts exist for Burundi, where the relationship is called *ubugabire* (Vansina 1972:195; Trouwborst 1961:4, cited in Vansina 1972:195; Lemarchand 1970, 1973; Weinstein 1976; D'Hertefelt, Trouwborst, and Scherer 1962). In the mythico-history, the Hutu refugees have radically denaturalized this relationship by overtly asserting that the gift of the original cow was the first in a long, historical series of tricks that the Tutsi deployed in order to gain power in Burundi.[28] What Marcel Mauss (1954) had to say, long ago, about the danger that inhabits gift relationships would have seemed very apt to people in Mishamo. By going back to the first gift, the first cow, and reconstructing what it seemed to have brought to its recipient, the refugees were stripping this relationship of the legitimacy of "tradition" and locating its foundations in one temporally insignificant moment. It was almost as if this moment were seen as an accident of history where the "trickery" of the Tutsi newcomers worked because of the innocence of the "natives." The exalted position of the Tutsi in Burundi, suggests the mythico-history, was founded, not on divine or natural premises, but on deception and ill-gotten power. Here, the denaturalization of hierarchical inequality operates by meticulous *historicization*.

The first gift represented only one of the many themes which together constituted a meta-commentary denaturalizing and "making strange" the hierarchical, castelike ordering of society in Burundi. A central dynamic of the mythico-history was the delegitimation of this hierarchy by appropriating themes from the dominant history and giving them utterly redefined significations.[29] This process of transformation was also reflected in the attention paid in the mythico-historical discourse to the politics of nomenclature, as the following section shows.

FROM ABANTU TO HUTU

The transformation from a docile *homo hierarchicus* to an antagonistic *homo aequalis* that was being asserted in the mythico-history was perhaps most tellingly expressed in the refugees' comment that, before the Tutsi came, the Hutu were not Hutu at all; they were simply *abantu* which, as mentioned earlier, signifies in Kirundi "the Bantu peoples" or simply, "human beings."[30] The singular of *abantu* in Kirundi is *umuntu*, "man" or "human being." (Both terms are linguistically related to the Kiswahili words of the same meaning, *mtu* and *watu*.) The name *Hutu*, the refugees said, was imported by the Tutsi from their home in the north and means "slave" or "servant." Thus, "we became their Hutu," "we became their slaves."[31] The Hutu refugees thus saw the arrival of the Tutsi as the cause of their own metamorphosis from "Human Beings" to "Servants".

Panel 7:

**FROM ABANTU TO ABAHUTU, FROM HUMAN BEINGS TO SERVANTS**

In the past our proper name was Bantu. We *are* Bantus. "Hutu" is no tribe, no nothing! *Kihamite* is the national language of the Tutsi. *Muhutu* is a *kihamite* word which means "servant." Having been given cows as *gifts* [by the Tutsi], the Hutu was used as a slave. It is indeed here that the name *Hutu* was born. The name means "slave." We are not Hutu; we are *abantu* [human beings]. It is a name that the Tutsi gave us. Having seen that those who were called the Bantu had already become Hutu, the Tutsi saw that they had us in their hand. They started to make, little by little, the monarchy, then. The Hutu were chosen to work and not to govern. Even during the Belgians. . . . The Belgians accepted this name, and then on the tax card one had to write "Hutu" or "Tutsi."

Hutu, it is a nickname, but we have accepted it. We have accepted it, but the fault can never fall on us; the Tutsi were more clever than our ancient ancestors. We do not call them men. These are monsters, the murderers. Our first identity is *muhutu*. We are Hutu.

If you ask a Tutsi, "Who are you?" he will never, never tell you that he is a Tutsi. Never. He will tell you that he is a Murundi quite simply, that he comes from the country of Burundi. But *we*, we will always say: "Yes, I am a Hutu, a *pure* Hutu." We do not fear. It is we who are the first inhabitants of Burundi.[32]

Such proud assertions of Hutu identity were ubiquitous in the refugee camp. On several occasions, a person could be heard to introduce himself thus: "Good morning, I am pleased to meet you. I am a Hutu refugee, and my name is ———." In contrast to analogous introductions among the Kigoma Hutu, no person in Mishamo was ever heard to introduce himself as *murundi*, a Burundian citizen. In conversation and passing reference to one another, the refugees used the name *Hutu*, and in discussions specifically focusing on naming and other markers of identity, the term *Bantu* was commonly brought forth. The distinction between national and ethnic self-definition was drawn with conscious deliberation, and it was made clear once again that the state of Burundi was not considered a true nation because it was ruled by the Tutsi, who were deemed to be alien to it. As one person in Mishamo pointed out, "In 1972, [the Tutsi] said, 'We are all citizens' and 'Do not fear,' but they killed many Hutu. This is why many Hutu are dead." At the same time, it was emphasized that, by referring to citizenship, the Tutsi strive to "hide their origin" outside of Burundi by calling themselves Burundians. In "hiding their origin," the Tutsi are also "hiding their true identity." This behavior was characterized as "malign."

The issue of purity resurfaces in Panel 7, recalling the link between autochthonous origin and purity. Thus, to be Hutu was to be in a subordinate position, but at the same time it was a sign of purity and pride. Here, as in many other narratives, the "caste" hierarchy was being constructed as unnatural, the result of sinister manipulation and trickery. The analogy made in Panel 6 between the biblical encounter among Adam, Eve, and Satan, on the one hand, and the encounter among Hutu man, Hutu woman, and Tutsi "trickster," on the other, powerfully expressed a connection with evil. Isolating and scrutinizing "manifestations" of evil was a central preoccupation in the discursive reconstruction of the past (and the present). This will be discussed below. Here it need only be noted that the figure of evil in its various manifestations throughout the mythico-history and the progressive negation of the humanity of the Tutsi implied each other (cf. Malkki 1990b). Both terms effected a categorical objectification of the Tutsi as "other" and as "enemy." This objectification, in turn, allowed for the creation of categorical equality between Hutu and Tutsi, an equality based on separateness and opposition.

In summary, the thematic cluster outlined here performed two key operations. The first was to constitute the category "Tutsi" as illegitimate in and alien to the "true nation" of Burundi, not only through asserting the Tutsis' status as newcomers and foreigners, but also through detailing a "malign" essential nature that rendered them morally unworthy of being a part of the "nation." By claiming a golden age of primordial, original nationness, and by aggressively redefining the Tutsi, the mythico-history was constructing a nation constituted specifically as a *moral community*. The second operation made a subversive objectification of the Tutsi-dominated caste hierarchy by denaturalizing, desacralizing, and *delegitimizing* it through historicization. Here, the histories of trickstering, deceit, and secrecy were the vehicles for unearthing the origin and *raison d'être* of inequality. Taken together, these mythico-historical operations established and continually strengthened the force of the antagonistic opposition between the primary categories, and they were an inseparable part of the production of a national consciousness *as Hutu* among the refugees in Mishamo.[33]

THIRD CLUSTER OF THEMES: THE COLONIAL GOVERNMENT
AS A PROTECTOR OF HUTU AND A MODERATOR OF EVIL;
FRANCOPHONE "CIVILIZATION" AS BENIGN KNOWLEDGE;
THE BLOCKAGE FROM EDUCATION

The mythico-historical visions of the Belgian colonial presence in Burundi are important, not so much because they said something about "the Belgians" themselves, but because these visions expressed crucial aspects of the relationship between Hutu and Tutsi. For it was in the context of explaining the Belgian role that certain key mythico-historical themes appeared again and again—for example, the contrast between benign or good knowledge versus malign, secret knowledge; and the constant opposition of good and evil.[34] What is more, narratives about the Belgians indicated something of the significance that the Hutu refugees in Mishamo gave to establishing and maintaining linkages to an "outside world" imagined as fair and impartial. As will become evident in this section and in the analogous section in chapter 3, the constitution of this "outside world" beyond the grip of local exigencies, and efforts to influence it and inform it about the "true history" of Burundi (and of exile in Tanzania), formed a pivotal concern in the mythico-history for some very specific reasons.

The refugees' construction of the Belgian colonial presence in Burundi is remarkable at first glance for the force of its positive, favorable valuation. This was a surprise; after all, the Belgians in Burundi were, like the Tutsi, a ruling group that dominated the Hutu. Given the historical record of harsh Belgian rule, especially in neighboring Zaire, one might have expected that the Belgian presence would be remembered as part and parcel of the tyrannical enslavement of the past.[35] Yet, this was not the case at all among the refugees in Mishamo.[36] On the contrary, the Belgians were quite widely remembered as a good, benign presence in many respects. Consider, for instance, this characterization in Panel 8.

Panel 8:

"THE BELGIANS" AS PROTECTORS AND MODERATORS

After independence, everything became worse. The Tutsi had then all that they had wanted at the same time that they sang of independence for everyone. [. . .] The Belgians were just; they were educated. They were just without regarding race! If a Tutsi has done something bad, he shall be punished. If a Hutu has done something bad, he shall be punished equally. The Belgians, they kept the Tutsi in the truth. [. . .] The Belgians judged justly. That is why the Tutsi had hate against the Belgians.[37]

Reactionaries and neocolonialists, of course, are only too happy to conclude from such remarks that the Belgians were well liked and to extrapolate from this that Africa colonized was a better Africa. A more critical reading would see in such recollections a form of nostalgia and the retrospective idealization of a historical era imperfectly remembered. But neither of these responses would accurately explain why the Belgians occupied such a visible position in the mythico-history, nor why they were so praised. For the praise, as was already suggested, was not so much a description of the Belgians as it was a way of characterizing the relationship between the Hutu and the Tutsi. "The Belgians," as a collective actor in the mythico-history, derive their significance in the mythico-history from this relation.

This relational significance was already suggested in Panel 8: the Belgians were important because they were seen to act and judge impartially without favoring the Tutsi, and to derive their standards of judgment, their "truth," from somewhere *beyond* the system created and deployed daily by the Tutsi against the Hutu. In this capacity, the Belgians were seen as *protectors* of the Hutu, champions of the underdogs (cf. Taylor 1992:53,55–6,61). (Hutu, Tutsi, and Twa alike were colonial subjects and thus "equal" in some curious measure.) Most of these themes of protecting the dominated, and of protecting "the truth" and justice, appeared in the domain of education. It is thus with reference to education and its historically particular meanings in the Hutu discourse that the role of the Belgians as "benign" and as "outsiders" will be pursued here.

The significance of education, academic or intellectual achievement, and "knowledge" in the mythico-history cannot be overemphasized. All the refugees—in camps or in towns—placed an extraordinarily high value on such attainments. The knowledge most valued was the kind seen to be accessible through schooling—ideally, schooling in the Francophone system. Thus, the ideal referred back to the system established by the Belgians in Burundi. (Cf. Greenland 1980.)

The knowledge imported by the Belgian colonialists was seen as *different in kind* from the manifestly dangerous kinds of "clever," "scheming," "evil" knowledge that wrought havoc in the primordial, egalitarian "nation" of Hutu and Twa in the wake of the Tutsi arrival "from the north." (Lemarchand 1970:31–2, 42.)[38] The knowledge of the Belgians was seen as *benign knowledge* and as an avenue toward equality for the Hutu. In other words, it appeared to lay out a clearly marked, open path of academic achievement ostensibly based on merit and achievement through industriousness. It was seen in sharp contrast to the ascribed status hierarchy of the Tutsi, a hierarchy in which the Hutu could never rise to the summit—if indeed they ever managed or dared to begin the climb. This hierarchy appeared impenetrable because enshrouded in secrecy and *malign knowledge*. Moreover, as many Catholic and other refugees in Mishamo stressed, the Catholic Church and its missionaries (likewise seen as principally Belgian imports) were the prime source of this highly desirable education, this *formation* (the French word bringing with it connotations or "civilizing" and "high culture," and the implication of a capacity to transform whole persons). Belgian education thus appeared to be an opportunity for upward mobility, with the impartial Belgians themselves there to ensure "fair game rules" and checks on procedure.

In the mythico-history, it was often emphasized that the Hutu were, in fact, the first to see the value of this education, and to "give their children" to it. This might be seen as yet another assertion of historical precedence in a domain that mattered a great deal to the Hutu refugees. Panel 9 recounts how the Hutu came to be the pioneers in education by default, as the "guinea pigs" of the Tutsi who mistrusted the mission schools, and how this Tutsi scheme then backfired.

Panel 9:

HUTU CHILDREN AS PIONEERS AND GUINEA PIGS IN THE FIRST
MISSION SCHOOLS

[. . . It] is the white missionaries who first influenced the Hutu children to go
to school. At this same moment, "the noble race" refused to send their
children to school. Oh yes!! For what fear? They had the idea that the
whites wanted to kill their children. They hid their children and guided the
missionaries to the enclosures of the Hutu instead. At that moment, we had
a preponderant voice to say. The first arrivals in school were the Hutu children. Having sent the Hutu children to school, the *mwami* [Tutsi king], the
chiefs, the subchiefs, all the clans of the Tutsi—the whole race of the Tutsi—
saw that the Hutu children knew how to write by the little letters that they
read, and [that] some progress was coming from the school. [The Tutsi]
started to wake up. They had slept at the moment when they refused school.
And seeing, further, that the missionaries began to give out work duties
among themselves, in some offices, in whatnot. . . . Yes, at that moment the
Tutsi started to send their children to school.[39]

This narrative emphasizes, then, the precedence, if unwitting, of
the Hutu in the valued domain of schooling. Informants further suggested that the Hutu had outperformed the Tutsi in schooling, being
more hardworking and possessed of greater intelligence. The Hutu,
then, should by rights occupy a higher place in the academic hierarchy
based on merit. These assertions of intellectual superiority were, however, always linked to another theme in the mythico-history: the
blockage of the Hutu from higher education by the Tutsi. It was said
that when the Belgian colonialists were still in Burundi, the Hutu students had a much greater chance of enjoying the fruits of their labor in
school; that they obtained the tangible proof, diplomas. After the Belgians left, people said, the Hutu were increasingly blocked from pursuing studies and were relegated to more technical and manual fields and
schools. They were not permitted to study "administration," "political
science," "sociology," or indeed, any of the "higher specializations"
because the Tutsi "were afraid that then [the Hutu] would try to take
power." The diplomas of the Hutu, it was said, even at the secondary
school level, were "kept in the Ministry of Education," and the Hutu
were not allowed to take them home, while the Tutsi students' diplomas were not thus confiscated. It was unfailingly pointed out among
the refugees that the Hutu were supposed to be the "workers" and that

their job was not to think, to "govern", or to "know about administration."[40]

Panel 10:

BLOCKAGE FROM SCHOOLING AND GOVERNING

It was said that "if the Hutu children are many [in the schools], they will
reign over us." So, since 1961 the Hutu cannot enter school. They said that
it is only the Tutsi who have intelligence, that the Hutu do not have anything
here [in the head]. Even in the army, there are Hutu, but if [the Tutsi] make
attacks, they diminish the Hutu. [The Hutu] are simple soldiers. Among the
children who enter school, forty are Tutsi and only three are Hutu children.
But like secondary school? No, no, no! Primary school, yes, yes. [. . .] Particularly the schoolchildren. . . . The schoolchildren are at the mouth of the gun,
always, always, always, always! There it was difficult. [. . .] In Burundi, it
was seen that the Hutu were more intelligent, stronger at school. They killed,
killed. . . .[41]

The "benign knowledge" derived from schooling was thus seen
as both liberating and dangerous. It brought power to explode the secrets of Tutsi domination, but—foreshadowing the 1972 massacres—it
was dangerous because it could attract the suspicion and wrath of the
powerful, thereby ultimately bringing death.[42]

In the end, the mythico-history shows, the Tutsi "outwitted" the
Belgians, the colonial period came to an end with the inauguration of
the independent First Republic, and the "evil" embodied in "the Tutsi"
as category was thereby granted free reign. And so, the "benign knowledge" brought by "the Belgians" ended up powerless against the "secret," "malign knowledge" of the Tutsi.

Panel 11:

THE DEFEAT OF "THE BELGIANS"

All that [the Tutsi] do, they hide, they hide. In Burundi, they do not want a
missionary, a foreigner, coming to work in Burundi because the missionaries
are at least, let us say, merciful—in the heart, pardoning. They have a weak
heart. They base themselves on the rules of God. And the Tutsi say: "Ah,
[the foreigner] comes to advise us. Tomorrow, tomorrow he will speak elsewhere his words." Now [the missionaries] are chased away [from Burundi].

The end of the colonial era was represented as a defeat of the
Belgians and of the Hutu by the Tutsi because "independence" signaled

freedom and self-determination only for the Tutsi (cf. Newbury 1988). But the role of the Belgians as representatives of a world beyond the Tutsi regime remained important in the mythico-history. A "world beyond" implied supralocal rules, standards, truths, and hierarchies. It was also valued as a "witness in absentia." There was great concern among the refugees that the outside world, or "international opinion," as it was often called by them, be knowledgeable about the events in Burundi, and that it receive "the truth" about conditions past and present there. This struggle "to set history right" will be studied in greater detail in chapter 5.

FOURTH CLUSTER OF THEMES: BODILY TRAITS, ESSENTIAL CHARACTER, AND CONTRASTING FORMS OF INNATE POWER

In the mythico-historical discourse, precise and lengthy descriptions of physical differences between Hutu and Tutsi abounded. It was clearly important that these differences be maintained and kept categorically unambiguous. The meticulously crafted maps of physical differences were superimposed in the mythico-history with analogous maps of what were seen as innate moral character differences. In this section I will briefly describe through the narrative panels, first, how physical difference was constructed and on what body parts the most significant difference was inscribed; second, how bodily differences were seen to express differences of "character traits" in Hutu and Tutsi, and how these differences of character and life-style were, in turn, seen to be legible from the body like symptoms; and, finally, how physical difference was related to social and political inequality, the meaning of labor, and qualitatively different kinds of power.

The mythico-historical constructions of bodily differences between Hutu and Tutsi bore a remarkable resemblance to similar descriptions to be found in the colonial records of Burundi: "The Batutsi . . . are of tall stature. Few are less than 1,80 m. They are in general of an extreme thinness, have a long head, a very aquiline nose, a fine mouth: such [types] among them recall in troubling fashion the type of the mummy of Ramses II" (Gahama 1983:276).[43] Further, "the race of the Batutsi is without doubt one of the most beautiful and most interesting of Equatorial Africa. In physique, the Mututsi is perfectly constituted. [. . . He] is a European under a black skin."[44] The Hutu, on the other hand, were considered "negroes properly speaking," bearing the "negroid" characteristics: "round face, thick-lipped mouth, an astounding nose, squat stature" (Gahama 1983:276). Even in recent years, among the whites in Tanzania who had had occasion to see (or to *think* that they had seen) both Hutu and Tutsi "types" and to hear the stereotypes recounted by other amateur naturalists, the same characterizations emerged. Thus, the Tutsi were supposed to be the tall, stately, thin people, and the Hutu the short, stockier, plain peasants. The fact that these distinctions were quite obviously heavily elaborated cultural constructs—ideal types confounded by the reality of physical diversity and variation—did not in the least detract from their power as classificatory tools, and trying to pin down their "objective" truth or falsity would be grossly missing their significance.

The fact to be explained is that the mythico-history reproduced these distinctions quite systematically, often in long lists, and accepted them as accurate descriptions. The highly conventionalized and stereotyped distinctions were replayed in detail: nose shape, color of tongue and gums, size of pupils, hair texture, prominence of ankle bones, protrusion of calves, lines on the palm of the hand were all markers of difference. It was also universally agreed that the Tutsi were more "beautiful" than the Hutu. In the mythico-history, as in the colonial record,[45] the markers of bodily difference were closely linked with and superimposed on moral and social difference. It is here that the meaning of the bodily differences in the mythico-history became intelligible at another level. The maps of bodily difference were not drawn for any intrinsic interest they might possess, nor were the distinctions seen as mere facts of nature. Rather, while the components of the body maps were accepted without rebuttal, they were deployed in new configurations of meaning which were highly significant and central in the mythico-history. They became symptoms and proofs for claims reaching far beyond the body.

Panel 12:

BODY MAPS

[. . . The] Tutsi are taller generally, [. . .] at the same time, thinner. . . . They are of a beautiful stature. They cannot do painful chores, for example, constructing houses in brick, in wood. [. . .] Their hair is not kinky, their eyes are a little round . . . also, their noses are more or less long. Their faces are more or less long. [. . .] They are real drinkers of no matter what drink.
[. . . T]he Hutu: This is a vigorous man being long or short. He likes to work very much—painful jobs are play for him. He is not a drunkard, since he

who loves painful work cannot drink much. The Tutsi did not know how to cultivate—up until today they have not learned [. . .]. The Tutsi are tall and light of build, and they are incapable of strenuous physical labor. They also have an aversion to hard work because they are lazy, and wish only to engage in the secret art of statecraft, administration, and chiefly duties. The whites of the Tutsis' eyes are brighter because they do not bend over hot, smoky fires.[46]

Thus, the body maps were articulated with distinctions of supposedly innate character traits such as laziness, and, further, with life-style and work habits. One might say that something like a curious caste difference was being inscribed on the body. The mythico-historical use of the body as a surface for the elaboration of other social differences did not end here, however; several other layers of signification were produced in the mythico-history, as will soon become evident.

### THE HEROIZATION OF HUTU PHYSICAL LABOR AND THE ATTRIBUTION OF TUTSI PARASITISM

The above narratives emphasized that the Tutsi "disdained" hard physical work. But they also asserted that the Tutsi were incapable of it, owing to their "delicate constitution." Various versions of physical incompetence existed in the mythico-history. This then led to a further assertion, namely, that the Tutsi who governed *depended* on the strong and skilled workers, the Hutu peasants, for their livelihood.

Panel 13:

"THEY EAT OUR SWEAT"

The Tutsi, they are lazy *to the cube*! (Calculus, you know.) To the cube, to the cube! They do not do anything. They want that we, the Hutu, be the workers. It is we who cultivate the fields, it is we who nourish the Tutsi. Yes! [. . .] It is we who feed the Tutsi. We are their granaries. We call them insects; they do not work; they just live, like insects. They eat our sweat.[47]

These characterizations are not unlike other characterizations of elite classes elsewhere, and all of them share an implicit statement about the power of the oppressed, and the ever-present vulnerability of the elite.[48] The Tutsi were relationally constituted as a parasitical category that was inessential to the existence of the "nation."

Considering Panels 12 and 13 together, one can begin to see, too, that an implicit opposition between two different *kinds* or qualities of power was being set up. The Hutu are "stockier" and physically stronger. They have "the habit" of hard work, and they are "good workers." Their power is located within the body. Internal, physical power is seen as a more or less constant, inalienable kind of power. It is augmented through imposing work on the body. Thus, the more a person works, the stronger he becomes. This equation suggests another one: the more a person is oppressed and constrained to work, the greater his physical power will become. In contrast, the less one works the body, the greater its depletion of power. Thus, the Tutsi are "weak of body." They govern through "malignity," "trickery," and "secrecy." Their power, then, is located *outside* the body and is thus more volatile, manipulable, and precarious. The ever-present references in the mythico-history to "the secrets of the Tutsi" as a hidden domain which excludes the Hutu and works against them strongly suggest this particular interpretation. Further, the image of Burundian society as a "population pyramid" where the Hutu represent the massive body of the pyramid and the Tutsi the small summit carried by it seems to express the same contrast of two different kinds of power.[49]

Being a good cultivator was very highly valued and heroized by the Hutu in Mishamo, and it seemed that putting hard work into the soil, cultivating it, not only signified an inalienable fund of physical power but also implied a right to the land. The Tutsi, being "insects" or "parasites" who put nothing into the land, should not, according to this scheme, profit from it. Moreover, it is well established in the ethnography of central Africa that parasitical "eating" (like "secret knowledge") is often a central metaphor for witchcraft, sorcery, and exploitative evil.[50] In a very general sense, then, what is being established is not only parasitism but also the moral unworthiness of the Tutsi to be members of the nation.

Thus, the physical markers of inequality on which the mythico-history and the colonial versions agreed were put to different uses in the mythico-history and thereby given new valuations which did not converge with the colonial ones. The stigmata of the "stocky," "sturdy" body in its naturalized physicality had become signs of virtue and power.

FIFTH CLUSTER OF THEMES: THE MIXING OF CATEGORIES; HUTU-TUTSI
INTERMARRIAGE

The mapping of difference on the body had the effect of establishing an indissoluble *categorical difference* between Hutu and Tutsi. The

mythico-historical themes to be discussed here reinforced the importance of maintaining this difference and laid out the danger embedded
in trying to blur categorical boundaries. Intermarriage between Hutu
and Tutsi was one of the key domains for discussing this danger. In the
forcefully didactic narratives to follow, the motives for intermarriage
are commented upon, and consequences are laid out as part of a more
overarching scheme of things. Panel 14 below makes a direct link between Hutu labor power and motivations for intermarriage. Having first
stressed the rarity of Hutu-Tutsi intermarriage, one person gave this
account of the conditions of its occurrence:

Panel 14:

### BEAUTIFUL TUTSI WOMEN AS BAIT INTO SERVITUDE

It seems to me that it is forbidden in their law to marry with the Hutu girls.
But if [the Tutsi man] is *very* poor, he will do it to have a cultivator, a slave.
But this does not usually happen. To see a Tutsi who has married a Hutu
[woman], this is hardly 2 per cent. The marriage between Tutsi women and
Hutu men happens a little more often, but from the majority point of view,
5 percent or 8 percent are Hutu with Tutsi girls [wives]. I can explain the
whys and wherefores to you. First, the Tutsi are lazy. Second, most of the
Tutsi are poor. They do not have enough money, they do not have enough
food. You see? Intrigue of the Tutsi: they demand when they see the wealth
of a Hutu. [. . . A] Hutu has cows, food. The father of the young Tutsi girl
begins to get along well with the father of the young Hutu boy: "Has your
son not yet reached the age of marrying? I have a daughter named Marie
Rose. She can be his wife. We have lived together. You have not hurt me
even on one day." This will be the deception of the Tutsi then. He deceives
the Hutu: "You will give me three cows only." At this moment he knows that
the father of this Hutu boy has cows. He also knows that there is enough
food [in the Hutu father's household]. He knows *further* that once his daughter arrives at the boy's [home] as his wife, his daughter will not work. She
will eat the sweat of her Hutu husband. The wife will be lazy while her
husband will work, work, work, provide, provide, provide! If the father of
the boy believes the lie of this Tutsi, [. . .] he will talk to his son. If the son
accepts, things will be very good for the Tutsi there. The Tutsi is content.
There is a third wherefore: The Tutsi girls are much more beautiful than the
Hutu girls. So, the pride of the young Hutu boy—a cultivated Hutu—who
has followed studies, that is—having had his diploma . . . or even a certificate. . . . He no longer wants to choose, at this moment, a wife among the
Hutu. He will immediately choose a wife there where there are beautiful

girls with altogether attractive faces. He forgets the laziness of a Tutsi, the evil of a Tutsi . . . At this moment, he no longer remembers this. He chooses a wife among the Tutsi. *This* is the third cause. *Fourth* cause: The Tutsi girls never like to marry their lazy brothers. [. . .] Because of what? [The girls] will receive nothing! The husband lazy, the wife lazy. . . . Then . . . ? *Fifth* cause: If the Tutsi girl gets married with a rich Hutu, the parents of the girl will receive much money, *much* help. If the husband is a worker of the government, like he who has a diploma, [or he who] is a medical technician, or a veterinary technician, or if he is a professor, or an artisan of these kinds of work . . . he receives a monthly salary [. . .]. There, the Tutsi wife has to oblige her husband to give a quarter of his salary [. . .] to the parents of the wife! [. . .] The wife says to her husband, "Mama has no clothes." Or, "Papa has failed to pay for his herds"—the tax, that is, for the cows. [. . .] [She can come to her husband] with numerous causes. She can also say that there is not enough food at her parents' house. At the very same time, the sisters of the wife—or then the brothers of the wife—live with their brother-in-law. They eat there, they drink there. It is the brother-in-law who buys clothes. At the moment when she imposes on her husband to help her parents, she refuses that the parents of the husband receive anything coming from the hand of their son. If once he gives, it is a fight in the night. Always! [. . .] *Sixth* cause: Once one gets married with a Tutsi woman, some children—*their* children that they receive—a few will resemble their mother. They have the beauty. The Hutu children—you find a form [that is] a little bizarre. And if the two races meet, you see that the two races *have met*. [The parents] receive fruits; their children are a little bit improved because several children take, let us say, the semblance of the mother. They will become Tutsi. If a Hutu man gets married with a Tutsi woman, four among five children will have the figure of their mother.[51]

In Panel 14, as in similar versions, the motives for intermarriage were presented in a highly conventionalized and didactic form. It is, indeed, appropriate to talk about "motives" and not simply "reasons," because whenever people discussed intermarriage, intentionality and calculation tended to be seen as driving forces. The Tutsi, it was said, suffered from "poverty" brought on by "innate laziness" and seized any opportunity to "trick" the Hutu man into a permanent arrangement of economic support. The beautiful Tutsi woman provided the means to accomplish this. She was bait to which the Hutu cultivator/worker was vulnerable. The motive of the Hutu man, then, revolved around the beauty of the Tutsi woman. In addition to her beauty, she also presented a possibility of "marrying up" in the Tutsi-defined hierarchy. The moral of the story was a simple one: falling into the trap of beauty brings lifelong servitude to the Tutsi woman and her family, and blocks the Hutu husband's means to provide for his own relatives. Thus, hypergamy of this kind was regarded as a form of now devalued "social climbing" fraught with danger.

The next panel begins by describing the same motives and emphasizes, likewise, that servitude and entrapment into ever harder work are the inevitable outcome of intermarriage. This version, however, brings the process to a much more tragic culmination. Death, not life, is seen to be the outcome of this "bad combination," this adulteration of categories.[52]

Panel 15:

**THE DEATH TRAP OF TUTSI WOMEN'S BEAUTY**

They [the Tutsi], they are the herders. They do not have food. All that which they use for eating, that comes from us, the cultivators here [the speaker points to the base of the population pyramid that he has drawn in the sand]. All right, here, at the summit of the pyramid, there is a certain Tutsi. The better to get food, he flatters a Hutu, a cultivator. He says, "I give you my daughter, even two or three cows." Like this. Then the Hutu, since he sees a beautiful woman with a long nose and [who is] very tall also in stature—elegant, if you wish—and who squanders smiles. . . . This is the means of flattering the Hutu, the cultivator who has perhaps five tons of beans and two tons of maize. [. . .] She sees a Hutu cultivator, slave. . . . Then the Hutu has to augment his cultivating since he gets married [with the beautiful Tutsi woman]. Well then, instead of seeing that he is overburdening himself—yes, that he is putting too much on his shoulders—the Hutu now has to cultivate *seven* tons of beans. But the Tutsi is not yet satisfied. This Hutu directly begins to despise the other Hutu because he is flattered and he boasts [. . .] about his Tutsi wife! And his parents are proud. It was like this in the past. [. . .] [I]n the years [between] 1800 and 1920, up to '72, the Hutu parents would have been happy [about a Tutsi daughter-in-law] perhaps. [. . .] One cannot condemn them. They did not understand in those times. *But!* From 1950 to 1972, *here* it is the [Hutu] *intellectuals* who did this! This is why our revolution will take a long time. It was very bad what [the intellectuals] did because they understood. The intellectuals should have tried to help. [. . .] If ever these intellectuals return [from Europe], they will seek to get married with a Tutsi woman. I ask myself. . . . So that the Tutsi would not look at him badly, [the Hutu intellectual] has to take a Tutsi wife. Even the three

Hutu ministers married with Tutsi women. So, the home of a Hutu minister is full of Tutsis—his wife and his servants. [. . .] Yes. He *has* to have Tutsi servants. If ever he were to have Hutu servants—he cannot. His servants *have* to be Tutsi. These are like spies. If ever he goes elsewhere during the night, [the servants] will know it. [. . . During] the genocides of '65, '69, and '72, the Tutsi—before killing the Hutu intellectuals—the Tutsi sought out the brothers-in-law of the Hutu who had married Tutsi women. That is to say that the brother-in-law is also Tutsi. They killed the Hutu husband and his children. So, why marry a Tutsi woman? I do not know—to show that he, too, that he has the power of marrying with this category. . . . Or to be able to pass the period of his life [in other words, to be able to live out his life without meeting with premature death]. [. . .]

For the marriage of a Tutsi woman and a Hutu intellectual: yes, this is done sometimes. But a marriage between a Hutu peasant and a Tutsi woman, no. Never, never! After '72, never! Even before '72, in general the Hutu peasants did not do it. [. . .] I will tell you something: I had a teacher who was my friend. Well, in 1970, my teacher wanted to marry a Tutsi woman, one of the teachers at the school. There were also several Hutu [women] teachers, four, all of them credentialed in pedagogy. So, when he told me that he was going to marry this Tutsi woman, I said: "Why have you chosen her? Because she is a Tutsi! There were four other women there! Four other, credentialed Hutu women! Not one was beautiful? Not one attractive? They were all antipathetic?" He said that love is blind. Me, I said: "I am sure that you will not get married with this woman." My teacher asked me why. I said: "You will see the evidence. I will make prayers for you." Three months later, in September of 1970, something happened. The Ecumenical Council of Churches in Geneva [. . .] gave him a scholarship for pursuing studies in theology [. . .] in Kinshasa. [. . .] The girl did not accept this. She cried, cried. She even tried to commit suicide, but someone caught her. This was in '71, now. He was supposed to return [from Kinshasa] in the month of June, '72, but the genocide had started in the month of April, the 29th. So, [after] that he was a refugee, a student refugee, in Kinshasa. [. . . He later wrote to me saying:] "If I had married this woman, I would be dead now." His mother, his sisters, his brothers . . . all, all, all were killed [while he was abroad]. [. . .] The Tutsi woman whom he had wanted to marry, she participated in killing the four Hutu girls, the credentialed. One of these Hutu girls had had two weeks of marriage when they killed her with her husband. They were roped together in their bed in the reciprocal position—let us say, like when they were in action. Then, [the Tutsi] said: "Do your actions so that your marriage should be very well completed."

They were thrown into [Lake Tanganyika]. These Tutsi, when they entered into their home, they were accompanied by the military people. Even in South Africa, that Pik Botha has never done this.[53]

The story of Samson and Delilah from the Book of Judges in the Old Testament was mentioned by many of the people who talked about the dangers or intermarrying with the Tutsi category. In the biblical version, Samson, the man of heroic physical strength, was brought down by the beautiful Delilah, his mistress and betrayer. That this story would have been of significance in the mythico-history is not surprising. For here, too, the beautiful woman was considered a betrayer intentionally and knowledgeably setting out to entrap the Hutu man into a marriage of enslavement. The young fiancée in Panel 15 was also portrayed as a willing participant in the killings that started in April of 1972.

The more problematic aspect in this sequence of events is that the Hutu "intellectuals" who "should have known better" so willingly married Delilah. As later panels will show, it was particularly the category of "Hutu intellectuals" who were among the first to be sought out and killed when the massacres started.[54] They represented, according to the mythico-history, the category which most threatened Tutsi dominance in Burundi. They had "education" and "knowledge" which might have allowed them to "discover the secrets of the Tutsi." But many were also seen as social climbers who sought to marry into the Tutsi category—whether for security or for ambition. Here it became apparent why the partial fusing of the two hierarchies described in the third cluster of themes was so problematic for the dominated category. Once again, the hierarchy of "civilization" brought by the colonialists was seen as the source of a benign, useful kind of knowledge which enabled the dominated to oppose and challenge the dominant. Yet, the "malign hierarchy" of the dominant was interpenetrated with the apparently "benign" one, and the Hutu had become captured by both.

The mixing of categories through intermarriage, then, was seen to breed, not life, but death. The 1972 massacre was seen as the historic culmination of such blurring of boundaries. The massacre was seen in this regard as a supreme moral lesson.

SIXTH CLUSTER OF THEMES: APOCALYPSE AND ACCOUNTS OF ATROCITY
The body maps[55] were put to further uses: according to the mythico-history, these physical markers served as clues during the 1972 massa-

cre as to who was Hutu and who was Tutsi; it was these that determined who would be killed. The differences therefore signaled the difference between life and death. This was very clearly expressed in a list given by a person in Mishamo in response to the question: How could it be possible to know a person's identity with certainty enough to kill?

Panel 16:

THE CONCRETE ENACTMENT OF THE BODY MAPS AND

THE LIFE/DEATH AXIS

There are . . . symbols. . . . There are symbols for recognizing a Hutu. [. . .] Well . . . so, the first symbol was this: In the hand of the Hutu there was an "M." Like this, you see? [Informant shows the lines forming an "M" on his palm.] Between the hands of the Tutsi and the hands of the Hutu there is a difference. One *had* to show one's hand [to the Tutsi during the massacre]. Like this they were able to recognize him who was the Hutu. But there were also other symbols on which one based one's judgment]. [. . . T]he second symbol was this: The Tutsi do not have these bones . . . [Informant bends to pull up the leg of his trousers, and points to his ankle bones]. Do you see? These bones here. The Tutsi have a straight line here. The third symbol—a Tutsi has a straight line here. [Still standing, the narrator pulls up the leg of his trousers further to expose his calf muscle.] A completely straight line here, while the Hutu has a swollen calf, like this. [He points to his own calf.] The fourth thing, one observed above all the gums—[. . . .] Yes, the gums. Especially the Tutsi have *black* gums. Exactly the majority of the Tutsi! Sometimes a few little red parts, but otherwise black. Altogether black gums. . . . One observed further the tongue. Their tongues are often black or blackish. For the Hutu, the gums and the tongue are always red or pink. Also, there are Hutu who have had the good fortune of having black gums and all the Tutsi symbols. Like this they have not been killed. There have been some mixtures of Hutu who have married Tutsi girls. [. . .] The fifth symbol was the language spoken—since the Tutsi do not speak like the Hutu. Their voice, their language. . . . They have a haughtiness in their language. . . . Example: For "you!"—do you understand? You! [. . .] So, for "you!" the Hutu says "sha!" The Tutsi says, "hya!" Or then the word for "goat": The Hutu says "impene." The Tutsi says "ihene." And other differences which differentiate the languages. It is a language which truly grates. With their pride! Arrogance! [. . .] The sixth symbol, it is the fashion of walking—[. . . .] If once a Hutu is walking, he walks—[The narrator gets up to demonstrate a brisk, energetic walk with arms swinging purposefully]—he walks vup! vup! vup! like this, fast. Whereas the Tutsi walks like he who has not eaten, who walks softly—like he who goes where he does not want to [go]. . . . We arrive at the—seventh symbol, I think. Yes, the seventh: One looked precisely at the nose. The nose of the Tutsi is a big nose—pointy—which goes in a *straight line*, a straight line, from the forehead to the pointed extremity of the nose. The nose is big—which has a straight line. It is a nose similar to [that] of a European, but I have made an observation: The Europeans have a curved line [at the base of the nose], like the Hutu. So, the eighth symbol. Let us go to the face. Almost always you find [the Tutsi] with shiny faces with slightly reddish eyes—when he is grown up. When he is still young, they are brilliant eyes! Clear! The eyes of the Hutu are not altogether red—at the same time, not altogether brilliant. An eye which is between white and red—when [the Hutu] are still little. For the Tutsi, this part—that which with you is blue—for the Tutsi that part is big, *immense!* He has the air of a timorous fellow! The rich Tutsi drink a very strong drink, so their eyes can become red. But the Hutu also have reddish eyes—here, they are adults. [The Hutu] have bizarre eyes, spoiled—with an old woman, tired eyes because of the smoke [from the cooking fires]. The Tutsi eyes are the eyes of a superior. You can determine that. Who has lived without working . . . one can see that. [. . .] The ninth symbol, this depends on the height. For the most part, the Tutsi are tall—but no rule without exception, as I have told you. There are also short Tutsi. There are also Hutu who are tall. When [the Tutsi soldiers] find him tall, it is the difficult problem whether he is Hutu or Tutsi. At this point, they utilized these other symbols. Looking at the hand, the legs, the calves . . . or then, walking. [. . .] Walking. They imposed: "Go get us that!" If he departed so fast, one knew that this is a Hutu. *But:* they did not kill him at this moment. They had to pass through all the other symbols.[56]

Again, the body maps described here were far from being naturalistic descriptions of inert features for their own sake. Essentialist projects to determine the "objective" truth or falsity of these body maps would not address the most complex or important questions concerning, precisely, their power as cultural constructs inextricably encoded in other domains of social practice, and capable of being put to many uses. One use, or effect, of such maps is to help construct and imagine ethnic difference. As Feldman has shown in his study of the body and political terror in Northern Ireland (1991:64), "the ethnicity of the body is built in its dismemberment and disfigurement. Violence constructs the ethnic body as the metonym of sectarian social space." Through violence, bodies of individual persons become metamorphosed into *specimens* of the ethnic category for which they are supposed to stand.[57]

The mythico-historical account in Panel 16 outlines how the categorical differences were deployed to calculate on bodies the axis between life and death. The body maps already discussed in connection with labor and intermarriage had become articulated in the mythico-history with yet another set of heavily physicalized maps, those charting the techniques of mutilating and killing during the 1972 massacre. These necrographic maps were extremely numerous and extensively elaborated in the mythico-history.

Two main types of narrative involving such necrographic maps were distinguishable. The first type of narrative was a description of events and procedures, presented with startling detachment and meticulous attention to "technical" detail. This type of narrative was a generalized, abstracted story without particular individuals as actors. Only the categories Hutu and Tutsi were acting subjects. Or, more specifically, "the -Tutsi" as categorical actor was cast as the subject, while "the Hutu" was cast as the categorical object and victim.

The second general type of narrative was a more specific, emotion-filled reconstruction, not only of techniques, but of particular events, whether lived directly by the narrator or told to him or her by others. These stories more clearly drew attention to the concrete experiences of the narrators as victims of atrocity. Despite this, the accounts of atrocity were also told at a generalized level where the relationship between the narrator and the victim(s) of atrocity was not explicitly defined.

Usually, the generalized, formalized stories of both types were told more often than personal recollections of deaths of a person's friends or family. When the fate of friends and kin was mentioned, what was more often stated was the simple fact of their dying. Thus, in most cases but not all, the necrographic maps were suspended in this context. One sometimes got the impression that the generalized accounts of either type were a means of recalling the more intimate deaths without talking about them directly.

Panel 17 gives accounts of the first, more dispassionately "technical" type.

Panel 17:

NECROGRAPHIC MAPS OF TECHNIQUES FOR DESTROYING THE BODY

[. . . T]here were many manners of killing them. [. . .] With the sisters [nuns]—you are familiar with bamboo? [. . .] They were split into two parts—of the length of 1.80 meters, 1.90 meters, or 2 meters, if you will. They were prepared with machetes, until the bamboo was pointed like a nail. So, a Hutu is placed on the ground. The bamboo is pushed from the anus to the head. It was like this that they did—to sisters, or *padres*—or to pastors. There are two other fashions. There are large nails, six centimeters, long, fat. It is planted with a hammer. The nail is placed on the head of a Hutu. Once hit, it begins to penetrate the head. *Several* techniques, several, several. Or, one can gather two thousand persons in a house—in a prison, let us say. There are some halls which are large. The house is locked. The men are left there for fifteen days without eating, without drinking. Then one opens. One finds cadavers. Not beaten, not anything. Dead. Or, [. . .] they were given an altogether weighty hammer—let us say, five kilograms. This was given to one Hutu among the Hutu seized. They were placed in a line. And then, the one who had received the hammer there received an order from the soldier to hit the hammer on the forehead of his friend, here. [The narrator motions splitting the forehead vertically in half]. They stay one behind the other [in the line]. I go with the hammer terminating one after the other. When I have terminated all of them, the soldier shoots me with a bullet. [. . .] Holes were made—trucks bringing cadavers, cadavers, cadavers. The cadavers were spilled into the hole. [In Gitega,] the *katepila* [Caterpillar bulldozers] were brought to make large trenches. [. . .] The trench was dug during the night. Very early in the morning, the Hutu seized were brought there. [An exact location is named and its geographic features described.] They were transported in trucks . . . perhaps twenty trucks. The people were arranged all around that trench and then the soldiers shot them. They fell in the hole. After, dust was put on top. The instrument which had dug the hole covered the cadavers. It is an instrument which moves on chains, which goes very slowly. It weighs a lot. This same instrument went on the filled hole [pressing down the earth] so that if by accident there is one still alive, he will not be able to climb out. Then the instruments and the soldiers left.[58]

In giving such generalized, technical, subjectless, and detached accounts, informants seemed preoccupied with rendering practical facts and details as accurately as possible. Accounts of this kind appeared to be part of a process of precise documentation and historical recording for preservation; each detail was reflectively presented as essential and significant.[59] The process of telling was often accompanied with body gestures which gave the accounts a hard visual commentary likewise demanding witness.

In panel 18, a series of narratives draws attention more closely to the fact that the events described *were* atrocities which had been lived and witnessed by particular persons known to the narrator. The accounts seemed to converge upon a number of formulaic key themes even more strongly than did the "technical" descriptions.

Panel 18:

### THE MYTHICO-HISTORY OF ATROCITY

The manners that the Tutsi employed—if, for example—yes, we are adults, well . . . for example: a pregnant woman (Hutu).[60] There was a manner of cutting the stomach. Everything that was found in the interior was lifted out without cutting the cord. The cadaver of the mama, the cadaver of the baby, of the future, they rotted on the road. Not even burial. The mother was obliged to eat the finger of her baby. One cut the finger, and then one said to the mother: Eat! [. . .] Another . . . another case which I remember—They roped together a papa with his daughter, also in Bujumbura. They said: "Now you can party." They were thrown into the lake. [. . .] My older brother, he was roped, and then he was made to roll, slide on the asphalted road behind a car. [The Tutsis'] intention was to equalize the population, up until 50 per cent. It was a plan. [My brother's] body was left in the forest. If it had been left on the road, the foreigners would have seen it, and they would have written about it. [. . .]

The girls in secondary schools, they killed each other. The Tutsi girls were given bamboos. They were made to kill by pushing the bamboo from below [from the vagina] to the mouth. It is a thing against the law of God. Our party would never do this. God must help us. [. . .] During the genocide, every Tutsi had to make an action [to kill]. In the hospitals, in the churches, . . . The Fathers had to kill each other, and to kill Hutu faithful. Even the sick were killed in the beds of the hospitals. The genocide lasted three months, from the twenty-ninth of April to the end of August. But the killing was started again in 1973, above all in Bukemba.

[In other cases,] a bonfire was lighted. Then the legs and the arms of the Hutu were tied. [Informant describes how the arms were tied in the back of the body, and the legs were fastened to the ground, so that a circle of captives around the fire was forced to bend backwards.] Then the fire, the heat, inflates the stomach, and the stomach is ruptured. You see, with the heat, much liquid develops in the stomach, and then the stomach is ruptured. For others, a barrel of water was heated, and the people were put into it. [. . .] For the pregnant women, the stomach was cut, and then the child who had been inside—one said to the mama: "Eat your child"—this embryo. One had to do it. And then, other women and children, they were put inside a house—like two hundred—and then the house was burned. Everything inside was burned. [. . .] Others utilized bamboos, pushing them from here [anus] until here [mouth].[61]

KEY THEMES OF ATROCITY ACCOUNTS

These passages suggest that there were certain body parts on which mutilation and destruction converged; and these body parts were also the points of thematic convergence in the narratives. While "techniques" or "manners" used were once again described in detail, it was the symbolic meaning of these events which was the more crucial aspect here. The sex of the body seems to have dictated the focal points for the infliction of violence on the body when the target was not a larger group. The mouth, the brain, and the head as a whole, as well as the anus, were focal areas on the bodies of men in particular. Women's bodies were said to have been destroyed largely through the vagina and the uterus. When the women captured were pregnant, the violence seems invariably to have focussed on the womb and specifically on the link between mother and child. In the case of the school girls, the violence was initiated through the vagina. In the case of both men and women, the narratives suggest, a systematic connection was made between the vagina or anus and the head through the penetration of bamboo poles. The bamboo poles (themselves stereotypically emblems of Tutsi categorical identity) were sometimes specified to be 1.8 or 2 meters long. It is perhaps not coincidental that these lengths correspond to the stereotypic height of "a Tutsi."[62] As reconstructed in the mythico-history, such connections did not appear haphazard or accidental. Rather, they seem to have operated through certain routinized symbolic schemes of nightmarish cruelty.

In the case of some informants, explicit links were made between these highly elaborated techniques of killing and their perceived symbolic or political intent. In other cases, the symbolic significance of the techniques was implicit in people's reflections on the "causes" of killing.

The disembowling of pregnant Hutu women was interpreted as an effort to destroy the procreative capability, the "new life," of the Hutu people. In several accounts, the unborn child or embryo was referred to, simply, as "the future." The penetration of the head through the anus, as well as other means of crushing the head, were seen as a decapitation of the intellect, and, on a more general level, as an effort to render the Hutu people powerless, politically impotent. (Reference was never made to any mutilation of the penis.) In particular, it was said that the intention was to squash the Hutus' efforts to gain higher education.

The anthropologist, upon hearing these accounts, predictably thinks of how in many societies, the linking of high and low, of the head with the anus or vagina, represents a profound form of defilement and humiliation, especially when these are linked through violent force. Similarly, the forcible penetration of the anus and vagina can only be seen as violent acts of humiliation and dehumanization. The implication of incest forced upon father and daughter by roping them together and forcing them to die in a sexualized position as they drown is likewise a cruel statement about their powerlessness to prevent either incest or death. How one dies is important here, as it is elsewhere in the world. And again, forcing a woman to eat the flesh of her own "flesh and blood," of her child, is imposing, not only cannibalism, but autophagy in the literal sense of devouring oneself. It represents a complete reversal of the "progress of nature" in which the mother's body nurtures, forms, and brings into the world "new life."

These accounts together documented a process of profound dehumanization of the Hutu as a people, of their objectification as something less than human and "natural." However, simultaneously, as these events and techniques were being described in the mythico-history by the refugees themselves, the dehumanizing gaze was necessarily turned against those who were considered to have produced and deployed the techniques of human destruction described. Thus, it was not specific individual perpetrators, but "the Tutsi" as a homogeneous category that had created the violence, perversity, and defilement. "They" are therefore seen as the source of the almost unimaginable evil and of the destruction of "the natural" as constituted in collective memory through the refugees' fifteen years of exile. The dehumanization of the Tutsi at this level acted as a culmination of earlier assertions in the mythico-history that the Tutsi did not belong to "the nation" in its pure, "natural" state. In narrative segments cited earlier, the Tutsi were cast as "the impostors from the north," "the foreigners," and further, as morally unworthy of membership in the nation because of their parasitism, thievery, and trickery. Here, then, the culmination of this reasoning was reached: Burundi as it is today is *not* and never can be a single harmonious nation, and the ruling Tutsi are the foreign, unnatural, evil element in it. They are not Bantu and not even human, *abantu.* In the mythico-history, the enemy of the "authentic nation" of Burundi is "the Tutsi."[63]

This form of categorical enmity was powerfully constituted on many levels of the mythico-historical discourse. But in several cases the very persons who described the apocalypse in these categorizing, objectifying terms also gave accounts of how individual Tutsi played an instrumental role in their personal escape. The position of these accounts of individual Tutsi saviors in the mythico-history is not clearly articulated, but they could be interpreted as a way of accounting for one's own good fortune in being spared from death. Three such stories encountered also seemed to emphasize the role of random chance and luck in the escape from death. They did not seem to attenuate in the least the categorical distinction otherwise drawn between good and evil, Hutu and Tutsi—if anything, these exceptions seemed to strengthen the categories.

The form of the Hutu refugees' accounts of atrocity as a whole can, perhaps, be compared with the accounts of other victims of extreme violence—survivors of Nazi concentration camps, of the Armenian massacres, of the current civil war in Bosnia, and of many other tragedies. In most of these cases, it is relevant to ask how the accounts of atrocity come to assume thematic form, how they become formulaic. This is not a euphemistic way of charging survivors of atrocity with selective amnesia, or of denying the fact of their experiences. Rather, it is to ask when and how both the perpetration and the memory of violence may be formalized.

The first thing to be examined in the present case is the extent to which the techniques of cruelty actually used were already symbolically meaningful, already mythico-historical. Acts of cruelty and violence, after all, often take on conventions readily. They become stylized and mythologically meaningful even in their perpetration. One need only inspect reports from Amnesty International and other organizations whose main purpose is to document human-rights violations to begin to see that the conventionalization of torture, killing, and other forms of violence occurs not only routinely but in patterned forms in the contemporary world.[64] Torture, in particular, is a highly symbolized form of violence. At this level, it can be said that historical actors mete out death and perpetrate violence mythically.[65]

Yet the accounts presented here were more than simple recollection. Clearly, they had sprung first from lived fear and horror. But the accounts of atrocity, remembered and retold, themselves became acutely meaningful themes in the mythico-history. They had, in other words, an order—more precisely, they had been incorporated into the overarching moral order expressed in the mythico-history. The stories of atrocity thus stand as ordering stories at an extraordinary level. In this specific sense, the collective reconstruction and memory of violence may also be characterized as mythical.

Thus, acts of atrocity are not only enacted and perpetrated symbolically; they are also, after the fact, stylized or narratively constituted symbolically. To debate about which of these levels is more mythologized is perhaps not the most interesting or important question, however. It seems more essential to point out that in this case in particular, fatal cruelty does not lie outside of the social, nor is it unconnected to other arenas of social practice. The organization of the related set of panels seeks to make intelligible precisely the ways in which highly elaborated and extreme violence was linked up with such other practices as the inscription of differentiating schemata on human bodies, visions of the mixing of categories that "ought" to be kept distinct, and the structuring of totalizing inequality. For the massacre was seen in the mythico-history precisely as an apocalyptic culmination of such "dangerous" tendencies and processes which had been formative of Burundian society for decades and even centuries.

WHY NOT BULLETS? SECRECY FROM OUTSIDERS AND THE DISPOSAL
OF BODIES

Hearing scores of accounts of cumbersome, difficult mutilation and killing, the listener eventually begins to become numb to their horror and to ask grimly practical questions. For instance: Would the process of killing tens or hundreds of thousands of Hutu not have been more efficiently pursued with guns and bullets? The Hutu refugees had several answers to this. The most "technical" and frequent answer was that "the Tutsi did not want to waste bullets."[66] Others pointed out that gunshots are noisy and could be heard by "the foreigners" or "the Europeans." Still another person gave a moral significance to the economizing of bullets: "But nothing frightens the Tutsi. They laughed while a man [was] in the process of dying . . . Many, many manners were used . . . It was said that the shot from a gun is the best death—the death of a soldier or of a Tutsi. This death, they said, is not designated for the Hutu." The meaning of an "honorable" or "normal" death was brought up by many, and it was generally believed that the Tutsi considered Hutu unworthy of bullets. There circulated, for example, a story of a man who succeeded in *buying* death by the bullet from his captors; this was said to have cost him 30,000 Burundian francs. He was shot. Another man said that had the Hutu simply been shot, they would not have fled, "because we do not fear death; but when the people heard *how* people were killed, they ran."

Another question that one might ask is: Why is so little known about the details of the massacre elsewhere in the world? The answer to this question brings up a theme which was central throughout the mythico-history but particularly marked in reconstructions of the apocalypse: the masterful manipulation of "secrecy" by the Tutsi. Theirs was the domain of "governing" and "administration," a domain that had to be kept secret to be effective. As one informant explained: "Among the Hutu, the intellectuals were more numerous than the Tutsi—*more* numerous. There were university people, doctors, whatnot, but from the point of view of administration, nobody is chosen as chief being Hutu. For what reason? It was that this Hutu, once chosen as chief, could *discover their secrets*. There are secrets that they make—when they are in their . . . their administrative conferences."

The Tutsi, it was repeated again and again, kept the massacre a secret from the foreigners living in Burundi by not shooting and by hiding the dead in mass graves and forests. As the person quoted in Panel 18 said, for example, "If [my brother's body] had been left on the road, the foreigners would have seen it, and they would have written about it." Another person explained: "The world knew that a war had exploded in Burundi, but the fashion of killing was not known. But the difficulty—the people who come from other countries, they arrive quite simply in the capital, and the Tutsi speak. No Hutu can converse with the foreigners—only the Tutsi." In these comments, there was once again the strong conviction that the foreigners, had they known what was going on, could somehow have protected the Hutu—or could, at least, have "written about it" and made the wider world aware of the apocalypse. But there was also a sense here that the mere act of exploding "the secrets of the Tutsi" would deplete their power, and that herein lay a special dimension of the importance of witnesses: they were destructive to secrecy.

The mythico-history identified several causes for the massacre. Informants seemed to feel a strong necessity to account for it—to explain its occurrence and extraordinary force in some comprehensible manner. Here, the different but interrelated thematic levels of explanation will be briefly considered.

A major cause of the massacre was unanimously seen as an attempt by the Tutsi to "equalize the population" on a statistical scale. Just as colonial ethnic/racial stereotypes had found a second life in the mythico-historical body maps, so did colonial demography get enlisted in the Hutu accounting of the arithmetic of genocide.[67] Everyone in Mishamo could recite the demographic configuration of Burundi's population: the Tutsi were 14 percent, the Hutu, 85 percent, and the Twa, 1 percent. The Tutsi, it was asserted, tried to change these numbers by killing as many Hutu as possible.[68] This, it was said, had been "the Tutsis' secret goal for a long time."[69] The goal was to "make Hutu 50 percent and Tutsi 50 percent also." Statistical reckoning of the effects of this "secret goal" was very common: "Before 1972, the population was 5,500,000. The Hutu had 4,900,000, the Twa had 100,000, and the Tutsi, 500,000. Then, more than 300,000 were killed according to the figures of the United Nations and what one hears on the radio. But this is not it. If we equalize *how* they killed in the countryside, we count 600,000. The 300,000 were in the *centers* of the provinces where the priests and the foreigners saw what was happening. In the interior of the country—mothers, children, men, even babies which were still in the belly. So, there remain 4,300,000 Hutu. In Burundi, there are 4,000,000 Hutu. The 300,000, that is us. Even South Africa has not had so many refugees."

It was said in the camp that by equalizing the population, the Tutsi would be better able to claim that Burundi was a democracy. While accepting this "secret goal" of equalization, people also agreed that there were particular categories among the Hutu which were the principal targets of the killing. The foremost category was quite unambiguously that of "intellectuals" and students. The second main category, missionaries, could be grouped together with the "intellectuals" because the missionaries were so closely involved in schooling in Burundi. Professionals of various kinds—politicians, doctors, nurses, lawyers, engineers, and agronomists—were another main category. Yet another category was formed by those who had intermarried with Tutsi women. They were considered a target because their close affinal connection to the Tutsi was seen to give them access to the "secrets of the Tutsi," thus making them a threat. Finally, the Hutu who were wealthy were also, to a lesser extent, isolated as a target according to the mythico-history. None of these categories, however, was as central as the "intellectuals."

Panel 19:

THE MYTHICO-HISTORICAL TARGETS OF THE MASSACRE

They wanted to kill my clan because my clan was educated. The clans which were educated, cultivated, they were killed. In my clan, there were schoolteachers, medical assistants, agronomists . . . some evangelists—not yet priests—and two who were in the army . . . in my clan. All have been exterminated. Among those [kin] who were educated, it is I alone who remain. [. . .] There are many persons who leave Burundi today because one kills every day. The pupils, the students. . . . It is because these are intellectuals—because if you do not study, you do not have much maarifa [knowledge, information]. One killed many Hutu university people.

The government workers. . . . They were arrested when they were in their offices working. The others also in their places—for example, an agronomist, when he was walking in the fields where he works, he was arrested. Or a veterinary technician: one finds him in his place, where he works. There were medical technicians, professors. . . . Or the artisans in the garage, or those who worked in printing houses or in the ateliers where furniture is made. They were killed there, on the spot. [. . .] The masculine missionaries and the feminine missionaries [. . .] were doing their work in the churches, in the schools as professors—or [. . .] in the hospitals as doctors. [. . .] They were not killed on the spot. [. . .] They were killed in the prison. [. . .] I think that the very first who were poured into the lake were the masculine missionaries and the feminine missionaries. [. . .]

Be you a student, this is a cause; be you a rich [person], that is a cause; be you a man who dares to say a valid word to the population, that is a cause. In short, it is a racial hate. One can say this. [. . .] If you are Hutu, yes. They killed missionaries, if you please. Only Hutu missionaries. [. . .] Many, many sisters were killed [. . .]. It is the sisters who can say words.[70]

The "causes" of the massacres, as listed here, do indeed agree with much of what is known about the targeted killings that have been called a "selective genocide" in Burundi (Lemarchand and Martin 1974).[71] However, it is necessary to note that one other often-cited "cause" of the killing (and the one most often cited by the Tutsi-dominated government of Burundi) was conspicuous by its absence in the mythico-history. This was the alleged existence of "plots" by Hutu revolutionaries to seize power and exterminate the Tutsi. Evidence for these accusations is confused, and such uprising as there was seems to have been a short-lived prelude to the much more violent wave of counterattacks or "reprisals" of the Tutsi-led government against the Hutu population (Lemarchand and Martin 1974, Lemarchand 1992, Weinstein 1976). The key point to be made here, however, is that, while an abortive uprising was occasionally mentioned among the Hutu refugees in Mishamo, it was not a much elaborated part of the mythico-history.

Another question the narratives of the killing raised was why the Hutu, who so massively outnumbered the Tutsi, were unable to resist the infliction of atrocity, or to stop it. Several variations on the theme of historically structured powerlessness emerged in response to this question. The powerlessness was of two kinds. The first concerned military force—lack of arms and a military organization—while the second focused on a powerlessness seen as embedded in "Hutuness." Giving an answer of the former kind, one person said: "These Tutsi, they are foreigners in our country. Nevertheless, they have killed many and *kill* many Hutu intellectuals. Because the Tutsi have the government, to kill Hutu is very easy. [. . .] We had no guns. To kill was easy. We were like women in the house." While there were allegations by the Burundi government that some Hutu "leaders" had stockpiled large quantities of arms and ammunition, certainly the vast majority of the Hutu who were peasant agriculturalists did not have firearms of any kind.[72] One person also said that it was "forbidden for any Hutu to have even swords."

The second assessment of powerlessness as something coming from within the "Hutu character" was related to many of the mythico-historical themes already laid out—particularly to the mythico-historical characterizations of the difference between internal Hutu power and external Tutsi power. The internal power was closely linked with the organic or "natural" physical power of the body, which was nevertheless vulnerable before the "malign" power of the Tutsi. In the accounts of the apocalypse, docility emerged as another constitutive feature of "Hutuness." Reference was made to a complete lack of resistance from the Hutu during the massacre, and the response of the Hutu was likened to the docility of sheep being herded. When asked about a Hutu uprising, one old man retorted: "There *was* no war. We were gathered like sheep, like goats. These are assassinations." Hutu docility was often described through such analogies to domestic animals. One Village Chairman in Mishamo, for example, explained: "The Tutsi, he is like the shepherd who guards the herds. So, it is easy for him to say, 'Today I will slaughter a cow.' It is easy. Or else, if one has chickens— one can slaughter them when one wants. We are like herds before the Tutsi." Gender supplied another metaphor for expressing docility and inequality of power for the Hutu men in Mishamo. In the words of one man (quoted above): "We were like women in the house." At yet another metaphoric level, Panel 20 constructed the "trait" of Hutu docility in biblical terms.

Panel 20:

**DOCILITY AS A HUTU TRAIT**

We are the descendants of Israelites. History says so. This was seen in 1972 when President Micombero proclaimed on the radio [that] we are Israelites. Our habits resemble very much the habits of the Israelites. All the Hutu who were captured to be killed, they behaved like sheep, and they did nothing but praying and singing only. This demonstrates how we resemble the Israelites. The Israelites, before attacking a country, first of all pray to God. We are the *first* Bantus who came to Africa. We are Bantus, thus Israelites. [. . .] This demonstrates that we had a democracy [before the Tutsi came]. It was good. There were no distinctions of race.[73]

Whether or not the Hutu responded with nothing but singing and prayer seems doubtful, but the descriptions of both docility and powerlessness can be traced throughout the accounts of atrocity, and their existence is in itself an ethnographic fact to be explored. Such docility, or submissiveness, seemed to be a source of shame to only a very few persons interviewed in Mishamo. For the most part, it seemed that this was a positively valued sign of peaceability and virtue. It could also be seen as an assertion of humanity and decency in contrast to the "inhumanity" and unnatural "evil" of the Tutsi category that the apocalypse powerfully served to establish in the mythico-history.

THE EXPLODING OF "SECRETS" AS THE FORMATION OF CONSCIOUSNESS

It is necessary to discuss briefly one further dimension of the narrative construction of the apocalypse in the mythico-history. It was commonly said that the massacre helped the Hutu to see once and for all what "the Tutsi" were like, and what their "secrets" were. Their "secret goal" had three principal versions in the mythico-history, as was implied above. The first was to kill all the Hutu intellectuals so that the Hutu might never govern, and so that they would forever remain the "workers of the Tutsi," or the "Hutu of the Tutsi"—as opposed to *abantu*. The second version concerned the Tutsi "plan to equalize the population" so that Hutu would no longer outnumber the Tutsi. And, in the third version, the Tutsi goal was seen as the elimination of "the whole race of the Hutu." It was emphasized that these goals had been a motivating force behind Tutsi actions for a long time before the massacre, and that the final moment of clarity came with the massacres.[74] The massacre thus stood in the mythico-history as the climactic moment of the discovery of "the secrets of the Tutsi." As one man put it: "Those Tutsi, we will conquer them because we know now their malignities. Earlier we did not know this. That is why they spoiled us. That is why they killed us." Another person explained: "If you are struck once, two times, three times—you think finally: 'Me, do I not have arms also?' It is this that happened in 1972. And it is in 1972 that the majority of the Hutu were killed." A third person added: "In general, the Hutu of today think of nothing else than the liberation of their country. Since all the ideologies employed by the Tutsi have already been discovered, [have become] known—this is why all the Hutu, there where they are to be found, think of nothing else but Burundi, the native country. What made us think about our country was the troubles of '72. The troubles of '72 awakened us because the Tutsi killed the children, the old people, the pupils in schools, the pregnant women and [. . .] all the inhabitants of the country of Hutu origin."

If the apocalypse itself was seen as a kind of *Kristallnacht* exploding "the secrets of the Tutsi" with finality, the arrival of tens of thousands of Hutu into exile in Tanzania was seen as the period when a collective, overarching understanding of the apocalypse began to be formed. Most Hutu came to the Kigoma Region, and it was especially in and around Kigoma township that they were massively concentrated at first. At least half of the refugees were collected in and processed

through the transit camp of Kibirizi near Kigoma township. The Hutu
refugees' descriptions of these initial stages of exile indicate that it
was here, in the cramped quarters of the transit camp and surrounding
squatter areas, that they first learned of the extent and nature of the
massacre in Burundi.

One person who had been "processed" through a transit camp
said: "It is after the meeting with the people of the different regions [of
Burundi, in Tanzania,] that we got the news. Me, what I saw [was] the
capture and the torture that the Tutsi race did to the people of the
Hutu race without their knowing for what they were [being] tortured."
Another person who successfully skirted the transit camp, but nevertheless was in its environs during his first months of exile, said: "The
cases [of killing and mutilation] which I myself saw happened in the
place where I was [in Gitega, Burundi]. The cases which were done in
other provinces, we discussed them when we arrived together in refuge
here. At the moment when we met—me, I am from Gitega—I met
those of Muramvya, of Bururi . . . The majority had come from Bururi,
very close to the frontier. It is the first thing that we did. Talk, t-a-l-k . . .
[about] what happened here, what happened here, what happened
there." Yet a third person explained: "Here [in exile] it is a meeting.
All the people from the different provinces of Burundi are reunited
here." What the refugees described was a kind of collective efferves-
cence of consciousness, an intensive period of intellectual and political
awakening. People from very different regions of Burundi who had had
little to do with each other prior to 1972 were thrown together in exile
with a strong consciousness of the fact that they were there because of
something they all had in common, their Hutuness.

THE BREAKDOWN OF RULING, COLONIZING IDEAS

The oppositional character of the Hutu mythico-history was rendered
more complex by the fact that the refugees' attack on the mythico-
historical versions constructed by the "other," "the Tutsi," implicitly *linked* them with precisely these versions. Thus, while the Hutu
mythico-history challenged by denaturalizing the ruling ideas (Marx
and Engels [1846] 1970) of the Tutsi version of a national history, it
simultaneously incorporated certain features of this opposing version
into itself. Acceptance of the "beauty" of "the Tutsi" is but one example. Far from claiming an alternative standard of beauty, people in Mishamo seemed to fully agree with what they themselves saw as Tutsi

criteria—and with what were in fact also, largely, colonial European criteria. In this sense, then, it seems that certain aspects of the "Tutsi version" had penetrated the Hutu mythico-history. But if the thought of the Hutu refugees was to some extent "colonized" by their Tutsi rulers,[75] it was equally clear that any Tutsi hegemony was subject, as all hegemonies are, to subversive reworkings. Thus even while the Hutu accepted the description of the Tutsi as "beautiful," they were busy revaluing beauty itself, casting it as a sign, not of nobility or virtue, but of evil and danger.

This particular example is a good illustration of the fact that the Hutu mythico-history was very much a world in the making. It was not a seamless version devoid of contradiction or ambiguity. Yet, the themes encapsulated in the panels above together reveal a breaking down and reworking of larger hegemonic, colonizing frameworks. The process illustrates how segments of a hegemonic worldview may be adopted, even as they are subverted, reinterpreted, and recombined in unorthodox ways. Indeed, the entire mythico-history might be described as a *subversion in progress.*

One starkly evident aspect of this dynamic and on-going process of subversion was that, in the mythico-history, the Tutsi were cast in many mythico-historical domains (such as the encoding and enacting of the body maps) as the primary subject, while the Hutu were cast as the symmetrical opposite, as that which the Tutsi were not. This reflexive self-definition could be seen as an implicit recognition of or a commentary on how the "self"/Hutu has been objectified by the dominant "other" or "others." This case very neatly illustrates that "the other" as categorical opposite or enemy is never passive in its relation to a collective "self".[76] Rather, the oppositional relation between "self" and "other" is characterized by the mutual, conflicting, and competing construction of either category. What has been documented in this case is the inscription of schemata by a dominant "other" upon a dominated collective "self" and the symbolic transformation of these schemata.

OBJECTIVIST DEFINITIONS OF HISTORICAL "TRUTH"

Much of the importance of the mythico-history would be missed if one were simply to seek an "objective" evaluation of the extent to which the themes and ideas of the mythico-history were "true" or "distorted" representations of reality, fact or fiction, scientific or fantastical (Comaroff 1985:4). Certainly, particular claims might be investigated and corroborated or refuted—indeed, this is an essential task for human rights workers, even if it is not my purpose here. And there is good reason to suppose that many of the refugees' accounts could be shown in this way to be substantially accurate, even as others would likely be revealed as growing out of rumors. But the mythico-history is misread if it is seen simply as a series of factual claims. For the "facts" it deployed, true and false alike, were only building blocks for the construction of a grand moral-historical vision. In this particular case, as with any other collective past, there exists no "God's-eye view" of history. The "worlds made" through narrations of the past are always historically situated and culturally constructed, and it is these that people act upon and riddle with meaning.[77]

Thus, the Hutu mythico-history is not seen here as "oral history," in the sense of a historical "source" that can be used to reconstruct "what really happened" in the past. Again, such a utilization of the refugees' narratives would be possible. But the more challenging approach to such narratives, in my view, is not to sort out "true facts" from "distortions" but to examine what is taken to be the truth by different social groups, and why. Different regimes of truth exist for different historical actors, and particular historical events support any number of different narrative elaborations. Such regimes of truth operate at a mythico-historical level which is concerned with the constitution of an ontological, political, and moral order of the world.

# three

We need history, certainly, but
we need it for reasons different
from those for which the idler
in the garden of knowledge
needs it, even though he may
look nobly down on our rough
and charmless needs and
requirements. We need it, that
is to say, for the sake of life
and action.

—Friedrich Nietzsche,
*Twilight of the Idols*

# THE USES OF HISTORY IN THE REFUGEE CAMP: LIVING THE PRESENT IN HISTORICAL TERMS

The dominant themes of the Hutu mythico-history of the past in Burundi having been outlined, it is now possible to place these themes in the contemporary sociopolitical context of the refugee camp where they were being remembered and produced, consolidated and transformed. Thus, while in chapter 2 the mythico-history appeared in the guise of narratives about the past in Burundi, here it will become evident how utterly contemporary and experientially salient this past was in the present of the refugee camp. Indeed, it will become obvious that the mythico-historical narratives represented a collective discursive practice, a vital form of social action, configuring and morally weighting virtually all domains of everyday life in the refugee camp, and giving form to the social imagination of exile.

There were three principal dimensions to the production and transformation of the mythico-history. First, the mythico-history of the Hutu past in Burundi served as a paradigmatic model and interpretive device for giving meaning to and acting upon the socio-political present of the refugee camp. Here, the past not only explained aspects of the present; it contributed to structuring social action in the present.

Second, particular aspects of the refugee camp served, in and of themselves, to further elaborate, to objectify, and, ultimately, even to produce the collective mythico-history of the past. That is, the camp with its constitutive techniques of power—its asymmetric structuring of authority, its organization and control of production, its system of schooling, its spatial isolation and its restrictions on mobility—was seen by the refugees to reproduce the hierarchical structure of the Burundian society they had fled in 1972.

Finally, this historically specific conjuncture of perceived relations between past and present was in the process of generating a mythico-history of the present, of exile. This is not to suggest that the mythico-history of the past and that of the present were distinct, independent processes; on the contrary, they were both integrally a part of the process of the mythico-history. Rather, the present was incorporated quite continuously and cumulatively into the mythico-historical discourse describing the past in Burundi—just as the past was, in a sense, inserted into the present. Thus, significant contemporary events of daily life in the camp were transformed into mythico-historical events.[1] These events became allegorical in that they had the same moral, didactic lessons embedded in them as did events in the more distant past.

This multidimensional process will be explored here by examining some of the actual events occurring in the camp that were seized upon in the mythico-history as being of key importance. Accounts of these key events very quickly circulated among the refugees, and, often in a matter of days, acquired what can be characterized as "standard versions" in the telling and retelling. These "standard versions" were not simply isolated accounts of particular events, told for the sake of telling and soon to be forgotten. Rather, they were accounts which, while becoming increasingly formulaic, also became more didactic and progressively more implicated in, and indicative of, something beyond them. In this sense, the "standard versions" acted as diagnostic and mnemonic allegories connecting events of everyday life with wider historical processes impinging on the Hutu refugees.

In his brilliant study of violence and the body in Northern Ireland, Allen Feldman has described processes similar to the narrative standardization of events in Mishamo. Referring to Lyotard's work (1973), Feldman writes:

[T]he relations between event, agency, and narrative are fundamentally *achronic* and not linear. [. . .] Narrativity is the condition for the identification of events, agents, and mediating sequence. Event, agency, and narration form a "narrative bloc" (Lyotard 1973:268) defined as the achronic engenderment of narrative, agency (narration), and event. Narrative blocs are plastic organizations involving language, material artifacts, and relations. [. . . .]. Narrative blocs may be internally achronic, but they fabricate temporalities and causalities such as linear time, which carry subtle valuations of agents, events, and effects. *Sequence and causality are both moral and metaphorical constructs."* (1991:13–4)[2]

Examining how events may be organized into "a configurational system, a mode of historical explanation, and a normative intervention," Feldman emphasizes, *"The event is not what happens. The event is that which can be narrated"* (1991:14).[3] This is a good description of how, in Mishamo, memories of some happenings melted and lost their shapes in the course of the everyday, while others became *events* that ended by being narrated into the mythico-historical process.

The new "standard versions" were interlinked with whole series of other "standard versions" concerned with the present and, further, with the mythico-historical themes from the Hutu past in Burundi. Very frequently, themes of the past were retold directly in the narration of the contemporary "standard versions." When appropriate, this structural mapping of the contemporary "standard versions" into themes of the past will be indicated by reference to panels in chapter 2. This referencing will also help to illustrate the social and narrative contexts within which themes of the past were invoked.

FEARFUL SYMMETRY: THE ANALOGY BETWEEN PAST AND PRESENT[4]
As in chapter 2, the panels to be presented in this section have been selected from those narratives which recurred with greatest frequency and similarity of form. Thus, each panel can be read as a condensation of other, close variations on the same mythico-historical theme. Where a quotation derives from an isolated comment by a single person, this will be indicated. The meanings of these standard versions are only understandable in relation, first, to other standard versions in the present, and, second, to the themes of the "past" in Burundi. The resulting constellation of meaningful relations and conjunctures—at once volatile and epic—was dazzling in its complexity.

SECTION ONE: EXODUS AND WILDERNESS
> Panel 21:
> EXODUS: FLIGHT, BORDER CROSSING, AND ARRIVAL INTO EXILE

We heard the guns: bum! bum! bum! bum! And then there were helicopters, and when they saw a group of men on the ground, they killed them. We, we left home. We went into the forest and hid ourselves in the rocks. Others, they took flight immediately, all the way to Tanzania, but we stayed three months in the rocks—from April until June. We put the children under the rocks, and then we looked around. If the soldiers were far, we went into the fields to find cassava, sugar cane, like that, to give to our children. [. . .] Then, in the night, at around eight o'clock, we began the voyage [toward Tanzania] having prayed to God so that he would protect us. That was the ninth of June [1972]. We walked for one day and two nights. We arrived in Tanzania. [. . .] We arrived with meat from our horses, with knives—with knives since we had been walking in the night. Knives and three radios . . . with money in our pocket, [Burundi] francs. When we arrived at the frontier, they said to us, "Approach, approach, our dear friends!" We were fearful. We asked each other, "What? The soldiers have reached here already?!" They said, "We are the soldiers of Tanzania." We had not known where the boundary was. We only walked like sheep, truly like animals. . . . We were very tired. Our children, their feet were swollen. The Tanzanian soldiers asked, "So, what do you have?" We said, "Knives, radios. . . ." Concerning the money we said nothing. The soldiers said, "Yes, approach." They said: "Sleep here on the sand first, near the lake." We slept perhaps two hours. Then they said, "Now we will take you to Kigoma." [. . .]

While we were going toward Kigoma, on the way, we thought that it was just us who had arrived there. We were 150, but then the others, they said, "No, no, no, we want to return to Burundi. There [in Tanzania] we will have a lack of food. We want to go home." So, 35 of us remained. But—sad—all those who returned then were killed, all. [. . .] When we arrived in Kigoma . . . oh, oh, oh! . . . we met many, many, many men, women, from *all* the provinces of Burundi. We even saw people from different provinces whom we had met in the church conferences in Burundi. *All of them,* they were all there! We had not *known* this! We asked them, "Where is your wife?" They said, "My wife, already killed; I ran alone." And then, "Where is the pastor of your commune?" They responded, "He, he was killed." Like this we learned the news. This one said, "Many, many killed in our parts." That one said, "In our region also." [It was like this that we learned.] The cases of killing which I myself saw, those were cases that occurred in the place where I was. The cases which were done in other provinces, we discussed them when we had arrived here together in refuge. [We met people from all the different provinces in Burundi.] The majority came from Bururi near the frontier. That was the first thing we did—talk, t-a-l-k . . . [about] what happened here, what happened there. [. . .] We stayed in Kigoma for eight weeks. Then the trucks, locomotives, came to take us to [the camp].[5]

Panel 21 is at once an individual account and a standard version of a class of historical events that was very widely shared among informants. That is, while the account is the product of one person's memory of fear and misfortune, it was a social fact that most other people in Mishamo held, to all appearances, very similar chains of events in their memories and spontaneously talked about them in much the same way, pausing to emphasize the same themes that this panel does. It was, indeed, remarkable that even with all the variations in personal experience, each account seemed to assert and illuminate a number of shared, generalized mythico-historical themes. Articulations of memory were thematically uniform. It was at this level that the personal accounts were positioned as "standard versions" in the mythico-history. The very fact that these more general themes echoed through many peoples' accounts made the conflation of the personal and collective levels of self-identification in the camp more readily visible.

The themes encapsulated in accounts like that in Panel 21 converged on three processes: fleeing, crossing the Burundi-Tanzania border, and arriving in exile. Together these processes helped to carve into the landscape a mythico-historical divide between past and present, locating the past in Burundi and the present in exile in Tanzania. That divide was, therefore, not only temporal but also spatial and political. Talking about "here" and "there" was a means of distinguishing two different periods, or worlds, of Hutu history. This politico-spatial constitution of historical time was characteristic of the mythico-historical discursive practice more generally.

The narratives concerned with fleeing and the border crossing, often told together, can be seen as expressions of one broader theme: the sudden, supplanting of a social order by an asocial chaos. Informants' accounts seemed to document, first, the transformation of a recognizable, familiar social landscape into an unintelligible chaos, an apocalyptic landscape, and second, the transformation of persons socially connected to their surroundings into mere bodies buffeted and propelled pell-mell through strange terrain—terrain made the more terrifying, one would think, by the awareness that it was, not long ago, *familiar.*

Fleeing was recalled as a process filled with apocalyptic confusion and fear; often it was also described as a very physical activity. Images of bullets grazing the skin and helicopters flying overhead, people being pursued and almost caught, people jumping and tripping over bodies, people carrying one especially valued possession that was weighing them down, and people hiding in bushes and rock formations—all these were remembered scenes of a totalized chaos.[6]

Sometimes people became quite preoccupied in developing detailed descriptions of how their bodies felt and reacted in the process of escaping. Sweating, body odors, muscle cramps, fatigue, unsuspected reserves of stamina, and lightness of body were among the sensations mentioned. For the listener, for me, these accounts evoked the picture of a momentary but total suspension of everything social, and of the violent condensation of all life into the body as an utterly physical organism. There seemed to be a recognition that social life had been overtaken by organismic life, and the sole purpose of the organism was to not allow itself to be extinguished.

The apocalyptic physicalization of the body and its functions was accompanied by another expression of chaotic formlessness, the unintelligibility of the physico-political landscape in which the bodies traveled. The narratives emphasized again and again that the fleeing refugees did not know where the national border was, or when they had actually crossed it. They continued to move on until they encountered Tanzanian border guards and military units.

The national boundary had a curious double aspect in the mythico-history. As a physical divide between the territorial states of Burundi and Tanzania, the border was apparently unclear and hard to make out. Yet it was seen as quite tangible on another thematic level: the border was the membrane between life and death. Many refugees in Mishamo described how persons known to them had decided to turn back while fleeing, and how they had invariably met with their deaths in Burundi.[7] Even in 1986 it was still considered extremely dangerous for a person to return to Burundi, even clandestinely. People were convinced that returning openly as a Hutu from Tanzania, and particularly as a *refugee*, might be tantamount to suicide. For this action would signify to the Tutsi authorities that the returnee was politically suspect and harbored "dangerous thoughts" against the regime in Burundi. The refugees said that their experience of exile had given them knowledge that would be considered dangerous by the Tutsi in power. The point to be noted is that while returning to the "homeland" was planned in the context of a collective, revolutionary return to a free Burundi, a premature crossing of the boundary was regarded as the crossing of the River Styx. In this era, it was a boundary permitting movement in only one direction.

The second aspect of Panel 21 to be remarked upon is that here, as in other accounts, the period of the massive concentration of Hutu refugees in Kigoma and its surroundings was seen as a decisive moment of clarity. It was here, among crowds of other Hutu, that people apprehended the full extent and scale of the events in Burundi, and, as they so often said, "discovered all the secrets of the Tutsi."

Most people seem to have fled from their homes in Burundi either alone or in relatively small groups (that were not necessarily kin groups) and consequently had but the vaguest conception of the numbers of other people who were escaping from all parts of Burundi, and whom they would find in Kigoma. The several weeks spent by most people in Kigoma were described as a period of extraordinary fermentation of a consciousness of what had happened to them. As one person said, "We realized that we were all here for one reason: because we are of the Hutu group." Kigoma at this time was characterized as a kind of melting pot for all Hutu from different regions of Burundi, and as a leveler of differences which may have been important before exile. (And there had been salient differences. Regional identifications had, according to some scholars, been especially important. Thus, within the category "Hutu" there were prominent divisions (and, in certain periods, antagonisms) between northern "mountain people" (*montagnards*) and southern "lake people," (*lacustres*). What was surprising was the *rarity* of references to region among the Hutu refugees during fieldwork; people mentioned "regionalism" as a problem of the past.)[8]

The refugees claimed that in Burundi they had not had much communication with Hutu in other regions, and that the Tutsi did not want them to be mobile. One informant noted with some glee: "Another evil plan of the Tutsi: we did not marry with [Hutu] people of other regions in Burundi because the Tutsi knew that if one region marries with some other one, we could inform ourselves. But unfortunately [for the Tutsi], the Omnipotent has reunited us all together here [in refugee camps]." A second informant explained it thus:

When I was in Burundi, I ignored categorically the Hutu of other corners. You understand, every country has four corners, west, east, . . . Now I know them, and I know many stories. This is because of [Burundi President] Micombero. It is for this that I rather like him. So, those of the east came here—with what? With their good and their bad. A man has to have these two things, the good and the bad. Those of the west came with their two companions, the good and the bad. Those of the north, ditto. Those of the south also came in this same fashion. And then there was me from the middle, the central region of Burundi. Now, here, we all know all these four corners of Burundi.

The establishment of the first permanent refugee settlements or camps generated another series of themes defining the initial stages of exile. Many of my informants in Mishamo had, by 1985, had experience of establishing not one but two camps. Some twenty-four thousand of the refugees living in Mishamo in 1985–86 were brought there during 1978–79 from Ulyankulu camp where they had already been settled for several years (TCRS 1984b: n.p.; Christensen 1985).[9] Panel 22 is a standard version describing the site near the town of Tabora in central Tanzania that was to become Ulyankulu, the first more permanent camp for the Hutu refugees.[10]

Panel 22:

**THE EXTRAORDINARY FOREST**

One has to believe that the good God is there. Most of the refugees were bitten by snakes. In this forest [to which we were brought by the trucks], there were all sorts of animals. Many died—some were bitten by the snakes, others were attacked by lions. It was a forest—an *extraordinary* forest—where there were serpents in colors that you have not yet seen! Lack of water to drink, nothing, nothing as food. . . . At that moment there were people like natives [living near the new camp site]. They taught us how to do whatever was necessary for life. [. . .] They [the government and international refugee agencies] showed: "Here is your place." That is all. A hoe, an axe, and a machete—these three things [were given to us]. The mother of the family also received a hoe. [They said:] "It is you who will combat the trees in your forest!"[11]

For the Tanzanian Ministry of Home Affairs and the international refugee agencies, the transportation of the Hutu into camps, or into sites for camps, was a significant step toward order, a spatial order that would provide the basis for establishing other kinds of order: medical and sanitary, social and economic, documentary and legal (Foucault 1979; Malkki 1985; Agrar-und Hydrotechnik 1978). Thus, the spatial ordering of the refugees was a necessary prerequisite for the "regularization" of their status and the "normalization" of their life. For the Hutu themselves, the arrival on the campsites seems to have been an awe-inspiring confrontation with a formless and dangerous wilderness. The refugee administrators had measured out and assigned plots of land for each household, but the refugees, it seems, saw only "the forest" and "the bush."[12] (In her study of Ulyankulu, Christensen (1985:97) describes her surroundings in similar terms: "A great variety of snakes and a number of monitor lizards in the dry areas and hippopotamuses in the river bed are remains of the once rich, wild and dangerous fauna of the site. The last lion was observed in 1977, when a refugee woman was attacked.") The allocation of the three implements for clearing and cultivating land was interpreted as an allocation of responsibility to the refugees for domesticating the wilderness. Thus, as Panel 22 concluded, "It is you who will combat the trees in *your* forest!"[13]

The magnitude of the "wilderness," the dangers that were imagined to be lurking in it, and the profoundly experienced, collective solitude of the refugees ensconced within it, emerged as the most powerful iconic reconstructions of this period in the mythico-history. The mythico-history did not for a moment claim here for the Hutu that native, innate mastery of "the bush" or of "nature" that has so long been attributed to "the African" in other settings,[14] nor did the mythico-history recreate the "extraordinary forest" in theological terms as "God's creation," *ergo* natural, benign, or neutral. Rather, the "extraordinary forest" was a terrifying, antagonistic force to be overcome. In William Blake's words: "Where man is not, nature is barren."[15]

Looking back to the myths of the foundation of the aboriginal nation of Burundi, it can be said that the refugees' confrontation with the wilderness in exile was another kind of foundation myth, another genesis story. The latter reconstructs the foundation, not of an autochthonous nation, but of statelessness and exile. And while the story of the "mole king" (Panel 2) sought to establish the rootedness of the early "Bantu" in the land of Burundi, the present stories show the converse, that is, the "uprootedness" and foreignness of the Hutu in the wilderness.[16] Indeed, biblical analogies describing the Hutu as Israelites wandering in the wilderness were explicitly made.

Further, just as the mythico-history of Burundi charted the transformation of the autochthonous "Bantu" into "Hutu," so the mythico-history of exile documented the transformation of the "Hutu" into "refugees." The transformation into refugeeness was a theme that ran throughout the mythico-historical discourse. Here it appeared in the discursive reconstruction of the beginning of exile as a battle with wilderness. This battle was conceived as having two main consequences. First, it was seen to have the effect of weeding out the weakest among the elderly and the young children. Thus, the ranks of the young and able-bodied became proportionally greater because they withstood the test of the early period.[17] Second, the mythico-history generated by this period gave a pervasive impression that in the initial stages of exile, the Hutu were what might best be called novice refugees—neophytes who had yet to face the trials that would make of them "true refugees." In other words, refugeeness entailed a process of *becoming*. It was a gradual transformation, not an automatic result of the crossing of a national border. (This vision of the transformation stood in striking contrast to that held by the refugee administrators. For them, the Hutu were refugees in their most unambiguous, pure form when they were most palpably victims and, on the legal level, from the moment that they—owing to a well-founded fear of persecution—crossed the national boundary.)

Cultivation of the land was a theme that made its appearance in many discursive domains throughout the mythico-history; it was also important in the narratives of early exile and, specifically, of the settling of the refugee camps for Hutu. The initial settling of Ulyankulu generated the mythico-historical confrontation with wilderness, as presented in Panel 22 above. The pioneering of Mishamo, on the other hand, produced themes focusing more directly on the cultivation of land by the Hutu. When the 24,000 people who had helped to settle Ulyankulu camp and had been cultivating it for six or seven years were transported in 1979 to the site of Mishamo to pioneer the settlement of a new camp, they saw this as one more phase in a repetitive or cyclical pattern of first domesticating wilderness, then cultivating it, and finally losing productive land. The following panel reflects the perception of this pattern. It is a mythico-historical narrative told in the context of listing all the prescribed services that the Hutu in preindependence Burundi were expected to render the *mwami* and his Tutsi chiefs, and of the "royal punishments" formulated for those Hutu who failed to serve.[18] This particular analogy with Burundi was recurrent.

Panel 23:

**VIRGIN LAND—CULTIVATED LAND—LOST LAND**

If once a *hutu* [used here to signify a slave] refused to do the duty obliged by a Tutsi, at this moment there were two things that could be done to him. First, to kill him with his family. If he was a little bit pardoned, one made him leave his domicile. If, for example, you were accused by the [Tutsi] chief governing the region where you lived, you could go to a chief who governed another region. He would receive you very well because you were a new *hutu* [slave] for him. You received a piece of land. You recommence to cultivate—once again—having left perhaps one square kilometer of banana groves in your old domicile. There were some Hutu who were lucky. Their new chief gave them the domicile of another Hutu who had been chased away by him. [Hence, the land was already cleared and cultivated.] If you, the new Hutu, had no luck, the chief gave you a savanna! Just like in Ulyankulu [camp in Tanzania]. We could not bring anything with us [when we were moved from Ulyankulu to Mishamo]. [. . .] Twenty-four thousand people were transported from Ulyankulu [camp to Mishamo]. Eleven thousand remained. In the beginning there were thirty-five thousand in Ulyankulu. There was not enough water there. We were told that here, in Mishamo, is a place where no matter who can cultivate without fertilizer. [Arrangements for the transportation of the people having been made,] the rains came to Ulyankulu, and the people began to ask: "Why leave now?" [. . .] We did not have the choice of going or staying. We were told quite simply, "This, this, this, and this [household] will leave, and that will stay." Then it happened that perhaps only one family stayed on one road, all alone [all the other households having been moved]. The eleven thousand stayed behind like those who have to live in a forest. Once again. Ulyankulu was a forest when we arrived there. [. . .] When we were transferred, harvests, houses, all this had to be left behind. [We were not allowed to take too many things on the trucks.] And Mishamo was the veritable forest.[19]

The Hutu loss of land in Burundi in 1972—while not explicitly mentioned here—was also represented as part of the cycle. Thus, in both the mythico-history of the past and that of the present, it was asserted that the Hutu had time and again faced wilderness, that Hutu labor power had made the wilderness agriculturally productive, and that through the agency of "others," they had then been obliged to abandon the land. That different reasons and historical agents may have provided the momentum for the closure of the cycles at these different times did not appear to be relevant in the mythico-history. The existence of the cyclical pattern and the implied fruitlessness of Hutu labor for the Hutu *themselves* formed a predominating theme here.[20]

Insofar as the settling of Mishamo had produced "settler myths" (Wilson 1964) of a peculiar kind among the refugees, it is relevant to note that there existed a structural analogy between the mythico-historical accounts of the ancient encounter between the Hutu and the

Twa in Burundi, and the meeting of the Hutu refugees with Wabende
people whose hunting grounds the area known as Mishamo was until
it became a refugee camp.

Panel 24:

FROM TWA TO WABENDE

[The Wabende] did not know how to cultivate, to wash themselves, to behave. . . . They did not know propriety. Completely naked, men and women.
They resembled the Twa from where we came. These are people who are
not interested in progress. They do not eat anything but grasshoppers. When
we first approached them [in the site that was to become Mishamo], they
took *flight!* They lived in poor houses with flies. It could be seen that these
were locals. They lived by the meat of wild animals and grasshoppers. They
nourished themselves also with honey and some grains of maize. [. . .] They
were altogether frightened to see us, *us, miserables!*[21]

Beyond this particular encounter, Wabende did not occupy a predominant locus in the Hutu mythico-history and will therefore be discussed no further. It need only be noted that, just as the Twa occupied
the third term in the pyramidal relationship of Tutsi : Hutu : Twa
in Burundi, so the Wabende occupied the nominal third term in the
relationship, Tanzanian administrators : Hutu refugees : Wabende
"locals."

In short, this clustering of narratives traced compelling symmetries between genesis stories of two imagined eras, between aborigi-
nality and refugeeness, and between land and dispossession.

THE REPRODUCTION OF HIERARCHY

Not surprisingly, perhaps, the relationship between the Hutu refugees
and their Tanzanian administrators in Mishamo had become, by
1985–86, a fundamental part of the mythico-history of the present. It
was possible to see, over time, how this relationship was constituted
in the course of the everyday, as "standard versions" about events and
practices in the camp emerged. Tracing these discursive processes
helped to illuminate how it was that "the Tanzanians" had become a
categorical, mythico-historical actor in the camp, and with what consequences.

It is perhaps well to begin this part of the inquiry with the most
totalizing characterizations given by the refugees of Mishamo. The following panel is representative, not only in regard to its substantive

content, but also in accurately mirroring the fact that the refugees tended to subject names, titles, labels, and terminology of all kinds to thoughtful, often parodying, scrutiny before adopting such terminology as their own. There was a keen sense of the provenance—or, one might almost say, ownership—of words, as if the words themselves carried some moral charge or quality of their original users. There was an ongoing, oddly one-sided war of words in operation in the mythico-historical discourse of the refugees. Thus, while Tanzanian government and UN officials insisted that Mishamo was a "refugee settlement" and not a "camp,"ᴸ the refugees had their own interpretation of these labels.

Panel 25:

"CAMP" OR "SETTLEMENT"?

There exist different kinds of camps. There are military camps. In these military camps there are Commandants, those who command the soldiers. Then there are refugee camps and settlements. A military camp is commanded, but a refugee camp is not. But I ask you: Who has the Commandant? It is we, refugees, here. Elsewhere, for example in the refugee settlements of Rwanda and Zambia, there are no Commandants. It is the refugees themselves who direct the affairs of the settlement, with the United Nations High Commissioner for Refugees. So, here this is not a settlement. This is a camp which has a Tanzanian Commandant. It is he who controls what happens in the camp. It is he who—in the name of the government—controls cultural, economic, and political affairs. It is the Commandant who decides. So, in our opinion, this is a camp. But UNHCR and TCRS do not want to say *camp* because the word has bad connotations . . . army, all that. They always want to say *settlement*.[22]

This panel summarizes in unequivocal terms the informants' vision of their own collective condition in Mishamo. By focusing on the figure of the Settlement Commandant and his official title, the mythico-history positioned him atop a clear-cut hierarchy in which specific functions and bureaucratic differentiations among the Commandant's staff tended to be irrelevant. He had become the archetypal "Tanzanian." All of the Tanzanian government employees under the jurisdiction of the Commandant in Mishamo were, in the mythico-history, members of a single category, "the Tanzanians" or "the citizens of here." Their persons and roles were categorically defined and set apart from "the refugees."

This structural and mythico-historical opposition was articulated

in everyday relations between the refugees and the Tanzanian administrators at all kinds of levels. It was expressed in such things as the
refugees' conviction that the loyalty of all Tanzanian employees in
Mishamo was first and foremost to the Commandant, and that all salient knowledge of activities in the camp would promptly be transmitted to him. Therefore, the categorical relationship had to be managed
continually.

It is worth noting that the Settlement Commandant was often
casually referred to as "the chief" [le chef], a term that harks back to
the chiefs and subchiefs of the mythico-history of the past in Burundi.
There these offices were usually held by Tutsi (see Leclercq 1973:11–
12; Vansina 1972). One appropriate way of interpreting the position of
the Tanzanians in Mishamo vis-à-vis the refugees is to establish this
analogy: Tutsi chief : Tutsi subchiefs : Hutu :: Tanzanian Commandant
: Tanzanian camp staff : refugees. In the mythico-history of Burundi,
all subdivisions and hierarchical distinctions among the Tutsi were
subsumed under the totalized, essentialized category of "the Tutsi,"
and so it was in the mythico-history of exile. The relevant, signifying
category was "the Tanzanians." That there should have existed such a
powerful analogy was not accidental. People continually brought forth
this analogy, and blew new life into it, in interpreting contemporary
events, processes, and relationships in the camp.

The overarching fact to be kept in mind here is that the organization of authority in the refugee camp was thought to reproduce the
structural asymmetry between the Hutu and the Tutsi in Burundi. The
refugees were acutely conscious of the fact that they were being governed, in exile as in the past, by an ethnically and politically distinct
"other." The insistence on naming their place of residence "our camp"
and not "our settlement" reflected this almost visceral awareness.

CULTIVATION

For many reasons, agricultural production was mythico-historically
very important. The primary economic activity in Mishamo was cultivation, and the bulk of administrative energy was channeled into the
organization and boosting of agricultural production there. It was
widely acknowledged by the organizations involved with the refugees
that the inhabitants of Mishamo were extremely productive cultivators.
Surveys on production, commissioned by TCRS and UNHCR,[23] indicate that on the basis of figures on sales to the NMC (National Milling

Corporation) and TAT (Tobacco Authority of Tanzania) alone, productivity for most crops was high compared to other regions in Tanzania. These figures did not account for sales on the black market. While the latter may have constituted a sizable percentage in comparison to the total sold to the NMC or TAT, black-market sales in Mishamo appeared to be lower than elsewhere in Tanzania due, largely, to Mishamo's isolated location.[24] Whereas the two other Hutu refugee camps in Tanzania—Katumba and Ulyankulu—were both relatively proximate to major towns (Mpanda and Tabora, respectively) as well as to roads and railway networks, Mishamo was in the middle of a vast, forested region. Further, as explained earlier, all movements to and from the camp were regulated—with uneven efficiency—by means of barriers and guards at the motorable entrances to the camp, and fourteen-day Leave Passes were required from the refugees before they were able to leave without fear of being arrested. This meant that, in the context of agricultural production, the refugees collectively ended up quite dependent on the channels of sale provided by the government marketing institutions. Panel 26 expresses the most common way of interpreting this system among the refugees during the mid-eighties.

Panel 26:

"WE CULTIVATE A LOT, THEY EAT A LOT"

And we left Burundi for this? Nothing has changed. In our native country, we were 85 percent of the population, we the Hutu. The Tutsi were 14 percent, and the Twa, 1 percent. The Twa are more or less like the Hutu. In Burundi, it is we who are the cultivators. It is the Hutu who cultivate the coffee, the tea, the cotton, the palm oil, . . . All this is exported, and foreign exchange is received. That is to say that the Tutsi, the minority, receive it. They, they do not cultivate. [. . .] So, we cultivate for the whole country. And here, what is different? We are the granaries of the Tanzanians. If we have a sack of beans, we cannot sell it to our friend. The government says to us that it is to be sold at two and a half [shillings] to the cooperative shop of the village. Same with the maize. Then the trucks of the NMC come to buy them. We, we do not go to Mpanda to sell them. They come here. [. . .] We are the granaries of the Tanzanians. [. . .] We are qualified workers, and they know it. They are savage. They are tutsianized. They are like the Tutsi, and not just concerning agriculture [. . .]. They do not want us to leave their country. We cultivate a lot, they eat a lot. We feed all the poor regions of Tanzania. From the big stores in Mpanda, food is taken to all regions of

Tanzania. Now they say that we are nothing but immigrants who came in search of new, good land to cultivate, but it is not true. We have become their slaves. We have been given a pet name here, "the tractors." They benefit by us. This is the wherefore that they do not want us to leave here. They tell you that the refugee will say, "I am a refugee of hunger because I did not have enough land to cultivate [in Burundi]." Lies![25]

The mythico-history represented the Hutu refugees as a "captured peasantry" in more ways than Hyden's (1980) original use of the term might suggest. Panel 26 reflects some of these aspects of the refugees' sense of encapturement. First, long observation of practices in the camp had convinced them that the Tanzanian authorities wanted to keep them within the bounds of the camp, cultivating. Second, people charged that by referring to the refugees as "mere" immigrants in search of fertile land, the Tanzanian authorities were giving further signs of their expectation that the Hutu would remain in Tanzania indefinitely. The third dimension of their encapturement was reflected in the rhetorical comment, "We are their slaves." This statement was truly ubiquitous and appeared in countless conversations about cultivation and other domains. Of course, the slavery issue was also central in the Hutu-Tutsi relationship in Burundi, where the Kirundi language signification of *hutu* as "slave" or "servant" was regularly asserted.

All these three dimensions of encapturement emphasized the exploitation of the Hutu cultivators by the governing "other." In this context, the relation of power was cast in exclusively negative terms. However, as in the mythico-history of Burundi, the relations of power impinging upon Hutu labor and cultivation were ultimately more complex. The references to the Hutu as the "tractors" and the "granaries" of the "other" were not simply a commentary on exploitation and domination. Examined in context, they were also an assertion of a particular kind of power, just as in the mythico-history of the past. The bodily, "internal" power of the underdog grew precisely from its exploitation, and as the laboring category became stronger, the elite category became at once more parasitical and weaker of body. In the parallel charges— "They Eat Our Sweat" (Panel 13) and "We Cultivate a Lot, They Eat a Lot" (Panel 26)—the power of the Hutu was also expressed as a kind of potentiality, as "something out there" (Gordimer 1984)[26] that might one day run wild and threaten to destroy the very category that had extracted labor and, unwittingly, given strength.[27]

A further dimension of the power relation operating in the domain of cultivation was that the status of the Hutu as cultivator par excellence was even more positively affirmed here than it was in the mythico-history of the past. Setting Panel 26 ("We Cultivate a Lot, They Eat a Lot") side by side with "The Extraordinary Forest" of Panel 22 helps to highlight an accomplishment of which people in Mishamo were quite pointedly aware: They were brought as unwitting, hapless pioneers to settle and domesticate a forest, an unfamiliar wilderness, and, through their efforts, it was transformed into a granary and a model settlement.[28] In light of the narrative memory of this metamorphosis, it was not surprising to find that the label "tractor" was not simply accepted as a stigma but positively, ironically, subverted into a heroizing marker of categorical identity.

Thus, not only was the Hutu cultivator heroized; his/her agricultural labor power was thought of as a definite force innate to the Hutu category. When people said, "It is we who are the cultivators," as they often did, they were not simply stating their occupation; this was a categorical, moral, castelike self-definition.[29]

What comes across most forcefully in the mythico-history as described thus far is that the hierarchy of Hutu/Tutsi relations in Burundi was structurally reproduced in the "refugee"/"Tanzanian" relations within the camp. Through the establishment of a categorical analogy between Tutsi and Tanzanian—through tracing "telling signs" of their likeness—the elaboration of a whole series of other analogic symmetries between these two categories was enabled.

TAXATION

People in Mishamo talked a great deal about what they called "taxes," and it emerged that these were another perennial domain of contestation in the mythico-history, a domain that was important for what it revealed about the day-to-day constitution of the Hutu-Tanzanian categorical relationship in the camp. Several different fees, dues, and levies were collected among Tanzanian citizens and refugees alike. The refugees, without exception, claimed that all such fees and levies were actually just taxes. They insisted that, according to international refugee law, refugees are not legally subject to taxation in their country of asylum. According to local UNHCR officials, the refugees were mistaken; the law stipulates only that refugees should not pay taxes other or higher than those required of citizens.[30] This, however, had not been made clear to the refugees at the time of the events to be recounted, and they consequently acted upon their convictions.

Panel 27 illustrates that a very well articulated blueprint or precedent for defining taxation was in place among the refugees in the camp. This blueprint was evoked repeatedly during the weeks in 1986 when the taxation issue was at its most controversial in Mishamo.

Panel 27:

**ETERNAL TAXATION**

We pay all that they ask of us, we pay, pay, pay the taxes for all things. That which is demanded from us, we pay. They have need of money for this, for that, for whatnot; we, we pay—like in Burundi. And they say that he who does not pay does not like the development of this country. In Burundi, one had to bring pots of beer to the *mwami* (king), like taxes. [And there were other duties toward the Tutsi as well. One Hutu clan had to bring pots of honey regularly. Another clan received the duty of cultivating for the *mwami*, another had to transport the *mwami*, and then there were the duties of carrying water and collecting firewood.] Let us go to the women and girls now. They had the duties of dancing, sweeping, carrying water.[31]

This account, much abridged here, was told in response to a series of new fees and levies in Mishamo.[32] Its interest in the present context lies in the directness of the analogical link it drew between the exaction of tribute in precolonial Burundi and payments due in the refugee camps.[33] This analogy made it possible to construe the paying of levies in Tanzania as a consequence of the refugees' social position and occupational specialization as cultivators in the hierarchy of the camp. It also reflected a consciousness that the castelike sociopolitical system in Burundi had been structurally reproduced in the camp.

In light of this analogical interpretation, it is not surprising that the refugees should have considered the various labels attaching to the special-purpose fees as efforts to hide their true nature as taxes. The labels were seen as a ruse intended to trick the refugees into paying the taxes without protesting their illegality. Many avoided the paying of the fees/taxes on these grounds. Others, particularly single or widowed women, said that they simply lacked the wherewithal to pay.

These issues were brought sharply into focus with the March, 1986, collection of the nationwide "Development Levy" (*kodi ya maendeleo*) in Mishamo. This was an annual levy applicable to all adults aged eighteen and over in Tanzania.[34] In 1986, the levy was set at Tsh. 200, which at the time of fieldwork was approximately one quarter of a month's minimum wage, or US$11.00. Certain events during the levy collecting in Mishamo will be briefly described here because this will help to show how particular, observed events gave rise to "standard versions" and how they became transformed into mythico-historical events.

In this particular year, 1986, district authorities from the district capital of Mpanda arrived in Mishamo during the night in the company of four armed soldiers. Early on the following morning (1 March 1986), the levy collecting was begun among TCRS and government employees in the Settlement Headquarters area, or Village Two. As the employees—citizens and refugees alike—had been unaware of the levy collectors' arrival, most were not carrying their levy cards. They were therefore unable to exhibit proof of payment of the previous, October 1985, Development Levy. The District authorities refused to allow them to return home to get their cards, suspecting that they would run away. By early afternoon, this issue had been resolved; a senior TCRS employee had agreed to assume full personal responsibility for any runaways, thereby enabling his staff, at least, to fetch their cards.

The presence of the armed soldiers made these events more visible as a spectacle of power. Small, quiet groups of refugees gathered in the Headquarters area, and subdued discussions appeared to be taking place among them. (I had driven there to use the TCRS radio transmitter.) Apparently, it was already known to everyone that the levy collectors had arrived in the camp in the middle of the night. Informants briefly encountered in the Headquarters area saw this event as a premeditated attempt to prevent them from hiding by catching them unawares. Arriving under cover of night was considered "malign." One refugee employed as a mechanic in the TCRS workshop said, cleaning his oil-stained hands angrily with a rag: "They come here with guns and all and all. Me, I have already paid, but my wife, she has not. Why [should she]? What has she *done* apart from cultivating?! There are people here who go a whole year without spending even one centime. Yes. And they, they have to pay if they do not have any money?" It was clear from the mechanic's reaction that he, like others in Mishamo, considered the sum in question as a tax on income and not as a Development Levy. Other men also reported in the course of subsequent days that they had not paid the levy on behalf of their wives, first, because their wives had not earned income, and, second, because their wives, staying close to their homes, were not in great danger of getting caught.

On March 2, a Sunday, the District authorities concentrated the levy collecting in two places, the Sunday services of the main Roman Catholic and Pentecostal churches in the Headquarters area, and the two main Sunday markets in Villages Two and Six. These were the two places where large concentrations of refugees (several hundred) regularly and legitimately gathered in Mishamo. Levy collection at the church services apparently failed. At both churches, people had detected the approach of the levy collectors' jeeps and scattered rapidly. The District authorities then went to the Village Six market and set up a levy collection center in the government jeeps. Levy collecting was in progress when the following events were observed. (I had given an acquaintance whose papers were in order a ride to the market.)

Several persons who had not paid the levy could be seen running at great speed from the market into the thickets of the surrounding forest. They were briefly pursued by the soldiers. The Assistant Commandant, supervising the operation with the District authorities, said when he saw me approaching: "There is no market today. The tax collectors have come. The people have run away. Oh, the situation is difficult." Indeed, no trading was being conducted. A group of perhaps two hundred spectators stood at some distance from the District authorities, watching and commenting quietly. Their attention was focussed on the white government Land Rover and the group of people surrounding it. Two men were checking peoples' levy cards, and some twenty refugees, men and women, were sitting on the ground next to them, in a tight cluster. A TCRS employee, himself a refugee, watched this from among the other spectators and explained that the group of twenty had been captured for having failed to pay the levy:

If they do not pay, they will be transported to the Commandant's office, and if they still do not pay, they will be put in prison for six months and will be expected to pay up after their release. For me, paying is not a problem, but how about single young women and old women who do not have money? How can they pay? But these people capture everybody. You *have* to pay. [. . .] This taxing started in '84. The first time it was not a problem. People paid, no problem. Why this has happened now, I do not know. I have never seen such . . . guns, army . . . and people running here and there like *rats*. [. . .] Many simply do not have money. Others do, but they do not want to pay. [. . .] The tax men will be here for a week. During that time, people will be hiding.

He then exclaimed: "Did you see?! Now they kicked that person!" The crowd of spectators made slight movements and a hum of quiet comments rose from them. The Assistant Commandant, observing the scene, said: "This time the collectors will be here for one week. Then they will return and go into the villages. They will go to every house, door by door. People are running away now. Let them run. The collectors will come again. This is a very difficult situation, very difficult. They do not want to pay. [. . .] After this, we will be going to the [Headquarters] market. The same thing will happen there. The whole place will become empty. People will run here and there to hide. If you want to buy something, go there now while the merchants are still there." I followed his advice, but at the Headquarters market, news of the levy collectors' intentions had already emptied the market, shops, and beer houses.

Elsewhere in the camp, word of the levy collectors' presence had also circulated promptly. Several of the smaller religious denominations had suspended church services. The village marketplaces, like the smaller churches, stayed empty. This was very unusual for a Sunday, ordinarily the only day of the week when larger crowds gathered in the village centers, not only for church services and markets, but also to pass time in the beer houses. Only a handful of people lingered tensely in the village centers that I visited. The doors of all the houses that I approached were tightly shut.

Three days later, on March 5, the levy collectors were still in Mishamo, having begun the door-to-door collection in the villages. During this time, most people were unavailable for prearranged interviews. Even those who had paid the levy avoided encounters with the District authorities. It seemed inappropriate at the time to pursue interviews in the villages that were undergoing the collection.

These events had many longer- and shorter-lived effects on the social life of the camp. One of the processes that was most compelling to watch was the mining of these events for familiar themes, and their placement in an intricate mythico-historical order of knowledge and memory.

Panel 28:

**THE DEVELOPMENT LEVY**

They say that this is a Development Levy, *kodi ya maendeleo,* but it is not. It is just a tax, quite simply. [. . .] The people have hidden themselves. They are scared. They do not want to be seen by the policemen. [. . .] Refugees should not pay taxes in their country of asylum. *Surely* that is against international law. Only in this country. They come here in the darkness of the night, and then they force us to pay. It is surely illegal. [. . .] The United Nations has a duty to protect our rights. They have "Legal Protection Officers," but where are they today? Is this not a situation where they would be needed here? They have no idea what is happening here. The Tanzanians make their own laws and demand our money. If you count how many of us there are—not only in Mishamo, but in the three [Hutu refugee] camps together— and then you estimate how many people over eighteen years of age there are, you can imagine how much money they get from us. They do not come like this, with guns, to demand taxes from Tanzanian villages. They do it to us because we are refugees. You see, everyone is hidden. . . . This is not just—or legal.[35]

Increasingly formulaic interpretations of the levy collection, emerging throughout Mishamo, visibly converged on certain thematic points. That the levy collectors had chosen to enter the camp under cover of night, "like thieves," and that they had hidden the true nature of the Tsh. 200 tax under the name development levy, gave evidence to the refugees of their malignity. But it was not only the particular officials and soldiers carrying out the operation who were thus pinpointed. Events of those weeks tended to be diagnostically interpreted as "symptoms" and "proofs" of the essential qualities of an entire category, "the Tanzanians."

Another focal point for standardizing interpretation was the refugees' own status and structural position in the camp. They believed that the use of soldiers to enforce payment and the (apparently) unusually high number of arrests in 1986 were directly attributable to two factors: the vulnerability of Mishamo's residents as refugees and, compounding their vulnerability, the virtual absence of the international agencies since the 1985 "hand-over" of the camp to the government.

The levy was also consistently interpreted as one among many means of exploiting the agriculturally productive refugee population. It was of little consequence to the refugees that the Development Levy

was, in fact, nationwide. Their eyes were on their own high productivity as refugee cultivators and on the benefit that "the Tanzanians"
derived from them. Many refugees tried to calculate the fabulous sums
thought to have been collected from the population of Mishamo. Here,
comparisons with the tribute paid by Hutu to Tutsi in Burundi were
also evoked with marked systematicity.

Another, larger process observed in the aftermath of the levy collection was the spontaneous generation of accounts of atrocity. Some
of these were located in the mythico-historical present and others in
the mythico-historical past. Two "standard versions" of atrocity from
the mythico-history of the present were recorded. The first of these
concerned the refugees who left their homes to hide for days and, in
some cases, for weeks in the thickly forested areas of the camp. In the
words of one refugee man who held an important administrative position in one of the villages: "They beat people. [. . .] We are living in
slavery. [. . .] If you go to the river, to the Rugufu, you will see *many*
women and children, *many*. They have not paid. They are hiding. They
are afraid to go back home. [. . .] [People] went there to tell them that
they cannot hide forever. It is better not to hide. They can be bitten by
the snakes. There are many animals. It is dangerous. And the river is
very dangerous now because of the rains." I asked him: "Don't the levy
collectors know that there are women and children hiding along the
river?" He replied: "No, if nobody tells them. But once they do go there,
the people will try to cross the river, and there will be many dead
people." It was in this context that some of the accounts of early exile
in "the extraordinary forest" were told. (See Panel 22). The dangers of
the "wilderness" (and of water most especially) were thus once again
provoked into narration.

The second "standard version" of atrocity centered on a particular
event, a confrontation between the tax collectors and a wedding party.

Panel 29:

### THE BEATING OF THE BRIDE

Each Saturday, the young boys and girls come for religious courses at the
Pentecostal Church [in the Headquarters area]. It is for those who want to
be married. The young people met with the little soldiers of the tax there.
[. . .] A certain young woman and her groom were coming from their wedding party there when the tax collectors stopped them. Of course they did
not have their tax cards with them. The little soldiers with their problems

began to beat them, and they said: "You are well dressed, you have expensive clothes—this must cost at least 500 shillings, that must cost 600—and yet you lack 200 shillings." [. . .] They had already paid the tax, but they had no proof of it. [. . . The] bride was beaten with the butt of the rifle, and her leg was broken. The soldiers beat the bride. Nobody did anything [. . .]. They were let go when the payment was alright. Refugees have certain rights, but they do not mean anything here. Who would be here to watch the protection of the rights? [. . .] The Tutsi like the Tanzanian hides his malignness. But in the presence of foreigners, he is a man, he is a lion. [. . .] Be it a pregnant women, a child . . . killing.[36]

The bride in this confrontation seems to stand out as a symbolically pure victim. This may be one of the reasons why the "beating of the bride" was so readily transformed into a mythico-historical "standard version." The reference to killing at the conclusion of Panel 29 led to accounts of atrocity in the mythico-historical past in Burundi. The bride as pure victim found an analogical counterpart in the pregnant woman disemboweled during the 1972 massacres. These figures together, the bride and the pregnant woman, exhibited perhaps more than any other the powerlessness of the Hutu as a category to prevent the perpetration of atrocities against themselves. And just as the humanity of the Tutsi category was negated through the narrative remembrance of the atrocities of the 1972 massacres in Burundi, so, too, did "the beating of the bride" become incorporated into the mythico-history as an analogous account of atrocity, an account on a more modest scale which nonetheless had the effect of dehumanizing "the Tanzanians" (Malkki 1990b).

THE POLITICS OF VACCINATION

It was the ongoing mythico-history of the atrocities committed in Burundi that also helped to make sense of the refugees' reaction to the TCRS/UNHCR vaccination program in Mishamo. When the program was first initiated, people feared this might be a secret plan for their mass sterilization. Explaining why Hutu women and children in the camp fled from any attempt to vaccinate them, a young pastor said: "In the year 1983, President Bagaza decided, instead of killing, to start a vaccination program. It was a massive sterilization program, directed at women—so that they could not bring into the world more people, us Hutu. But officially it was said that it was an ordinary vaccination campaign. The campaign continued for two months. Then the leader of the [PALIPEHUTU] liberation party [in Mishamo] put an end to it. He wrote to international organizations about it. They sent spies into Burundi, and they observed that the rumor was true."

A Village Chairman also remembered the fear that people initially had in the face of the TCRS nurse who was coordinating the vaccinations and distributing milk powder in the villages: "They knew that [the nurse] had spent two or three years in Burundi before coming here. When she made milk with powder, they said: 'That will kill us.' But we, the chiefs of the villages, we drank this to show [it was safe]—also our wives and children drank it. The people said: 'You are going to die.' But they came to see that it was not dangerous. Now the women like [the nurse] very much."

In 1986, several years after the first vaccination attempt, informants claimed that the *rumors* that the vaccination program was a sterilization program targeting Hutu refugees had been planted by camp authorities. It was further claimed that this was a conspiracy to sow seeds of fear and mistrust against the international agencies among the refugees and also to sabotage the TCRS health program. It is interesting to note that in this instance as in other spheres of camp life, the international agencies (TCRS and UNHCR) were ultimately a "neutral," inactive presence in camp life. Primary historical agency was attributed to the category "the Tanzanians." Thus, in the mythico-historical narratives concerned with the vaccination program, it was not the program in itself that became key but rather, the alleged Tanzanian conspiracy to sabotage it.

THE DISTRICT COMMISSIONER'S TOUR

Another key event in Mishamo to have become incorporated into the mythico-history was a tour of Mishamo's sixteen villages by the District Commissioner (DC) from Mpanda. The tour occurred shortly after the levy collection (which had likewise been directed by the District Commissioner). The most remarkable aspect of this visit was not anything the District Commissioner himself did; it was that every refugee encountered at this time knew the outline of the District Commissioner's speech practically by heart and seemed almost compelled to recite it. Each of the points made by the District Commissioner was reproduced and "diagnosed" with startling uniformity. He probably never knew that his speech had such an afterlife. A "standard version" of the District Commissioner's speech is given at some length in Panel 30 because it condenses and illuminates several central themes of the mythico-history of exile.

Panel 30:

### THE DISTRICT COMMISSIONER'S TOUR

"[The DC] had several subjects. The first, he said that we are cultivators. He said that we are peasants. He said that we came here as peasants in order to cultivate. So, we have to stay quiet and cultivate and follow the development of Tanzania. [. . .] He said that we are here so that we can be protected, and that we should stay here and cultivate peacefully. [They say that the people from Burundi may try to come and kill us.] Second, he said that we are thieves. He said that in our camp there are many thieves. He said we steal in the store, and spare parts—and then we take them to Burundi. He works for the government! He could not say that the citizens steal. He said that we are cultivators—and that we must not squander, spoil the favor we [derive] from this. This is to say that to be a cultivator is an elevated thing, agreeable for us. He started with the cultivator, then the thief—. So, if we are thieves, we squander this—being cultivators! It is for this that he first spoke of cultivators, and then of thieves. He wanted to show us . . . that one is to be a good cultivator. Third thing, he said that we kill many of the elephants of this country. He said that Burundi was the first in the Common Market [in ivory exports] because we, we kill elephants here and take them to Burundi. He is in the process of trying to prevent us from doing this. He said: "If you take a lot of ivory there, you help your enemy to prepare himself. How can your [liberation] party allow this?" Fourth thing, concerning our party [PALIPEHUTU], he said that our party has no official status in Tanzania or in the OAU [Organization of African Unity], and that if we want to have this thing, we have to ask the OAU to accept it first. Then he said something on the dues we pay to our [liberation] party. He said that what we have paid is stolen from us, and that restaurants and hotels are built with our money instead. He said that we should no longer think about the return to Burundi, to our native country—that there are already too many people in Burundi, and that we would have no place there. He said that Burundi is even smaller than his District, Mpanda. They do not want us to leave the country. They need us. We cultivate a lot. [. . .] But we said that we are *refugees*. Burundi pays those who govern us here because the Tanzanians have the possibility of making meetings like the DC's meeting here. Burundi wants to know what is happening here. [. . .] The government of Burundi has sold us to Tanzania. [. . .] The chief of the camp [Commandant] gave programs to the Village Chairmen, and they had to try to convince people to come and listen to what the DC wanted to say. [. . .] He also spoke about "adult education" [saying that we should attend more]. This is the means of making us stupid. It means that we are stupid because we do not even know how to plant maize! They teach us to plant, to put chemical fertilizer. Ha! This, and one also learns to read and write—also little mathematics exercises, two plus one. They understand very, very well that we are cultivators.[37]

This rendering of the District Commissioner's speech drew together, in the form of an itemized, systematic list, many themes that had become pivotal in the mythico-history of exile. Among these, yet again, was the theme of cultivation and the maintenance of the Hutu refugees as the cultivating category. Here, as in previous panels, the rationale for the refugees' spatial confinement was traced to their value as a fund of agricultural labor power. The assertion was once again made that "the Tanzanians" had need of the Hutu as "cultivators" and "peasants"—in other words, as *hutu* and not as "refugees." The narrative accounts of this panel also revealed how attuned people were to any signs of the other's attempts to define the Hutu, and to establish its own definitions as true. Mapping the refugees' diagnostic interpretations of the motives of the other shows on the one hand that they tended to essentialize the Tanzanians. But on the other, such mappings also, necessarily, demonstrate how inescapably relational is the social imagination and enactment of collective identity. For the refugees' narratives ended up suggesting that without these particular categorical antagonists—"the Tutsi" and "the Tanzanians"—Hutuness would be something quite different.

The adult education classes promoted by the District Commissioner were widely scoffed at, for if the Hutu were such powerful cultivators, why did they need to be taught to plant and fertilize by those whom they fed? The question answered itself neatly in the mythico-history, and the classes were simply considered as one further prong in the "Motivation Programs" designed to increase the productivity and "usefulness" of the refugees.[38] People in Mishamo had a well-articulated consciousness of being the collective object of a series of processes which would simultaneously increase their docility and decrease their "apathy."[39]

BLOCKAGE FROM HIGHER EDUCATION

The themes of education and intellectualism had been transferred into exile with the Hutu refugees and were considered just as central to their collective condition as they had been in Burundi. (Cf. Panel 10, "Blockage from Schooling and Governing," chapter 2.) It appeared that in education, as in so many other spheres of life in the camp, the mythico-history of Burundi and that of exile were mutually constitutive. In other words, narratives on Hutu education in Burundi were often generated by observations of the state of Hutu education in Tanzania, and, conversely, Hutu education in Tanzania was interpreted by reference and analogy to schooling in Burundi. This is not to say, of course, that nothing had changed, or that no changes were acknowledged by the refugees; the question of education, like so many others, had been transformed in exile.

Seven primary schools had been built in each of the sixteen villages in Mishamo. All shared an identical academic curriculum that was designed according to national standards by the Ministry of Home Affairs Education Coordinator and her staff in the camp. There were no secondary schools in Mishamo. One reason given for this by the education coordinators was that all secondary schools in Tanzania accept students from the entire country, and that Mishamo would be too remote a boarding school for most nonrefugee students from other regions of Tanzania. It should also be noted that while very few Hutu refugee students gained entry to the secondary schools, it was by no means easy for Tanzanian students to obtain places in them, either.[40]

The corps of teachers in Mishamo included both Hutu refugees and Tanzanians resident in Mishamo. Most of the headmasters were Tanzanian. All education in Mishamo was supervised by the Education Coordinator, who at the time of this research was the wife of the Settlement Commandant.

Some scholarships for refugees in Tanzania were provided by the UNHCR, but these were exceedingly scarce. One UNHCR official who had recently interviewed prospective applicants said: "The scholarships are very, very few. This year we can give five to only the top, top, and absolutely best [. . .]. Remember: all the applicants need to get a recommendation from the Commandant in order to be considered. We can't do anything otherwise."

Regarding the progress of schooling in Mishamo, one resident headmaster gave this assessment:

From 1979 to 1982, there was a lot of trouble in schools. Parents did not like it. When we got places for secondary school in 1983, they were more satisfied. They saw that if you go to school, you can be somebody. [. . .] I think it would have been better if all the refugee pupils would have been in boarding schools because then you can change them more easily. The parents influence the pupils a lot. You can see it. You can learn so much about the family through the pupil. [. . .] In Swahili Studies we teach them kind words, how to behave nicely, how to be clean and so. But this class is only two times per week. It is *too* little. Then the students go home, and they hear different things, see different things, and then they do not learn. It is a problem, very difficult. We have problems with pupils, but this is so in all schools—not only refugees. Some are very rough; they do not obey. Many are lazy. In general, they do not subscribe enough to the things we are teaching. This is a big problem. [. . .] Usually, if they are not good, we give them work outside, [. . .] work in the fields, hoeing, weeding.

The parents of these pupils had priorities quite different from those expressed by the headmaster. While they valued education in general very highly—indeed, as one of the highest achievements to which a person can aspire—they saw education in the particular context of the camp as fraught with problems and dangers. First, they saw that, whatever the reasons, the structural asymmetry between themselves and the Tutsi in the domain of schooling had been reproduced in exile. That is, in both places the Hutu had been blocked from higher education for reasons which, in their eyes, had remained constant throughout their history. What people had to say about schooling reflected this understanding: that the Hutu were categorically defined as "the true cultivators" by themselves and by the "others," and that they were in a real sense captured within this essentialized category.

Panel 31:

### TECHNICAL SCHOOL FOR HUTU, HIGHER EDUCATION FOR OTHERS

There were two categories of school—one for the children of the Tutsi chiefs, another for the Hutu children. The Hutu were taught—are prepared for agriculture, and the Tutsi are prepared to govern. It is like this today in Burundi. The Tanzanians also have schools for themselves where they learn—how is it called?—the social rights—for example, the politics of the country. For the Hutu it is the *métiers* like mechanics, construction, and carpentry. These are their chosen schools for us, the technical schools. This a bad thing because our generations of the future will not know that place from where they came, they will not know their country of origin. At the same time, this is to kill the ideas of liberation. [And that is the] final point.

[. . .] At the time of the arrival of the Belgians, the Tutsi employed the malignness [. . .] of telling the Belgians that the Hutu are accustomed to cultivating—by that token, therefore, they should be taught agriculture.[41] You see that. This was an evil ideology parented by the Tutsi. Even today, the Hutu [in Burundi] will tell you that "me, I am accustomed to cultivate." If you ask: "What do you think of your country?" they will say this. [. . .] The Belgians *discovered* this secret because they governed Burundi for many days. [. . .] The ideologies employed by the Tutsi are already discovered, known. [. . .] The schoolchildren are at the mouth of the gun [in Burundi], always, always, always, always! There, it was difficult.

And here? What is there? Nothing! Education here in Tanzania is truly bad. Our children are taught by our enemies. They do not learn anything here. Even at the end of primary school, not a word of English![42] Our friends who went [fled] to Rwanda or to Zaire have their children in schools, and they advance. They go to secondary schools, they. Here, no. [In Tanzania . . .] they have primary school and then what?! Nothing. The intelligent, the stupid, the lazy—no difference. After primary school, they go home to cultivate, cultivate, cultivate."[43]

The mythico-historical analogies between past and present that people in Mishamo so habitually and expertly mapped allowed them to diagnose, not just the reproduction of structural inequality in exile, but also the replication of the *motives* compelling the governing "other" to exclude the Hutu from higher education. This exclusion was, of course, linked to that very thing—the power to grow things and feed people—that gave the Hutu value in the terms of the other.

The categorical definition of the Hutu as "the true cultivators" was a double-edged sword in much the same way as the earlier mythico-historical claim to autochthonism (cf. chapter 2). When people called *themselves* "true cultivators" the name carried a positive value, and it was not considered that cultivation and education should be mutually exclusive. But when "true cultivators" was a label affixed by the antagonistic other (Tutsi or Tanzanian), it had the effect of capturing the Hutu in castelike subordination, in *hutu*ness, and of naturalizing their blockage from education and intellectual pursuits.

The account of how the Tutsi "employed the malignness" of telling the Belgian educators that the Hutu should be taught agriculture because they were "accustomed to cultivating" was one expression of this struggle over the meaning of *hutu*ness. In light of this theme of trickery, the adult education classes in Mishamo acquired a peculiar signification; in the refugee camp also, the Hutu cultivators were being taught to cultivate because they were cultivators.

In an effort to describe the significance of this blockage in Tanzania, one man posed the question; "What if I wanted to study philosophy?"[44] He did not mean that he was intellectually incapable of studying philosophy, but that philosophy epitomized the intellectual pursuits from which he was excluded by virtue of his membership in the "Hutu cultivator" category. There was a cluster of scholarly subjects which people in Mishamo identified as perpetually closed to the Hutu. They were variously named "philosophy," "political science" or "politics," "social rights," "history," "the humanities," and—as I was once told—"those studies which you do here." It was evident that these subjects signified "intellectual labor" as opposed to manual or bodily labor and that they produced "knowledge." "Knowledge" was a valorized, almost sacralized resource. It might not be inaccurate to suggest that the mythico-historical construct "knowledge" was in itself a way of referring to a particular kind of power.

It is likely, too, that the high, almost spiritual, value placed on education and intellectualism by the refugees in Mishamo is directly traceable to the now well-documented patterns of "selective genocide" in 1972 in Burundi, where intellectuals and other schooled people were the first victims of lethal categorical hatred (Lemarchand and Martin 1974). The caricature of the hapless old Hutu in Burundi who said, "Me, I am accustomed to cultivating" (Panel 31), seemed to document how the colonizing of Hutu thought had happened. "The Hutu" was able to say this of himself because he had interiorized a certain definition of himself and his proper station, a definition that had been fashioned by those who had the long habit of governing him. But the mythico-history drew a clear distinction between this old figure and the Hutu person in exile. It asserted that those Hutu who had survived the massacres in which "the intellectuals were killed first," and who had become refugees, were not colonized in this manner. Thus, consciousness of what had happened during the massacres and what it meant was forged in exile when Hutu from all the regions of Burundi were thrown together in refugee camps. In the mythico-history, exile had brought the final, collective discovery of the "secrets of the Tutsi."

The mythico-history constructed, however, analogous dangers of intellectual and spiritual colonization in exile where the governing other had become the category "the Tanzanians." Again and again, different people in Mishamo said that to block the Hutu refugees from education was an effort to make them into domestic animals. In the words of one informant: "Schools [are] closed to Hutu children. This is a means of *nous rendre bête.* If I could continue school, what would the capacity of my thoughts be? I ask myself." These remarks, spoken in French, were interesting because of the ambiguity of the French expression *rendre bête.* The statement could be read "blockage from schools makes simpletons of us," or "blockage from schools makes animals of us." Schools were seen as the primary channel to benign knowledge and powerful thought, and without schooling, there was a danger of becoming less than a social being. This was a danger not just for the individual Hutu person but for the whole category—so that when specific schoolchildren in Mishamo were denied further education, the entire people was denied it at the same time.

In the mythico-history, one potent means of refusing and combating "intellectual animality" was to know the collective history and systematically to unearth the "malignities" of the "other." Parents often said that the most important things for their children to learn were taught to them at home. They would say, "We try to tell them where their country is, and why we are here." And "Even a child here knows who the Tutsi are."

Time was acutely experienced as a force working against the adult generations who wanted to teach the younger refugees things that were not written into any school curricula. Several parents observed that their many years of exile had taken a heavy toll on the language skills of their children. And people often remarked, regretfully, that the children mixed Kirundi and Swahili in their everyday language.[45] The impossibility of learning French in school in exile was likewise keenly regretted. But, in the absence of French, learning English was valued as a substitute because it, too, was recognized as an "international" language—a language that enabled the Hutu refugees to try to maintain articulate links to the imagined international community "out there."[46]

Finally, the blockage of Hutu refugees from secondary schools and other institutions of "higher learning" was also interpreted as an effort to quell political activism and organizing in the camp. One person put it thus: "I think it is difficult for us to have a secondary education because they [the Tanzanians] think that if we are educated, we will not cultivate anymore, that we will do nasty things. They think that we will go and fight in our own country." On several occasions, it has been evident that the government of Burundi has suspected the Hutu refugee camps in Tanzania of being bases for armed training of guerilla forces.[47] The Tanzanian government was, of course, anxious to ensure that this was not the case, and that it would not be drawn into conflict with Burundi.[48]

This cluster of themes on schooling, intellect, and knowledge should be seen as central to the mythico-history as a whole rather than as an isolated theme. Schooling had a direct bearing on the mythico-historical oppositions between cultivating and governing, Hutu and Tutsi, refugee and Tanzanian, and even on the moral distinction between internal and external forms of power. Ultimately, these issues fed into a broader mythico-historical struggle over power, knowledge, and truth.

SPATIAL CLOSURE, SOCIAL INSULATION

The precisely planned ordering of space in Mishamo—and, indeed, in any refugee camp—was an intriguing issue, not only in terms of the rationalization of that ordering, but in terms of the socio-political *effects* that different kinds of spatial regimes might be expected to produce. The creation of disciplinary spaces for the purpose, not only of containing, but also of normalizing people has been explored by Foucault (1979) and others. In a refugee camp where people are contained for one overarching reason, their statelessness, the compartmentalization and regulation of space comes to have heightened practical and political significance.[49] For there, normalization occurs first of all at the level of categories—most of all, national categories. Just as it is unlikely that a zoo keeper would put creatures of different species in a single cage, so it seems to be standard practice that different national "types" or "kinds" are segregated as a matter of course in the administration of refugees.[50] This practice is by now so standardized that it hardly even seems to need rationalization.

In Mishamo, the issue of keeping order among different "nationalities" obviously did not arise, except insofar as the Tanzanian camp authorities and most of the remaining TCRS staff tended to live apart from the refugees. Space within the camp had been, however, rationally organized for various other purposes. Perhaps chief among these were, first, the provision of space for maximum agricultural productivity over the long term, even as new cultivators came of age, and, second, the ensuring of the relative, collective immobility of the cultivators, and of their crops. Both processes necessitated the planning and regulation of space.

While it would be worthwhile to study in detail the compartmentalization and monitoring of spaces within Mishamo, and within each of its villages, these subdivisions of space inside the camp were not explicitly generative of continual mythico-historical elaboration and will therefore be bypassed. The aspects of space that were a part of the mythico-history were broader. They concerned the location of the camp in a forested nothingness, a green wilderness, and the regulation of its outer boundaries. Ultimately, then, the question of space centered on issues of isolation and the control of movement.

As was noted earlier, any person desiring to leave the camp legitimately had to apply for a Leave Pass from the office of the Commandant. Obtaining the fourteen-day Leave Pass was in turn linked to other bureaucratic requirements such as the paying of levies and fees. A villager seeking a Leave Pass had first to apply to the Village Chairman for a letter of authorization. This was granted if the applicant had paid all dues and presented a "legitimate" reason for traveling. (Visiting family in other camps appeared to be the most common reason given.) The applicant would then take the authorization letter to the office of the Commandant for approval and might be interviewed further. The refugees also said that anyone who had publicly marked himself or herself as a political activist or troublemaker would be denied exit.

If the camp had been located in the proximity of railway lines or larger towns, this system of regulating movement and space could not have been so efficient. It was precisely the remoteness of Mishamo from any other habitation or transportation that acted to bar movement. The vast, 2,050 square kilometer area of the camp was not surrounded by fences or walls, simply by miles of forest. It was the overabundance of undomesticated and forbidding space that acted as the barrier—and together with the curtailed period of legal travel time—conspired to make travel to and from the camp a problematic issue among the refugees.

Panel 32:

**CONTROL OF MOVEMENT/SPACE/TIME**

They [the guards at the road barriers of Mishamo] ask for taxes [before permitting travelers] to pass—or they steal quite simply. They also interrogate you: "Where are you going? Why?" We are not supposed to leave our camp without authorization from our Commandant. [. . .] The Leave Pass is easy to get if the Commandant wants to give it. . . . "Leave Pass" it is called. . . . One receives a letter from the Village Chairman. One takes it to the Commandant, then one pays fifty shillings. But sometimes it is necessary to pay more. [. . .] The permission is only for fourteen days, not more. Always fourteen days. [How far can you go in seven days? How long can you stay where you are going?] It is not desired that we leave the camp. It is desired that we stay here. You see, the [Tanzanian] government tricked the United Nations in saying that this is a settlement. It is a camp because we cannot leave when we want to. Sometimes people nevertheless leave even without permission, but it is difficult. It is much better to have the permission. If, for example, you use the [footpath] that goes from Village Eleven to the lake, there [at the lake] there are many government officials who may ask you for your papers. If you do not have them, they can put you in jail.[51]

Narratives like this one suggested that the refugees experienced their isolation as repressive; but there was also another dimension to their experience of the ordered space of the camp. A particular kind of power was being generated by the spatial closure of Mishamo and by the concentration of the refugees within it. One thinks again of Foucault's (1979) juxtaposition of the dungeonlike prison in the murky recesses of which the prisoners are invisible to their guards and the modern panopticon where they are compartmentalized in such a way as always to be accessible to the gaze of administrators. Mishamo could perhaps be described as a system intermediate between the dungeon and the panopticon. For in this particular case, the inhabitants of the enclosed, compartmentalized, and visible space were nevertheless enabled to manipulate and subvert the interior space in more ways than would ever be possible in the panopticon. In the account to follow, a certain mastery of the space enclosed in the camp is expressed.

There is an insect which makes threads—a spider. If a fly touches the threads, this will be known. [Whatever happens anywhere in the web, the spider who built it will know.] This camp is like those threads there. If something happens in the twelfth village, in some hours Village One will know it. If something happens in Village Three, in a few hours Village Six will know it. People meet each other along the road and tell each other the news [while walking]. This is a good means of communication. The "feeder roads" are like the little threads [in the web], and the "main roads" like the principal threads. But when we were in Burundi, it was difficult to know information. Each family on its own hill. . . .

In Burundi, we did not get news. The families lived separately—no villages. No villages such as here. [. . .] Here [in the camp] it is a mixture, a meeting of people from all the different regions of Burundi. [. . .] In the year 1983, our party suggested that *all* refugees should be moved into camps.

The metaphor of the spider's web was unique to one person. But the significance of its imagery was more widely shared. Many people remarked on the fact that they walked a great deal between the different villages in the camp, exchanging news and thoughts along the way. In effect, their descriptions conjured up the image of a discreet relay system for circulating information of all kinds. Whatever happened in the camp, people said, all the refugees would quickly know about it. It was claimed that nothing of importance occurred in Mishamo without everyone's knowledge.

It is compelling to think of the spider as the mythico-history itself, a discursive practice consuming all "digestible" things in its path—that is to say, things that were intelligible and significant as potential elements of the mythico-history. This perpetual, self-conscious circulation of ideas or knowledge was perhaps one of the reasons why the camp had become such an intensively signifying context, and why the mythico-history had acquired such a deeply narrative form. At the same time, tracing these paths of narrative production indicates one of the ways in which spatial isolation and concentration had become a positive technique of power, a technique helping to *produce* mythico-historical knowledge.

INSULATION FROM THE OUTSIDE

The refugees' descriptions of space and movement gave an impression of Mishamo as a place where the boundary between inside and outside was so clearly delineated that it became easy to know what crossed that boundary. It also became important to know what came in and went out—not only for the camp authorities but also for the refugees. In this sense, the camp had become an inward-looking system. However, this did not mean that the refugees within the camp were unaware of or unconcerned with events and processes occurring beyond the camp boundaries. Indeed, the opposite was the case. Perhaps partly because of their very boundedness, the refugees were acutely conscious of the existence of the world outside their camp and desired to know about it. They gained information through the oral circulation of news and stories, through the collective use of the scarce radios owned by people in the camp, and through any accessible printed material.

The spatial closure of Mishamo was not seen as unambiguously negative or bad in and of itself; only the deployment of the disciplinary techniques made possible by the fact of closure was experienced as "malign" and repressive. Fault was found with the *uses* made of the spatial regime by the governing other but not with the spatial enclosure of the camp itself.

One of the "malign" purposes most commonly ascribed to the spatial isolation of the refugees was that of preventing news of the refugees' plight from reaching the outside world. Here an analogy was frequently drawn with the insulation of the Hutu from benevolent foreigners by the Tutsi in Burundi.

Panel 33:

INSULATION FROM THE OUTSIDE WORLD

When journalists come here from Europe or America, they are watched all the time. They come here to see how the refugees are living, but they can never talk with them. They do not hear us. Sometimes we try to be nearby when they come to the villages; we are in camouflage, but we never manage to talk with them. They come in cars and together with many Tanzanians. [The camp authorities] bring the guests through by car and show them the schools, the godowns, the dispensaries, and so on, but not the problems. [. . .] [T]he difficulty—the people who come from other countries, they quite simply arrive in the capital [Bujumbura], and the Tutsi speak. No Hutu could converse with the strangers [. . .] about the Hutu. Here [in Mishamo] it is the same thing. Many times—above all, if the visitors speak French—one does not permit them to converse with the refugees who speak French. Sometimes this happens. If the visitors come to villages, the Tanzanians do not understand French, and they think that the refugees make accusations, and that they do not speak the truth. Telling others, it is difficult. We are private. We do not have the liberty to tell in particular—or in sum.[52]

Many evaluation teams from international and church organizations, funding agencies, and other institutions, as well as government officials routinely made tours of Mishamo. This camp was a popular site for visitors because of its reputation as a success story, a "model settlement." Reports resulting from these visits, like project reports, were singularly devoid of commentary by the refugees. This fact did not set them apart from most other reports on refugee projects else-where, but in the context of the Hutu mythico-history this became a meaningful fact. It was transformed into a sign of the refugees' struc-tural muteness. In talking about their inability to converse with visitors from the world beyond, the Hutu seemed to be expressing the lived experience of being objectified as "the refugees."

THE POLITICS OF LANGUAGE

The choice of language was a politically charged issue in the camp, as is suggested above. Most people in Mishamo spoke Swahili in addition to Kirundi, a great many spoke French, and a very few knew English. Only some of the elderly and some women were unable to speak Swa-hili.[53] It can thus be said that for most refugees, the choice of language depended not just on competence but on context. People seemed to prefer speaking Kirundi and French, treating both languages as their own, as part of their cultural and linguistic heritage, while associating Swahili and English with life in Tanzania. English was also considered important as a means of communicating with the outside world. Speak-ing French occupied a particularly interesting position in the camp con-text; it was a means of communication that was unintelligible to the Tanzanian authorities. For this reason, it was not generally used in the company of the authorities. This would not only have given offense; it would have exhibited open defiance and signaled the existence of "secrets." In these contexts, Swahili was usually spoken. Perhaps be-cause of the very fact that French was a language not spoken by the governing other in exile, it had become like a second "native language" among the refugees.

ANALOGY, ALLIANCE, AND EQUIVALENCE

Thus far, the following arguments have been made in this chapter: First, the Tanzanian camp authorities had come to stand for the gen-eralized, essentialized category of "the Tanzanians" in the mythico-history. Second, the perceived or experiential structural asymmetry between the Hutu refugees and "the Tanzanians" was seen as a repro-duction of the castelike hierarchy of social life in Burundi.[54] Third, through numerous comparisons—in domains such as cultivation, taxa-tion, vaccination, education, the control of movement, and the ordering of space—the analogy between the Tutsi and the Tanzanians had be-come progressively more significant and forceful. Thus, through the metaphoric links expressed in the foregoing panels, the Tanzanians and the Tutsi had been analogically mapped onto each other as the dominant and governing "other(s)" in the mythico-history.

Further, it was believed that the Tutsi and the Tanzanians were not only analogous but actively allied. The allegation of alliance appeared in Panel 30, "The District Commissioner's Tour," where it was claimed that the District Commissioner and the camp authorities, having direct access to the refugees (while the government of Burundi did not), functioned as a channel of information for the Tutsi.

This claim was further supported by a visit to Mishamo by the Consul of Burundi stationed in Kigoma Township near the Burundi-Tanzania border. This visit occurred after fieldwork had ended, but accounts in letters from refugees in Mishamo were detailed. It was observed that the Consul arrived after dark, stayed for several days, and toured villages in the company of the Commandant, and that no explanation of his visit was provided to the refugees. The numerous letters seemed to suggest that the Consul's visit was also in the process of becoming a "standard version." (This visit, which one person referred to as "the nocturnal voyage," will be mentioned again in the Postscript).

The belief in the existence of an alliance between the Tutsi-ruled government of Burundi and the camp authorities, and between "the Tutsi" and "the Tanzanians" as broad mythico-historical categories, was explained in several ways. First, it was concluded, as in Panel 30, that "the government of Burundi has sold us to Tanzania." This belief often appeared in connection with cultivation; it was conjectured that the Hutu as a fund of agricultural labor (as *hutu*) had been sold to the Tanzanians by the Tutsi. People in Mishamo were adamant that the camp authorities had received money from the government of Burundi, and thought that the Tutsi had thereby accomplished important objectives.

First, as long as the Hutu in exile remained in the camp under the management of "the Tanzanians," they would be less likely to return to Burundi in order to "make a revolution." In the words of one informant: "There is a confidence[55] between the government of this country [Tanzania] and UPRONA [the ruling party in Burundi]. We are told all the time in the public meetings that we have to leave this thing [the liberation movement]. But us, we are ready to die because we know that the government of Burundi has evil habits."[56]

Second, "the Tanzanians" might convince the Hutu to become

immigrants and to foresake their links to the "homeland." The District Commissioner's attempt to persuade the refugees that they "would have no place" in Burundi was interpreted as one among many conspiracies to break these links. Finally, it was asserted that "the Tanzanians" gave the Burundian government information on activities among the camp refugees, and the Burundian Consul's visit seemed to provide rich evidence of this.

It should be noted here that the alliance between the categories "Tutsi" and "Tanzanians" was also conceived as an alliance between governments, and that "governments" were generally conceptualized as opaque apparatuses wielded by the "governing other." In the mythico-history, then, the art of statecraft entailed practicing the "malign knowledge" of the "other" to the exclusion and certain detriment of the "Hutu" category.

One further dimension of the Tutsi-Tanzanian relationship emerged in the narrative constructions of camp life. At key points in the mythico-history, the relationship between "the Tutsi" and "the Tanzanians" became not only one of analogy or alliance, but of actual equivalence. The Tutsi and the Tanzanians as categories had become similar, then allied, and, finally, interchangeable. The most visible indication of such a fusion came in narratives where discussion shifted almost imperceptibly from one category to the other. In many cases, it was unclear to which category the pronoun *they* referred. This elision occurred, for example, in the abundant lists of the "traits" of the enemy, one of which was presented in Panel 5, "The Theft of the Aboriginal Nation in the Absence of Civilization."

The second, more significant axis of equivalence was the transference of specific "Tutsi traits" onto the Tanzanians. In the mythico-history, the "character" of the Tutsi and the Tanzanians as categorical actors merged. The *Leitmotiv* was once again "malignness," and particular remembered or experienced cases of trickery, ruse, secrecy, and theft became symptoms of the more generalized malign-ness. The assertion that was sometimes made—that the Tanzanians were "tutsi-anized"—would seem to be best understood in this context.

As was noted earlier, the categorical equivalence did not extend to the ascription of physical "traits" or attributes. There were no body maps of the Tanzanian category, and in the mythico-history of the present, there were no body maps of the Hutu, either. These, as was suggested in chapter 2, were left in the past, where "the Hutu" was reflexively constituted as the opposite of "the Tutsi."

One exception to the general absence of physicalizing body maps in the mythico-history of the present was to be found in the area of cleanliness. This narrative, too, emerged in the context of yet another list of physical differences between the Hutu and the Tutsi.

Panel 34:

CLEANLINESS AND CATEGORICAL PURITY

It is like this that the Tutsi were able to distinguish who the Hutu was; the Hutu does not like dirtiness. He does not like to live with the calves of cows, with animals. He likes to change his clothes from one day to the next, but the Tutsi always wear the same clothes. You see that we change our clothes every day—more often than the Tanzanians. It is a beautiful sign [. . .]—a beautiful sign of life. It shows the difference between the Hutu and the Tutsi—and the Tanzanians. [. . .] In brief, one can say that it is the mode of life. We are different from the citizens.[57]

It is perhaps too easy merely to dismiss accounts such as this as slanderous prejudice, without asking how such accounts had come to be generated and what they might mean. As an empirical question, of course, "cleanliness" is of little interest, but considered as a form of social commentary on the relations of opposition in which people found their lives embedded, it becomes more significant. For the claim of cleanliness seemed to fit together with other mythico-historical claims regarding the ubiquitous oppositions between good and evil, purity and corruption, Hutu and Tutsi. In this field of oppositions, the contrast between the Hutu and Tanzanian categories was ultimately secondary to the one between the Hutu and the Tutsi. However, both oppositions were in some sense expressions of one and the same thing. They expressed the importance of marking and imposing essential, moral, *categorical* difference between self and dominating "other." In exile, this categorical difference had also become aligned with a distinction between "refugees" and "citizens," as the conclusion of Panel 34 above suggests; it was not stated whether the term *citizens* referred to the Tanzanians or to the Tutsi. Yet merely marking difference was clearly not sufficient in the mythico-history; difference was accompanied by the assertion and affirmation in everyday practice of *categorical antagonism*, or enmity. Both "the Tutsi" and "the Tanzanians" had acquired the status of "enemy" in the mythico-history. Thus, symbiotic hierarchical relations between the Hutu and the Tutsi were broken and supplanted by antagonistic equality in the wake of the 1972 massacres, later, similar antagonistic equality was extended to the Hutu-Tanzanian relationship in exile. So long as the Hutu insisted on their refugee status, they need not accept as permanent an unequal symbiotic relation with "the Tanzanians."

INTERNATIONAL ORGANIZATIONS AND THE "INTERNATIONAL AUDIENCE"
In chapter 2, it was shown that the category, "the Belgians," occupied a special position in relation to the Tutsi-Hutu-Twa hierarchy in Burundi. It was suggested that the mythico-historical reconstruction of the colonial administration in such a positive light stemmed from the status of the Belgians as the key source of "benign knowledge," a kind of knowledge independent of and qualitatively opposed to the "malign knowledge" monopolized by the Tutsi category. It was emphasized that the central importance of the Belgians in the mythico-history should be seen in relation to the system of schooling which they, principally, had imported to Burundi. Finally, it was concluded that the Belgians were so significant because they seemed to stand apart from the trilevel hierarchy of Burundi society and, therefore, to be ultimately independent of this hierarchy. Whereas the Tutsi were the "malign foreigners," interlopers who pretended to nativeness, the Belgians were remembered as the "benign foreigners" who checked the evil of the Tutsi.

In the mythico-history of exile, the trilevel pyramid of Tutsi-Huta-Twa had been structurally reproduced in another pyramid: that of Tanzanians-refugees-Wabende. The fourth, quasi-independent term, "the Belgians," had likewise found its homologous counterpart. "The Belgians" had been replaced by another "foreign" category, the international organizations concerned with the refugees.

The primary position within this category was occupied by the UNHCR and by the United Nations as a whole. The secondary position was occupied by TCRS and, less directly, by the Lutheran World Federation (LWF)—this despite the fact that TCRS, as the implementing agency, had the greatest day-to-day presence in the camp. While other international organizations were known to the refugees and were encompassed by the totalizing category "the international organizations," the UNHCR and TCRS were more prominent in the ongoing production of the mythico-historical narratives. The category of "international organizations" was often simply referred to as "the UN," or "the United Nations." While most refugees were perfectly aware of the institutional distinctions among these organizations, their differentiation seemed to be irrelevant in the larger mythico-historical context. This operation of fusing lent further support to the interpretation that these organizations were most relevant in the mythico-history as a single, totalized category. Accordingly, the identities and actions of specific individuals in the employ of the international refugee agencies were not salient. In short, the "UN" construct was operative as the categorical fourth term in the mythico-history. The agencies mentioned were regarded as the local instantiations of wider and more powerful organizations based elsewhere. This supralocal link to the main offices elsewhere was very significant in the mythico-historical constitution of the relationship between these international agencies and the refugees.

As in the case of "the Belgians" in Burundi, the predominant importance of the category of "the international organizations" in Tanzania derived at once from their ultimate externality to local hierarchies and from their perceived protective capabilities. It was not the specific qualities or aims of the organizations that were elaborated in the mythico-history, but the way that they affected the dominant opposition between Hutu and "other," be the latter Tutsi or Tanzanian.

Panel 35:

**THE "BENIGN FOREIGNERS"**

There in Burundi, you know, the foreigners, they know our problem, and it is us that they try to help, but now the government has become angry because of this. But the whites, they are for us. [. . .] And now, who protects us? What laws touch us? Those of the government or those of the High Commissioner? The Commissioner cannot help us a great deal. But at least we are still in the hands of the UN. [. . .] At the very least, the UN still supports us. They are for us, the refugees.[58]

The favorable valuation of the international organizations, so evident in Mishamo, might appear paradoxical at first glance because, in accordance with the Tri-Partite Agreement, UNHCR, TCRS, and the Ministry of Home Affairs, all participated in the spatial, social, and economic, and political design of Mishamo. The international organizations were, therefore, equally the architects of Hutu confinement in this remote camp. But this fact did not seem to have made the international organizations "malign" or to have identified them by any means as the category that governs or oppresses. The "malign" aspects of camp administration were understood as Tanzanian trickery; the international organizations were seen, not as complicit, but as uninformed or deceived.

While a structural homology existed between the role of the Belgians and that of the international organizations in the mythico-history, exile had produced a significant transformation in the substantive significance of this role. Stated summarily, the Belgians were significant in the mythico-history on four levels. They had imported a system of education which was seen to empower the Hutu. They were seen as protectors of the Hutu underdog. They were constituted as a force moderating evil in the opposition between good and evil, or Hutu and Tutsi. Finally, the Belgians established a link to an "international audience," a benevolent entity beyond local struggles and parochial ruse.

The most fundamental transformation in exile was that the international organizations were no longer the source of education. Their "benign power" now derived from the fact that by their very presence they affirmed the status of the Hutu as *refugees* and that, ideally at least, their mandate was to care for and protect the refugees. In practice, the international organizations—perhaps inevitably—fell short of the ideal in protecting the refugees' rights as the refugees themselves conceived them. When key events like "The Beating of the Bride" (Panel 29), "The District Commissioner's Tour" (Panel 30), or the Burundi Consul's visit (above) occurred in the camp, the refugees routinely posed the questions, Where are the international organizations now? Does the UN not know what is happening here? It was often simply assumed that the camp authorities managed to "hide" happenings in the camp from the international organizations headquartered far away in Dar-es-Salaam.[59]

The presence of UNHCR and TCRS employees in Mishamo was reduced to a handful of TCRS staff following the official "handover" of Mishamo to the Tanzanian government in August, 1985. The August ceremony, attended by high officials of the Ministry of Home Affairs and by representatives of UNHCR and LWF from their European headquarters, signaled the end of the operative stage of the Tri-Partite agreement between the Tanzanian government, UNHCR, and TCRS. Even before the handover date, the ranks of TCRS and UNHCR staff actually residing in the camp had been systematically scaled down in phases. The refugees seem to have watched this process closely. Fieldwork for this project began less than two months after the handover ceremonies. Already at that time, a collective vision of this transition had formed itself in Mishamo, and the ceremonialized moment of the handover had become a watershed event for the refugees. It was seen as an augury of a new, more difficult era in their collective existence in the camp.

It is not surprising that the handover should have become elaborated; signs of it began to appear in so many areas of life in Mishamo. Writing of Mishamo and other refugee settlements in Tanzania, Armstrong (1988:65–6) has observed: "The post-handover years demand a considerable readjustment to less amenable circumstances as settlements tend to become neglected, facilities and services run down and the refugees have to confront the major problems of living in a type of remote rural ghetto, without any political voice and living in an impoverished, economically beset nation." The refugees saw the decline in the services and physical structures of the camp, but they also closely followed signs of their own growing vulnerability and powerlessness.

Panel 36:

**HANDOVER**

There will be many changes after this handover. This has already started. For example, we pay taxes under force. TCRS, they gave us to the government in August [1985]. This time [after handover], the tax men came with force. If we imagine what will come later! Eh. [. . .] We are in slavery. [After the handover, we also have to cultivate more.] In this season of cultivation, we have been obliged to cultivate two hectares of sunflower [per five-hectare household plot] for their new factory in Mpanda, a factory which will produce sunflower oil for all of Tanzania. This is an order. We, the refugees in Mishamo and Katumba, have to cultivate the sunflowers. We have further to give two sacks of sunflower seeds without receiving even a single centime. [. . .] These two sacks should be considered as theft. For the people, to accept or not accept the cultivation of sunflower seeds—here where we are, the answer has to be yes. If, for example, they desire that you kill your mother, here, also, they desire the answer, yes. Not proper, this. But we are like slaves.[60]

Other key events described in foregoing panels in this section were also either seen as a consequence of the handover or considered to have been aggravated because of it. The international agencies, it was believed, had served to keep the exploitative actions of "the Tanzanians" in check. In short, the handover of Mishamo was compared to "The Defeat of 'the Belgians'" (Panel 11) by the Tutsi at the end of the colonial era in Burundi. It was considered that the Tutsi had outwitted the Belgians: "independence" was yet another Tutsi "trick" that signaled only Tutsi independence from the Belgians but no true independence for the Hutu masses.[61] In the case of Mishamo, it was believed that a similar transformation was in progress, and it was feared that the power of the Tanzanian administrators over the Hutu cultivators would become less and less moderated by outside forces. In this connection, it was frequently repeated that the handover was the beginning of "real slavery." The phrase "they gave us to the government" might be interpreted as another expression of this theme of slavery, a theme continually renewed in the mythico-history. The renewal happened through the acute detection of "signs" or "symptoms" of the evolution of a more crystallized form of "slavery." Such signs included the collection of the "Development Levy" (Panel 28), the District Commissioner's tour of the camp (Panel 30), and the new program implemented in Mishamo for the cultivation of sunflower seeds.

The most serious consequence of the handover in people's eyes was that their very status as *refugees* seemed to be threatened by the withdrawal of the international agencies. It now becomes more intelligible why the refugees should have reacted so unanimously to one particular paragraph in the District Commissioner's speech: the charge that the Hutu were mere immigrants in search of fertile land to cultivate. (See Panel 30.) The speech challenged the Hutu refugees' status as refugees and ultimately, therefore, the very reality of the events that had made refugees of them in the first place. In this light, the District Commissioner's comment signaled danger for the refugees. For in the mythico-history, the possibility of immigrant status led to the comment that "we are their slaves," which in turn signified that "we are their *hutu*." The symbolic significance of this equation was considerable. In the mythico-historical scheme of things, the refugees' acceptance of *hutu*ness or "slavery" in exile would have meant that they had traveled in a circle from *bantu* to *hutu* to refugee, and back to *hutu*. There was a great deal at stake, then, in not allowing that circle to close.

Even when the international organizations were no longer palpably present in the camp (as was practically the case during fieldwork in Mishamo), the link to them as a generalized, totalized category was vigorously maintained by the refugees.[62] There were several ways of going about this task. The most immediately visible means of maintaining the link was to have discussions about the nature of the duties and capabilities of the international organizations, and reciting details of international refugee law. It was surprising how knowledgeable ordinary people were about these laws and conventions. As one TCRS employee said, rather in exasperation: "They are very clever, those Bahutu. They know their rights as refugees. They will cite to the UNHCR officials Article so-and-so of the Geneva Convention! *They* chase after the *UNHCR!*" Ordinary villagers did not form delegations or go to the UNHCR head office in Dar-es-Salaam, but many knew about such delegations and discussed them with interest and concern. An extraordinary number of refugees in Mishamo also took the initiative of writing to the main offices of the international organizations in Europe, and not just to refugee organizations. This correspondence appeared to be principally unidirectional from the camp to the outside, but this fact was not a deterrent. People's purpose in sending these letters into the "world beyond" was not to receive return mail but, rather, to document in conscientious detail all those aspects of their collective condition and of events in the camp that appeared to be in violation of their rights as refugees. These letters seemed to be meant as a constant reminder to the world: We are still refugees and still under your mandate.

The number of international agencies known to the refugees was considerable. Many of these (again, often one-sided) contacts were made through the UNHCR *Refugees Magazine* which provides subscriptions free of charge and which apparently sometimes publishes addresses of international organizations around the world. To these addresses, people sent, not only letters documenting exile, but also retrospective accounts of the massacre of 1972 and other events in Burundi past and present. Yet others were engaged in preparing manuscripts on the history of the Hutu people and in submitting essays on other topics to French-language journals and magazines (see Malkki 1994).

People in Mishamo were convinced that their voice would be heard as long as it was the voice of "the Hutu refugee." Their letters were apparently also well known in the head offices of the international organizations and in the Ministry of Home Affairs in Dar-es-Salaam. Many of the letters were produced in triplicate or more and sent to all institutions concerned. There was some frustration about "these refugees' letters" in the international organizations because, as a UN representative explained, the main offices in Europe, which likewise received copies, periodically contacted the Dar-es-Salaam offices, inquiring what was going on. This intensive, remarkably collective preoccupation with maintaining links to the international organizations made a peculiar contrast with the overwhelming spatial isolation and remoteness of the refugees in Mishamo. Yet, it seemed to be this particular combination of isolation and linkage which had helped to elaborate and intensify the refugees' preoccupation with what Said calls a "thereness" (1986a:28). The world beyond was conceived as an international and impartial audience for the documentation of the "true history," not only of Burundi, but of exile. It was a Hutu history which was being documented, then—lived and generated locally but needing supralocal documentation. Deposited with an international audience, it became a part of the larger struggle over history and historical truth in which the Hutu were engaged with the dominating "other."

# four

# TOWN REFUGEES: A PRAGMATICS OF IDENTITY

The previous two chapters have described the pervasive historicity of identity and consciousness among the Hutu refugees in Mishamo. The role of what I have called the mythico-history of exile was so powerful in Mishamo that one is tempted to think of it as the central and constitutive feature of the Hutu refugees' consciousness, the symbolic core of their lifeworld (cf. Gilroy 1991:17). Not all of the Hutu refugees in Tanzania lived in camps, however, and not all ordered their lives in mythico-historical terms. In this chapter, it is precisely the relative absence of mythico-historical orders among the town refugees in Kigoma that is the central social fact to be explored. In order to render this absence intelligible, rather than merely stating it, it is necessary to explore what else *did* exist in Kigoma, what other conceptual and practical processes meaningfully ordered people's lives. This question will be approached through exploration of particular domains of everyday practice among the town refugees; through these, it will become possible to see the rival constructions of order and morality that held sway there. In this way, it will ultimately become possible to understand the challenge that the town posed for the mythico-history in the camp.

The argument of the chapter will be presented in three main sections. First, it will be shown how the town refugees tended to pragmatically manage a series of different identities in preference to a primary self-definition as refugees, and how this "pragmatics of identity" contrasted with the heroization of a single collective identity among the camp refugees in Mishamo. The examination of this management of identities lays the groundwork for the second main section of the chapter, an exploration of three key axes of assimilation among the town refugees: intermarriage with "citizens"; legal or documentary "naturalization"; and the narration of personal socioeconomic trajectories. Finally, the third section raises the broader question of the town refugees' relationship to their past, to their history, by describing how they formulated and debated the question of a return to Burundi.

### THE CIRCUMVENTION OF BUREAUCRATIC ENTANGLEMENT

As was shown in chapter 3, the international organizations occupied a significant position in the living and narration of exile in Mishamo; they were also related to the mythico-history of the past insofar as they occupied a structural position analogous to that of "the Belgians." Both categories, "the Belgians" and "the international organizations," were significant as benign outsiders; both were considered benign largely because they were supralocal. The international organizations' image as protectors of the Hutu was very salient among the camp refugees of Mishamo.

In Kigoma, the situation was very different. The international organizations were never much discussed, and they were not perceived as a categorical actor. Even when town refugees were directly asked to express their opinions of these organizations, their responses generally revealed a rather vague sense of their function and, more to the point, a lack of interest. When asked to describe the role of TCRS, for example, one person said that "its role is to give aid to refugees of the camps, like to someone whose house has burned down, and so on." Another person offered, "It is often said that they have constructed schools and dispensaries [in Kigoma Region] because of the refugees." A third person said, "Me, I think that the advantage [of having the UNHCR here] is that they receive the new refugees who arrive here in Kigoma." In short, a good deal of variation appeared in such answers, and, clearly, the social cost of not knowing the *raison d'être* of the international organizations was not high.

It is also relevant to know that many (though by no means all) refugees in town actively *avoided* any contact with the UNHCR, TCRS, and the Kigoma Settlement Commandant's office. This caution was reflected in the following response to a question about the proper role of the UNHCR:

If truth be told, I do not know what the people of UNHCR do. In the past, a Zairean refugee advised me to go to the office of the UN to get a refugee card, but I do not know how to do it. I do not even know where the office of the UNHCR is. [. . .] For the moment, I am thinking of going there, but I am afraid that they will not give me this refugee card because I came a long time ago, in 1972. They could ask me, "Where were you all this time?" Or else they might think that I am a newly arrived one, and, by consequence, [expel] me, or take me to the camp. [. . .] And it is for this reason that I try to hide myself, my nationality, for fear of the immigration agents.

This man, like many others, avoided contact with "offices" of any kind. The international organizations were not classed apart from other, local and regional government offices because all were perceived as points of potential bureaucratic entanglement, places where the refugees might be swept along in processes beyond their control. (One thinks of the poor old man in Ousmane Sembene's *The Money Order*). The most important concern appeared to be the possible loss of the power to determine one's own status and place of residence.

STRATEGIES OF INVISIBILITY
As has already been noted, the Kigoma township and its environs were a heterogeneous, socially complicated, and cosmopolitan crossroads of human and other traffic. The town's resident population comprised many different, interspersed categories of people sharing neighborhoods, and continual streams of visitors, travelers, mobile merchants, and other less permanent inhabitants. This plurality and continual mobility meant that the person in the street was not to be fixed and classified simply by virtue of his or her locale. It also meant that it was often impossible to discern who among the residents might be a refugee from Burundi. For the refugees did not live in ethnically homogeneous, bounded neighborhoods (though some neighborhoods were generally known to be more populated by refugees than others), and they were just as mobile as other residents in the township. This heterogeneity was a fact about the social setting itself, and the Burundi refugees in town had come to make deft use of it. Another feature of the sociocultural landscape that aided the town refugees in their quest for a shelter-

ing anonymity was the preponderance there of ethnic Waha, whose language, Kiha, was very closely related to the refugees' own Kirundi.

Whereas people in Mishamo readily and spontaneously introduced themselves as "refugees," those in Kigoma did not do so. Indeed, at the outset of the research, it was singularly difficult to locate informants at all. Many denied that they were refugees—a pose made credible (or at least hard to disprove) by the plurality of identities available in their complex urban context.

In Mishamo, everyone (with the exception of the camp authorities and a few conspicuous outsiders like myself) was by definition a Hutu refugee. Moreover, the question of identity was a heavily idealized, moral, and political one. There, identity was a matter of profound essences, traceable to the ancient depths of time. A person was a "Hutu" and a "refugee" by virtue of historico-political forces more formidable (and more important) than his or her own will or desire. In Mishamo, one's self-identification was always made in reference to the larger collectivity of "a people" in exile. Both the individual and the collectivity were categorically defined.

By contrast, most town refugees did not define themselves primarily as members of the marked collectivity "Hutu refugees" and, indeed, expended a good deal of creative energy in circumventing this identification. Far from being heroized, refugeeness was instead often negated and supplanted by a series of alternative identities and labels. The number of persons who openly defined themselves as refugees regardless of context was remarkably small. Most people managed one or more adoptive identities or labels that were already given and rendered workable by the lived-in settings in and around town. Thus, some claimed to be Burundian immigrants from the colonial era and, thereby, Tanzanian citizens. Others staked a claim to citizenship by asserting that they were Waha.[1] Yet others explained that they had adopted Islam and Arabic names and thus, implicitly, Tanzanian identity (there being very few Muslims in Burundi, they said). All of these adoptive labels converged to negate any uniform, collective self-definition, and they were individualistically pursued and deployed. The social uses of these multiple identities were shaped by many different nexuses of relations with diverse categories of people, and in a multitude of shifting contexts. Much like protective coloration, then, these multiple identities operated as strategies of invisibility.

It seemed at first that the quest for invisibility was the effect of a generalized fear of conspicuousness among the town refugees, and that this fear structured the initiation and management of social relationships, as well as shaping other domains of social action. The most readily observable expressions of this fear—or of the desire for anonymity—where the circumvention of any bureaucratic entanglement that might require an official declaration of personal legal status and, also, a quickness to avoid involvement with strangers, particularly when this entailed revealing one's status. However, it would be misleading to characterize these strategies of invisibility only as products of fear. The fact that worry and caution informed many aspects of the refugees' social relationships with others should not conjure up an image of them as "cringing, huddled masses."[2] Indeed, when worry was evident, it seemed to have more to do with the practical consequences of being identified as a refugee in some particular mundane situation than with a more generalized fear of persecution. People believed that juggling identities could facilitate numerous routine activities of daily life: avoiding harrassment by immigration agents and other officials; securing jobs; traveling; obtaining licenses for petty trade, market spots, and fishing; spending leisure time in bars and night spots; and conversing with strangers. Such creative management of identity is, of course, a recurring theme in the ethnography of central and east African town life. Shifting categories, Islam, etc. are all well documented aspects of urban life in the broader region, as Vincent (1971, 1982), Bujra (1975, 1978–79), L. White (1990), Leslie (1963), Parkin (1975), and others have shown.

For the Hutu refugees in Kigoma, then, juggling identities was not just a simple knee-jerk reaction of fear; it was, instead, a specific form of a much more general kind of strategy employed by urbanites throughout the region. The refugees' expertise in manipulating categories of identity was deployed both to resolve specific difficulties raised by their refugee status and to achieve other, broader ends that were not directly related to that status. Their strategies of invisibility formed an enabling, empowering device in the ordinary conduct of many domains of life in Kigoma. But these strategies became most readily observable when a person was challenged or called upon to identify herself or himself as something more taxonomically objectified than simply "local." In the following sections, it will be shown what specific identities or labels were commonly drawn upon and how these were made credible through the orchestration of social relationships. The inventive management of situational identities[3] by the town refugees turned upon their denial of refugee status, and it is therefore necessary to begin by examining the social construction of that status.

## THE NEGATION OF THE REFUGEE LABEL

In the camp, refugeeness was at once a protective legal *status* and a politico-moral *condition*, mythico-historically elaborated. In Kigoma, refugeeness tended to be considered from an entirely different basis. Here, it could not be described as a protective status because, as was noted earlier, the international organizations that were the source of legal protection and material aid played little role in the lives of most town refugees. Thus, the status of "refugee" was neither particularly useful nor desirable. As an idealized moral condition, refugeeness was not workable, either. This had once again to do with the fact that people did not imagine for themselves a categorical, collective existence as "refugees." Refugeeness in the Kigoma context is perhaps best described as a *label*—a generally hindering, stigmatizing label.

The meaning of the "refugee" label could be seen both in casual conversation among informants and in responses to more structured interview questions. Several dimensions of informants' comments are of interest here because they suggest how refugeeness was socially constituted and experienced and thus help to explain why the "refugee" label was eshewed.

Perhaps the most important aspect of the town refugees' comments on the label was that, when talking about "what it means to be a refugee" or "life as a refugee," they tended to situate their comments temporally, in the early years of their lives as newly arrived refugees in Tanzania. This temporally bounded period of "the early years" seemed to be considered the appropriate backdrop for any discussion of refugeeness.

The early period was unanimously remembered as one of extreme social and economic hardship. Poverty, hunger, lack of work, and problems of housing were, for understandable reasons, well-trodden areas of reminiscence. In the present context, social hardships of a particular kind are relevant. Informants chronicled "social problems" in their relations with "the citizens" and talked especially about the "insults" that were often directed at them as refugees in the early years. These remembered insults seemed to serve as retrospective inventories of the kinds of stigmata that could be expected to attach to refugeeness.

The following excerpt of an interview summarizes points brought up by many informants in their chronicles of early hardship.

Apart from problems of food and lodging, the gravest problems were only that the citizens considered us to be savage animals. I say this because, sometimes, if one hit a Burundian, it was said, "Hit harder, it is a refugee." For this, we found ourselves to be without value in their eyes. [. . .] The citizens insulted us in the beginning because they said that we had left our fields, our plantations of palms, coffee, cassava, and had come here without bringing anything. For this, they said that we had come to eat their food. We were not liked because of our poverty. [. . .] For the moment, the situation has changed; we have bought palm plantations, we have built our own homes, we have become accustomed [to living here].

The following testimony shows clearly that the early years were associated with social problems and hardships, but it is also of interest because, unlike the mythico-historical accounts of early exile in Mishamo, it fails to make explicitly categorical or essentializing judgments about the "locals" or "citizens." No inherent "traits" are excavated. Indeed, while most people mentioned that early exile was characterized by insults and jokes, they also hastened to add that not all "locals" were alike, and that this problem had to do with particular temperaments, particular situations in the labor market, and particular social contexts. The most frequently made retrospective assessment of the problem was, in the words of one person, that "[t]hose who insulted us and did not like us were above all the drunkards. Sometimes they said that if a refugee dies, it is like an animal dying. But all this was said especially when beer had been bought. All this happens in beer clubs and cabarets." Yet another person put it thus: "I think that [the insults] were a way of condescending to us. But it was not everyone who insulted us. In general, it was very few persons. It was those who were dishonest, persons who were habitual impolites, those who did not even get along with other citizens."

Another significant aspect of the passage cited above is its suggestion that it was somehow understandable for the local, well-established population to resent refugees "because of their poverty." It acknowledges that "danger" and criminalization may attach to extreme poverty.[4] Poverty was here seen as a source of stigma; the appropriate remedy was not a protestation of injustice, but an overcoming of poverty.

Other stigmata of refugeeness were like poverty in that they, too, were acknowledged, not denied. Indeed, for most people in town, the whole figure of the refugee appeared to be constructed from these stigmata, and to be devalued, even pathologized. Many informants said that they hated "this name of 'refugee,'" and that being called a refugee caused them to "feel bad" and "ashamed." Others claimed that someone wishing to insult them could simply say: "You, refugee!" Another man, responding to the question, "What is a refugee?" said: "Nobody loves the name 'refugee.' Nobody detests liberty." Yet another person who was himself a recent arrival from Burundi explained why care should be exercised in asking people (and especially younger people) whether they were refugees: "The young . . . they came here at the age of four, let us say, and they are now sixteen, eighteen, even twenty years old. Their parents did not like to speak their national language. So, these young do not know a single word of Kirundi, and they have no love for their old country. So, they call themselves Tanzanians. If you tell him that he is a refugee or a Murundi, he is very embarrassed. This is especially here in town. In Mishamo it is different; the children speak Kirundi. Here, no."

When informants produced more formulaic definitions of a refugee in the context of interviews, the following points were commonly listed: (a) a refugee is always afraid that he will be transported somewhere against his will; (2) a refugee cannot vote or be elected to office; (3) a refugee cannot be a member of a political party; (4) a refugee always has to worry about Leave Passes; and finally, (5) a refugee does not feel free. It is significant that all these aspects of an imagined refugee's status were hindrances and constraints. The leitmotiv among them was the curtailment of liberty or freedom. Freedom here referred to personal freedom in the contemporary context, in distinction to the more collective, revolutionary freedom envisioned by the camp refugees for a Burundi of the future. In the words of one man in town: "No, I do not prefer the name 'refugee,' because to be a refugee, it is to lack all liberty. You do not feel free at all. Each person looks at you like a being without value, inferior, particularly when you are having an exchange with a person who has done bad things to you." Having talked in this way about the lack of freedom of refugees, several informants interestingly pointed to the camps—and, specifically, to Mishamo—as the place where the "real refugees" were to be found.

After chronicling the social hardships of early exile, people often went on to describe how their lives had improved since the beginning. By improvement they meant, not the augmentation of their moral or political worth as refugees, as did informants in Mishamo, but rather, the betterment of the social and economic conditions of individual lives. This trajectory of improvement was linked precisely to the fact that it had become possible for many in Kigoma to escape the refugee label.

Paraphrased for the sake of brevity, the common themes appearing in many informants' reconstructions may be reproduced as follows: When, starting in April of 1972, tens of thousands of Hutu crossed the border into Tanzania and converged upon Kigoma, the arrivals formed a highly visible collectivity. They were "the refugees," a spectacle of bodies *en masse*. Squatting in the region by the thousands and quickly becoming a source of cheap labor, they necessarily disrupted everyday life in Kigoma, not least because they brought down the wages of other residents. If considerable ill-feeling attached to them at this time, it was because they were so many, and so poor. So long as the refugees remained a visible group, rendered conspicuous by their very numbers, they were all vulnerable to the blight of stigmata and insults. When, in subsequent months and years, the bulk of the refugees had already been transported into camps elsewhere, away from this border region, those who remained in Kigoma could finally become less conspicuous. It became possible for them to act as individual persons and to start sloughing off the stigmata.

In Mishamo security derived from being a member of the larger collectivity known as "the Hutu refugees." In town, however, it was better ensured by the very opposite, by being unclassifiable. One informant put it like this: "No, I do not like the name 'refugee,' particularly here in town. I prefer the name 'citizen'; it is for my security [. . .]." In the end, there is justification for suggesting that although the same word, *refugee*, was used in camp and town, it referred to two quite different figures in the social imaginations of these settings.

MURUNDI VERSUS HUTU, NATIONAL VERSUS ETHNIC CLASSIFICATION

But camp and town were different not only with regard to their imagining of refugee status; they also diverged in another important aspect of self-definition. When the refugees in town referred to themselves collectively, they tended to use the term "Burundians" (*Barundi* in Kirundi, *Warundi* in Swahili, *burundais* in French) in preference to

"Hutu." There was nothing extraordinary in this usage until it was set side by side with that of the camp. There, "Hutu" was the spontaneous designation. As was described earlier (Panel 7), the camp refugees had highly elaborated reasons for the names ascribed to categories, and the meaning of the name *Hutu* was mythico-historical. They displayed great unanimity in defining themselves as "Hutu," in express opposition to "Barundi."

The town refugees, on the other hand, expressed a motley variety of both strongly and casually held opinions about these designations or (as they often put it) "names." Many seemed to be puzzled at the very question of nomenclature and wondered why this was important to know. (I did not have a good answer at the time.) For most, nomenclature as an academic question was a rather inconsequential one; it did not matter much which term was used.

The most common answer given to my terminological question was, "It is preferable to be a Murundi instead of a Hutu." One man had a historical reason for preferring the name "Murundi": "I am a Murundi because the name Hutu . . . it was the Tutsi who named us that because we were their servants." Another young man reasoned thus: "Me, I am a Hutu; the Murundi is he who is in Burundi." On a separate occasion, an informant arrived at the opposite conclusion: "Burundi is a country and the Barundi are the three races of Burundi, the Hutu, the Tutsi, and the Twa. So, the Murundi is he who is on the exterior of the country." His father interjected, "Muhutu and Murundi, it is the same thing." The son then replied: "If I have to choose, I am a Hutu first, Murundi second." Yet another man explained at greater length why "Murundi" was better. "Yes, I like to be named a 'Murundi.' That is good. But the name 'refugee,' truly I do not like it. [. . .] 'Muhutu'? That is the same thing as a Murundi. But in any case the name Murundi is preferable. For example: if a citizen passes through here, and if I call him 'You, Muha!', he will not be as pleased as when I call him, 'You, Tanzanian!' [. . .]" This man did not always call himself Murundi, however; sometimes he was Muha.

Despite these significant variations and fluctuations of opinion, it became possible to draw some general conclusions. National classification generally took precedence over ethnic classification; "Burundianness" generally superceded "Hutuness" in the Kigoma context. What needs to be emphasized here is that for the town refugees, nationality was closely interlinked with citizenship in a state. Hutuness had not formed itself into a competing, challenging nationality. In Mishamo, by contrast, nationality was not coterminous or interchangeable with citizenship, just as the nation was not equivalent to the state. It was considered that contemporary Burundi was not a true nation but only a corrupt state ruled by interlopers. True nationness was being prepared in exile.

The equivalence of nationality and citizenship in Kigoma became very clear in an interview with a successful tailor who, being at work, clearly had more urgent matters at hand than these: "I do not ponder anything. I consider myself as a citizen [of Tanzania]. I am trying to *become* a citizen. [. . .] If someone asks, I am a Murundi. One bases oneself on nationality."

This man considered himself a citizen of Burundi even when in Tanzania. Others more quickly assumed that by fleeing Burundi, they had lost their citizenship there. For example, my research assistant asked a friend of his, "Can one exist without any nationality at all?" His friend answered: "Yes, it is possible. For example, myself: I have no [CCM] party card, I am not a citizen [of Tanzania], I am not even a citizen of Burundi. For this, it seems to me that I have no nationality." Similar deductions were made by many other informants in Kigoma.

Finally, in Kigoma it was considered inappropriate in a way that it never was in Mishamo to use "tribes" as a form of identifying and classifying people. It was also considered rude (just as it was in Tanzania at large). As one person said: "Here in town one does not use the name of the tribe. One says 'Murundi.' Me, I say that I am from Mpanda, from Katumba. Then they think that I must be Mfipa and then I explain like this, like this. I say that I come from Burundi quite simply."

THE JUGGLING OF LABELS

The rejection of the "refugee" label and the significations of "Hutuness" and "Burundianness" having been explored, the stage is now set to explore the play and management of other labels and identities in Kigoma. The range of these alternative, often fictional identities was, not surprisingly, circumscribed by the wider social landscape in which the arrivals from Burundi found themselves. Thus, some refugees claimed to be Burundian immigrants who had arrived several decades ago, or descendants of immigrants who had come to Tanzania in the colonial days in order to escape the harsh labor practices of Belgian rule. Others claimed to be Waha and therefore Tanzanian citizens. Yet others appealed to their adopted religion, Islam, as a way of indicating, in a more circuitous fashion, that they were citizens. Still others simply referred to a locale, a home area, in Tanzania in support of their claim to citizenship.

It can be said that at least two levels of permanence and social investment existed in this play of identities. On the more shifting, changing level, people chose labels or names depending on specific situations. Thus one person might at one time refer to himself or herself as Murundi and at another, as Muha. This was workable especially in town, in the company of casual acquaintances and strangers.

The more permanent, fixed level in the play of identities seemed to entail greater commitments. Several people had adopted only one label or identity and stuck to that one. This demanded that a person pay attention to various details of his or her life in order to ensure that "everything fit." That these strategies were socially efficacious seems quite clear. But it could also be suggested that they had become, for some, an accustomed mode of conducting social relations even when their use did not appear to be practically necessary. The following comment by one town refugee suggests this. "I do not like to be called a 'refugee.' That word, 'refugee,' I *detest* it. But, also, I do not want to be a Tanzanian citizen. I like that one should call me a 'Murundi Tanzanian citizen.' With this word I would be pleased because then one knows right away that I am not a refugee or a citizen, but a Tanzanian Murundi." This passage does not reveal what labels or identities the speaker managed, but it does make plain that, like many other town refugees, he wanted to keep his options open. He wanted to be neither a "citizen" (mzalendo) nor a "refugee" (mtoro, mkimbizi). He did not want to be fixed by a taxonomy beyond his control. Security and freedom, for him and others like him, derived precisely from the possibility of social and spatial mobility or, put in other words, from being socially unmarked.

THE "IMMIGRANT" LABEL

The claim to Tanzanian citizenship by way of immigrant status was validated by the fact that a sizable, well-established Burundian immigrant population had existed in the Kigoma region since the colonial times and even earlier. This fortuitous situation was frequently put to use by more recent arrivals seeking to conceal their "refugee" status.

As noted above, the predominance of ethnic Waha in the Kigoma area facilitated such strategies, since Kirundi and Kiha are mutually intelligible languages.

Such usage of an "immigrant" identity to hide oneself was revealed in a particularly vivid way on one occasion when I paid a fieldwork visit to a refugee household composed only of an elderly woman, her adult daughters, and their children. They were thrown into such a state of fear by the arrival of myself and my companions that all the women of the household vigorously claimed to be immigrants from the colonial era, and to know nothing about any refugees. They also immediately offered money in exchange for being left alone. The best reassurance was clearly to accept their declared status instead of challenging it, and to leave as quickly as possible.

Interestingly, the town refugees' assessments of their actual relations with immigrants, particularly in the early years of exile, varied substantially. Some said that Hutu refugees and Hutu immigrants had got on very well together, and that a good deal of cooperation had existed between them. Others believed that the Burundian immigrants in Kigoma had desired first and foremost to distance themselves from the more recently arrived Burundian refugees. All informants knew of cases where the immigrants had shunned contact with the refugees. In the words of one person, the immigrants "do not even want to say that they came from Burundi. They came to work . . . without passports; it was a [constant] come-and-go [between Burundi and Tanzania]. The immigrant tries to stay away from the refugee, and he even tries not to speak the national language [of Burundi]."

People tended to account for the social distance maintained by the immigrants in one of two ways. First, it was believed that the better-established immigrants had been ashamed to be associated with the refugees. Informants did not appear to be surprised that they themselves should have caused shame or embarrassment to the immigrants. After all, for them, too, a refugee was a disparaged figure. As one man put it, "[the immigrants], since they have already installed themselves here in Tanzania, they are not proud of us, being refugees."

The second reason usually given by the town refugees for the distance between themselves and the Burundian immigrants turned upon fear. Informants surmised that the immigrants avoided associating too conspicuously with the refugees for fear that they themselves might be mistaken for refugees and transported into refugee camps.

Since the fear of being moved away was strong among the town refugees themselves, it is not surprising that they should have seen it as a reasonable reaction on the part of the old, established immigrants.

The "Muha" label appeared to be most frequently deployed among the town refugees (*Muha*, sing., *Waha*, pl.). As in the case of the other labels, being Muha facilitated traveling, forestalled unnecessary questions, and smoothed other matters of the everyday. It was also claimed that when camp refugees came to town, they sometimes found it expedient to travel as Waha.

My research assistant sometimes found that he was obliged to talk with people as if they were Waha, all the while knowing for a fact that he was talking with a Burundian refugee. After a conversation with one such town refugee, he commented: "[He] does not want to be a citizen of here. If somebody calls him a refugee, that hurts him in the head. He calls himself a Muha. Many here in town, except for the intellectuals, call themselves Waha. Even some people whom I knew [previously] refused [to admit] that they were Barundi. It is almost the same thing as with someone who has changed his name. [. . .] They are hiding themselves."

Exploring the uses of this particular identity led to interesting questions which are too complex to be fully discussed here. But it is worth mentioning their existence, even if briefly. All informants considered Waha to have close ethnic and historical links with the Burundian refugees. Indeed, as scholars of the region have documented, the Burundi-Tanzania border cuts through a wider culture area.[5] Many refugees said, "The Waha are our brothers." Nonrefugee Ha informants agreed. One elderly man also said that "the name *Muha* means 'servant' just like 'Hutu'" and that both Hutu and Waha "had Tutsi rulers."

Other informants made an even stronger link between Hutu and Waha, saying that "they employ the name 'Waha,' but ethnically they are Hutu." In two cases, this kind of link was made: "[Waha,] it is the same thing as the Hutu. Waha are immigrants who came from Burundi. When the colonialists asked them, 'Who are you?' they said, 'I am *nduwaha*'—which means 'I am from here.' Hence, the name 'Waha.' They were afraid that if they said 'Murundi,' they could be chased away. This is how it happened. This was more than forty years ago."

While these histories of the relationship between Hutu and Waha were very common in Kigoma, in the camp Waha were scarcely mentioned. They did not seem to play any part in the mythico-history. The town refugees, for their part, said that the camp refugees could not know anything about the Waha because they had not lived in Kigoma.

Yet, interspersed with the town refugees' assertions of Hutu-Ha equivalence were other comments which distinguished the two groups and actually ranked them hierarchically. One person remarked: "I hear it said that a Muha is he who cultivates the fields of others (for a salary), or he who carries baggage for others." Another informant confirmed: "Here in town it is often said: 'Mzigo mzito mpe Muha,' 'heavy baggage, give it to the Muha.' They are a little bit despised."

These devaluing stereotypes do not in themselves necessarily distinguish the Hutu from the Ha. More explicit hierarchizing comments were made, but these too contained paradoxes and ambivalence: "Waha, there is not a great difference between them and the Burundians. It is the same thing. Above all it is said that Waha are people who are very timid. And then it is said that they were late in knowing civilization. And it is said that it is thanks to the refugees who came from Burundi that the Muha now feels himself to be a little bit evolved. [. . .] One can see a big difference between a Muha and a Murundi. [. . .] The Murundi always goes about in style."

Another stereotypical characterization turned upon a particular kind of supposed "fearfulness": "If you see [Burundian] immigrants mixed together with Waha, you can see the Waha because of their fear. It is said that a Murundi can pass in front of the police even if he is carrying fraudulent baggage, but a Muha could not. He would tremble too much." (That this stereotype actually reveals more about the town refugees themselves than about the Waha will become evident below.)

Whether the Waha were called brothers or distinguished in hierarchizing terms from the Burundians depended on context. When the history of the region and its inhabitants was at issue, Waha were said to have old links with the Burundian refugees. When talk turned on trade and what may be called "business sense," Waha appeared in a less complimentary light. What presented itself as ambivalence and paradox to the outside observer did not, however, in any way hinder the efficacious use of the Muha label as a strategy of invisibility by the Burundian refugees.

THE "MUSLIM" LABEL

The adoption and social performance of aspects of Islam comprised another strategy of invisibility among the town refugees. They explained that since there were "no Muslims in Burundi," a Muslim would naturally be assumed to be a Tanzanian citizen. In some cases, people had adopted only Arabic names; in others, the transformation was more thoroughgoing. The following account of such a metamorphosis gives a sense of what this specific strategy potentially entailed.

"I do not like the name 'refugee,' particularly here in town. That is why I have even changed my name. If you ask for me by my Christian name (Albert) here, they will say that they do not know him. For now, my name is Hamisi. This name, I like it, but that is not to say that I am a Muslim; it is only a fashion of living. I go to mosque often. If I do not go, it might become known that I am a liar. To be a citizen . . . I would like to be a citizen in my country [not here], but I simply hide myself as a means of living." His friend added, "He does not want to be a citizen of here, but hides as a citizen to protect himself."

On a later occasion, the same man gave a longer account of his change of identity. (At that time, he was also using yet another name.) He recalled that when he first arrived in Tanzania in 1972, he went directly to Ujiji, where he found work as a day laborer in the palm and banana plantations of Luanda (a basin near the Luiche river). An old Muslim woman was the overseer of the laborers. "It is she who was our patron. If you got along well with her, you lacked nothing. After a long time, she advised me to change my religion. [. . .] In those days I had nothing, like all refugees. But I should not say 'all' because there were refugees who came with a lot of money. But I had no means of receiving [money], and the money that I received by working was a very, very low sum. Because of this, the old woman counselled me to change my religion. She promised me many things, and having heard these promises, I decided to change my religion." The old woman apparently promised the young man that he would receive a higher salary and be moved to the head of the other workers. Later, his patron also arranged for him to marry two Muslim Ha women. He had four children by his two wives. He called himself a citizen, and still lived in Ujiji at the time of the research. His relationship with the old woman had become a quasi-kinship relation; she referred to him as her grandson. He said he had no need of refugee identification cards or passports because he was already considered a citizen.

Another informant reported that while living in Ulyankulu camp, he had begun to come periodically to work in Kigoma and had found it expedient to change his name to a Muslim one at that time. The adoption of this token of a nonrefugee identity, he said, "was a means of living well in town." Subsequently he also decided to take two wives, reinforcing his identity as a Muslim and, by implication, as a citizen of Tanzania.

## THE PRAGMATIC CHAMELEON

The identities managed in Kigoma were situational identities embedded in pragmatic concerns and in shifting relations with a rich variety of different social actors.[6] Sometimes fictional, sometimes not, these adoptive identities were cloaks of protective coloration that lent their bearers security and a range of options in complex social arenas. Hence, these identities involved elements of individual choice and calculation.

These aspects of identity among the town refugees stood in vivid contrast to the historicity and collectivization of identity in Mishamo. Among the camp refugees, identity was drawn from an essentialized, collective unit, a people, and personal identity was scarcely separable from this collective one. Identity was a matter of belief and moral judgment. Operating as a fundamentally oppositional construct, it entailed judgments of good and evil. In Kigoma, the play of identities operated on a more individual basis and was thought of as responding to the practical needs of the immediate, lived present.

## ASSIMILATION

In the foregoing sections it has been suggested how the management of situational identities served as a technique of invisibility in the flow of ordinary life in Kigoma. The groundwork is now in place for going further and examining processes of assimilation among the town refugees.

It will become obvious that the term *assimilation* is used here advisedly. It is not meant to suggest what "assimilation studies" have too often assumed: that the social world into which the refugees were trying to insert themselves was itself a stable, fixed point of reference to which the newcomers had to "adapt." On the contrary, the "locals" of Kigoma seemed caught up in the same fluid, contingent social field as the refugees; their own identities were not fixed and unequivocal models to which newcomers could simply "assimilate" in some uncomplicated way. Assimilation, for the town refugees, rather comprised a series of tactical moves and performative poses that were empowering in specific, sometimes fleeting, social contexts; like so much else in Kigoma, it was a matter less of cultural essences than of practical conjunctures.

The strategies of invisibility discussed in the previous section clearly involved the simplest kind of move toward "assimilation" in that they expressed the desire of the town refugees to stay in the township and to "pass" as locals. Yet these strategies did not in themselves show which social relationships and arenas were chosen by the town refugees as means to insert themselves into the social setting of Kigoma, nor was it apparent how permanent were the solutions. Two very different axes of assimilation will be considered in this section. The first concerns citizenship, "naturalization," and the social uses of identity documents. The second axis will be that of intermarriage with "citizens" and other nonrefugees.

CITIZENSHIP AND THE DOCUMENTATION OF IDENTITY

As Foucault (1979) has demonstrated, documentation can come to be a very efficient technique of power by means of which people can be fixed and objectified and, in the process, rendered more visible as objects of knowledge and targets of "care and control" (Malkki 1985).[7] The very fact that the town refugees were not spatially isolated and concentrated in a camp made them less accessible to technical and bureaucratic interventions than were the Mishamo refugees. This fact about the wider setting in Kigoma, combined with people's own strategies of invisibility, meant that documentation was not an effective means of social control—or, more precisely, that documentation did not produce the effects that may originally have been intended. For spatial and sociopolitical reasons, then, the generation of objectifying knowledge about the Burundian refugees in town was singularly encumbered. Surveys, evaluation reports, census information, and other documentation were widely acknowledged to be unreliable. The town refugees' inaccessibility also influenced the degree to which it was possible to issue them identity documents. Here, key documents included the refugee identity cards issued by Tanzanian government representatives in conjunction with the UNHCR; naturalization documents; and the CCM (*Chama cha mapinduzi*) party cards of Tanzania.

It is hardly surprising that many town refugees did not carry any of these three kinds of documentation. The management of ethnic,

religious, linguistic, and other signs and symptoms of naturalized identity obviated the need for refugee identification cards as well as for a
Tanzanian passport. Successfully claiming to be Muha, or a Muslim,
or an immigrant, or simply a citizen from some region of Tanzania was
sufficient proof of legitimate residency for many of the town refugees.
The use of these signs of identity can, indeed, be considered a form of
de facto naturalization. For if the use of a given identity was convincing,
if it worked, its user was in effect taken to be a citizen.

There was a lively appreciation of the workings of this de facto
citizenship in town. Some said that it was only necessary to marry a
citizen, this providing all the security that was necessary. Others had
discreetly arranged to get CCM party cards and found that these worked
as efficacious proof of citizenship. Some combined these options. One
man, for example, had converted from Catholicism to Islam, married
two Ha women, and carried a CCM card. He had neither a refugee
identification card nor Tanzanian citizenship documents. It was surprising at first to discover that he explicitly equated his conversion,
marriages, and CCM card as practical alternatives to the two latter
forms of documentation. One person attempted to clarify these intricate social webs, giving the impression of dispassionately guiding the
listener through a known procedure. "If one is afraid of having to leave
one's belongings, of being chased away from town, one marries with a
Muha woman. Like this it is very easy to hide oneself, and to say that
'I am Muha.' Then one tries to obtain all the necessary documents, the
party card, . . . Like that." It is unlikely that such procedures were ever
so cut-and-dried in motivation, in feeling, or in actual execution, but
it was a crucial fact that this kind of knowledge—about the fashion-
ing and use of signs of citizenship—abounded among the town refugees.

The documents in question had come to serve purposes and to
circulate in ways that had not been intended by anyone in particular,
and different significations had seeped into them as a result. Thus, the
CCM cards (or, perhaps, copies thereof) seemed to be in wide circulation. Other kinds of cards also facilitated trading, traveling, and other
affairs. In the assessment of one person: "It is hard to distinguish [the
refugees] because even the citizens do not all have identity cards. There
is the card of the [CCM] party for the members. Then there is a service
card for the citizens who work in the service of the government. Even
among the privates [private employers], if they have more than ten

employees, they may have cards. This is above all in town because sometimes they search for people who do not have their work cards—so that they can be returned to their villages."[8] These various types of cards apparently also circulated among the town refugees and assured them of their continued ability to live in town.

Even the UNHCR refugee identity cards appeared to have uses adapted to the social landscape in which they traveled. As mentioned earlier, relatively few of the town refugees had such documentation, and those who did have it usually also had other assurances of continued residency in Tanzania—a very secure job, greater-than-average wealth, or one or more Tanzanian spouses. It was not possible to obtain reliable or thorough information on the number of refugee identification cards that were actually being carried, but it appeared that they were more numerous in the town and its immediate environs than in more distant or inaccessible villages in Kigoma Region as a whole. It can also be suggested as a general pattern that those town refugees who were well known in the township, and who were rendered socially visible by their occupation or post, were more likely to carry the refugee identification documents. Another group carrying these documents comprised those camp refugees who traveled between camps or between camps and towns, buying and selling merchandise. Informants cautioned, however, that the refugee identification cards could not always be taken as reliable proof of a person's identity. It was said that petty merchants and even spies came from Burundi, concealing their identity by showing fraudulently obtained refugee cards.

Official naturalization had also been considered, but among people who were not wealthy, this option was often unattractive. Many said it was natural to want to be a citizen, but not in someone else's country. When asked, "Would you like to be a citizen?" one person said: "Of course, but in another country. I like to be a citizen in my paternal country, there where I was born. Because even if I am a citizen in another country, I cannot forget my origin." People also pointed to the expenditure of time and resources that would be swallowed up by the process of transforming oneself into a legally documented citizen. In one interview, the question of citizenship came up among five town refugees, young married men all of whom were engaged in cultivation and petty trade. All five agreed that going through the process of naturalization was an unwise way of spending one's time and resources.

One of the young men, evidently echoing the sentiments of his companions, said: "No how! I do not even have the idea of it. For what reason should I nationalize myself? Nobody even knows that I am a refugee." He was then asked: "So it suffices to call oneself a citizen quite simply?" To this he replied: "That suffices. What counts is to live without difficulties. [. . .] The immigration agents have never come to our street searching for refugees. They often habitually arrive at the port and ask for documents from people who are newly arrived in their view, people who carry baggage, like that. [. . .] They look mainly in the ports and then at those who are vagabonding." Each of the five men seemed to have a kind of good-humored expertise about the routes and habits of the immigration agents.[9]

Another informant said much the same: "I do not have money to squander in buying a nationality. [. . .] Even though I am not a citizen, what matters is living without difficulties. If nobody disturbs me, why think of it? [. . .] In any case, the immigration agents have never come to my house." Like the others, he too went on to explain where the immigration agents could be relied upon to go. The idea of purchasing a nationality—anathema to any patriot or nationalist—seemed to be an eminently sensible one in the social setting of Kigoma. For the mythico-historically inclined refugees of Mishamo, in contrast, buying a nationality would have been like buying oneself a new soul.

There was one category of town refugees for whom "buying a nationality" or securing official documentation of some kind was deemed more necessary than for others. These were the refugees who had become very wealthy (or arrived that way) and who owned such immovable property as land, houses, or restaurants, or valuable items like lorries, taxis, other cars, boats, and heavy machinery. This necessity was clearly acknowledged even by those who were not themselves wealthy. It was considered that wealth on the scale described made a person more visible, and so more likely to be noticed and visited by immigration agents. My research assistant, having talked with men of conspicuous wealth, explained: "Even Hutu immigrants do not have these sorts of documents. But there are immigrants and refugees who came [to Tanzania] being already rich and being well known, and they had to get the nationality. They were obliged since the immigration agents came almost all the time to ask for their documents. It is almost the same thing as for the travel documents; one pays a sum of money in secret. This happens especially here in town. The agents do not arrive in the farther villages very often, I think. [. . .] The rich merchants see that if they do not nationalize themselves, it could be that they do not receive their permits for commerce."

Another informant knew of estimates as to the costs of obtaining citizenship and affirmed that, for the wealthy, it was indeed necessary to invest in becoming documented. "It is difficult to get [a nationality]. There are some who have paid even Tsh. 60,000 to get it. Others, Tsh. 30,000. It depends on their situation. But you see, in general it is the rich merchants who want the nationality because it is they who have the houses, and so it is they who have the difficulties. They do not want to leave all this. [. . .] If, by chance, there were a change of government, they would return, I think, even if they had Tanzanian nationality. It is not that they like the Tanzanian nationality so much; they are obliged to do it. There are practical reasons."

The social significance of citizenship and other forms of documented identity was clearly complex and changeable in the Kigoma context. Particular documents did not have a fixed one-to-one correspondence with particular courses of action or particular degrees of commitment to place among the town refugees. For some, identity documents were simply another technique of invisibility. For others, the same documents were a means of extralegal de facto naturalization signaling permanent residence in Kigoma and the intention to make a new life in Tanzania. Legal naturalization, too, meant several things. For some, it was a pragmatic expediency not necessarily indicating anything about a person's political loyalties or long-term plans. For others, however, it was a statement of the desire to live the rest of one's life as a legal citizen in Tanzania.

The range of different meanings attaching to citizenship and to the documentary construction of identity shows how inadequate is the common assumption that when a person "assimilates," he or she simply "gains" aspects of a new cultural identity while "losing" something definite from the old identity in the bargain. Just as citizenship was always something more than a simple matter of have or have-not for the town refugees, so, too, was that messy, vital phenomenon that scholars so passionately gesture at by saying "identity." Rather than revolving around a transition from one fixed, rooted identity to another, the lives of the town refugees celebrated what Deleuze and Guattari have called "rhizomes":

[U]nlike trees or their roots, the rhizome connects any point to any other point, and its traits are not necessarily linked to traits of the same nature; it brings into play very different regimes of signs, and even non-sign states. [. . .] It is composed not of units but of dimensions, or rather directions in motion. It has neither beginning nor end, but always a middle (*milieu*) from which it grows and which it overspills. [. . .] The tree is filiation but the rhizome is alliance, uniquely alliance. The tree imposes the verb "to be," but the fabric of the rhizome is the conjunction, "and . . . and . . . and . . ." (Deleuze and Guattari 1987:21, 25).[10]

INTERMARRIAGE

Intermarriage was a second important axis of 'de facto naturalization' and another domain in which the *absence* of the camp refugees' mythico-historical approach to the dilemmas of exile was especially striking. For in Kigoma, unlike in the camp, categorical orders were collapsed, not reaffirmed, through marriage.

Reliable statistical information on the frequency of mixed marriages among the town refugees was unavailable. However, it is possible to say that well over half of all married informants had nonrefugee, non-Burundian spouses. Intermarriage was not the exception or categorical aberration that it was in Mishamo. It was very common and acceptable. No town refugees with whom marriage was discussed expressed moral or political criticisms about those who had intermarried. As in other social arenas among the town refugees, normative judgments about the affairs of others were scarce. This does not imply that intermarriage did not raise complicated issues—only that the ethnic origins and nationalities of spouses were not in themselves seen as *causes* of problems.

It is perhaps well to begin with an examination of the reasons given by the town refugees for intermarriage, and for marrying in general. Three kinds of reasons emerged in conversations with people. The first was situated in the early years of hardship in Tanzania. Informants very commonly talked about the quest to marry a citizen in order to survive in the beginning. Hunger and the need for security were said to have compelled the early alliances. For reasons that never became fully clear, one iconic figure was retrospectively evoked by many: the figure of a young Hutu woman helpless without her family in a foreign land. It was she who contracted what were called "marriages of hunger" with citizens. Many family groups were separated in the course of fleeing from Burundi into Tanzania, and in some cases, even years elapsed before they were reunited. It was therefore not unexpected that many young women might have found themselves alone in Kigoma. One would also expect to have found as many young men in the same predicament, but it was possibly easier for men to find employment and to manage as single adults than for unmarried women.[11] The fact remains, nevertheless, that the young, unmarried refugee woman was a compelling figure, even for nonrefugees. One citizen noted, rather ruefully: "If I had not been a child in 1972, I would have married several Hutu girls then. It was so easy."

The "marriages of hunger" were often mentioned in the course of explaining that various practices were necessary for refugees if they were to "get along," to "manage," or "to get out of difficulties." The solitary, young refugee woman seemed at times to stand as an icon of extreme, "pure" need and of the absence of recourse. Perhaps she embodied evidence of the pressing necessity of assimilation for all the town refugees.

It was said that many of the early marriages dissolved when the parents of a young woman moved into a camp. Particularly when bridewealth payments had not been concluded, as was frequently the case with these early marriages, the parents worried that their daughter might not be properly cared for, and that she might end by "vagabonding" in town without anyone to look after her.

The second reason for intermarriage also cited necessity as the mother of invention. This neediness was, however, not quite so "pure" as that of the stranded young woman because it was not equally extreme. It was clear in informants' comments that they had considered various options before they settled upon marrying a "citizen." Their motivations involved not only hunger and other palpably immediate needs but also "profits," "advantages," "comfort," and the more long-term security of social standing and residence in town. It is noteworthy that this series of reasons was expressed almost exclusively by Burundian men, for whom intermarriage meant marrying a "citizen-woman," usually a Ha woman. On the one hand, discussions of this kind of marriage were a commentary on the structural vulnerability of refugees; but on the other, they told of a kind of prowess. This prowess, or competence, was manifested in the words of one Burundian man—a thirty-year-old cultivator living in one of the villages surrounding Kigoma township—who began an explanation of his personal arrangements thus: "I can tell you how I succeeded in marrying two citizen-women." He went on to give a lengthy account of name changes, a conversion, and the juggling of jobs and residences. When asked if he had thought of marrying a Burundian woman, he replied: "As you know, I changed my religion [to Islam]. I tried to search for a Hutu Muslim girl, but by bad luck I did not succeed." My research assistant told me later that in his judgment the young man was not "serious" because he knew perfectly well that "there are no Muslim Hutu women in Burundi."

Several young men said that marrying a Burundian woman who still had family was impractical because her family would demand prompt and high bridewealth payments. Others said that "with a citizen-girl, at least, one could receive profits," and that with her "there would be means" to become well established through the help of her family. Many reported, for example, cultivating land that belonged to in-laws. By far the most common reason given in this context, however, was "security," which meant that marrying a citizen enabled the town refugees themselves to pass for citizens and, thereby, to be protected from immigration officers and other problems.

The third set of reasons given for intermarriage was perhaps the most interesting one in terms of the comparison between Mishamo and Kigoma. In Mishamo, wider categorical oppositions dictated the choice of marriage partners, and the very topic of intermarriage with non-Hutu nonrefugees produced normative judgments and categorical prohibitions. In Kigoma, by contrast, the number of potential groups or categories from which a spouse might be chosen was much expanded. The pool of eligible partners was not definitively bounded at all, but open and changeable. Further, choices were never made in accordance with pregiven categorical rules but were expected, on the contrary, to depend on such things as chance, luck, love, taste, and other personal considerations. It is for these reasons that marriage provides such a good example of the less categorical thinking that seemed to prevail in the social life of the township. By this, I do not, of course, mean to imply that the thought of the town refugees somehow made no use of categories (marriage partners, for instance, were chosen according to various categories, such as beauty or personal characteristics); the point is only that the relevant categories were different from, and subversive of, the reified, moralized ethnic-national categories of the camp refugees' mythico-history.

The very range and variety of potential marriage partners seemed to fascinate many of the town refugees, and it was a popular subject of conversation among both married and unmarried men, town refugees and citizens alike. Unfortunately, however, it was difficult to get information about how women in Kigoma may have seen these issues, and most of what follows is based on discussions with men. As in Mishamo, women were often very shy about being approached by outsiders, and as it was difficult enough to coax even the men into interviews, it did not seem wise or appropriate to pursue interviews too aggressively where cooperation was not forthcoming.

Men's discussions of marriage partners spanned the range of possibilities and considered the "characteristics" of different "types" of women, often in a playful, lighthearted spirit. It is not entirely clear why so many informants should have produced rank-ordered lists of different ethnic and national categories of women preferred as wives. It is possible that the form of my research assistant's questions evoked them in some cases. I think that he heard these lists on a regular basis during interviewing and then, sometimes, conducted a further interview following that format. However, I myself also heard such lists in conversations about marriage and domestic life without ever soliciting them. Several Tanzanian informants also gave similar lists of preferred marriage partners.

One refugee listed his marriage preferences as follows: "(1) A Murundi—my race; (2) a Muha—it is the same language; (3) a Rwandese Hutu—almost the same language; (4) a Kenyan—she is African, same color, and also, she is accustomed to the African life; (5) a European—although she might not be able to endure our African life; (6) a Tutsi—to save my life quite simply; that is to say, I could marry a Tutsi woman if there were a rule which tells me: 'If you do not marry with a Tutsi, you will be killed.'"

Among lists made by Tanzanian men, the positions of Waha and Burundian (Hutu) women were reversed, and usually Tutsi women were preferred to European women. The majority of the town refugees made one categorical distinction: they put the Tutsi women at the bottom of the lists. Interestingly, most did not completely exclude this category and described scenarios in which marrying a Tutsi woman might be possible or necessary. Distinctions were also drawn between those Tutsi who had been implicated in the massacres of 1972 and those who had not. It was further pointed out that "There are many Tutsi in Ujiji, immigrants who came long ago. The Hutu know that they had nothing to do with the massacre of 1972. The Hutu and the

Tutsi of Kagera, Ujiji, marry each other, no problem. The only objection is that the Tutsi girls are usually lazy." A young man (who had arrived in Kigoma recently and had been a university student in Burundi) added that "there has always been much intermarriage among the Hutu and the Tutsi, especially among the intellectuals." The fact that Burundian refugee women (Hutu) were placed at the top of the lists was explained in one of two ways. Some informants simply said, "She is of my race." Others said that they would prefer to marry someone who knows the difficulties of being a refugee. Interestingly, even those who had themselves married "citizens" placed Burundian refugee women at the top of their lists.

In this limited sense, the discourse on marriage among the town refugees was categorical. The lists of ideal partners in marriage reflected a keen interest in ethnic, national, and racial categories. However, in Kigoma, the categories were numerous, shifting in meaning depending on the social domains in which they appeared. In contrast, in Mishamo, the categories were essentialized, and stood in dual opposition to each other (Hutu : Tutsi :: refugee : Tanzanian). These mythico-historical, opposed categories structured virtually every aspect of social practice in the camp. In Kigoma, however, the social and symbolic significance of these categories was continually challenged, unsettled, and played with. This was very visible in the domain of marriage. The categories that were momentarily established and idealized in the lists of potential partners were just as easily dissolved when questions of taste and fortune, circumstance and "divine will" intervened. These comprised the third kind of reason that people gave for their marriage choices. These not only collapsed the ethnic and national categories; they seemed to negate them.

All informants with whom marriage was discussed agreed that these unpredictable personal considerations were paramount. Thus, for example, one person said: "Me, first of all I appreciate her beauty. After that, I observe her comportment, if she is impolite or not. Then I make enquiries if in her family there are contagious diseases, leprosy or TB. After that, love." In another case, that of a cultivator and petty trader living in Ujiji, God's will and love were seen as decisive forces: "First of all, it has to be understood that for us men (and even women), it is God who chooses who will be your wife, or who will be your husband. Even if you choose, even if you do no matter what, if God does not want, you will not be able to marry the one you want. I say this because, me, I had two fiancées, one citizen and another Hutu. If truth be told, I loved them both, and it was difficult to choose one and leave the other. But, as in our Christian religion it is prohibited to be a polygamist (to have more than one wife), I decided to marry with the citizen because it seemed to me that she loved me more than the second one. For this I can say that it is love quite simply." Another person who had been faced with the same dilemma of choice between two fiancées married the Hutu woman. Notably, he reasoned his choice exactly as the former person had. In both cases, God's will and love were considered decisive. Again, a third person who had married a citizen appealed to love, observing that it is natural to marry those women whom one is accustomed to seeing, no matter what their origins. When this man was asked about the categorizing lists that had been spontaneously designed by other informants, he responded: "A woman is a woman. What counts is love." This person had on an earlier occasion said that he had married a "citizen" for "security," in order to become less visible as a refugee. But clearly, love and strategies of invisibility were not necessarily contradictory reasons for marrying. As one town refugee said, when reminded that he had claimed to have married for practical advantages of de facto citizenship: "That is for sure, I married for these things, but she also had the two other reasons, love and beauty." Beauty was an important criterion for many informants, but no mythico-historical "body maps" were made, and specific features of the bodies of women were never consistently enumerated.

The mythico-historically meaningful "traits" ascribed to Hutu women in Mishamo, as well as their mythico-historical plainness in comparison to Tutsi women, failed to appear in discussions of marriage among the town refugees. If "traits" were discussed at all, it was "wifely qualities" or "characteristics" that were at issue. The qualities of a "wife," potentially found in any woman, superseded the qualities of a woman as a member of an ethnic category. In Kigoma, neither citizens nor refugees characterized Hutu women as plain or unwitty. Tanzanian informants characterized Burundian refugee wives as "not often adulterous" and as women who "do not like to separate from their husbands" and who "respect their husbands." Many nonrefugees also said that refugee women may be expected to be more loyal and courageous than others because of the hardships that they have endured. These personal qualities were considered to be particularly important in town, where adultery and separations were commonplace.

Many refugee men agreed with the citizens' characterization of Hutu women in general but also emphasized that whether a particular woman had grown up in a camp with her parents or lived for "too long" alone in town influenced her "qualities." Reportedly, some town refugee men had elected to go to the camps to find suitable wives.

The following lengthy passage from a conversation with the former university student who was quoted earlier seemed to summarize the views of other town refugees on intermarriage as a matter of individual taste; it also seemed representative of many town refugees' opinions of the camps, where marriage was first and foremost a categorical matter. Thus, discussing intermarriage among town refugees, the young student said:

I think that there *is* a certain remorse, regret, but they do it nevertheless—for many reasons. Tastes and colors cannot be debated since everyone does not share the same tastes. Normally, for the Bantus it is all right because the languages are married. From the point of view of character, behavior, culture, [. . .] for the Bantus it is almost the same thing [. . .] for example, the preparation of meals, the taste of one or another thing. There is not a neat difference. What motivates intermarriage [. . .] First of all, in Mishamo, they are there among themselves; that arranges itself like that. But here in town, it is not the same case, since one cohabits with many different types of people. One is attracted by this or that physical trait, one has the habit of this or that kind of girl [. . .] So, one no longer thinks only about the same tribe. But the people who have never left Mishamo or the camps, they to their girls. It should be added also—let us say—the conformism to the culture which is stronger in the camps, which absolutely necessitates taking a woman who shares the same customs, the same language.

Here again, idiosyncratic considerations of taste and emotion, as well as the vagaries of history, intruded upon and superseded categorical loyalties of "peoplehood." Also, the significance of "race," "tribe," and "nation" as exclusive ordering principles in marriage, or in other domains of social practice, was subtly undermined. Such challenges were sometimes put with even more force. One person (a town refugee cultivator who converted from Roman Catholicism to Islam, and lives with his two Ha wives and their children in Majengo [Ujiji]) questioned the direction of the questions he was being asked, saying, "[Marital] disorders do not present themselves because of tribe." Another person (who had himself married a Christian Hutu woman and lived with her and their three children in Kagera) said: "What counts is love quite simply.

[. . .] The marriages which separate do not depend on questions of nations. They depend often on the characters of the persons who have, perhaps, bad hearts."

Everyone agreed on the fragility of marriages in Kigoma, whether ethnically or nationally endogamous or not. Marriages were considered to be more temporally durable in camps and also in rural villages in general. The consensus of opinion was that in town, there were more temptations to adultery by both husbands and wives, to drunkenness mainly by husbands, and to wives' excessive desire for "beautiful, modern clothes." These temptations then led, it was said, to jealousy and fights, financial problems and hunger, and, finally, to separations.

While it has been underscored throughout, and with justification, that categorical distinctions among "peoples" were subsumed in other considerations and even actively negated in Kigoma, it would be mistaken to derive from this too simple a picture. For the point is not that all people in Kigoma thought uncategorically. It is, rather, that there was tremendous *variation* in peoples' thinking, in contrast to the startling unanimity of Mishamo. Moreover, there was one domain in which even informants in Kigoma were preoccupied with the *potential* significance of national categories. This was the unresolved question of whether it would ever become possible for the refugees to return to Burundi.

It was only this question of return that brought up expressions of doubt and uncertainty about the categorical loyalties of spouses and raised as a problem the existence of "mixed marriages." Informants did not reflect on this as a problem concerning the whole category of refugees; usually the question arose in the course of reflections on one's own circumstances. And, as in other spheres of life among the town refugees, opinions and predictions varied widely. For those few informants who openly declared their desire to stay permanently in Tanzania as documented citizens, the issue was relatively unproblematic. Most people, however, were de facto citizens only in social terms (through marriage to a citizen and other means), and for them, the possibility of return was most problematic. Some expressed confidence that, of course, their Tanzanian wives would follow them to Burundi: "[T]here is nothing strange in that." Others were more doubtful, at times even cynical. Upon contemplating the chance of his Tanzanian wife accompanying him to Burundi, one man (reputedly a drunkard) said: "Why not? But this will depend on her. If she wants, I will return with her; if she does not want, she will stay here." One Pentecostal man married to a Pentacostal Tanzanian woman had doubts of a different kind; he thought of how his Tanzanian wife would be received in Burundi: "Despite the [shared] religion, it is a little bit of a shameful thing there in the interior [of Burundi] to bring a foreign wife." These imagined arrangements for the future should not be taken to mean that all town refugees had the conviction or the desire to return to Burundi, for this was an open question for many of them. These questions were like most others in town: not without form, but open.

AN IMMIGRANT MYTHOLOGY? THEFT, WORK, AND WEALTH IN TOWN

In the arena of social practices that is the subject of this section, questions of work, wealth, and financial security were paramount. However, as will quickly become apparent, the purpose here is not to explain whether the town refugees were poor or wealthy, needy or economically self-sufficient.[12] It is, rather, to delineate an arena upon which a great deal of cultural energy and imagination was concentrated by them: the social imagination of work and financial security, poverty and wealth, success and vagrancy.

Like marriage, this arena was productive of much chronicling in Kigoma. Often people related their own life trajectories spanning from the time of arrival in Tanzania to the present moment. But their imagination might be captured equally by the trajectories of others and particularly by those lives that touched the more extreme poles in the possible range of economic or material circumstances. There was interest in the trajectories of those "rich men" who had come to command visible signs of wealth and success, but also in the possibility, or the imagined proximity, of poverty and of "the vagabond." Most informants could be situated in the middle ground between the two extremes, having places to live and regular nourishment and engaging in some combination of cultivating, fishing, and petty trade. Most also situated themselves thus, in the middle. It was for the people occupying the middle ground that the socially visible, spectacular poles occupied by the "rich man" and the "vagabond" were most meaningful and fascinating.

These two figures did not represent entirely different orders of social worth, nor were they subjected to a one-dimensionally moral classification of "good" and "bad." Quite the contrary—the vagabond encapsulated the possibility of becoming something else, perhaps even a "rich man." By the same token, there was a suggestion that the rich man might one day find himself metamorphosed into a vagabond. The range of socioeconomic and material possibilities was conceptualized as an unstable, bustling continuum along which status positions never got really firmly fixed. For the majority of the town refugees, the two poles were a preoccupation, not only because of the wealth and the poverty that they augured, but also because at the extremes—beyond the unremarkable mainstream—a person was more likely to become socially visible, a spectacle.

Two different kinds of trajectory were at play in this imagined socioeconomic arena. The first, connecting vagabond to rich man, was an *ideal* trajectory charting the variability of the refugees' fortunes in the new land. The second traced the more intimate particulars of one's own life course. Often in the course of conversation the latter was placed side by side with the former, the ideal serving as a benchmark against which one's own fortunes could be assessed. Both these trajectories, ideal and personal, were construed as the paths of *individuals*, not as the collective path of the Hutu refugees as "a people." Of course, reference was made to the fortunes of others, and comparison of oneself with other refugees (and nonrefugees) was frequent. But these comparisons did not amount to that vision of a collective subject, a "people," that was so central among the camp refugees.

The chronicles of particular informants varied widely in details, but cumulatively, they revealed certain thematic convergences. Their accounts tended to share an understanding of the years lived in Tanzania as a series of successive stages. First, the early years were described as a period of profound poverty and need, when people "had nothing." Second, there were recollections of how necessity came to be the mother of invention. Here it was described how theft and other kinds of more or less illicit activities were sometimes simply necessary for progress. Third, there emerged images of "having made it," of having achieved material success and social standing.

The first theme, emphasizing the poverty and vulnerability of the newly arrived refugees, was much like the descriptions of the stigmata of refugeeness seen earlier. The town refugees' commentaries suggested that they had familiar knowledge and understanding of the circumstances that conspired to make poverty a dangerous condition: "In the beginning, social life between the citizens and the refugees was bad. The citizens, seeing that we are refugees, considered us as inferior beings. It was difficult to associate with them because they were afraid that we might steal their food, because of hunger. For this, many thought that we are thieves, that we could not live without stealing because of the lack of food. They considered us as ferocious men, that we kill persons without pity. People told us a lot of nonsense."

This explanation was not flatly judgmental; rather, it suggested that the fear of poverty was understandable. The following passage reflects the same reasoning. Neither comment denies that some town refugees indulged in theft. It was recognized that hunger and necessity bred theft, just as it was acknowledged that theft was dangerous to the better-established, better-off residents of Kigoma. It was also recognized that among the thousands of people in Kigoma there were "bad apples" as well as good ones. Thus, categorical ascriptions of virtue on the scale found in Mishamo never seemed to find a foothold here.

> There were not *so* many problems with our hosts [citizens]. Only, when we had first come [in 1972], and when there was theft, it was said, "it was the refugees." [. . .] [Stealing,] that depended on the refugees who were numerous. Many of them did not have money, food, and for this it was believed that it was the refugees who stole. [. . .] For now, the situation is not bad. First of all, the refugees have diminished. Many are in the camps. We who stayed here, some of us have palm trees, we have cultivated cassava, and some even have more cassava than the citizens.

The removal of the more spectacular *masses* of refugees from Kigoma into the camps, it was recalled, improved and eased the circumstances of those who remained in town. When the refugees numbered in the tens of thousands in Kigoma, there were of course more hungry mouths to feed and fewer jobs to go around. This situation drove down the wages of the nonrefugee residents, arousing their resentment. As one person said:

> When we arrived in Kigoma, we started looking for work. For this, we were engaged in, say, construction companies, and because we were paid very small salaries, the citizens' salaries were diminished where they had been paid a lot before. For this, the citizens saw us as bad persons who diminished the daily salary so that we could receive work. In the neighborhoods, those who had lost their jobs because of us insulted us, and said many things to us, like for example: "You, you are imbeciles, animals. You work for nothing because of hunger. You will die here in Kigoma." But for others of us, the relations were not very bad.

These accounts of the early years were all similar in that they offered a social logic of the effects of poverty and necessity—in a nutshell: "If a refugee is rich, people are not afraid of him. This is said very often. I know that it is true. I remember when I lived in Kagera [Ujiji], if somebody was poor, he was considered a thief."[13]

The second stage in the town refugees' life chronicles can be thematized as that of necessary, productive theft. Far from denying that theft existed, these reminiscences acknowledged and sometimes celebrated it. In what is to follow, an interesting distinction is made between productive, directed theft and petty, aimless theft.

The thieves of the fruits of palms and banana trees are mixed from Waha and Burundian refugees. The big number of the fruit thieves are the Waha. Waha thieves steal in no matter what plantation and sell to others. The money received they use for drinking beer and adultery. In point of fact, that is all. The Burundian fruit thieves are rogues [wajanja in Swahili,[14] malins in French]. First of all, they begin by renting the plantation of somebody and then cut the palm fruits from the plantations bordering the plantation they themselves have rented. The Burundians often seek wealth. When they have received a lot of money, they leave off stealing and start to make commerce, and that is why the Burundians very often become rich. They start to do little things; then they become rich.

Another person added: "Even the refugees themselves say this: 'The Burundians are clever.' They steal in order to have progress." There was a clear difference for informants between unproductive theft, where the fruits of one's efforts are frittered away without a thought for tomorrow, and constructive theft which, through foresight and self-discipline, leads to "progress" and wealth. The latter genre of theft was a kind of prowess, a competence. Informants' comments reflected an amused appreciation and even an idealization of the control and canny strategizing that were required for the use of theft in the building of more durable personal wealth. It was not only the transformation of illicit dealings into legitimate business that was being idealized, but the capacity for canniness and ruse in itself. The following comment, distinguishing different calibers of thieves, reflects such idealization: "The city thieves steal from the village thieves. The one from the villages does not know all the manners that are employed in town. So, he too is robbed. And the city thieves say: 'They are silly little thieves. They steal fruits! They should be stealing money.'"

The third stage of the ideal trajectories constructed by the town refugees reflected the imagery of success, of the enjoyment of the results of one's labor (and of one's constructive theft, as the case may be). Here, those relatively few who had most visibly succeeded, the rich "merchant refugees," were central figures. In the figure of the rich man, the transformation from theft to commerce had been accomplished. And just as theft was a form of prowess, so too was skill in commerce. Indeed, many informants declared that the Burundians were "good merchants" and that "the Burundian likes wealth."

In addition to the "rich men," there were also people who might be characterized as self-made men. They were more modest versions of the rich men, or perhaps potential rich men in the making. Both the rich men and the self-made men shared one thing: they generated personal success stories, or rags-to-riches chronicles. These success stories concerned not only the obviously wealthy merchant refugees who stood out from all the residents in Kigoma; they also followed the trajectories of those who had had "nothing" and were now managing—and managing without constructive theft. So, these stories established a progression from utter poverty and destitution to the condition of working for others and huckstering, and from this, to being independent as a petty trader, or a fisherman, or a cultivator, or a combination of these. There was decided pride in these paths of success. In the words of one town refugee (himself, at the time, on his way down economically): "Sixty percent of the merchants in the Kigoma market are Burundians. They *tried* more than the nationals—let us say, following the difficulties that they had had. They were, then, more active than the citizens. The citizens, one can say, have learned much among the foreigners." This assessment was widely shared among informants, and it is remarkably reminiscent of the lore that so often mythologizes immigrants elsewhere in the world, and perhaps particularly in the United States. "We had to try harder" is a very familiar theme.

Taken together, these three idealized stages celebrated canny strategies and knavery, or malign cleverness. But it is important to realize that here malignness had quite a different signification than in Mishamo, where "the malign" was systematically identified as a "Tutsi trait" and was, in effect, a synonym for evil. In the town refugees' idealization of malign cleverness, no connection to "the Tutsi" as a category was articulated. Indeed, cleverness, trickery, and malignness were generally seen in a much more lighthearted way, and certainly not as attributes essentially opposed to Hutuness.

Together, then, the three discursively imagined "stages" of life in Tanzania form what may be likened to Horatio Alger stories in which, relying on his wits, a young man creates "something from nothing" and makes a place for himself in the world as he finds it. Other comparisons might be seen in the late-nineteenth-century robber barons of American lore, or in the Canadian Duddy Kravitz story. All of these stories deal in some measure with wealth that was not inherited but made in the course of one lifetime—thereby presenting on a human-sized scale the chance for the listener to achieve the same.[16]

It is appropriate that all these points of comparison should feature young men, because these stages along the path to success were on the whole configured for a male protagonist—and even more specifically for a young man. Here, it is possible to do no better than wonder how different such accounts might have been for the girls and women among the town refugees if circumstances had permitted this research to be conducted equally among them.

There is a further, important feature that these imagined life trajectories shared. They were, without exception, initiated at the moment of arrival in Tanzania, and not in a distant past in Burundi. This does not mean that Burundi was not frequently discussed, only that in the particular domains in question, the starting point was the arrival. Both the past and the present were encapsulated in the period following the arrival in Tanzania. Thus, as was said before, "the past" signified the early days of exile, and "the present" meant today, or now. Early exile was remembered as the period that had been overcome and lived through. Thus, when people talked about the "early days," they were chronicling something that had long since passed and changed. This usage struck an essential contrast with Mishamo. There, exile was conceived as a perpetual present because it was so intimately related, through opposition, to the historico-spatial past left in Burundi and to the future, again located in Burundi, the "homeland" to be.

Now, if one reverses one's direction on the idealized rags-to-riches path imagined by the town refugees and follows it downward for a good while, one will encounter the "vagabond." This figure was as captivating to the social imagination in town as the "rich man"; and the kind of people who would be expected to be associated with it included the unemployed, women, and the elderly. This typology of three figures had superposed on it another typology: thieves, prostitutes, and beggars. Thus, the unemployed were potential thieves, women were potential prostitutes, and the elderly were potential beggars. Whether the former were transformed into the latter was seen to depend on the particular circumstances of individuals and on chance. These three potential categories of vagabonds were apparently not equivalent to the thieves discussed earlier. It was acknowledged that the unemployed could become pickpockets and even thieves, but this depended on their other circumstances, such as whether their family and kin networks were located in town. It was also explained that the "little merchants" who did not have licenses could be chased away as vagabonds by the authorities.

The danger in "vagabonding" was in being identified as one and being sent away from town. According to local knowledge, this danger was subject to seasonal variations. The rainy season, starting in the month of November, was identified as the most dangerous time for vagabonds because it was the season when police were most likely to "arrest and chase away from town" people who looked like vagabonds. The reason for this may have been that the coming of the rains also initiated the sowing season. It was therefore a busy time for all cultivators, and the ranks of those who had spent time in town during the dry season would be thinned when time came to sow. The remaining people would then more conspicuously stand out as having "no place" and "no connection" in Kigoma township.

The vagabonds were possibly such compelling figures because they seemed to embody the deeply sensed precariousness of *all* the town refugees' prospects of permanent residence in Kigoma. The vagabonds, then, were a human refraction of those uncertain, unpredictable circumstances that seemed to necessitate the numerous strategies of social invisibility discussed earlier. For these strategies were, of course, also designed to shore up people's residential stability in town.

One final aspect of the socioeconomic arena in Kigoma must be drawn out further. Town refugees' views on the varieties of work and trade that a person could engage in were conspicuously free of moral evaluation. This is not to say that all illegal or illicit practices were celebrated—only that people tended to describe various practices such as "theft for progress" without morally judging them. Even in the case of ivory smuggling, which had sinister significations in Mishamo, town refugees tended to describe, not to judge. In accounts of the routes that the ivory took, for instance, it was the spectacle of the risks, the danger, and the intrigue that usually predominated. Upon concluding a long account of how ivory smuggling was done in the region, one person said, "It is a very dangerous affair, but also, there is a lot of money that one can receive" (see Harland 1988).

## "THE RETURN IS IMAGINARY!"

Not surprisingly, the question of a return to Burundi was problematized for most town refugees. Everyone had clearly been called upon long ago to make certain decisions regarding the desirability and possibility of a return. These decisions seemed to be a complex mixture of prediction and desire, and a remarkable degree of variation emerged in people's views on this question. The variation in opinions seemed to turn on two questions: Is it possible or not? and Is it desirable or not? These two issues always seemed to be somewhere present in people's thoughts about going back. The question of possibility, involving a practical prediction about the political future of Burundi, appeared to be less problematic than the question of desire.

The number of informants who unequivocally stated their personal convictions and hopes about returning was smaller than the ranks of those who were ambivalent or frequently changed their minds. The wealthy tailor quoted earlier on the topic of citizenship also had definite views on repatriation: "Concerning the future? It is but to live with our neighbors. The future is that which we are doing right now, I believe. Working, attracting the clientele, exchanging niceties with the neighbors, assuring our futures. These are the fundamental ideas of life." Being a relatively rich man, he was among the few who were socially conspicuous enough to need formal documentation of their status. This tailor said he was in the process of applying for Tanzanian citizenship and carried a refugee identification card in the meantime. He fully intended to "put down roots" in Tanzania and said that whether or not it became possible for the refugees to return to Burundi, he would stay. He added, however, that being in a position to visit Burundi regularly, he knew how unlikely the regime was to change. He rather cheerfully observed: *"Plus ça change, plus c'est la même chose."* Another person who likewise had a visible and documented status said: "I do not think that it will be possible to return. There would be too many problems. Returning does not appeal to me because the problems are always there. I plan to stay here—where I see that life goes better."

There was an evident tendency for those town refugees marked by their socioeconomic status or occupation to have taken a firm decision one way or another, but there were others of equal socioeconomic markedness who had not. Further, many who were of modest means also told of firm decisions. Thus, social status and degrees of wealth were not an altogether reliable clue to a person's thoughts on the question of the future.

For the purposes of the comparison with Mishamo, the most important aspect of the town refugees' ways of locating and imagining the future was that they were concerned with practical queries and considerations, weighing advantages and disadvantages, and not with contemplating a millennial return. One person assessed the situation like this: "Many have started to naturalize themselves. They have no hope of return. And as they are starting to have good houses, shops, to manage well, they will stay." Here, as in numerous others' words, predictions about the feasibility of returning and statements of one's desire never were fully distinguished. A person might say, for example, that a return would not likely be possible and then add that he or she planned to stay in Tanzania in any case; or: "I am thinking of staying here in Tanzania if there is no means of returning to my country. I do not like to stay in another country, but what can I do?" This comment resembles the next one in that both link repatriation to a change of regime in Burundi in rather abstract, dispassionate terms. "About my future, me, I think I will stay here in Tanzania, except if the Hutu receive power. I was in Burundi a few days ago. Really, if you are used to living here in Tanzania, you cannot even have the *idea* of returning to Burundi. The Tutsi look at you always. If you arrive in Burundi, you are asked for your passport, your Leave Pass, whatnot. . . ."[17]

The clauses "if the Hutu receive power" or "if the regime changes" were markedly vague and disengaged in comparison with the camp refugees' unequivocal, apparently unanimous statements about reclaiming the nation. Whether the possible change of regime was temporally near or distant did not appear to be of urgent concern to most people in Kigoma, and the change of regime was mentioned somewhat as one might refer to a phenomenon of nature—a lightning storm or a flood—beyond human efforts. There might be another way of interpreting this apparent passiveness, however, and it is expressed in the following assessment of the possibility of return: "Myself, I want to return, but I see that it is not easy. There is a possibility [to go back], but it is not easy. Maybe after several years. I do not think that Mr. Bagaza will do as Mr. Museveni has done, to call back all the refugees. It would not be easy for Mr. Bagaza. If we return back to this leader, it is very difficult, it is bad. I have gone there in 1982 for a visit. [. . .] But I did not enjoy [it]. They want to know what you are coming to do if they see you there."

Again, the future was seen to depend on "Mr. Bagaza" and the Burundi state.[18] This passage suggests that the appearance of passiveness was possibly related to the town refugees' conceptions of the state. The state still appeared to be seen as the proper locus of authority, and in this sense, the Burundi state was more of a legitimate entity to the town refugees than to those in Mishamo. But more important than the question of legitimacy was the underlying implication that any change of regime in Burundi was ultimately linked to the Burundi state and not to any forces outside the state, not to the refugees massing just beyond its boundaries.

CASUAL BOUNDARY CROSSINGS

In the course of discussions about the return to Burundi, another interesting contrast between camp and town appeared. In Mishamo, a mythico-historically premature return to Burundi by isolated individuals was often predicted to bring death. In Kigoma, by contrast, the Burundi-Tanzania border appeared to be quite casually crossed (and there was regular boat traffic between Kigoma and Bujumbura). People might mention informally that they had been to Burundi for one thing or another and make no further comment about it.

Ironically, in Mishamo, where the boundary was perceived as closed and dangerous, an eventual collective return was widely predicted and desired. In Kigoma, where the boundary was continually being traversed by individuals for purposes of trade and visiting kin, a collective return was considered impossible by many, if not most people. Indeed, people in town said that precisely *because* they had visited Burundi, they knew that a return was not possible. The tailor, once again, put it succinctly: "Me, I have gone several times to Burundi—in 1981, '83, '84, '85. [. . .] So, me, I am *au courant*, and I know that the return will not be possible. No, it is not possible. Me, I will stay here. After five years, after ten years, after twenty years, I will be here!"

The town refugees did not speak of their years in Tanzania as a collective (or, for that matter, an individual) *preparation* for a return. Indeed, it would be misleading to describe their lives as being in a state of exile. For "exile" implies a "thereness" (Said 1986a:28) and a vital link to a "homeland," or an "origin," or a "proper place." Among the camp refugees in Mishamo, exile was a lengthening but always *tempo-rary* period of trial in an overarching historical process spanning from the legendary foundation of Burundi to the still utopian, still nonexistent "homeland." History in Mishamo was the monumental path of "a people." In Kigoma, there was no such millennial path. There were instead individual life trajectories spanning from the "early days" or "the beginnings" in Tanzania to the present. The future was not firmly localized in Burundi, or anywhere. For in Kigoma, the question of what links existed with Burundi, and whether Burundi was "homeland" or "home," was a difficult one. The link was made more tenuous by such axes of manifest and symbolic assimilation as marriage with nonrefugees and forging wealth and financial security in the new land. In sum, what was "exile" in Mishamo was simply day-to-day life in Kigoma— just as "the homeland" was simply Burundi, and "the people" was simply a collection of different people pursuing a multiplicity of unstable, crisscrossing trajectories. In this sense, the absence of a Hutu mythico-history in town was replaced by a partial, potential immigrant mythology. Immigrancy seems to imply the permanent "rooting" of one's life in another country, but in the case of the town refugees the question of permanence was clearly undecided and tentative. They seemed to feel most at home in the borderland that was Kigoma, a zone of sheltering vagueness where national or categorical "species"-allegiance was not continually being extracted from them. Their lives recalled this observation about displacement and the movement of people: "to some people the very 'state of movement' is being 'at home'" (Marianne Forró, cited in Tabori 1972:399).[19]

CONCLUSION: THE TOWN REFUGEES' RELATIONSHIP TO HISTORY
The conditions for the absence of a collective Hutu mythico-history among the town refugees have now been laid down. But it is still necessary to examine the relationship of the town refugees to their history in Burundi. It could be argued that this relationship consisted of a simple *denial* of history among the town refugees. After all, their strategies of invisibility entailed a denial of the identities that would root them in Burundi. Likewise, gestures of assimilation, in marriage as in trade, seemed to anchor their lives nonhistorically, in the present, in Tanzania—or, at least, to allow an escape from the monumental, epic history of "a people." Finally, the ambivalent question of the return to Burundi

opened at least the possibility that the *future history* of Burundi might not encompass those who were currently refugees in Kigoma.

Yet, as must be evident by now, the town refugees tended to structure their lives and conversations in such a way as to leave both their immediate and more distantly perceived options open. Perhaps, then, it would be more appropriate to identify in this context an indefinite suspension of history instead of an outright denial? No hard-and-fast answer to this question emerged, and definitional questions may not be the most constructive approach here. It is possible, nevertheless, to suggest that for the town refugees "the past" did not signify a heroized or epic history of a "people" or an "antagonistic past" as it did in Mishamo.[20] Rather, "the past" had multiple significations. On the one hand, it signified the early days of social and economic hardship in exile, and was, at this level, a past that had been overcome. On the other hand, the past was that which had been left behind in Burundi. For most informants, this past had simply passed; it was not a predominating, structuring force in their everyday lives in a positive sense, in the sense of a "charter" (cf. Appadurai 1981:202).

By the time that fieldwork for this project reached "the Kigoma phase," the things so passionately remembered by the Mishamo refugees had roughly crystallized in my mind into the thematic configurations that were presented in chapter 2. It was in pursuit of similar mythico-historical themes that I spontaneously set out in Kigoma. This research direction was quickly frustrated, however, not least by the denial of refugee status by many potential informants. Informants (when at length they began to be found)[21] enquired why their history should be of interest to me, or anyone. I had come to assume that the importance of history would be considered obvious by "any Hutu," and so had no good reply to this reasonable query. In town, history did not enjoy the status of an overarching, indispensable explanatory device. Most town refugees did not consider it a privileged lens for achieving an understanding of their lives, or for getting at "truth." In the camp, the questions of "truth" and "history" had been so meaningful (and so intertwined) because their referent was a categorical collectivity, the Hutu people. Without "a people," the monumentality of history in Kigoma was pulverized.

When the past in Burundi was broached by the town refugees, it was almost invariably in the context of formal interviews and directed conversations where question and answer succeeded each other. No spontaneous, oratorical, didactic monologues about the history of the Hutu emerged. Knowledge of history was not generally a highly valued skill. Indeed, it was said that the old people who liked to live in the camps were the persons who knew about the past. Knowledge of history, then, was widely considered to be a specialized skill mastered by elders and by historians. The elders were "repositories of the past," like books. In short, "history" among the most town refugees tended to signify a limited body of specialized (sometimes even arcane) knowledge, not a foundational, essential dimension of life, not life's blood.

A further distinction needs making. Whereas history in Mishamo moved where "the people" moved, the town refugees, to all appearances, took "history" to mean the history of Burundi as a fixed, territorial state. This state-centered vision of history also seemed to be experienced as a "received history," a narrative authorized elsewhere. This was reflected in people's conversational preambles: "According to what I learned in school . . ." or "In the books it is said . . ." or "I have heard it said . . ."

The body of knowledge that was history in Mishamo, by contrast, was an oppositional, challenging recasting of fundamental truths. Forms of "received history" or "school history" were usually classified as history according to the Tutsi and ingested by the mythico-history as yet another symptom of the "malignness" of the Tutsi. In Kigoma, the question of who had created the dominant, accepted history was not seen as crucial or life threatening. There, "historical facts" were more likely to be treated as neutral or inert. And for most people, these "facts" did not form into larger chains of political or moral significance. They did not link up into a mythico-history.[22]

It is not an accident that some of the most popular topics of conversation among the town refugees should have converged into certain thematic clusters: the dangers and stigmata of refugee status, the "unmarking" of oneself as a stranger, the adoption of workable, efficacious identities, marriage with citizens, working toward material success, "making it," and, finally, the problematic return to Burundi. The return was in some senses a logical culminating question to the other axes. Thus, what happens after all this assimilation? Where does it leave us? Do we return when and *if* the others (the "real refugees" in the camps) return? Is the forging of a new order in Burundi still going to be relevant for *us?* Because of the problematic connection to Burundi and the undecided question of permanence, the chronicles in this chapter cannot be satisfactorily defined as "immigrant myths" or even as a "mythico-history of immigrants." Posing the key questions as either/or options—Do I return or stay forever? Is home here or is it there?—may not be the right move, at least not for many of the refugees. As was described earlier, the question of a collective return to the "homeland" frequently brought up mentions of casual, even routine visits to Burundi. There is good reason to expect that the either/or question will never get an either/or answer and that some of those people who have here been called town refugees will continue to straddle both places, calling both "home" or, more likely, finding "home" somewhere in between.

# five

# THE DANGER OF
# ASSIMILATION AND
# THE PURITY OF EXILE

It is perhaps evident by now that there was an unmistakable, if not extravagant, self-consciousness to the actual, day-to-day living of exile among people in Mishamo—indeed, that exile was a vitally relevant experiential dimension of the life-world of the camp refugees (Gilroy 1991:17). Delineating the proper conduct of collective and personal lives in exile, control over the purity of identity and politico-moral purpose, and taking a position in the face of assimilative social or economic processes—issues like these were constantly being reflected upon and struggled over by people in Mishamo. That the shape of everyday life looked different for most town refugees does not mean, of course, that they had no self-consciousness about their circumstances; but it is relevant to question whether the term *exile* best describes these circumstances.

One of the richest sites for the further exploration of these questions about exile, identity, and morality is the bundle of social and imaginative relations that had been formed *between* camp and town. How people in these two sites imagined each other informed the ways in which they imagined and identified themselves.

This dialectical relationship between camp and town was most generally constructed as one of opposition and antagonism. The opposition, however, was not symmetrically weighted. The fact that not all refugees lived in camps was more important an issue for the camp refugees in Mishamo than the existence of camps was for the town refugees in Kigoma. The town refugees and their ways of life were a challenge and a threat to the mythico-historical order that so fundamentally structured life in the camp. The town refugees were themselves a categorical actor in the mythico-history of the camp. In town, by contrast, the camp as a particular imagined place posed a different set of concerns. For the town refugees, the prospect of being transported to a camp was a pragmatic concern, a specter of the loss of certain kinds of personal freedom and the stripping away of a socially empowering categorical anonymity.

The structuring of this asymmetric opposition will be described here in the following order: First, the town refugees' views of and relationships with the camps will be discussed. It will be suggested that while "the camp" was positioned as a particular kind of social construct in the local knowledge of the town, it was neither a part of any urban mythico-history nor a predominating concern in everyday life. Second, the social construction of "the town refugees" as a mythico-historical category operative in Mishamo will be described. This will be embedded in a wider discussion of the politico-moral implications of assimilation in general, as seen from the camp. Intermarriage, legal naturalization, and commerce were seen by the Mishamo refugees as three key channels to assimilation and will be discussed in this order. Here, the presentation of the mythico-history begun in chapter 2 will be taken up once more. For the town refugees had become a mythico-historical category paradigmatic of the dangers associated with the relinquishing of displacement and refugeeness. Their place in the mythico-history of the camp shows how assimilation had become equivalent to a loss of purity. Purity and its endangerment form the central issue of this chapter.

## THE DISTANCE BETWEEN CAMP AND TOWN

Kigoma township and the three Hutu refugee camps were spatially distant from each other. (Mishamo was 200 kilometers by car from Kigoma.) But this spatial distance, while considerable for people without regular means of transportation, was exaggerated in the mutual perceptions between camp and town because such a great *social* distance had come to be inserted between them. The appearance of distance, then, was another expression of the social construction of difference between camp and town. This does not mean that there was ever a total lack of contact between Kigoma and the camps. Indeed, kin ties and trade networks routinely straddled these different locales. It is unnecessary to map out in detail how the straddling was accomplished, but a few general observations should be made. First, as regards trade and commerce, the primary links appeared to be those between Kigoma township and Katumba camp, near Mpanda. This was surprising at first glance because Mishamo was geographically closer to Kigoma than was Katumba. However, Katumba was located near a railway line (as was Ulyankulu camp near Tabora, in central Tanzania), while there was not even any regular bus service between Kigoma and Mishamo. Thus, of the three Hutu camps in Tanzania of the mid-1980s, Mishamo was the only one severely isolated through lack of transport and vast buffers of forest and bushland. These facts of politico-spatial landscape partly accounted for Mishamo having less traffic with Kigoma than the other two Hutu refugee camps. Paradoxical as it might appear, this isolation also helped make Mishamo the "ideal type" of a refugee camp in the imagination of those living in town. When town refugees spoke of "the camp," Mishamo could usually be expected to be the place they were thinking of, not Ulyankulu or Katumba.

One frequently reported camp-town link was one of double residency: people registered as residents of a camp, but came to Kigoma for several months at a time for commerce or fishing. These seasonal movements had left a human residue of permanent settlers in town. As for kin links, it was said that especially the young liked to live in town, while their parents tended to stay in the camps. Likewise, men often left their wives and children in the camps for extended periods while they worked in Kigoma. Some of these men had begun by building a house and clearing land for cultivation in a camp, then later started gradually to build another house in town. The possible permutations in these camp-town links were numerous, then. But again, they did not appear in the imagery that either locale wove of the other.

THE CAMP AS A SPECTER AMONG THE TOWN REFUGEES

For the town refugees who were interviewed about their views of the camps, the choice of residence was a *fait accompli;* they had chosen to live in town, and none of them were planning to move to a camp. Some had parents and other kin in the camps; others had no living relatives in exile. Ties of kinship did not appear to have determined where people ended up living. Moreover, the town refugees took active measures to ensure their continued residence in Kigoma. One important reason for the management of the fluid, situational identities discussed in chapter

4 was precisely to avoid being objectified and fixed as a "refugee"; by extension, the goal was to circumvent the possibility of being transported into a refugee camp. The same may be said of marriage with "citizens" and of the de facto naturalization described earlier. These means of adopting socially protective coloration were designed, not so much to escape being sent back to Burundi, but rather, to avoid transportation into camps.

At the time of this research, rumors of a new camp to be established for Hutu refugees were widely circulating in the township. People expressed great worry that it was especially they, the town refugees from Kigoma and its environs, who would be transported there so as to induce them to cultivate. Even the crops were speculated about: the camp would be near Mbeya in southwestern Tanzania where conditions were favorable for cultivating coffee and tea, cash crops. The new camp was seen as an exclusively commercial proposition. As one person said: "It will be still another place for cultivating, a *machine* for cultivating." He, agreeing with other town refugees' assessments, concluded: "There is not one person who likes this. It is by force. To be taken to a new camp, people say that it is like dying. There will be large, very hard trees. Always new forests." The threat of this new camp was the more formidable because at the time of these rumors, so-called merchant refugees had been expelled from Tabora and Mpanda and sent back to the camps at which they had been officially registered (Ulyankulu and Katumba, respectively).[1] As my research assistant explained: "In Kigoma, in the market and in town, the refugees are scared to identify themselves [as Hutu refugees] because they think that they will be transported into the camps like happened to the merchant refugees of Tabora and Mpanda. They were taken to Katumba and Ulyankulu last month, in April [1986]. Many of them already had plots in the camps to which they were returned, but they had to leave behind their businesses, their houses, et cetera, in town." Both the expulsion of the merchant refugees and the rumors of the new camp were ominous to the town refugees because they lent substance to the fear of being uprooted from life in town.

Upon confronting the town refugees' unwillingness to identify themselves as refugees, my research assistant (himself a camp refugee) said: "They are afraid that I will help to transport them into camps. [. . .] The refugees in town think that the refugees who are in camps are not free—that they are like prisoners since they cannot leave,

go anywhere, without permission . . . that they are always guarded,
like that. They are afraid of that. Here [in town] they are free. They
can go wherever they want without any question of passports, Leave
Passes. . . . Above all, people do *not* like Mishamo because they say
that it is a very isolated place; there are no communications."

The steps that townspeople took to ward off transportation into
the camps were in themselves the most powerful social commentary
on the camps. The loss of freedom and the prospect of isolation, as
explained above, tended to dominate the town refugees' impression of
the camps. Living in the camps signaled undesirable forms of social
and economic control. Notably, it was not only the discipline exercised
by the camp authorities that was at issue. For the refugee inhabitants
of the camps themselves were seen by many as the agents of unwel-
come forms of control. It was specifically *moral* prescriptions and proscriptions that were foreseen by those in town. The camp refugees
would, it was believed, contribute to the loss of personal freedom by
expecting compliance with the interests of the idealized community of
the Hutu refugees as "a people" in exile. Thus, the more individualistic,
varied, and often unpredictable trajectories of the town refugees' lives
would be swallowed up and dissolved by the collective trajectory of the
refugees in the camps (and perhaps especially in Mishamo).

The camp refugees were not heroized in town. And they were
frequently characterized as moralistic and even naively judgmental, as
this (previously quoted) assessment by a town refugee suggests: "[F]irst
of all, they are there among themselves; they do not see further than
their own noses [. . .]. We should add also—let us say—the conformism
to the culture which is stronger in the camps."

In sum, the camp was not heroized as a privileged locus of knowledge or consciousness by the town refugees. Instead, it tended to be
skirted as a place of incarceration and insulation. The occasional gloss-
ing of the camp as a rural or pastoral idyll did not erase its disciplinary
aspects. And while cultivating the land was an essential part of the
town refugees' nostalgic reconstruction of the camp, cultivation was
not seen as a source of bodily, internal power, as it was in the camp
itself.[2] In the end, it seemed that the camp was for the town refugees
a locus of powerlessness, a confining place where inhabitants were fixed
and objectified as "the refugees" and "the cultivators." Significantly,
several informants in town said that the "real" or "true" refugees were
in the camps. They were thereby marking a difference between them-

selves and those in the camps. And, finally, historicity was not seen as an empowering mode of social action but rather more inertly as a form of living in the past.

## THE VIEW FROM THE CAMP: TOWN REFUGEES AND
## THE SPECTER OF ASSIMILATION

It is now possible to return once more to Mishamo. How did Mishamo accommodate the fact of Kigoma and the rival constructions of the town refugees? What meanings were attached to assimilation in the mythico-history? As was noted in the opening sections of this chapter, the town refugees had become a categorical actor in the mythico-history of the camp. They stood for and even embodied imagined processes of assimilation and were thus a dangerous category.

### INTERMARRIAGE AS A DANGEROUS MIXING OF CATEGORIES

In light of the analogical relations between past and present that animated other dominant themes in the mythico-history, it is not surprising that Hutu intermarriage with Tanzanians should have become aligned with Hutu-Tutsi intermarriage in Burundi. As with cultivation, governance, education, and other themes discussed earlier, conversations about particular marriages tended to evoke more sweeping commentary on intermarriage both in Burundi and in exile. At times, it was unclear where the narratives were spatio-temporally located, in the past in Burundi or in the present in exile. The analogical relation was so powerful here that it almost seemed to suggest a peculiar causal link: if intermarriage with "the Tutsi" was dangerous, then it must be so with "the Tanzanian." The following narrative emerged from camp refugees' reflections on intermarriage with women of the Tutsi category in Burundi.

Panel 37:

**SAMSON AND DELILAH IN EXILE**

Hutu men do not marry Tanzanian women. Why? Because our thoughts are still in Burundi. A Hutu woman with a Tanzanian man—a small quantity. In a thousand Hutu women you can find one who has married with a Tanzanian. It is always between a Hutu woman and a Tanzanian man. Always only this. But if one day we gain our country, she will separate from her husband. [. . .] It is not good to marry with the Tanzanians. To mix with the Tanzanians is equal to mixing with the Tutsi. One does not do it. If this ever happens, there is not even a religious ceremony, nothing. Remember the writings of the Bible. Remember Samson, a good Israelite. It is to lose nationality. Up until today, the [Tanzanian] government has not found a means of nationalizing us. The journalists have heard [from the Tanzanians]: "[The Hutu] do not mix. They always think about their own country."[3]

Interestingly, here, as in the mythico-history of Hutu-Tutsi intermarriage, the story of Samson and Delilah was retold. Among biblical analogies, this was a regularly recurring one. It associated marrying the other with betrayal and deception, just as it did in the mythico-history of the past. The Delilah in the past, the archetypal "beautiful Tutsi woman," was cast as "bait" for enticing Hutu men into servitude and, finally, into death. The connection between intermarriage and danger was quite concrete, and Delilah's betrayal was attributed malicious forethought and instrumentality. In the mythico-history of the present, her betrayal was posed in less instrumental and less directly causal terms, and the issue of the physical beauty of the categorical other as a trap did not arise; nor was intermarriage with "the Tanzanian" associated with bodily death.

In addition to these thematic transformations, the mythicohistorical roles of the Samson and Delilah figures had been reversed. The Tutsi woman had been replaced by the Tanzanian man. Thus, it was no longer the "malign" Tutsi woman who trapped the Hutu man, but rather, the Tanzanian man who, by virtue of his membership in a "tutsianized" category, was seen to be essentially "malign."

The position of the Hutu refugee woman was not very fully articulated in the mythico-history; it was unclear what motivated her to cross the categorical boundary. It was not that her beauty in any way "caused" intermarriage; here, as throughout the mythico-history, the Hutu woman was cast as aesthetically powerless and unmarked. Her virtues and her claims to affection resided in attributes other than physical beauty. However, discussions of individual cases of intermarriage in Mishamo underscored the asymmetry of power and authority between the imagined figures of the Tanzanian groom and the refugee bride. It was suggested that men in positions of authority in the camp were able to persuade refugee women (in particular, younger women) to marry them simply by virtue of their authority and not because this alliance promised wealth or security.

These transformations in the theme of intermarriage could be examined in finer detail, but for the present it is more relevant to try to pinpoint why the Tutsi-Tanzanian analogy lodged in the theme of intermarriage was so potent. Intermarriage in exile was seen as a channel into more permanent agricultural servitude under the dominant other, and as an implicit acceptance of the naturalization of a status which ought to be kept unnatural and at bay. It was also emphasized time and again that this combination of categories was necessarily weak and impermanent; it would not withstand the moment of return to the "homeland" nor even the harshness of refugee life in a camp. (The logical possibility that the refugee bride would leave the camp with her citizen husband was never brought up by informants; in the single recorded case of intermarriage that was observed during field-work, the couple stayed on in the camp while the marriage endured.)

In sum, marriage with "the Tanzanians" was a category mistake, a bad combination, in the mythico-history of the camp. Given the constitution of "the Tanzanians" as a "malign," "tutsianized" category, and given the manifest structural inequality between them and the refugees, it seems mythico-historically logical that this form of mixing categories should be proscribed as evil and dangerous. This account would be incomplete, however, were it not emphasized that marriage with a nonrefugee—and, particularly, a citizen of the country of asylum—threatened the transformation of exile into irreversible, naturalized assimilation. As such, it symbolized forsaking the true and proper nation of the refugees.

The relative socio-spatial isolation and remoteness of Mishamo from Tanzanian towns and villages, as well as the small size of the Tanzanian community in the camp, conspired to make the problem of intermarriage largely a hypothetical "taboo." There was little *within* the camp to pose a significant challenge to the prohibition against marrying the other. However, the mythico-historical order of categories and boundaries was challenged from *without* by the town refugees in Kigoma. For, as was described at length in the previous chapter, the refugees there routinely married categorical others for a variety of reasons. Some reasons were formulated as a practical necessity. At this level, marriage with a "citizen" was part of the "pragmatics of identity" discussed earlier. It might be described as a form of social naturalization. But another level of explaining marriage among the town refugees contained a more explicit rejection of the meaning and importance of categorical thinking. Ethnic and national categories and boundaries were subsumed under more universalizing questions of taste and attraction, chance and God's will, habit and love. People in town emphasized that "tribe" and "nationality" were not proper criteria for choosing spouses and often pointed out that these concerns typified thinking in the camps.

The marriage practices of the town refugees were problematic in the mythico-history and in the camp on several levels. First, the mythico-history encompassed the town refugees in a particular way: they not only symbolized but seemed to play out the specter of assimilation. Marriage with a "citizen" was a potent gesture toward mixing categories and toward producing new generations of persons who would in time be neither "pure Hutu" *nor "pure refugees."* Second, the town refugees were also problematic because they had never become aligned with "the Tutsi" or with "the Tanzanians" as an externalized, essentially distinct enemy category. They were not excluded from "Hutuness" by the camp refugees but were claimed as members of the nation in exile—albeit morally suspect members. Intermarriage challenged the Hutuness of the town refugees, however. Finally, insofar as intermarriage in town was seen in terms of the biblical allegory of Samson and Delilah, the town refugees were thought to be endangering themselves and all Hutu refugees. For the problems of loyalty and trust were often evoked in discussions concerning non-Hutu spouses. These problems derived not only from the non-Hutuness of the spouses but also from their nonrefugee status. It was expected that a person who had not lived through the flight from Burundi or through the hardships of exile would have insufficient understanding and endurance to withstand the trials that might yet lie ahead for the refugees.

But more than this, the Hutu in Kigoma were considered to be flirting with the easy life and courting a "tutsianized," dangerous category. This opinion revealed that the camp refugees believed many of the alliances between Hutu and Tanzanians to be casual, not "true" or "permanent" marriages. All of these qualities attributed to intermarriage in town were believed to cloud or blur the fund of benign "knowledge" and illumination that the Hutu refugees' collective condition in exile had generated and, therefore, to cloud also their vision of a return to the homeland.

THE DANGER OF "NATURALIZATION"

In Panel 37, "Samson and Delilah in Exile," it was prescribed that intermarriage with the Tanzanian category is "to lose nationality." The threat of this loss was also articulated in the discursive spheres of im-

migration and "naturalization." The legally recognized status of the
residents of Mishamo as refugees was crucial in the mythico-history of
exile. Ultimately, it involved not merely a technical question of legal
status but the "true identity" or "essence" of the Hutu refugees in their
own eyes and, they thought, in the eyes of the world.[4] Again, being
a refugee signified both a legally protected status and a mythico-
historically elaborated condition, a moral condition that was an inalienable part of the collective trajectory of exile.

Refugee status was not taken for granted in the camp; its maintenance was thought to demand continual vigilance against those who
would strip the Hutu of it. Having followed events and heard policy
statements from government officials over many years, the refugees
believed that the Tanzanian government would prefer to treat them as
immigrants and not as refugees. After the handover of the camp to the
government, it was thought, the government would have a freer hand
to realize this intention—no longer having to negotiate the administration of the camp with the international organizations. Thus, the standardizing narrative interpretation of these processes tended to target
the signs or even symptoms of the gathering threat to the refugees'
status in everyday life in the camp, and the status in itself became
something that had to be protected. In these circumstances, it became
important to exhibit and emphasize signs of true and legitimate refugeeness.[5] Even subtle challenges by outsiders to the authenticity and
legitimacy of Hutu refugee status were taken as a betrayal and even as
a plot to render the Hutu powerless.

The specific kind of powerlessness that people conceptualized involved a "spurious rooting" of their identities in a place to which they
did not think they belonged. It involved becoming subject to the laws
of the land of exile and, simultaneously, being stripped of formal recourse to the international refugee agencies' assistance and losing the
protection of international refugee law. This was clearly in evidence
in the standard versions of the District Commissioner's speech in
Mishamo (Panel 30). Reflecting on the threat of status loss, one elderly
informant said: "They consider us as 'immigrants.' In my thinking,
basing [it] on the idea of a 'visitor,' the signification of 'visitor' is that
he *has* a place to return to. Thus, he must return home. [. . .] Oh no!
To tolerate staying here, oh no, oh no! Only because we do not have
the power to advance to other countries, to claim *our* country—I ask
myself. . . . What the government obliges, we have to do. It is necessary

to obey the law. But we are like slaves. Were we citizens, nothing would change. We would by no means get all the rights of citizenship." Another person, also discussing the unadvisability of accepting citizenship, expressed doubts about whether the Hutu could freely leave Mishamo even if they were to become citizens of Tanzania.

The desire of the Tanzanian category to strip the Hutu of their refugee status was a perceived threat that continually renewed itself, as was reflected in this standard version:[6]

Panel 38:

**A METAMORPHOSIS FROM REFUGEES TO IMMIGRANTS?**

They try to make us immigrants quite simply. We cultivate, we are taxed, like immigrants. They get a lot of benefit and money from us. Yes, they want us to be "integrated" because we are beneficial to them. But this is only on the economic level, not otherwise. We would be "economic citizens." [. . .] Look at the Rwandese [Tutsi] refugees [in Tanzania], for example. They were nationalized, but they do not have full citizenship rights. They cannot vote, for example. [. . .] [The Tanzanians] would be happy if we would accept citizenship, but we resist. We would not be full citizens. We do not *want* citizenship. And neither do we want to be immigrants. We are not allowed to elect our leaders. We are not free. As refugees we have at least some rights. We will wait, and then we will return to our home country.[7]

These issues about status and rights were a prominent feature of everyday conversation in the refugee camp. Often they were sparked into narration by particular events that people witnessed and identified as symptomatic of the endangerment of their refugee status. At other times, they were repeated with didactic intent independently of specific, mundane events. Yet a third mode of narration existed for the crystallization of the status issue on a mythico-historical level; the standard narrative versions at times lectured upon with sober didacticism were at other times reproduced humorously. Here, the "performative efficacy" (Tambiah 1985) of the narratives as oratory was most powerful. The opening words of the panel below were uttered in tones of bemused sarcasm.

Panel 39:

**HAVE WE COME HERE TO HAVE OURSELVES NATIONALIZED?!**

And further, [the Tanzanians] invite us to nationalize ourselves. We *refuse!* Yes! With this really . . . tsk! tsk! . . . they are not happy. They want us to stay as their slaves like. . . . Have we come here uniquely to have ourselves nationalized?! Did we not have our own country? The best that we have now, it is that we are still in the hand of . . . of . . . wait . . . *Umoja wa mataifa*, that is to say, unity—the Organization of the United Nations, UN. This is why we still have the best, because the UN still supports us—at least. But once we accept the nationality of here, we will be like what? One will oblige us like one obliges their dogs or their cats, or no matter what domestic animal.[8]

Once again, "integration" through immigration—as through intermarriage—was constituted as a perilous progress, a descent into servitude. While the refugees continually charged that theirs were lives of slavery in the camp, in the context of status questions servitude acquired another dimension. That is, a distinction was made between the temporary, unavoidable, and illegitimate "enslavement" of the Hutu as refugees on the one hand, and a permanent, accepted, and legitimated "enslavement" on the other. The implication was that the latter form of "enslavement" was a *naturalized* condition. And if "naturalized," the Hutu must accept and internalize it. In this case, they would be defining themselves once more as *hutu*, as the "natural," "traditional" category of "slaves" that they were in Burundi. They would be docile like the domestic animals envisioned in Panel 39 above, and their consciousness would thereby become fully colonized by the malign other.

As was described in chapter 4, the meanings attaching to refugeeness in Kigoma township were entirely different. Far from being a status to be protected, a status signaling a link with the imagined homeland, identification as a refugee in Kigoma had become a source of stigma and numerous everyday problems. There, it was accepted as a matter of course that many people chose to reject the refugee label and also the Hutu label. The pragmatics of identity among the town refugees largely centered upon this rejection. The camp refugees in Mishamo were aware that these processes occurred in town. In their moral and mythico-historical interpretation, the "pragmatics of identity" in town became a shameful, cowardly "hiding of identity." It was also referred to as "denial of the origin" of the Hutu refugees. (The denial of originary identities had a formal parallel in the mythico-historical account of how the early Tutsi "hid" *their* origins in the North, outside of Burundi, but this connection was not explicitly made by informants.) In contemplating the town refugees' practices, people in Mishamo emphasized again and again that "here in the camp, even a child knows what a Hutu is." Others spoke in a similar vein: "Here we are not ashamed of being refugees"; and: "Here we are not afraid to say that we are refugees."

Indeed, this unequivocating self-identification as Hutu and as refugees could be seen in ordinary social interactions in the camp. On several occasions, it was possible to observe how a person in Mishamo introduced himself to a visitor from outside the camp: "Good day, I am a Hutu refugee from Burundi and my name is ———." This declaration of identity was spontaneously offered with first greetings. In casual conversation, likewise, the terms *Hutu* and *refugee* occurred together as two facets of one name, or interchangeably. While people in Mishamo were well aware that others might attach negative or derogatory meanings to the label of refugee, there was never any suggestion that they themselves felt ashamed or stigmatized by the designation.

It did not matter in the mythico-history of the camp whether the town refugees adopted legal citizenship in Tanzania or simply passed themselves off as citizens. Both actions were deemed to amount to a denial of origins and a hiding of identity, and both signified disloyalty to the Hutu as "a people." For exile was envisioned as that post-massacre era that finally taught the Hutu "what a Hutu is" and prepared people for the return to the place where the Hutu "belong." By becoming, or even posing as, citizens in the land of exile, the town refugees were tangling and muddying these larger, collective directions of exile. Assimilation at the level of naturalization, as at the level of intermarriage, was irreconcilable with the more overarching collective purpose.

## RESISTANCE TO HIERARCHICAL ASSIMILATION IN MISHAMO

In the mythico-history it was clearly desirable and, indeed, crucial *not* to relinquish "uprootedness" and to ensure that the Hutu remained in a categorical state of displacement, both legally and socially. This refusal to root was perhaps the most important form of positive sociopolitical resistance in the camp—resistance which the camp itself had helped to invigorate. Other forms of resistance were, in turn, structured by this refusal. As long as the Hutu were liminal and not a permanent or naturalized category of Tanzanian society, they were successfully resisting not only "integration" or assimilation in general, but incorporation into hierarchies past or present. It is not surprising that Tanzanian society should have been seen as hierarchically asymmetric by the

Mishamo refugees; in the peculiar context of the camp, the Tanzanians were the sociopolitical, minority category whose task was to administer and govern the mass of the Hutu refugees, and the camp as a bounded spatial entity existed because it was planned so by the administrators.

Thus, while living within the hierarchy of the camp, the Hutu could not be transformed into immigrants or into naturalized "slaves." The camp in itself served to legitimate the claim to separateness and displacement because it was specifically "a place for refugees." This opposition implied another. The Hutu as refugees had constituted an antagonistic equality with the dominant other (Tutsi or Tanzanian) by insisting on categorical separateness and by transforming the other from natural chief to enemy. By the same token, the formerly "natural" and "traditional" asymmetric "symbiosis" between Hutu and Tutsi was broken and denaturalized. "Natural," castelike inequality was "made strange," not only for Burundi but also for the camp in Tanzania. The opposition, then, was between antagonistic equality and separateness, on the one hand, and symbiotic, docile, natural inequality, on the other. This antagonistic equality was a means of maintaining categorical purity vis-à-vis the other, the "enemy," through separateness.

In Kigoma, relations with others were not so visibly or systematically nested in a single hierarchy as they were in the camp or in Burundi. Thus, in the lives of the Kigoma refugees, a concrete transformation from hierarchy as a hegemonic, organic order to relative equality had occurred. It is ironic that this transformation was not elaborated by the town refugees, as it was by the camp refugees for whom such a transformation had not occurred. For, as was described in chapter 3, the relations between the Mishamo refugees and the camp authorities were hierarchical and interpreted by the refugees as such—hence, the refusal of any kind of incorporation. It seems, then, that a degree of lived, experiential equality and sociospatial mobility in Kigoma rendered irrelevant the continual mythico-historical challenge to asymmetry that was so evident in Mishamo. As one person in Mishamo observed, "It is we who have the Commandant."

COMMERCE AND WEALTH AS POLITICO-MORAL EVILS

Thus far it has been described how the town refugees posed a challenge to the mythico-historical order of things in the domains of intermarriage and immigration. There remains one further arena which is crucial for understanding, not only the social construction of the camp-town relationship, but also the wider meanings of assimilation and exile in the mythico-history: the arena of commerce and wealth. This was indeed the domain in which the opposition between camp and town was most fully elaborated and which most sharply reflected the mythico-historical role of the town refugees as the "enemy within."

The town was the mythico-historical place for "merchant refugees" and "dangerous wealth." It posed two identifiable kinds of danger in the mythico-historical order of things. First, insofar as the practices of trade and commerce necessitated close relations with "other" categories, these practices in themselves served to anchor the refugee merchants in local networks, thereby deepening and diversifying their assimilation. Second, wealth in itself was a suspect, dangerous category because its pursuit was seen to corrupt the town refugees morally and politically, by causing them to stray away from the collective trajectory of exile which, if "properly," "virtuously" lived, would culminate in a collective return to the homeland.

It is significant that the category "town refugees" was seen as a homogeneous category of "merchant refugees." The mythico-history did not seem to allow for much differentiation, if any, within the category of the town refugees; it did not include "cultivators," "intellectuals," "students," "priests," "clerical workers," "domestic workers," "professionals," or other nonmerchant categories. The very fact of their residence in town, then, implicated the town refugees in the dangerous circuits of wealth and commerce. They were "merchants," the categorical opposite of "cultivators," the camp refugees.

When the time approached for my research to move from Mishamo to Kigoma, informants in the camp offered a series of different warnings and instructions for living in town. It was most often said that great care should be exercised in choosing conversation partners because "you never know to whom you may be talking." It was emphasized that since so many "different kinds of people" lived in town, it would be impossible to know whether one was talking with a Hutu or a Tutsi. It was not believed that the "body maps" charting physical differences between Hutu and Tutsi (Panel 12) would help in the identification process. The social scene in the township was considered to be difficult to navigate and therefore always potentially dangerous.

Many of these caveats also produced longer characterizations of the town, accounts that tended to converge on the themes of wealth and commerce as a courtship with danger and evil. Some of the panels to be presented below emerged from such caveats.

DEALINGS WITH THE DEVIL

There seemed to be, in the mythico-history, two main orders of discourse on wealth and commerce, evil and danger. The first order was supernatural in that it concerned dealings with the Devil. The second was only mundane in that it involved dealings with another kind of mythico-historical "devil," the "enemy." The rich abundance of accounts centering on the supernatural was mystifying at first, but when these accounts were set together with the second order of dangers, their meaning became more accessible to interpretation.

The dangers of the first order encompassed such things as the use of harmful and even deadly "talismans" procured from *waganga* ("healers"; *umupfumu* in Kirundi) for the purpose of obtaining another's wealth; the use of "nocturnal slaves" to augment one's agricultural output at no cost; the use of only children as fishing instruments (*ikimara*); the writing of letters in blood to Satan; and other techniques. It is not necessary to reproduce accounts of all these different techniques; examples suffice to make the argument clear. It should also be noted that whether the beings or forces described here as supernatural derived from Christianity or elsewhere seemed to matter little. Similarly, the distinction between "the supernatural" and "the mundane" orders of danger was not centrally important in the narratives to follow because larger mythico-historical themes about danger and evil were at issue.

Of course, these kinds of themes—tying material goods to sorcery, secrecy, and evil intent—were not unique to this instance; they appear very widely in many parts of Africa in one guise or another (Comaroff 1985; Ferguson 1993; Geschiere 1988). The point is that these widely distributed ideas about wealth were pressed into service when people in Mishamo were thinking about the town refugees.

The first panel concerns the augmentation of wealth through fishing in a very particular manner. It entails the trapping of people, or their spirits, into unbreakable, captive relations of exploitation.

Panel 40:

AN ONLY CHILD AS A FISHING INSTRUMENT

If you are an only child,[9] if you go to ask for employment from the fishermen there [at the lake], pay attention. Never admit that you have been born an only child. If you say that you are an only child, you are killed by the fishermen, and you will be an instrument for fishing, for catching many *dagaa*. The fisherman has killed you uniquely to get many fish. This is the object desired by that diabolical spirit. It is you who goes searching no matter where under water and pushing the fish toward the pirogue [boat][10] of the one who has killed you. During fishing, there have to be two persons on the boat: the master of the boat and then the servant, a chauffeur, in other words. Well, the servant there cannot see you. Only the master of the boat sees the action of the cadaver there. You, the cadaver, gather fish into your arms [and herd them toward the pirogue]. And then the one who has done this manner [of fishing] will never be lacking in fish, or in little fish, *dagaa*.[11] A man killed for this reason is called *ikimara* in Kirundi. He is killed to search for *dagaa* for his master.[12]

The relationship between the only child and the owner of the boat, the captive and the master, is invisible to everyone but themselves. It is a hidden, secret relationship. The theme of the theft of labor and of slavery becomes even clearer in the next panel.

Panel 41:

NOCTURNAL SLAVES

One can see that the Muslims are very rich, but from morning till evening, they do nothing but sit on their mats. They have cars, Hondas [motorcycles], beautiful houses. . . . How? Well? How can they have these riches? It is said that they employ spirits to cultivate for them during the night, spirits of persons who are dead. They are their slaves. It is like this that they have their riches! You go to sleep at night. In the morning you awaken and your feet are very dirty. You ask yourself: "Eh?! How? Did I not wash myself in the evening before going to bed? How can I be so dirty?" You get up and your body aches. You feel tired, your arms ache, your back aches. . . . You do not understand. But during the night, you have gone into the fields to work, and you have cultivated during the whole night. Just before the sun, you return to bed. If one is killed with talismans, if his spirit is taken, this person will appear dead. Others will think that he is dead and they will bury him. This is but burying a piece of wood and thinking that it is a person. He who has the talismans can do this. It is always a question of wealth. Those who do this are really pushed [driven] to receive wealth, earthly wealth.[13]

The story of the only children who become fishing instruments and the story of the nocturnal slaves[14] intimately wove together wealth and the surreptitious entrapment of people.[15] This relation always appeared to involve the deployment of a malign knowledge that depended for its efficacy on secrecy and ruse, on hidden capacities. Further, in both panels (as in other analogous themes) this clandestine relation was forged through death. In chapters 2 and 3, the theft of labor as a necessary corollary to slavery was a recurrent theme, and this is in some measure parallel to the two panels above. For in each case the dominant other was endowed with apparently contradictory qualities: parasitism (suggesting weakness) and, at the same time, formidable danger and power.

There was yet another series of mythico-historical themes that defined wealth, and even the desire for wealth, as fundamentally suspect. This series is perhaps best described as Faustian; it asserts that wealth necessitates dealings with the Devil. Doctor Faustus undeniably hovers about in the following conversation in Mishamo concerning letters written to Satan.

AN OLD MAN: You can write a letter with your blood to Satan. Then you bring it to the cemetery during the night. You leave it there somewhere. Then, it is possible that after some time, you will find a response, a letter from Satan!! AUTHOR: Also written in blood? OLD MAN: ?? . . . I do not know. No, I do not think so. In ordinary ink, I believe. AUTHOR: Why would one write such a letter to Satan? OLD MAN: Pfff! One can ask for riches. If one desires money. He wants something from the bad spirits who are the satans. It is always done in order to get a lot of money. The person can write [to the satans]: "I am poor, so, I present myself before your High Benevolence that I may become rich like the others." At that moment, he might receive an answer to this letter that he has written with his own blood. [. . .] Then he who has made the request receives some obligations. He can ask you to kill your wife or else your child, those whom you love very much. Or he can ask you not to go to church, or to no longer make gestures to adore the good God. At this moment, you depend on your patron, the Devil. [. . .] It is done for wealth.[16]

This explanation (given in derisive tones) implies that the hunger for wealth demands abominations—such as the abandonment of basic loyalties toward those whom one loves in life. But there were other stories of ordinary Hutu men, residents of Mishamo, who had nothing to do with this order of evil. They drove TCRS lorries[17] for a living, made good money on the side, and yet found their deaths magically. One person explained:

we have already buried many Hutu drivers, those who worked for TCRS. [. . .] It was because of jealousy. If a lorry-driver drives from here until Dar-es-Salaam, he can take [passengers] on the way where they want to go, and he earns a lot of money—maybe 100–200 Tsh. per person. So, the other truckers are jealous of him because he has money to buy all sorts of goods, and one day he will be able to buy his own truck. Well, if one uses a talisman, that can trap him even at—let us say—Mbeya [i.e., at a great distance]. Even on paved road. Only the driver dies, and the others in the lorry are not even hurt, and there is nothing the matter with the lorry. Only the driver is dead within.

Here, it was not that the lorry drivers were evil; foolishness was their main vice. But their fate brought home the point yet again that money will soak up trouble from far and wide.

More generally, all of the foregoing panels together converge on the process of personal enrichment as evidence of expertise in clandestine, nefarious techniques of power. All treat it as axiomatic that wealth requires dealings with the Devil. That these links should have emerged in the mythico-history is not in itself remarkable. As in so many other places in Africa and elsewhere, wealth was tied to subterfuge and witchcraft (cf. Taussig 1980).[18] But the camp refugees were not simply asking, How can those people be so rich when we are so poor? In fact, it is not at all clear that the camp refugees were on average poorer than the town refugees (or other groups). While reliable information on incomes would be very difficult to obtain, there is justification for suggesting that greater differences of wealth obtained among the town refugees than in the camp and that economic fortunes were more variable in town. Cultivating seemed to provide greater security and regularity of income in the camp, if not spectacular wealth. The point here, however, is not level of income but rather the fact that wealth was suspect for reasons of a quite specific kind, as we shall see.

But before proceeding, it is perhaps worth noting that dealings with the devil and witchcraft in the service of dubious ends were considered endemic in town, while people in Mishamo did not ordinarily have to contend with such dangers. The town was a locus of danger because it allowed for the mixing of categories which in the camp were separate or absent.

Panel 42:

### URBAN SORCERERS

There are more sorcerers in town, for example, in Kigoma [than in Mishamo]. There one has to pay attention. There are more of them! Because there in town, all sorts of people meet each other. There are refugees, Zaireans, *bazungu* [Europeans, whites], Tanzanians, merchants, Indians, fishermen. . . . And for all trades there are many clients—for the merchant, for the mechanic, for the driver, even for the sorcerer. Yes, one has to pay attention.[19]

The linkage of the Kigoma refugees to impurity in the mythico-history was also evident in specific accusations of what may be called moral pollution, such as laziness and the avoidance of hard work in the fields, vagrancy and prostitution, drunkenness and petty theft, and, more seriously, smuggling ivory to Burundi, to the "enemy," and finally—most dangerously of all, acting as paid informers to the Tutsi-led government in Burundi. These different levels or varieties of moral fault seemed to form a mythico-historical set, so that even apparently trivial misdeeds (laziness, for example) were related by association with acts of the gravest seriousness (smuggling, informing, betrayal).

Two dimensions of these attributions of impurity are of special note. First, a continuity between the "merchant" refugee category and all of these states of impurity was powerfully asserted in the mythico-history—indeed, these dangers were seen to spring from the merchant category. As we saw before, the town refugees themselves acknowledged a relation between the thief and the merchant, but this was a heroizing relation. It did not express a moral continuum but rather celebrated prowess and competence.

The second dimension of this mythico-historical chain of progressively greater impurity and danger is that all of the accusations were in one manner or another linked with the dangers of assimilation. The danger lay in the careless denial of the importance of categories and in their willful mixing. By starting from petty theft and commerce in Kigoma and culminating in dealings with Burundi, the mythico-historical chain established that the town refugees were not only "mixing with the Tanzanians" but also fraternizing with the Tutsi, the primary categorical enemy. In this light it was not surprising that some of the accusations leveled at the Kigoma refugees should have borne a formal resemblance to the mythico-historical characterization of the Tutsi. (The Tutsi, too, were constructed as lazy, unwilling to engage in physical labor, prone to the "theft of labor," and expert in ruse.)

The following panel encapsulates popular views from the camp concerning the contradiction inherent in being both a merchant and a refugee. It was considered dangerous and improper for true refugees to immerse themselves too deeply in this-worldly concerns, whether trade or smuggling. Here, this-worldliness referred, not to the religious axes of life and death or heaven and earth, but rather to assimilation in the land of exile.[20] The other-worldly, the imagined homeland, was always present in narratives such as this one by an old farmer:

Panel 43:

THE CONTRADICTION OF RICH REFUGEES

The merchants [. . .] were chased away from Kigoma—and the other merchants also. Having gotten money, they bought clothes and instruments necessary for a man . . . *every sort* of merchandise. They became rich. They have cabarets, hotels, restaurants . . . *being refugees!!* So, all their riches were seized by the government. [. . .] They were chased from the towns. Now they are in camps.

Here again there was the implication that commerce of this kind was dangerous *specifically* for refugees, that being a refugee naturally suggested, even demanded, certain kinds of social conduct while closing off others. Being a refugee entailed prescriptions and prohibitions, duties and moral responsibilities. It was not a mere label or legality; it was a status and a collective condition with its own moral weight.

In this framework, being a merchant also became more than a pragmatic occupation, more than a simple means of making a living. It, too, became a mythico-historically elaborated social location, and ultimately a moral condition bearing its own foreseeable consequences. It was expected that a person be either a refugee or a merchant, not both equally: "In town it is those who make commerce. But we have not come here to make commerce. We are refugees."

Panel 44:

THE MERCHANT REFUGEES AS TRAITORS

The ivory traders are in Tabora, Mpanda, and Kigoma. If a Hutu refugee walks toward Ulyankulu [camp], the authorities will push him and question him: "Show your travel papers!" They never want a Hutu to frolic about or to promenade in the town of Tabora. These Hutu were not polite toward the authorities; they showed themselves as rich. Well, they were sent back. To return where? To Ulyankulu, to their camp. We are very well pleased because our rich comrades, our merchant fellows, were chased from the towns. We are very well pleased! They sold us. [. . .] By doing what? By giving money to Burundi, even going to Burundi, accusing and telling stories.

Those [refugees] who were rich in Burundi, or those who had a job which furnished them with money, it is they who are now poor [in exile]. Why? Because they did not want to put themselves into the movement to kill these beasts. What beasts? The elephants. [. . .]

Another great fault: The ivory there is transported to Burundi for selling it to our enemy, [President] Bagaza. Well, this is why that Bagaza has become the first in the Common Market [in ivory exports]. The country of Burundi has no elephants! Bagaza was poor before this! Because of these Hutu egotists, the wicked Bagaza found the means to have a lot of ivory— and to go and sell [it] to the Common Market. For this reason, Bagaza furnished a lot of ivory, and then he got gifts from those who bought it. [. . .] And something else that Bagaza did at that moment: he bought the strongest weapons. Because of the wealth, he bought the strongest weapons. He has them currently. This is why the Tanzanians do not like the Hutu. This is a bad thing that the Hutu have done. It is imbecility. [The merchant refugees] are interested to get much money, but they ignore what the enemy is thinking. [These merchants] are rich. They are interested to stay here [in Tanzania] with their riches.

Panel 44, drawn from a conversation with the old farmer cited above, is centrally important in the mythico-history because it establishes a continuous set of links between commerce and the desire for wealth, on the one hand, and politico-moral danger and evil, on the other. The merchants who became successful enough to enter the business of ivory smuggling forged relations with Burundi, where a large market for local ivory continues to exist. (cf. Harland 1988) Carrying ivory to Burundi was considered a betrayal of the Hutu people in exile because that ivory sustained and empowered the enemy; and the stronger the enemy, the more gravely compromised the return of the refugees to the homeland. Here, as in the case of the blood letters to Satan, commerce was seen to demand the abandonment of categorical loyalty and purity. In this light, it was not surprising that many of the camp refugees should have expressed views such as this one: "Those who are in town, those are merchants. The merchant can be an enemy—finding money because [the township] is so close to Burundi and Burundi has a lot of money. The merchant very, very much loves money. So, it is easy to be an enemy of us who are in the camp."

QUISLING EVIL AND RETRIBUTION

For the Mishamo refugees, "the people" was the relevant politico-moral actor. "The people" included all Hutu largely because it was an oppositional category, drawing its vitality of meaning so directly from the categorical enmity with the Tutsi. The Kigoma refugees were problematic for this collective, inclusive mythico-historical framework because they failed to fit the ideal and yet were recognized as a part of it. Moreover, through their actions, the town refugees were said to "give a bad name" to *all* Hutu refugees in Tanzania, thereby making everyone's collective status more precarious and vulnerable. They were thus a curious sort of "enemy within." The evil they symbolized was a quisling evil. But their actions had not caused them to be excluded from the collectivity of "the people"; nor had they become an externalized enemy, like the Tutsi and the Tanzanian categories. In spite of their categorical aberrations, their membership in the nation in exile was accepted. The view from Kigoma was rather different. There the concept of a people with a shared, collective trajectory was not universally meaningful. For the Kigoma refugees, the camp refugees tended to be more of an absence, a distant "they."

The encompassing, inclusive force of the mythico-history vis-à-vis the town refugees became evident in people's predictions and accounts of retribution and rehabilitation. Particular events that were current and fresh in people's minds during fieldwork eventually became "standard versions" about what happens to refugees who become merchants, mythico-historical quislings.

Three specific cases were most often evoked during this period. The first concerned the already mentioned April 1986 expulsion of Hutu merchant refugees from Mpanda and Tabora. The merchants were transported back to the camps in which they were registered and where they already had plots—Katumba and Ulyankulu respectively. They were obliged to leave behind their businesses and houses in town. In Kigoma, the expulsion set rumors spiraling; it was a threatening event because it gave substance to people's worries that they, too, might be subject to forced removal into one of the camps. In Mishamo, by contrast, the expulsion was seen as a logical, reasonable outcome of "dealing with the devil": everyone knew that commerce and exile were irreconcilable processes. Many in Mishamo even expressed their pleasure at the expulsion and thought it might serve well as an object lesson.

The second case was one of augured retribution, involving persistent rumors about the establishment of the new camp for Hutu refugees near Mbeya that was mentioned earlier. These rumors began long before representatives of the international organizations had publicized any such plans, although it was clear by the end of fieldwork in October 1986 that such a camp was indeed being at least officially discussed.[21] The new camp, a specter for the town refugees, was welcomed by the camp refugees insofar as it was seen as a means of curbing the "dangerous" activities of the merchant refugees in town. Moreover, its establishment was seen as a direct result of the "corrupt" activities of the merchant refugees.

The third event to be interpreted as retribution for politico-moral impurity in the mythico-history occurred in April 1987, after fieldwork for this study had ended. The material presented here derives from letters from refugees and nonrefugee informants, as well as from newspaper articles. For reasons which are not entirely clear, the government of Tanzania decided to expel approximately five thousand "irregulars" from the Kigoma region. The category of "irregulars" included those town refugees who did not have identity documents. Some reports identified this as a measure to control black marketing (magendo) in Kigoma, historically a social and commercial crossroads that has been called "the capital of all the traffics" (De Barrin 1986). Other reports suggested that this operation was a retaliation by Tanzania for the expulsion of Tanzanians from Burundi (and Kenya) in March of 1987.[22] Although there was no authoritative account of the motivations for this operation, there certainly was an abundance of conjecture. Under pressure from the Government of Burundi, the UNHCR in Kigoma and Tanzania, and "several Embassies," the Government of Tanzania suspended the operation on 7 April 1987.[23] The significance of these events derives in the present context from the explanations given them by the refugees themselves. Letters from Kigoma[24] reported that houses had been pillaged and that many people had gone into hiding in the countryside surrounding the township. Relatively soon, however, many informants wrote that conditions had returned to normal and that those expelled had immediately turned around and started trickling back into Tanzania. Several letters mentioned that those who had thought to pretend to be Tanzanians when questioned by Burundi authorities, and to act as if they did not understand Kirundi had been released and sent back. Letters from Mishamo, by contrast, contained information about the refoulement (forced repatriation) for a somewhat longer period of time. The operation was diagnosed, on the one hand, as a conspiracy between the Tutsi and the Tanzanians and, on the other, as retribution for the activities of the merchant refugees. It was believed that the merchants had profoundly angered the Tanzanian government with their display of wealth and with smuggling and black market business. (Other aspects of the *refoulement* will be discussed further in the Postscript.)

THE CAMP AS A PLACE OF PURIFICATION

Many camp refugees saw a clearcut solution to the problem of the town refugees: "Bring all the refugees into the camp." As one person said in discussing the rumored plan for a new camp and the extension of Katumba camp: "They will move [the town refugees to the new camp] also. I think so. You know, they are rich, playing with the easy life. So, why shouldn't they come here to help us?! They will move them from Kigoma, Tabora, and so on. I think it is good. They *should* do that." The camp was clearly antithetical to the "easy life" with which the town refugees were considered to be toying. But more importantly, it was conceptualized as a place of purification or even rehabilitation, a place where the contradiction between merchant and refugee would be resolved.

It might have been expected that since no refugees living within camps were rounded up during the 1987 *refoulement*, the camps would present themselves as an attractive option—a safe haven—for at least some town refugees. If many had had their homes and fields burned, they might have gone to begin again in the camps. This does not seem to have happened, however. Letters from both Mishamo and Kigoma confirmed that no new arrivals had entered the camp from the town. The camp was evidently still not an option for those in town.

THE MYTHICO-HISTORICAL CONSTITUTION OF PURITY AND EXILE

As has already been suggested in the foregoing sections of this chapter, the camp refugees' views of the town refugees and of assimilation were fundamentally structured by the mythico-historical meaning of exile. The town refugees' actions were being morally judged according to an ideal, correct way of being a refugee and living in exile. In this final section, some of the most important aspects of the mythico-historical constitution of exile will be summarized.

First, exile was part and parcel of a more overarching historical trajectory of the Hutu as "a people," a trajectory which was traced back to the misty origins of the autochthonous nation of Burundi. The 1972 massacres which catapulted the Hutu into exile were seen as a moment of illumination and, also, of the violent, productive rupture of relations with the Tutsi. The beginning of asylum in Tanzania was, in the mythico-history, the "first birth" of a nation in exile. The culmination of exile was necessarily the future return to the "homeland." The realization of this millennial return was considered to depend on the way in which exile was lived by the collectivity of the Hutu. In this sense, exile represented a period of tests and lessons, a process of purification, which would make the Hutu as "a people" worthy of regaining the homeland. The achievement of purity, then, was gradual and required not only vigilance but hard work. Here was yet another source for the heroization of labor and industriousness that ran throughout the mythico-history.

Panel 45:

**TRIALS IN DIASPORA GIVE PURITY AND KNOWLEDGE**

Instead of nationalizing ourselves here, we can accept all the difficulties, all the miseries, in seeking our country. Those who have accepted all these difficulties, all these miseries, will receive their native country. Once somebody hurts us, once we suffer, this means that we are being educated. We are being educated, I think—to know how to act and. . . . You know, for example: Someone who refuses to give you food gives you a good means of avoiding laziness. [You then say to yourself:] "Why not look for my own? I will work, and in no time, I will receive my own food. I have to do everything possible to gain my own." We congratulate them very well, we congratulate them. [. . .] They begin to educate us as refugees—who have nothing, refugees who have nothing, as their very own. [. . .] They teach us to research our lost good. It is this pretty fashion that they show us. Can you live without your own [things?] when you once had them, if you will? [. . .] In the Bible it is said also: "Without being servants, you will not be served." Yes, yes. If you want to become an honorable man, be first of all yourself a servant of others. You will be honored, you also. [. . .] One receives according to what one gives.[25]

The themes in this panel were very enabling in the effort to understand the mythico-historical constitution, not only of everyday social details in camp life, but of the grand sweep of exile as a social process of purification. They suggested that the techniques of power characterizing the camp—while experienced as repressive and exploitative by the refugees—were simultaneously interpreted in a positive light, as productive forms and practices. The camp might repress, control, govern, and exploit those it encased, but it was at the same time recognized as that place that had taught the Hutu how to be refugees. As the panel said, "They begin to educate us as refugees."

Earlier, it was suggested that the mythico-history cast the Hutu in the initial stages of exile as novice refugees who were not yet "real" or "pure refugees," and that the condition of refugeeness required a process of *becoming*. This interpretation is also supported by Panel 45, for the "trials and tribulations in exile" constituted a long test of strength and moral worth, a test of epic proportions, in the mythico-history. It was only through this path of hardship that "the people" would achieve and deserve the reward, the return home. In this context, servitude, too, became productive, for "if you want to become an honorable man, be first of all yourself a servant of others." In short, anything might transform itself into a productive "lesson" to empower and illumine.

Now it becomes possible to pursue the transformation that the Hutu as a distinct category had undergone in the mythico-history. In chapter 2, Panel 7, it was charted how the "original," "aboriginal" Bantu peoples living in the "autochthonous nation" were transformed from *bantu* (human beings) into *hutu* (slaves, servants) by the Tutsi "impostors from the north." The massacre then catapulted the *hutu* into exile, transforming them into (what I have called) novice refugees. The trials and tribulations of exile taught them to become "true refugees." It is this condition that was heroized in the mythico-history. For it was only through becoming "pure refugees" that they could achieve the transformation into "pure Hutu." And *hutuness* and Hutuness were categories that were set side by side so that they might be distinguished from each other. In the former state, the *hutu* were still "servants" of the Tutsi, and in the latter, they had become—and were still becoming—"the Hutu" as "a people." They were creating a nationness, first, through undergoing the hardships of exile and achieving moral worthiness and, second, through separating themselves as a category from "other" categories and resisting any hybridization. The camp had proved to be an ideal locus for the continual distillation and disciplining of this categorical purity. The transformations charted here serve to underscore that "purity" was not considered a categorically ascribed status but, ideally, a status achieved through the will and agency of the collectivity of the Hutu refugees, the categorical protagonist.

PURITY AND "AUTHENTICITY"

The camp refugees' insistence on a collective identity as a distinct people also found expression in another theme in the camp: authenticity. This term appears to have been first used by the leader of the

PALIPEHUTU liberation movement, Gahutu Rémi, but circulated among other people in the camp as well. Even when this particular word was not used, people stressed the importance of maintaining a kind of cultural purity among themselves, in large part through disseminating knowledge of their collective history.

Panel 46:

"OUR QUALITIES AND TRADITIONS"

We try to teach people not to think that this place is their home. Our home is Burundi, not Tanzania, and we have no rights here. Our hosts, the Tanzanians, do not like to see people teaching each other about their traditions. We should keep our qualities and traditions.[26]

The maintenance of "authenticity" was considered to require continual effort, particularly as it always appeared to the refugees to be under threat from the categorical "other" of exile, the Tanzanians. Several informants asserted that "the Tanzanians" had "a conspiracy to make us forget our traditions." These claims underscored the distinctness of a "Hutu tradition," a tradition that I initially translated as "culture." But as will presently become evident, this equivalence was more complex than one might have expected.

THE SIKUKUU CELEBRATION

On 5 February 1986, an anniversary celebration of the birth of the *Chama cha Mapinduzi* (CCM), Tanzania's Party of the Revolution, was held at the stadium of the Settlement Headquarters area in Village Number Two, also known as Ifumbula. I and a neighbor of mine, a recently arrived TCRS water engineer from Bombay, were invited to attend. As we settled into our seats, I had the overwhelming sensation of having stepped through the looking glass into the script of a play about state power—and I had, in fact, stepped into a ritual. I, along with the Settlement Commandant's spouse, the new Assistant Commandant, a school headmaster, a church leader, and various other TCRS and Ministry of Home Affairs (MHA) staff, sat in the shade, on a covered, elevated concrete podium, with a sweeping view of the stadium field glimmering in midday sun. Directly below the podium, facing us, was a semicircle of quiet children in fresh uniforms. At the edges of the stadium stood a few other people (perhaps the parents of the performers), looking on. Presently the children began to dance and drum and sing. They separated into smaller clusters, and one pupil in each cluster led the others with whistle and song. Rhythmically moving rows and circles of children formed and unformed before us. In the middle of the dancers were four young boys on their knees, drumming. All the song lyrics and dance imagery praised the Party of the Revolution, and Tanzania.

The second segment of the program featured a speech by the spouse of the Settlement Commandant. Raising a fist in the air, she called out "[long live] Chama cha Mapinduzi!" and everyone raised their voices in echo. She then talked about matters of development (maendeleo), cultivating, and the importance of work, and concluded with a volley of political slogans. Her speech was followed by another segment of dancing, drumming, and singing by the schoolchildren, who by now were looking rather sweaty. There was one more speech by the new Assistant Settlement Commandant, who talked more about work and the party. The celebration came to a close with a final segment of dance, drumming, and song by the children, and lunch for those on the podium.

Sitting next to me during the dance segments of the Sikukuu celebration, the Commandant's spouse was able to explain what the different dance sequences and gestures meant. At one point, the young dancers had wooden sticks in their hands. She said that these symbolized hoes: "They are singing that we have to plant and cultivate now; this is the time for cultivation." My neighbor, the water engineer, asked her if the songs the children performed came from books or if they were of their own composition. She thought that they were all designed by the children in school.

I was still thinking about the Sikukuu celebration on the following day when I met an old tailor from one of the villages near the headquarters area. I asked him whether the children had really written the Sikukuu songs themselves, for this seemed to me doubtful. He responded: "Of course not, it is the monitors who write them—it is the principal of the school, rather. They, they do not know how to write music, the pupils. [. . .] to sing these songs, it is an obligation. [. . .] The songs do not come from the heart. They are the songs of this country, not ours." The small group of schoolchildren that I queried likewise said that their teachers had told them what to sing.

It was sometimes easy to overdramatize what one saw in Mishamo and therefore necessary to try continually to discipline one's eye and frame of mind. (But this is probably true of all anthropological fieldwork.) It did seem to me, however, that the dancing children's faces expressed an unblinking understanding of an obligation to sing. While the performances were at times energetic and engaging, the children's expressions tended to be quite grave.

The Sikukuu anniversary celebration seemed to demand that one think critically about what "culture" and "tradition" meant for the different people in this momentarily and self-consciously shared ritual context. This must remain, for lack of information, an open question for the Tanzanian camp administrators who were present. Quite possibly, they thought little of it, taking it as one social obligation among others. But for the Hutu refugees who either witnessed or traded accounts of the anniversary in the days following it, the stakes were clearer to see. It was in this connection that many refugees brought up their perceptions of a "conspiracy" to make them "forget [their] traditions." The core of the conspiracy appeared to be that they were being naturalized against their will. For, as was evident in the formal speeches of the Sikukuu celebration, and in the District Commissioner's speech (Panel 30), the refugees were regularly urged to keep their minds on the soil instead of dwelling unproductively on the struggle for Burundi.

Another intervention in the sphere of "culture" came in the efforts of a French nurse to introduce new crafts to the Hutu. Employed by TCRS, she was a longtime resident of Mishamo.[27] Early in 1986, she took a holiday on the island of Madagascar and brought back to Mishamo a brilliantly colored multiplicity of Malagasy baskets, weavings, and other handicrafts. She then announced a workshop to teach the Hutu refugees to make similar artifacts because, as she put it, "these refugees have no culture." Her intention was to introduce culture into what was, for her, a fractured space or a pathological void resulting from the "apathy" of refugee life.[28] Interestingly, in her effort to help the refugees by encouraging the revitalization of their cultural life, she was convinced that *any culture*, even if imported from Madagascar, was better than none.

The camp refugees themselves did not appear to be much concerned with culture in this sense of "customs" or material culture. The nurse's intervention on the customs side of culture was not resisted; it was just irrelevant. For it was not "Hutu customs" or "Hutu handicrafts" that defined Hutuness.

The concept of culture is problematic to use here in any sense, if for no other reason than its absence from the everyday discourse of the refugees. People in Mishamo never spent time trying to enumerate the "contents" or "substance" of their culture in that exhaustive, earnest, un-self-conscious manner that the ethnologist of old has led us to expect of people. If there was anything stereotypically folkloric in their imagination of "culture," it was incidental—or gestured towards in a lighthearted, even offhanded way (as in the case of the traditions of drumming in Burundi, traditions associated with the monarchy).[29] The meaning of *qualities* and *traditions* (the words that appear in the panel above) was at once more essential and more relational, consisting in the memorable historical shapes of the agonistic struggle with the other (cf. Fanon 1965; Gilroy 1990a).

The most relevant meaning of *traditions* in Mishamo seemed to be, not culture or customs in any quaint or colorful sense, not crafts that could be peddled or museumized, but a raw and living history of struggle and loss. Indeed, this sense of *traditions* seemed in many respects to be in concord with Ernest Renan's moral vision of the nation:

Man is everything in the formation of this sacred thing which is called a people. Nothing [purely] material suffices for it. A nation is a spiritual principle, the outcome of the profound complications of history [. . .]. A nation is a soul, a spiritual principle. [. . .] [S]uffering in common unifies more than joy does. Where national memories are concerned, griefs are of more value than triumphs, for they impose duties, and require a common effort. A nation is therefore a large-scale solidarity, constituted by the feeling of the sacrifices that one has made in the past and of those that one is prepared to make in the future. (Renan 1990:18–20)

*Qualities* seemed to mean those essential signs that distinguish a "Hutu" from a "Tutsi" or any other category, just as surely and naturally as the stripes of the tiger distinguish it from the spots of the leopard. What was less immediately apparent was that these species-like distinguishing markings were not so much "cultural" or "ethnic" as *moral* traits, and morality was as fundamental and essential an identifier of difference as blood and genes are in other places. These issues offer evidence, yet again, that the dividing line between biology and culture, materiality and morality, does not lie stably in the same place everywhere.[30]

Gilroy has written about the "metaphysics of Britishness" (1991: 47). In Mishamo, the metaphysics of Hutuness was at stake. This is indeed the proper term to describe the refugees' discursive construction of "qualities and traditions." It would be inaccurate to gloss this simply as "culture"; its real reference was to an *imagined moral essence*. Hutu identity, or the metaphysics of Hutuness, was about the construction and transformation of human categories defined in terms of good and evil and, by extension, about the proper (or even "true") order of the world. So, what was being kept pure was not so much customs but moral essence—indeed, the mythico-history was a history of the transformations of and struggles over this moral essence.

Whereas for the European nurse, authenticity was that which had been lost, or left in the past of the homeland, for the Hutu refugees, authenticity seemed to mean the here and now, and the relation of present circumstances to the future. Indeed, the insistence on authenticity, refugeeness, and Hutuness together necessarily stood as a statement about the future: As long as the Hutu remained "uprooted" and "displaced"—"a people" on foreign soil (Malkki 1992a)—they manifestly had a connection to the place from which they had originally fled. Exile by definition implied a "thereness" (Said 1986a), a place from which one was absent. Similarly, refugeeness represented, not only the will to return, but also the ultimate, if distant, *possibility* of return. For if the Hutu were to accept immigrant status or citizenship in exile, they would be relinquishing uprootedness from the "homeland." Without this link, exile would no longer be intelligible as an era of preparation for the return home. The linear, forward-looking momentum of the mythico-history of exile was founded on the belief that exile was temporary. And the millennial return was a clear and present utopia that was in some sense already being lived and imagined.

THE NECESSITY OF TEMPORARINESS

The camp refugees' unfaltering belief in the temporariness of exile might appear surprising when it is considered that exile had lasted over fourteen years at the time of my fieldwork, and the moment of return still appeared at that time as an abstract vanishing point on the sociopolitical horizon. (But see Postscript, below.) This conviction, however, was clearly necessary if the mythico-history as a whole was to be intelligible and meaningful. The end of exile was much discussed in the camp. Sometimes people indulged in fanciful predictions based on the symbolic significance of particular calendrical dates or numbers. But most of the time, biblical themes were what gave proof of the inevitability of an ultimate return.[31]

Panel 47:

"EVEN JESUS WAS A REFUGEE"

Even Jesus was a refugee in Egypt. When his enemy, Herod, died, he came back. Herod was pursuing him. Then, when Herod died, Jesus did not stay in Egypt. He returned to his country. We are Hutu, natives of Burundi. We will never be natives of Tanzania, never.[32]

Sitting at a smooth old wooden table in his house on a quiet afternoon, one person was discussing with his friends the "integration" project of which the Hutu refugees in Mishamo were the object, and he concluded: "We will never see this as our home country." He then rose to fetch for his guests an issue of the newsmagazine *Africa* (April 1985, 25–7), containing an article on the Israeli airlift of the Falashas from Ethiopia. He pointed: "Look, the Ethiopian Jews were refugees for who knows how long—hundreds of years! Now they have finally returned to the country of their ancestors. They were 'airlifted'; the Jews of Israel arranged it."

It is interesting that this man should automatically have considered the Ethiopian Jews as refugees. This suggests that refugeeness was thought of as something that was inherited from one generation to another as long as exile endured. The suggestion of the generational inheritance of refugeeness was so evident in informants' comments that this question eventually was explicitly pursued. Everyone interviewed on this topic agreed that this was indeed the case. "If I am a refugee here, of course my child is a refugee also—and so is his child, and his child, until we go back to our native country." Thus, any legal provision granting automatic citizenship to children born to refugee parents in the asylum country would have been irrelevant here.[33] The "well-founded fear of persecution" that legally defines a refugee was passed on socially in Mishamo from parents to children.

PREPARING FOR THE RETURN

Insofar as the culmination of the mythico-history was the return to Burundi, life in exile consisted in marking time. However, marking time was not sufficient; the refugees in exile (it was thought in the camp) had to prepare for the return voyage. In the course of preparing for the return, a vision of the place to be returned to, the "homeland," was longingly elaborated.

As mentioned earlier, it was considered that returning to contemporary Burundi would be tantamount to death because it was still governed by "Herod." (See Panel 47 above.) Contemporary Burundi was not yet equivalent to the "homeland" in the mythico-history, nor was it a "true nation." Rather, it was a "mere state" governed by the Tutsi, those who were originally "the impostors from the north." The "homeland" to be regained was constituted as an "authentic nation," a nation that needed a transformation—or, perhaps, a restoration—to its "original" and "pristine" state. The myths of foundation in the first of the narrative panels gave form to this mythico-historical construct, the "homeland," which was still located in the abstract future (and, also, in the remote past).

In the mythico-history it was the exiled natives, the refugees, who had the kind of knowledge to empower them to achieve the transformation of Burundi into a "true nation." Thus, just as in the myths of foundation the "first birth" of the nation was constituted as the moment when the legendary hunter, Burundi, and his people came to the land of the aboriginal Twa, so the "first birth" of the future "homeland" was seen as the moment of the Hutu refugees' return to a new Burundi. The only question was whether the return would be, as the popular expression went, "by peace or by the sword" (par la paix ou par l'épée). Thus, whereas the town refugees talked in more abstract terms about "a change of regime" and always situated the impetus for change in the hands of those Hutu people actually living in Burundi, in Mishamo the force of change was epicentered in exile. In sum, exile was an era of political empowerment.

DISPLACEMENT AS PURITY

In the camp, the resistance to putting down roots was central to the affirmation of a collective identity based on the past and on the lost homeland. The apparent limbo of refugeeness allowed the Hutu refugees to maintain their distance from the two hierarchies into which they might most easily have been incorporated, those of Tanzania and Burundi. The separation made possible an antagonistic equality between Hutu and "other" and closed off any possibility of a reinstatement of hierarchical "symbiosis." At the same time, being a refugee signaled a tie with the homeland and, hence, the possibility of an eventual return. Finally, being a refugee meant being categorically pure, not blurring boundaries. Curiously, the very status "refugee," which ordinarily acts to make people interstitial or liminal—and hence polluting (Douglas 1966, Turner 1967, Malkki 1992a)—in the national order of things, had here been transformed through a curious social alchemy into a state of purity. While they were by definition, as refugees, boundary crossers (and thus problematized by other actors like the international organizations and the Government of Tanzania), this particular crossing was actually the beginning of a categorical purification in the refugees' own eyes. This link between categorical purity and refugeeness was being produced in a sociohistorical context ideally suited to its production, the refugee camp. And Mishamo, among all three of the Hutu refugee camps in Tanzania, had become the privileged locus of this categorical purity. The purity of refugeeness was an unintended and yet seminal product of this technology of "care and control" in the forest.

# CONSCIOUSNESS AND LIMINALITY IN THE COSMOLOGICAL ORDER OF NATIONS

The core chapters of this study have been animated by the challenge of describing and accounting for the striking historicity of thought and social action among the Hutu refugees in Mishamo camp—and for the equally evident desire of the town refugees on Lake Tanganyika to escape the monumental patterns of history in which a categorical identity such as "the Hutu" seemed enmeshed. The concern throughout has been to explore the lived, experiential circumstances which had made it possible for historical and historicizing forms of consciousness to become dominant in the everyday social action of some and not others. In this sense, the project is an ethnographic exploration of two quite specific local contexts, and of how these helped to give form to a historical-national consciousness, on the one hand, and a challenging cosmopolitanism, on the other.

The study of this historicity in the process of transformation—and of the disparity between camp and town—has made it possible to see that more was at issue in these everyday processes than historicization. For here constructing history also entailed the innovation and transformation of categorical social orders—specifically, the order of national categories. This final chapter traces some of the central effects of the linkage between historicity and nationness, with a view to revealing something of the *kind* of power that animates the national order of things and to suggesting why national thinking should be explored, not just as a more or less autonomous political ideology, but as one among several powerful, familiar categorical forms of thought and practice. The nature of these interlinked forms is complicated by their being always local and at the same time transnationally meaningful, and always both cultural and political. For the nation form (Balibar, in Balibar and Wallerstein 1991: 86ff.) is also a cultural form—a cultural form that in this era presents itself as both necessary and uniquely natural.

CONDITIONS FOR THE TRANSFORMATION OF HISTORICAL CONSCIOUSNESS

The comparison between camp and town constitutes a study of two dramatically different conditions for social production and invention. The camp has turned out to be a fertile ground for producing historicity and categorical nationness. The township, on the other hand, is a place that has inhibited the production of historicity and nationness and has instead given form to what may be called cosmopolitanism.

In the cosmopolitan scheme of things, the insistence on a historically rooted categorical purity was experienced as a disabling variety of parochialism that would hinder social mobility, and falsely, unnecessarily fix people in social locations not of their own making. This is not to say that the town refugees had no awareness of their history, or that they had no relationship with it. Rather, it can be suggested that the town refugees, while being knowledgeable about the past, had with history a relationship consisting largely of denial.[1] That is, insofar as history was relevant in the town refugees' lives, it often presented a problem that had to be erased or subdued. This can perhaps be rephrased as a desire not to allow history (or refugeeness) to define the present. In being relegated to the realm of "the past"—that which has long since passed—history was rendered more neutral and hence docile. In the camp, on the other hand, the cosmopolitanism of the town refugees signified a different set of problems and dangers: the betrayal and abandonment of categorical loyalties; the hiding of true identity; the dangerous neglect of the history that brought the Hutu into exile; and the putting down of roots in "alien soil." All these "quisling evils" amounted to a loss of purity.

Thus, history represented an entirely different creature in the two settings of camp and town. In the one, it was seen as a source of power, knowledge, and purity; in the other, its meaning and effects were negatively conceived as cumbersome and threatening, or even as irrelevant. To borrow Nietzsche's terms in a somewhat unorthodox manner (Nietzsche [1873–76] 1983:67ff.), the species of history in Mishamo was at once monumental and critical, a transformative ordering device of epic scale; while in Kigoma, history was more often placed in an antiquarian realm for the use of specialists and parochialists, or glossed as a personal past (a life history).

Both the Hutu in the camp and those in town had lived through the genocidal months of 1972 and, it may be presumed, had been a part of the broader historical processes and political relations that culminated in the massacre. Both groups shared the fact of exile. Yet, only in the camp had a mythico-history come to be created. Given the very different relationships to, and social uses of, history that the two groups of people had developed, it would not be satisfactory to locate the "source" or "origin" of the mythico-history or of the historical consciousness it expressed in the "past": both camp refugees and town refugees experienced the events that displaced them, but they lived their consequences very differently. The massacre of 1972 and the processes that led up to it can be assumed to be implicated in the deep historicity observed in Mishamo but cannot alone account for it.

The comparison of Mishamo and Kigoma forcefully suggests that, in order to explain this historicity, it is necessary to look deeply into the more contemporary circumstances of life in exile, and especially into the peculiar circumstances imposed by the institution of the refugee camp itself. What is at issue, then, is not so much a "history of the present" (Foucault) as an account of the presentness of history. This was attempted in a limited manner in chapter 3 for Mishamo and in chapter 4 for Kigoma. While the circumstances of life in Kigoma promoted individual strategies and the dissolution or manipulation of collective identities, it was suggested that a number of the constitutive features of the camp had the effect of historicizing and collectivizing the lives of its inhabitants.

First, by grouping the Hutu together into an immense collectivity, and by enclosing them all together in a place set apart and marked especially for them (a place which systematically excluded others), the camp fixed and objectified them as "*the* Hutu" and as "*the* refugees." Life in town, on the other hand, was marked by continued interspersing of people and negotiation of relationships and did not provide the possibility of such an efficacious, homogenizing objectification. Indeed, it actively denied it.

Second, the direct relations of control that existed between the camp administrators and the administered had further objectifying effects. All the techniques of control—the control and monitoring of mobility with Leave Passes, the issuing of refugee identification cards, the tours by District officials, the reports and project evaluations, the visits from international funding agencies and "experts"—all these practices of authority had the effect of helping to constitute and produce the Hutu as refugees and, hence, as a categorical object of interventions. The camp, then, produced "refugees" in a way that the township never seemed to do. Indeed, as was noted earlier, many informants—whether in the town, in the camp, or in the organizations administering them—said that the "true" or "real" refugees were to be found in the camps, not in town.

The camp did more than pick out the refugees as a collective object, however. As was suggested in chapters 3 and 5, the very objectification of the camp's inhabitants as "the Hutu refugees" conspired to help transform them into a collective subject. The refugees as a collectivity had become an essential part of the mythico-historical trajectory of the Hutu. Refugeeness was a further transformation of Hutuness, and one that was crucial in the longer march toward regaining the homeland lost to malignness. If correctly and virtuously lived, refugeeness promised to combat and undo illegitimate Tutsi domination. "The people" in exile became the subject of their own history. Even the objectification of themselves as refugees was encompassed in the mythico-history. Informants in the camp often pointed out proudly that it was because of them that the camp was established. The camp, then, ended up verifying that its inhabitants were not just a chance assortment of individuals but a well-defined, recognized collectivity worthy of the power that was continually exercised over them.

The camp was a locus of hierarchical, asymmetrical power in which the overwhelming numerical majority of inhabitants, the refugees, were subject to the authority of the small minority of the Tanzanian administrators. This minority controlled important aspects of the refugees' economic and social lives and was experienced as exploitative and illegitimate. With or without the mythico-history, the camp was an antagonistic social setting. The refugees were in a situation where collective resistance to the Tanzanian minority category was called for; it was this situation that made of the camp a fertile ground for the elaboration and production of the mythico-history. Given this situation, the hierarchy of the camp set up a multitude of analogies with the asymmetry of Burundi society as the refugees had known it. These analogies continually reaffirmed the themes of domination and slavery, parasitism and malignness, ruse and secrecy. The Tanzanian minority thus easily, almost perforce, came to occupy the categorical position of the Tutsi in the mythico-history. They became the "tutsianized" other that was to be mistrusted. The need to resist "the Tanzanians" is one central dimension that made the mythico-history so useful and necessary in the pragmatics of everyday life in the camp. The mythico-history required the struggle with "the Tanzanians," but also, crucially, the struggle with "the Tanzanians" required the mythico-history. This was visible in the numerous contestations between the refugees and their administrators regarding the place of history in camp life.

Indeed, the camp administrators' relationship to, or perceptions of, the historicity of the refugees was itself a productive axis in the reinforcement of historical consciousness and categorical solidarity. Unlike the town refugees, the camp administrators did not see the historicity of their wards as a docile, nostalgic form of living in the past. The refugees' historicity (sometimes dubbed an "obsession") was accorded much more power and danger. Mentioning the past implied consideration of a historical trajectory, and of a possible return to Burundi. The administrators therefore apprehended this history (correctly) as a code for political organizing, and unrelenting historicity as a sign of what might happen in the future. Not surprisingly, then, the camp administrators actively discouraged talk of Burundi and the past and exhorted the refugees to cultivate and "live peacefully" instead. (See Panel 30, The District Commissioner's Tour). Given the refugees' profound mistrust of the administrators as "tutsianized" antagonists, it is not paradoxical that the latter's admonition to forget Burundi should have been received as an expression of "malignness." The attempts by the camp administrators to discourage history unwittingly merged with and reinforced already vital mythico-historical themes.

In sum, just as local pragmatics worked against collective identity and nationness in town, conditions had been created in the camp where history became immediately relevant and useful in the present, and where collective identity became a strikingly concrete, palpable frame of reference.

### THE CAMP AS A TECHNOLOGY OF POWER

Power "produces reality; it produces domains of knowledge and rituals of truth" (Foucault 1979:194). The refugee camp as a "technology of power" produced its objects and domains of knowledge on two levels. On the one hand, it helped to constitute "the refugees" as an object of knowledge and control. On the other, the camp served to produce "the refugees" as a categorical historical subject empowered to create a mythico-history of a people. Its local, particular pragmatics conspired to produce—independently of intentions—historical narratives which reordered the lived-in world. Thus, as a technology of power, the camp ended up being much more than a device of containment and enclosure; it grew into a locus of continual creative subversion and transformation.

Just as Foucault has shown for prisons and clinics, the refugee camp as a technology of power was both limiting and productive. Within it, certain kinds of political action were possible, others impossible. Certain kinds of socio-political forms and processes, and certain kinds of objects and subjects, emerged while others did not. Such transformations occur not only in refugee camps and prisons but in a wide range of disciplinary institutions. In *Discipline and Punish* (1979), Foucault wrote, not merely an analysis of the prison, but an exploration of disciplinary techniques of power that may become emplaced in any number of different contexts. Thus, for example, van Onselen's careful study of mine compounds in the former southern Rhodesia could serve as a point of comparison. "For," as van Onselen wrote (1976:151), "the compounds belonged to a distinctive set of institutions which have been described as having an 'encompassing or total character'—like prisons or mental hospitals—and within them black men were the objects of a process of 'perpetual colonisation.'" Here van Onselen is citing Goffman's work on "total institutions" (Goffman 1961a,b), which also makes an illuminating comparison with refugee camps.

The field of comparison might be extended to yet another technology of power, the old-age "home." These, too, are technologies having many systematic effects. They serve to transform old age into a medicalized and therefore specialized "problem" or object on which documentation accumulates. Old age institutions make it possible for those on the outside to believe that suffering refers to arthritis, incontinence, or loss of memory—and not to any anguished fear of an old person that in the dark quietness of nighttime, death is eating their body faster than it can in daylight. In short, such old-age institutions have the effect of creating conditions for the invisibility of aging and death.

Prisons, old-age institutions, mining compounds, and refugee camps: these are transformative technologies of power in which collectivities of persons become fixed and objectified as "the inmates," "the elderly," "the labor force," and "the refugees." But it is also relevant that such technologies of power can, and often do, become generative, productive sites for social and political invention and transformation—just as the refugee camp has become the privileged locus for the creation of a mythico-history. It is possible to imagine how any one of these technologies could provide conditions for transformations of consciousness. And if this is accepted as a possibility, then this has implications for conceptualizing the production of historical consciousness in the present case.

### THE TRANSFORMATION OF HISTORICAL CONSCIOUSNESS AS A SITUATIONAL PROCESS

Ethnographic exploration of the Hutu refugees' case suggests a number of more general implications for the transformation of historical consciousness. Some of these will now be sketched out. Most obviously, historical consciousness is not a capability typifying a particular stage of development, nor does it entail a process of unidirectional evolution—neither can the formation of consciousness be represented as a teleological trajectory tending toward a point of perfection or completion. Trying to imagine, hypothetically, either a total absence of consciousness or a state of perfect consciousness reveals the chimeric quality of seeking to pinpoint "stages" of consciousness as a naturalist might pinpoint taxa. To do so would necessitate first typologizing and then hierarchizing all social collectivities into those that "have" consciousness and those that do not "have" it in some evolutionary scheme of unbroken continuity (Foucault 1977:146). Such a continuity, implying a collective *destiny*, is often constructed by historical actors themselves—such as Hutu people in exile—but as Foucault shows, it is not the proper task of the anthropologist or historian to "pretend to go back in time to restore an unbroken continuity that operates beyond the dispersion of forgotten things" (Foucault 1977:146).

Foucault's words evoke one of the most well-known debates in anthropology on the issue of historicity and historical consciousness: that between Lévi-Strauss (1966:245–69; 1976:323–62) and Sartre (1960; 1963). There are a number of points in Lévi-Strauss's essay "History and Dialectic" (1966:245–69) which are of relevance here.

First, Lévi-Strauss traces, through his discussion of the operation of chronologies and totalizations, the analytical frailty of teleological historical continuity, and concludes that "alleged historical continuity is secured only by dint of fraudulent outlines" (1966:261). Such continuities become symbolically and politically especially meaningful, if not crucial, when the history in question is a "national past." Such pasts are constructed as collective trajectories of "a people" and as such, necessitate continuity.[2] (Cf. Spencer 1990.)

The second relevant point is Lévi-Strauss's attack on Sartre's distinction between "historical humanity" and "original humanity" (1966:248). Examining the link between historical consciousness and humanness (or subjectivity) in Sartre's thought allows Lévi-Strauss to illuminate the mysticism of Sartre's vision of history. He goes on to point out that "aspects of the savage mind can be discovered in Sartre's philosophy," and that it is therefore first-rate as an ethnographic document (1966:249n.). For in Sartre's thought, history, truth, consciousness, and struggle form a single, continuous trajectory or figure. As will be presently suggested, this is not unlike the constellations to be found in the mythico-history.

In the same essay to and against Sartre, Lévi-Strauss makes yet a third related point, namely, the impossibility of a single, "objective," "totalized history." Taking as a case in point the French Revolution, he argues that the Jacobin and the aristocrat necessarily lived and constructed different versions of its events. "When one proposes to write a history of the French Revolution one knows (or ought to know) that it cannot, simultaneously and under the same heading, be that of the Jacobin and that of the aristocrat. *Ex hypothesi,* their respective totalizations (each of which is antisymmetric to the other) are equally true" (1966:258).

Lévi-Strauss is correct at one level—when decoupling truth and history in Sartre's terms—in saying that "historical facts are no more *given* than any other. It is the historian, or the agent of history, who constitutes them by abstraction and as though under the threat of an infinite regress. [. . .] [F]or a truly total history would confront them with chaos" (1966:257). Thus: "History is therefore never history, but history-for" (1966:257).

However, saying in absolute terms that "truth is a matter of context" (Lévi-Strauss 1966:254) presents problems. My gestures here to Lévi-Strauss's relativistic demystification of historical "truth," like the references elsewhere to Goodman's concept of "world-making" (1978), are not intended to suggest that history is nothing more than a matter of competing versions. It is not the case that all versions of history should be accorded equal validity, or that a retreat into thoroughgoing relativism is politically or morally defensible. If all versions were equally true, it would be possible to insist that the Holocaust never happened in Europe, that Hiroshima was a dream, that forced relocations never occurred in South Africa, or that the categorical massacres of Hutu in Burundi in 1972 were in fact massacres of Tutsi. There are "wrong" versions of historical events in this sense.

Yet it remains the case that the study of "objective history" as the reconstruction of a universal and unsituated historical truth needs to be challenged. And clearly this has been done in much insightful work by scholars like Hobsbawm and Ranger (1983), Wright (1985), Foucault (1972a,b, 1977, 1980), Appadurai (1981), and others. The literature on the anthropological uses of "oral traditions" has likewise had to address the question of versions (Vansina 1985; Schoffeleers 1988: 487–8; Cohen 1989). Haraway's discussion of "situated knowledges" (1991) is a powerful way of reconciling the idea of situatedness with objectivity.

The conceptualization of the production of historical consciousness as a transcendent "rising to" (or "attaining of") consciousness is open, not only to theoretical objections such as those made by Lévi-Strauss, but to empirical objections as well. In the simplest terms, actors do not discover orders of the world that existed before they made them. As many recent studies (Anderson [1983] 1991, Hobsbawm and Ranger 1983, Mitchell 1988, among others) have shown, consciousness is not a "thing" existing absolutely, independent of social action and invention or of the contingencies of the lived. The notions of "rising to" and "discovering" historical consciousness ignore the created or invented character of such consciousness by implying a purposive struggle toward illumination or enlightenment and precluding all that is accidental or unforeseen. This is another dimension of the continuity problem discussed above, which easily becomes an issue of national pedigree.

A strong parallel to this heroizing conception can once again be found in the Hutu mythico-historical discourse. In the mythico-history, the attainment of "benign knowledge" and the explosion or discovery of "the secrets" of "the other" can perhaps be interpreted as a commentary on historical consciousness. The Hutu mythico-history heroizes the formation of consciousness in this way, as a struggle for, and a rising to, consciousness. The question of consciousness is posed as one of discovering, or *seeing*, by those who are in the process of transforming, subverting, and creating politico-moral orders. It is an activity of discovery and, as such, a process of empowerment. The process of discovering and of unearthing the hidden, the secret, is a fundamentally transformative act. It is heroizing because it implies the necessity of a struggle to explode the hidden, and because it also necessitates a heroic protagonist in a way that acquiring knowledge of something that was simply unknown does not. The secret is hidden by someone, and therefore has to be unearthed by a subject empowered to do so.

If teleological and evolutionary theories of historical consciousness are themselves mythico-historical, then how are we to understand moments of intense historicity like that of the camp refugees? Lévi-Strauss shows that conceptualizations of history like that of Sartre are mythical, but he does not spell out how it is that such mythical, order-making histories come about. The case explored here suggests that historical consciousness is lodged within precarious, sometimes accidental processes that are situated and implicated in the lived events and local processes of the everyday. Underscoring the conjunctural and the contingent in the production of historical consciousness is not intended to imply that the forms of such a consciousness are thoroughly haphazard or lacking in structure. This will become evident momentarily. The purpose is, rather, to challenge "the existence of immobile forms that precede the external world of accident and succession" (Foucault 1977: 142). It is to challenge also the turning of randomness into inevitable continuity, and of "chance into destiny" (Anderson 1983:19). Thus, the intent in this book has been to make an ethnographic exploration of the observable ways in which historical consciousness is embedded in and emerges from particular, local, lived circumstances—in this case, the camp and the nexuses of relations centering around it. There is no single origin that can be privileged as the point of "birth" for this historical consciousness but rather, an irreducible multiplicity of circumstances and complex relationships—many of which converge in one way or another around the camp.

One of the central conclusions to be drawn from this case, then, is that nationness and historicity are produced and elaborated as a result of exigencies of everyday practice. In other words, collective histories flourish where they have a meaningful, signifying use in the present, as they did in Mishamo. In contrast to the evolutionary view of historical consciousness as a capability typifying a particular stage of development, it is being argued here that actors produce historical consciousness where they need it "for the sake of life and action" (Nietzsche [1873–76] 1983:59).

The Hutu case also suggests another conclusion, which has already been implied. Instead of looking at historical consciousness as a *thing* already formed, it may be more profitable or true to life to focus on the *processes* of its formation and transformation. Indeed, the Hutu case underscores the fact that here, historicity does not culminate in any closure which might permit it to be examined as a finite, bounded entity or structure. Rather, it is an ongoing process of which some episodes have been presented here, through the eyes of the observer. This historicity is cumulative, dynamic, and capable of continual transformation, not a static structure fixed outside of time and place.[3] The spider's web—the analogy used earlier to describe how everyday events become transformed and standardized into mythico-historical events[4]—could also serve here to describe historical consciousness itself, insofar as it entails a process of dynamic transformation, an active seizing of events, processes, and relations in order to ingest and subvert them and, finally, to build something new.

HISTORICAL-NATIONAL CONSCIOUSNESS

The exploration of the contemporary, ongoing processes converging to create the Hutu mythico-history has also produced another outcome of some interest. It has provided an unusual opportunity to study the interrelationships between historical and national consciousness. This relationship was asserted in chapter 1 and threaded throughout the core chapters of this study. It is now possible to offer some more synthetic observations about it and to suggest how this particular case may help to recast classical questions in the scholarly literature concerned with nationalism and historical consciousness. Living historically, as the Mishamo refugees did, seemed to imply the creation of nationness, and conversely, the formation of the construct "nation" was necessarily historical.

The mythico-history was characterized as a form of collective discursive practice concerned with the history of the Hutu as "a people." It is therefore necessarily the history of a *collectivity*. The Hutu refugees constitute the principal subject, the categorical protagonist, the "people." It was argued earlier that this construction of a shared, collective past (operating simultaneously as a charter and as a "destiny") was essentially also the creation of a *national past*. Thus, the mythico-history heroized and revalued the categorical protagonist (by separating any "other" from its collective trajectory) and constructed what may be described as an imagined moral community.[5]

The mythico-historical themes presented in the panels of chapter 2 outline the imagining of the moral community at several different levels. The foundation myths seeking to establish the historical precedence of the Hutu in Burundi use autochthonism to legitimate the status of the Hutu (and the Twa) as the true members of the imagined aboriginal nation. Second, the mythico-historical accounts of how the Tutsi category arrived as "foreigners" and "aliens" from their own home "in the North" and how they "stole" power by nefarious means, establishes the impostor status of the Tutsi, thereby making their membership in the true nation not only illegitimate but unnatural. This theme further consolidates the Hutu claims to nationness as natural and primordial.

A third level in the mythico-historical creation of Hutu nationness occurs in the panels charting the contrasting relationships of Hutu and Tutsi to labor and bodily power. By claiming that the Tutsi category is averse to, and actually incapable of, hard work, and that the Tutsi therefore have to steal the labor of the Hutu cultivators, the mythico-historical narratives are establishing the parasitical status of an elite minority ruling the nation illegitimately. As parasites, the Tutsi are in yet another way categorically unworthy of membership in the moral community.

A fourth level of legitimation/delegitimation revolves around the mythico-historically significant population statistics: 1 percent Twa, 85 percent Hutu, 14 percent Tutsi. Here the charter of nationness is lodged in the power of the sheer numbers of bodies: surely, those who form the massive body of the society should by moral and political right govern themselves and forge their own destiny. Democracy was imagined as an inalienable feature of this moral community.

Finally, we come to a level of legitimation and delegitimation which perhaps more than any other serves to establish the boundaries of the moral community: the genocidal killings of 1972. As was shown in several panels, the mythico-historical reconstruction of the events of that year was very extensive and careful. The body maps of physical "traits" of the warring "peoples," as also the maps for destroying the body, served to negate the very humanity of the Tutsi category. The cataclysm canonized the inhumanity and evil of the "other," thereby fundamentally purging the "other" from the moral community. That the Tutsi category still ruled in Burundi meant in mythico-historical terms that contemporary Burundi was a mere state, a false and corrupt entity, and not a true nation.

Several conclusions can be drawn from this summary of the mythico-history. First, it should be clear why the mythico-history has been characterized here as an ever-changing, dynamic set of ordering stories. The narratives of the camp refugees were centrally concerned with the ordering and reordering of sociopolitical and moral categories; with the construction of a collective self in opposition and enmity against an "other"; and ultimately, with good and evil. Thus, the mythico-historical narratives ingested events, processes, and relationships from the past and from the lived conditions of the present and transformed them within a fundamentally moral scheme of good and evil. These were moral ordering stories on a cosmological level. In the mythico-history, all protagonists are categorical, and they are attributed essential, constitutive characteristics, much as in other classifying schemes. Here, the term *cosmological* is intended to be understood in a classical anthropological sense, much as Tambiah has defined it:

Cosmologies [. . .] are the classifications of the most encompassing scope. They are frameworks of concepts and relations which treat the universe or cosmos as an ordered system, describing it in terms of space, time, matter, motion, and peopling it with gods, humans, animals, spirits, demons, and the like. Cosmogonies consist usually of accounts of the creation and generation of the existing order of phenomena, explaining their character and their place and function in the scheme. [. . .] [A] classification as a system of categories in the first place *describes* the world, and [. . .] this description usually also implies and entails evaluations and *moral premises* and emotional attitudes translated into taboos, preferences, prescriptions, and proscriptions. (Tambiah 1985:3–4; second emphasis added)

Tambiah's formulation is helpful because it underscores the level of totalization and encompassment at which the mythico-history comes to be deployed. That is, assertions of nationness involve claims about the categorical order of the world in a very fundamental sense. Tambiah's distinction between cosmology and cosmogony is also important here because of the echo it finds in the mythico-history. On the one hand, the mythico-history described a contemporary order of things, persons, and relationships; on the other, it also reconstructed in detail how and *why*, through various transformations, the present order emerged.

Such categorical orders as have been described here do not arise out of an antecedent void or formlessness. The making of cosmological, mythico-historical order necessitates the destruction and subversion, encompassment and ingestion, mutation and revaluation of previously existing or antagonistic orders. This is why the mythico-history was described as a spider ingesting those things that happen to be captured in its web. The spider eats and thinks its prey, thereby recreating the ordered web in which it lives. Thus, neither disparate, antagonistic orders nor dissenting "others" are ever passive in this process.[6] Insofar as these orders are spun in an oppositional context, in struggle, making history inevitably implies the unmaking of somebody else's history. Such processes are always agonistic. They are a kind of cosmological praxis, a form of acting upon the fundamental order of the world. The mythico-history represents simultaneously the processual making and unmaking of orders at a moral and cosmological level.

One of the most important aspects of the mythico-historical ordering stories is that they powerfully articulate the close interrelationships between the production of historical and national forms of consciousness. The debate about history in Mishamo had high stakes because it was also a contestation about what categories had the right to exist, or what the system of categories should be. The mythico-history centrally concerned the legitimation of the moral right of the Hutu to act in the world as a categorical protagonist. This is why it seems accurate to suggest that historical and national forms of consciousness were mutually structuring to the point of indivisibility in this case. History became a way of defining nationness, and conversely, the nation was necessarily historical. Talking about or acting in terms of one implied the other.

It is clear that the Hutu mythico-history dealt centrally with the moral right of its actors to exist as collectivities, and that it asserted this right in the face of opposition. True, the dominant categorical antagonist, "the Tutsi," was bodily absent in exile and had been replaced by a secondary "other," the Tanzanian category. Yet the mythico-history continued to order itself ultimately in opposition to the dominant "other" in Burundi. And this "other" was not silent. It, too, constructed oppositional orders. The Tutsi-dominated Burundian government of the mid-eighties did not speak directly to the Hutu in exile, but it did have to legitimate its own ordering of the world, both to itself and to the broader, imagined "international community."[7]

The following case in point shows clearly the agonistic character of the mythico-historical order and also the ways in which historical and national-categorical contestations became locked into a single figure. The case focussed on one point of opposition in particular: the reconstruction of the 1972 massacre. The Hutu narratives concerning the massacre were laid out in chapter 2. Therefore, only the version presented by the Tutsi-dominated Burundi government of the 1970's will be discussed here. The story that unfolds, as will become apparent, is much more than a "struggle over versions" of the events of 1972. It is all at once a struggle over historical events and over categories and cosmology.

A little over one month after the beginning of the massacre in Burundi, the Permanent Mission of the Republic of Burundi to the United Nations delivered its account of the events of April and May 1972 in Burundi in a paper entitled *The White Paper on the Real Causes and Consequences of the Attempted Genocide against the Tutsi Ethny in Burundi*. This peculiar document opens with the following words: "Peace has been restored throughout the Republic; the enemy has been impeded from doing further harm. It is therefore possible for us to fulfill a pleasant duty towards our friends, both local and foreign: the duty of truth." The document then proceeds to lay out in detail the events and "causes" of the apocalypse. It is too long to be reproduced in its entirety, but certain sections will be excerpted (verbatim) here when they are particularly relevant in the context of the Hutu mythico-historical themes discussed in this chapter.

Throughout the *White Paper*, explicit reference to "the Hutu" as the culprits is meticulously avoided, and the terms "enemy," "criminals," "evil forces," "rebels," and "gangs" are used instead, with the suggestion that the impetus for the massacre came from *outside* Burundi. The document states: "ABOUT 25,000 PERSONS BOTH LOCAL AND FOREIGN, MAINLY MULELISTS, WERE TRAINED, OUTSIDE BURUNDI, IN THE ART OF USING WEAPONS AND SABOTAGE. THE PARTICIPANTS WERE UNITED BY [OATH] NEVER TO BETRAY ONE ANOTHER, IN ANY CIRCUMSTANCE. CONTACTS WERE MADE WITH OTHER CRIMINALS RESIDING IN BURUNDI" (Government of Burundi 1972:5). The principal actors' identity was in this way first externalized and then criminalized, and Hutu were never presented as the categorical culprit. Indeed, several references to the role of the Hutu in defending the "Fatherland" against "the criminals" appear: "IN ALL THE INVADED REGIONS, CIVIL AUTO-DEFENSE GROUPS COMPOSED OF HUTU AND TUTSI ARE APPOINTED UNDER THE AEGIS OF THE PARTY [. . .] AND THEY SECOND THE DISCIPLINARY FORCES WHO HAVE DISPLAYED THEIR REMARKABLE COURAGE" (Government of Burundi 1972:3).

In oblique reference to the Hutu category once again, the document states: "BUT IT IS COMFORTING TO NOTE THAT MANY WHO DID NOT BELONG TO THE ETHNIC GROUP FACING EXTERMINATION PREFERRED DEATH, RATHER THAN ASSASSINATE THEIR BROTHERS" (Government of Burundi 1972:3). The implication is that those "noncriminal" Hutu persons who did not join the Mulelists were often killed by "the criminals."

These indications of Hutu loyalty to the "Nation" or "Fatherland," as Burundi is called in the White Paper, are consistent with the overall argument of the paper, which emphasizes "national unity" and places citizenship in the nation-state above all other classifications. This is a significant point to note because the nation of the White Paper is not the same as the one constituted and recognized by the Hutu refugees. The following excerpts make this point. In criticizing the response of the international press, the paper states: "This same press, we know for a fact, is in the service of those who cannot bear to see BURUNDI UNITED, STRONG, AND AMONG THE PROGRESSIVE NATIONS OF AFRICA. It is in the service of evil forces who desire to see Africa and Burundi humiliated, divided and on its knees" (Government of Burundi 1972:1). Later in the paper, it is written:

DO NOT FORGET THAT GENOCIDE IS UNKNOWN TO OUR HISTORY AND CULTURE, AND EVEN THE WORD IS INEXISTANT [sic] IN OUR LANGUAGE. HOW CAN IT BE DIFFERENTLY? TRIBALISM WAS UNKNOWN BEFORE THE ARRIVAL OF THE WHITES. BEFORE COLONIALISATION [sic], OUR SOCIETY HAD REACHED A DEGREE OF COHESION AND NATIONAL UNITY THAT MANY EUROPEAN COUNTRIES LACKED. IF YOU HAVE ANY DOUBTS, QUESTION YOUR ETHNOLOGISTS AND HISTORIANS.

In the circumstances, it seems improper to speak of tribes in a nation where, since centuries, all the inhabitants speak the same language and worship the same God (Imana), and are subject to the same laws and authorities. If tribalism is to be mentionned [sic], think of the one you dissipated into our society. You craftily took advantage of the [naivete] or the cupidity of certain *of our citizens. In a few years you destroyed the secular product of our ances-tors. You distinguished between the Burundese citizens libelling [sic] them as Hutu and Tutsi. You did not stop there. You convinced Hutu of the necessity of massacring Tutsi.* (Government of Burundi 1972:9–10)

In glaring contrast to the Hutu mythico-history, where the colo-nialists were seen as protectors of the Hutu "natives" against the Tutsi "impostors," this version asserts an original nationness encompassing both Hutu and Tutsi and charges that an original state of "cohesion" and "national unity" was destroyed by the colonialists who sowed the seeds of tribalism.[8] Thus, in both Hutu and Tutsi versions, the source of evil is located outside the nation—with the significant difference that, for the Hutu, the Tutsi are the outsiders, while for the Tutsi, the colonialists and other, less-defined "evil forces" and "criminals" are the foreign element to blame: "WE REALIZE THAT THIS ENTIRE ROWDY CAMPAIGN IS LED BY FOREIGN ENEMIES, WHO DO NOT WISH TO SHOULDER THIS RESPONSIBILITY. [. . .] IN ORDER THAT THE IMPERIALISTS BEAR THE FOLLOWING IN MIND, WE HEREBY EXPOSTULATE OUR WILL AND DETERMI-NATION TO OVERCOME THE FORCES OF EVIL" (Government of Burundi 1972:7).

In seeking to establish the truth of this version, the paper details accounts of atrocities which are near mirror images of the Hutu ac-counts described in previous chapters:

They are not satisfied only with killing their victims; first they mutilate chil-dren, regardless of age, and in front of their parents slaughter them, then they attack women who are made to undergo undescribable [sic] atrocities; they are [disembowelled] if found pregnant, and finally it is the lot of men and the elderly, who are savagely assassinated. [. . .] IT BECAME APPARENT VERY QUICKLY THAT THESE CRIMINALS MASSACRED IN A DEFINITE PATTERN: [. . .] THESE BRUTES WERE GUIDED BY INDICATIONS TO VICTIMIZE PEOPLE BELONGING TO THE *SAME ETHNIC GROUP* [Tutsi]. (Government of Burundi 1972:3)

The similarity to the Hutu accounts—if the victim-killer relation is reversed—is startling. This reversal is heavily emphasized: "CER-TAINLY A PLAN OF GENOCIDE WAS ESTABLISHED BY CERTAIN TRAITORS OF THE NATION, A GENOCIDE OF TUTSI" (Government of Burundi 1972:7). The paper further cites "evidence" which is said to "MORE THAN PROVE THE FACT THAT THE AGGRESSORS WERE NOT ONLY DESIROUS OF OVER-THROWING THE INSTITUTION OF THE REPUBLIC, BUT HAD A MINUTELY

DRAWN UP PLAN OF SYSTEMATICALLY EXTERMINATING A COMPLETE ETHNY—TUTSI" (Government of Burundi 1972:4).

Finally, the *White Paper* seeks to establish the legitimacy of its own attack upon—or retaliation against—the "rebels" by emphasizing several times that "ONLY THE GUILTY WERE PUNISHED" (Government of Burundi 1972:5, 9–11). Thus: "WE DO NOT SPEAK OF REPRESSION BUT OF LIGITIMATE (sic) DEFENSE BECAUSE OUR COUNTRY WAS AT WAR" (Government of Burundi 1972:10). And further: "OUR COUNTRY, WITH ITS SECULAR AND HUMAN CULTURE, IS AWARE THAT EVERY MAN IS RESPONSIBLE ONLY FOR HIMSELF. ONLY THE GUILTY WERE PUNISHED" (Government of Burundi 1972:5). This last passage seems to attempt to deny that the government retaliated against the Hutu as a category, or that this category as a whole was held responsible. Again, the argument for national unity encompassing both Hutu and Tutsi is implied here by the anonymous label "the guilty." For the same reason, this passage also represents a claim to humanity, or human decency, and argues that it is not inhuman to punish "the guilty." In its conclusion, the *White Paper* once again makes this appeal to humanity, rationality, and legitimacy: "AT ALL EVENTS, THE PUBLIC AUTHORITIES IN BURUNDI AS IN ANY OTHER COUNTRY OF THE WORLD HAVE THE RIGHT AND THE DUTY TO PUNISH THE GUILTY. ADHERENCE TO AN ETHNIC GROUP IS NOT REASON ENOUGH FOR PENAL IMMUNITY ANY MORE THAN IT CONSTITUTES [AN] OFFENCE" (Government of Burundi 1972:11).

Considering all the points made in the *White Paper* together with the key themes of the Hutu mythico-history of the massacre, it becomes evident that in both versions, a common set of issues is at stake. Foremost among these is the composition of the nation, the identity of its true or legitimate members. In the *White Paper* the nation is harnessed to citizenship in a sovereign, territorial nation-state, and no claims are made to legitimacy stemming from autochthonous origins. Ethnic loyalties are denied in favor of citizenship in the state. In the Hutu version, by contrast, the deconstruction and delegitimation of this "inauthentic," "Tutsi" definition of nationness was crucial. Citizenship in the nation-state was denaturalized and made strange by reference instead to the autochthonism or nativeness of the Hutu and the Twa. The latter categories are thus the "natural" members of a primordial nation, while the Tutsi category represents not just a "race of aliens" but one of "impostors." Thus, as was shown in chapter 2, the Hutu refugees' answer to the Tutsi version is encapsulated in this rhetorical question: "The Tutsi do not like to admit that there are three tribes in Burundi, but if that is so, why are we here [in a Tanzanian refugee camp]?"

In seeking to refute the kinds of claims to nationness and "national unity" that were made in the *White Paper*, the Hutu mythico-history would seem to leave itself vulnerable to the charge of tribalism. But it is not entirely accurate to label the mythico-historical process as an expression of a "tribal consciousness" (cf. Leclercq 1973). For from the point of view of the Hutu refugees, at least, what is being asserted is *national*, not tribal, identity. As was argued earlier, "Hutuness" properly refers to a nationness, that is, a historical-national consciousness. Insistence on the existence of three separate, distinct "tribes" or "races" in Burundi challenges the Burundi government's assertion of nontribal national unity.[9] The *White Paper* insists that tribalism was of colonialist manufacture, a malign policy destroying an original unity and harmony. And it is, indeed, quite probable that the ethnic and racial stereotyping of the European colonizers are implicated in contemporary, postcolonial constructions of ethnic difference (Lemarchand 1994).[10] That is neither here nor there, however, as far as the mythico-historical significance of these categories is concerned. For one of the most crucial claims of the mythico-history is that the Tutsi category does not belong to the moral community of the authentic nation. The status of "Hutuness" as a morally legitimate, national category is also asserted in the liberation movement briefly discussed in the last chapter. The very name of the liberation party reflects this: PALIPEHUTU, *Parti pour la libération du peuple Hutu*, "Party for the Liberation of the Hutu People."

For both sides, the Burundi Government's *White Paper* and the Hutu camp refugees' mythico-history, the legitimation of the categorical claims of the actors necessitates laying claim to a history. And this is not just any kind of history. It is a totalizing, collective historical charter which defines its dominant subject, and the "rights" and "destiny" of that subject. Ultimately historicity and nationness become forged into a single figure. It is in this sense, then, that history—through contestation over the proper essence of nationness—is bound up with questions of cosmological order.

The claims to legitimacy embedded in the Hutu mythico-history are expressed in a particular form: that of oral narrative. This narrativity should not be taken for granted. As Comaroff and Comaroff (1987) have shown, where historical consciousness is thought to be absent, it may simply be finding expression in nonnarrative forms. Where legitimation *does* take narrative form, the role of the imagined *audience* would appear to be crucial. Specifically, insofar as claims to legitimacy imply an "outside world" as an audience, or as a consuming public, they almost necessarily demand a narrative form.

In the mythico-history, a prominent place was accorded to a generalized, agentive figure of "international opinion" as a final arbitrator in the Hutu struggle over truth and history (Malkki 1992b, 1994). It could be said that "international opinion" itself had the status of a categorical actor within the mythico-history. Among the refugees in Mishamo, there was generally an abiding faith in the awareness and concern of "international opinion" regarding the condition and problems of the Hutu people. There was a conviction that the "Hutu plight" was on the world map, like the South African struggle. This was often discussed. Many times people in Mishamo asked what people in America and Europe thought of the Hutu problem, and the answer (that the majority does not even know of the existence of people called Hutu or of Burundi) met with surprised disbelief and consternation. It was said that surely the Hutu case merits attention equal to that of the South African case because the Hutu case is "even worse." To paraphrase a frequent argument made by Hutu refugees: in South Africa it is the white who dominates and kills the black, but in Burundi it is black killing black—and further, in South Africa, at least, it is known what is happening because the government publishes what it has done. If only four or five South African blacks are killed, this is reported in the newspapers, while in Burundi, hundreds and even thousands die without so much as a mention in the papers.

The concern with the "outside world" and "international opinion" was also reflected in the fact that a remarkable number of the Hutu refugees in Mishamo were engaged in writing down histories and chronicles. There was a proliferation of written documentation of the 1972 massacre, the history of Burundi and its ethnic relations in general, and, also, conditions in the refugee camp. The authors of such written histories were concerned that they reach "international opinion," and several ways of attempting to launch these histories into the "outside world" had been devised. One such means was to collect addresses of international organizations and to write to these, as was described in chapter 3.

In this context of supralocal legitimation, it was not sufficient to produce oral narratives. It was necessary to transform narrative legitimation into written, documentary form. Written texts were thought to have greater power to circulate and to be accepted as true. Thus, one might say (with Appadurai 1986) that written documents were thought to be capable of "a social life" of their own in a supralocal, international arena where oral forms were not similarly empowered.

REFUGEES IN THE ORDER OF NATION-STATES

Looking for a moment longer at the implications of the Hutu mythico-historical construction of "international opinion" or "the international community" is worthwhile for what it reveals about the status ascribed to national, categorical protagonists. The mythico-history did not imply a supranational or a cosmopolitan world but rather (and precisely) an *inter-national* one. This is a vision of a community of distinct "nations" entering into relationships with one another. That the mythico-history is not commensurate with cosmopolitanism becomes patently clear in the position of the Kigoma town refugees in it. The quisling evils attributed to the town refugees center upon beliefs about the latter's disregard for Hutu nationness and its categorical purity.

The mythico-historical constitution of what may be called an imagined international community is not dissimilar to many scholarly and theoretical conceptions of the international. A striking parallel can be drawn from Mauss. Having defined "the nation" in deeply moral, categorical, and indeed, mythico-historical terms ([1920?] 1969:627, 629), Mauss goes on to distinguish internationalism and cosmopolitanism as follows:

[T]he current language is misleading. It confuses, in effect, two quite distinct types of *moral attitude.* We propose to reserve the term, cosmopolitanism, for the first attitude. This is a current of thought and of actions as well that actually lead to the destruction of nations, and to the creation of a morality where nations would no longer be sovereign authorities, the source of laws and supreme goals worthy of sacrifice to a higher cause, that of humanity [. . .]. [Such ideas] are but the end result of pure individualism, whether religious and Christian, or metaphysical. This politics of "Man-Citizen-of-the-World" is but the consequence of an ethereal theory of man as monad, everywhere the same, agent of a morality that transcends the realities of everyday life; a morality conceiving of no other country [*patrie*] than humanity, no other laws than the natural ones. [. . .] An internationalism worthy of the name is the opposite of cosmopolitanism. It does not deny the nation. It situates it. Inter-nation is the opposite of a-nation. Consequently, it is also the opposite of nationalism, which isolates the nation. *Internationalism* is, if we may be granted this definition, the set of ideas, beliefs [*sentiments*], and rules, and collective organizations whose goals are to formulate and manage the relations among nations and among societies in general. (Mauss [1920?] 1969:629–30)[11]

Both for Mauss and for the Hutu mythico-history, cosmopolitanism represents an absence of order and of categorical loyalties and rules. The stakes in the mythico-history concern the right of the Hutu to be (or become) a collective actor, a historical subject, in the domain of interrelationships among nations. At issue is not the denial or denaturalization of the order of nations but the attainment of a legitimate place in that order, a seat at the table.

It is ironic that the refugees who were spatially isolated and insulated because of their categorical liminality and danger in the national order of things (Malkki 1992a) should have set about so single-mindedly to reconstruct another nationness. In this light, it was perhaps Kigoma that was the more profoundly subversive site of historical transformation because it was there that national categories were continually being dissolved and subverted. The town refugees challenged the order of nations, de facto, by approaching it (or appropriating it) as a strategic game, sometimes cynically, sometimes playfully. National categories in the township were most meaningful, not for their essential content, but for their changeable, contextual social meanings and effects in the mundane pragmatics of identity.

The contemporary, categorical order of nations, I would suggest, always presents the two distinct possibilities, tending in opposite directions, which Mishamo and Kigoma exemplified. The first possibility is that a liminal collectivity tries to make itself fit into the overarching national order of things, to become a nation like others. This was the case in the camp. The second possibility entails an insistence on, and a creative exploitation of, another order of liminality. To take this path, as most town refugees seemed to have done, was to try to elude national categorization altogether. This had the effect of destabilizing nationality as a moral and essential trait. In the camp, liminality was understood to be like a rite of passage: a temporary state preparing the way for membership in a recognized and honored category ("true nationhood"). In town, liminality was not so orderly; it was the "noise" in the system, the cosmopolitan disorder that awaited no necessary resolution into national order.

This study seeks to illuminate, not only the forms of Hutu consciousness in exile, but also the hegemonic order of nations within which the refugees operated. As suggested in the introduction, displacement, exile, and refugeeness can provide new dimensions to the study of the global order of nations and the nation form on two levels. First, they can show how nationness—and historical-national consciousness—may come to be formed in the absence of a state apparatus or a territorial base—or, indeed, other characteristics usually taken to be necessary properties of nations. Second, the interventions and correctives that almost necessarily come to bear on refugees and other displaced collectivities illuminate exactly how it is that national and international orders constitute totalizing, categorical orders entailing mythico-historical ordering processes, and how they operate to normalize and domesticate liminality. The question of liminality here problematizes the contemporary order of nations, thereby forcing us to confront our own uses of the nation as an analytical concept and as a unit of study (cf. van Binsbergen 1981). Just as we now assert critical distance to Durkheimian ideas of social cohesion and organismic functionalism, so should we assert the same toward nations as self-evident units of cohesion within a global, totalizing organic solidarity. In the case of the Hutu in exile, Anderson's way of conceptualizing nationness goes much farther toward helping one to understand the different processes that have been explored here:

Part of the difficulty is that one tends unconsciously to hypostatize the existence of Nationalism-with-a-big-N—rather as one might Age-with-a-capital-A—and then to classify "it" as *an* ideology. [. . .] It would, I think, make things easier if one treated it as if it belonged with "kinship" and "religion," rather than with "liberalism" and "fascism".

In an anthropological spirit, then, I propose the following definition of the nation: it is an imagined political community [. . .]. Communities are to be distinguished, not by their falsity/genuineness, but by the style in which they are imagined. (Anderson 1983:15)

Following Anderson's characterization of the nation as an imagined political community, this study has sought to show how, in a particular case, the nation becomes first of all an imagined *moral* community—and how, ultimately, such an imagination elaborates itself into a *cosmology* of nations.

Denying nations their objective "entitivity,"[12] their status as a natural order, and their evolutionary or teleological trajectories, and proposing instead that they can be seen as mythico-historical is not a way of writing them out of existence or reality. On the contrary, it is to emphasize that they are social inventions capable of very real and formidable sociopolitical consequences.

CONCLUSION: "THE TYGER"

Tyger Tyger, burning bright,
In the forests of the night;
What immortal hand or eye,
Could frame thy fearful symmetry?

In what distant deeps or skies,
Burnt the fire of thine eyes?
On what wings dare he aspire?
What the hand, dare sieze the fire?

And what shoulder, & what art,
Could twist the sinews of thy heart?
And when thy heart began to beat,
What dread hand? & what dread feet?

What the hammer? what the chain,
In what furnace was thy brain?
What the anvil? what dread grasp,
Dare its deadly terrors clasp!

When the stars threw down their spears
And water'd heaven with their tears:
Did he smile his work to see?
Did he who made the Lamb make thee?

Tyger Tyger burning bright,
In the forests of the night:
What immortal hand or eye,
Dare frame thy fearful symmetry?

**—William Blake**

The nation as a social construct, and often, as an analytic concept, has embedded within it a host of other concepts which it is necessary to pull to the foreground. These include race, type, and culture. In a study of a different kind it would be possible to give fuller discussion to such interconnections, but here only a few of them can be suggested.

The conflation of the concepts of race, type, culture, and nation does not detract from their power; quite the contrary. The imprecise, shifting meaning of each term can also empower it to operate in a wide array of contexts, for any number of purposes, and with an infinite variation of effects.[13]

Perhaps one of the most central operations implied in all of these terms is that of *typologizing* collectivities of various kinds into national *categories*. One of the most frequent modes of typologizing is achieved through constructing a "history-of" and a "culture-of" for each collectivity.[14] These constructions also, crucially, serve to distinguish various collectivities according to their degree of nationness—or the degree to which the collectivities approximate an ideal. Elsewhere (Malkki 1989), I have suggested how the construction of such typologies and their arrangement according to a variety of criteria in smaller and larger (and higher and lower) concentric circles in relation to an epicenter of "real" nationness necessarily entails hierarchization. Typologizing is never the mere marking of difference among social collectivities. It evokes scales and standards erected out of the bulwark of "Western civilization," scales which are visible in so many aspects of "inter-national relations," from commerce to scholarship.

Having explored the implications of constructing national typologies, Handler suggests that imagined national communities represent themselves to themselves as "types" and as "species" and that the concept of "race" often comes to be tied in with these (1988:40,43–5; cf. also Balibar, in Balibar and Wallerstein, 1991). Thus, "the species metaphor implies a set of attributes similar to those suggested by the collective individual. The collectivity envisioned as a species or as an individual organism has fixed boundaries, describable qualities, and an environment and history which have made it what it is" (Handler 1988:45).

Such species and type metaphors commonly structure relationships and hierarchies among nations. The boundaries of a species in biological terms are defined by the capacity to produce fertile offspring. Insofar as nations are conceived like species and taxa, the "mixing of categories" can become a bad combination, an unproductive union. This was clearly visible in the Hutu mythico-historical narratives concerning intermarriage and other relationships with "others." Thus, species, type, race, and nation can all be seen in this context as *forms of categorical thought which center upon the purity of the categories in question.* They, all of them, tend to construct and essentialize difference. But more, such categorical types also operate to naturalize and legitimate inequality. In the most extreme case, the construction of one category may imply the denaturalization and even dehumanization of another.[15]

This is not to imply that racism derives directly or simply from national typologies, or from nationalisms. As Anderson has suggested (in reference to the work of Tom Nairn), "Nairn is basically mistaken in arguing that racism and anti-semitism derive from nationalism—and thus that 'seen in sufficient historical depth, facism [sic] tells us more about nationalism than any other episode.' A word like 'slant', for example, abbreviated from 'slant-eyed', does not simply express an ordinary political enmity. It *erases nation-ness* by reducing the adversary to his biological physiognomy" (Anderson 1983:135). (Cf. Nairn 1977: 337,347).

The linkage between humanness and nationness is a central one (see Arendt 1973 [1951]:294,300; Balibar 1990; Mazzini 1891 [1849]; Joseph 1929). But Anderson's conclusion from this becomes less certain in light of the present case. He writes: "The fact of the matter is that nationalism thinks in terms of historical destinies, while racism dreams of eternal contaminations, transmitted from the origins of time through an endless sequence of loathsome copulations: outside history. [. . .] The dreams of racism actually have their origin in ideologies of *class,* rather than in those of nation [. . .]" (Anderson 1983:136).

Insofar as being a nation is equivalent to being a historical subject with a "national past," denying the nationness of an "other" is denying its subjectivity, even its humanness. When the construction of nationness happens in an essentially oppositional, antagonistic context, as in the Hutu mythico-history, it very readily involves the destruction of opposing orders and the annulment of the "other." The case of the mythico-histories involved here suggests that those processes we call nationalism and racism are parallel constructions capable of interpermutations. Both are forms of categorical, mythico-historical thought. In some sense, class, too, is such a form, as Anderson implies in evoking the symbolic color spectrum of aristocratic blood and the complex business of breeding aristocracy (1983:136).[16] Mythico-categorical thought almost necessarily involves categorical purity and omnipresent "dreams of contamination," just as it may involve visions of "historical destiny."[17]

A genocidal massacre is one of the most extreme ways in which humanness and subjectivity can be denied to a social collectivity. But the possibility of such denial is there in all national thinking. The mythico-historical body maps charted in chapter 2 can perhaps be read in two directions. On the one hand, they describe and reflect the annulment of the Hutu category; but on the other, they end up canonizing the inhumanity of the Tutsi category. The annulment of an "other" is the flip side of nationness, the "fearful symmetry" inherent in the nationalist beast.

Like Blake's tyger, categorical and mythico-historical thought commands a terrible beauty. It is at once compelling and frightening. Its aesthetic and emotional attraction sometimes blinds us to its danger. But seeing it as only dangerous or only terrifying does not help to explain where its great power is generated.

The purpose here is not to pass judgment on the tyger but to look at it with denaturalizing eyes and to ask Blake's question: "In what furnace was thy brain?" How does it happen that such a form of thought has come to dictate its awesome powers so hegemonically? And why does it hold such beauty for so many people when the sinister side of its symmetry has time and again seized visibility? For Blake, the furnace was God. Here, one might say, the furnace had become a convergence of processes: a massacre, a long exile, and a camp. This particular convergence is, of course, not the only possible site where mythico-historical production can ever occur; but it was, without a doubt, a key site.

# RETURN TO
# GENOCIDE

Since the first draft of this book was completed in early 1989, historical and political transformations of profound importance have taken place in central and eastern Africa. The people who live in this region, as citizens and as refugees, have seen their circumstances change dramatically, often tragically. So rapid and consequential have many of these transformations been that they have, time and again, overtaken any effort to offer an accurate, up-to-date interpretation of them. The text to follow is therefore an account of social conditions and frames of mind that are characterized, first and foremost, by profound uncertainty and flux.

This account will contain only a bare outline of recent political events and transformations of which I, writing from distant California in April of 1994, have no firsthand knowledge. But my aim is less to describe or analyze the flow of events in the region than to consider how these various events have been experienced by the refugees in western Tanzania with whom I worked and lived. There is every reason to believe that their circumstances have been radically altered by political events in Burundi, Tanzania, and Rwanda since the summer of 1993.

It is my hope also to suggest —through describing the particular case of the Hutu refugees from Burundi—how complicated and confusing the question of a return "home" can be for people who, having been victimized by extreme forms of violence, have lived in exile for many years. As Finn Stepputat (1993) has pointed out, there has been a great deal of research on displacement and the pain of "uprooting," but much less on people undergoing repatriation. Perhaps we tend to assume that since the people repatriating are returning to their own, "native" country, they know what to expect and how to manage. They are returning home (cf. Mankekar, forthcoming, pp. 20, 26). And, of course, in returning to their *patrie*, they reenter its domain of national sovereignty, thereby quite automatically disappearing from the domains of international refugee law, international assistance, and scholarly research on "the problem of refugees." But " home" is not necessarily a familiar place, or a safe place, and it is not always wise to assume that those returning after a long absence know what awaits them. And, finally, when the collective return of a very large group of people is in question, it is possible that their very presence in that "homeland" will set in motion processes over which they have little control.

A very brief outline of recent political events (from 1987 to 1994) is given in the following paragraphs. The remainder of this postscript traces some of the consequences of these political upheavals in the Hutu refugees' lives, and explores (as well as the available information allows) their interpretations of them.

The year 1987 saw a successful coup against Burundi's President Jean-Baptiste Bagaza by Major Pierre Buyoya, who suspended the constitution; power was seized by a Committee of National Redemption, according to the *Los Angeles Times*, 4 September 1987, p. 6. Under Buyoya, the country saw the beginnings of a program of liberalization and political transformation. Bagaza's repressive policies toward churches were relaxed or abolished, and freedom of expression was encouraged. In December of 1987, Buyoya's regime also "expressed its willingness to give serious consideration to 'the question of national unity'" (Lemarchand 1994:119). These important shifts in policy raised the "anxieties of Tutsi hard-liners" and "nurtured Hutu hopes for a further acceleration of the move toward liberalization" (Lemarchand 1994:19). The following year, 1988, was marked by countless incidents of violence, political persecution, and protest as political tensions (often in the form of both hope and fear) mounted. These finally culminated in August 1988 in another episode of mass executions, principally carried out by the government security forces, in the northern communes of Ntega and Marangara in Burundi. The army's retribution was once more phrased as a restoration of public order. An estimated 15,000 people died at the hands of the government troops, and tens of thousands fled, this time mostly to Rwanda.[1] This brutal episode apparently catalyzed a significant shift in thinking in Burundi's ruling circles. Increasingly serious attention began to be given by the Buyoya government to questions of national reconciliation. It was also more and more widely recognized that the repatriation of the Hutu refugees would have to be a key element in the long and fragile process of establishing peace and security. In response to this shift in policy, some Hutu refugees from Tanzania did begin to repatriate in small numbers.

In October 1990, a civil war in neighboring Rwanda was touched off by the advance into Rwanda of the FPR (Front Patriotique Rwandais/ Rwandan Patriotic Front [RPF]) from Uganda. The RPF is a mainly Tutsi guerilla force that has been based in exile in Uganda for many years, battling the Hutu-dominated Rwandan government. This battle was closely watched inside Burundi, as well as by refugees from Burundi.

In the summer of 1993, the national reconciliation process in Burundi culminated in the first democratic elections in the history of independent Burundi. The result was an overwhelming and (to the Tutsi-dominated government) evidently surprising victory for Melchior Ndadaye and his opposition FRODEBU party (Front pour la Démocratie au Burundi). At this time, it appears, large numbers of Hutu refugees began to make applications for repatriation from Tanzania or to undertake repatriation unofficially.

Ndadaye was in office for 100 days. On 21 October 1993, President Ndadaye was killed in an attempted coup allegedly orchestrated by high officials of the Burundi army. (Both former Presidents Jean-Baptiste Bagaza and Pierre Buyoya have been suspected of collaborating in this coup attempt.) The assassinations of the president and a large part of his government provoked a spontaneous uprising in Burundi. Many people, presumably mostly Tutsi, died in the course of the uprising until the army once more moved to "restore order." The army, in turn, directed a massive program of killing against people identified as Hutu, on a scale comparable to the repression in 1972. It is estimated that more than one hundred thousand persons died in these mass killings, and that at least 1 million people became refugees in neighboring countries.[2] The coup eventually collapsed, and the democratically elected government was reinstalled, though it was clear to all that the civilian government remained at the mercy of the Tutsi-dominated army. The political situation gradually became quieter in Burundi, but incidents of small-scale fighting and continuing political persecution have been reported.[3] President Ndadaye was succeeded by Cyprien Ntaryamira, also of the FRODEBU party and also belonging to the Hutu category.

On 6 April 1994, the President of Rwanda, Juvénal Habyarimana, and the new President of Burundi, Cyprien Ntaryamira, were killed in a plane crash on their way home from a regional meeting of heads of state, a meeting whose purpose had been to find a way to bring peace to the region, and specifically to Burundi and Rwanda. The crash continues to be widely regarded as an assassination, although there are various accounts of who might have been responsible, and with what motives. In response to the deaths of the presidents, very severe violence erupted in Rwanda. There is a terrible process of mass killing going on now, and a fierce battle between the Rwandan (mostly Hutu) army and the RPF forces that came in from Uganda. This time the majority of the dead have been Tutsi, victims of the Rwandan army (especially of the Presidential Guard), or of gangs of young Hutu men reportedly terrorizing the capital and the countryside.[4] While fighting is heavy in Rwanda, the situation in Burundi has, surprisingly, remained relatively quiet thus far. Some were becoming more hopeful that it would remain so. But on Sunday, 24 April, there was another (unsuccessful) coup attempt in Burundi, suggesting that the situation is far from stable. At this writing we are still in the midst of these unspeakably sad events, and very far from understanding them.

I have been in regular correspondence with twenty-five to thirty people from Mishamo and Kigoma since leaving Tanzania in late 1986. The many letters that people have written—in friendship, as in hopes of informing and witnessing—represent by now a substantial body of documentary accumulation on a number of different topics and themes. In what follows, I have judged it useful to quote extensively from some of these letters so that they might, at least, shed more light on the very fragmentary and generally uninformed news coverage of the region. Sometimes the letters treat matters that never made their way into newspapers, but are, nevertheless, of great collective significance. I have chosen to highlight themes and issues with which many of my correspondents were concerned (rather than quoting passages of a more personal nature, for example), and to order these themes into a roughly chronological sequence. The most recent, and horrible, violence will appear below, in its place in the chronology.

1987: THE REFOULEMENT OF HUTU REFUGEES

The early months of 1987 were an eventful and, by all accounts, alarming period for the Hutu refugees living in western Tanzania, whether in town or in the camps. In April 1987, a roundup operation described by the Government of Tanzania as a systematic effort to expel so-called irregulars, people living and working illegally in western Tanzania,[5] was briefly attempted. This operation (already introduced in chapter 5 above) became a roundup of Hutu refugees who were sent to Burundi against their will.[6] It targeted mainly people who have here been described as "the town refugees."

In all, sixteen letters from camp and town described the refoulement operation (or expulsion) that had been centered largely in and around Kigoma and Kasulu.[7] One person, living near the center of town in Mwanga, sat down to write an account of it on the very day that the operation started there, 3 April 1987:

Now it is 16 hours in Tanzania, it is Friday, the 3rd of April, a good number of Hutu refugees have been loaded into lorries with the destination of their famous country of origin. For you to pose yourself the question, what the Tutsi power in Bujumbura has in store for them. The agents of immigration, of security, and the police, gun in shoulderstrap, enter in each of the homes of the refugees. The latter (refugees) present their identities [identity cards] which sometimes are torn up by certain immigration agents. Very serious, and worse still, they have a list of some people who are sought by the Government of Burundi. Even if you have the necessary papers, you are made to board the special lorries that are there to accomplish this dramatic mission. On the exterior of Kigoma, it is bad. The operation [there] started on the 31st of March where many refugees were directed to the Tanzano-Burundian border during the night. Once arrived in the land of the wolves, they were received by the local authorities, the officers, the army . . . N.B. The men, the women, as well as their children are all affected, that is to say that the operation spares nothing. The Tanzanian government lies [claiming that] that those who were expelled were Burundian migrants[8] who live in Tanzania illegally. But sincerely, this is not true, they are true refugees. [. . .] It is not just that, Liisa, there are also students who came from the collège of Gitega (the second city of the country) who sought refuge in Tanzania and who were taken by the police. On the following day, the immigration agents at the border handed them over to the Burundian authorities.

The same person wrote back on 10 May 1987 in response to further inquiries from me.

For each house [. . .] there were four to five persons. There were in question one agent of the police, one agent of the immigration service, one agent of security, and two militias, guns in the shoulderstraps. One refugee [with whom my correspondent spoke of the matter] testifies what happened to him, and I cite: "They knocked on the door toward six o'clock in the morning; I (the father) and all my family were still asleep. I came out half dressed. They told me to go and get dressed. After, they made us get in a 'LANDROVER' without any form of procedure." This proves that this was no longer the control of identities [identity cards], but, maybe, as one still doubts, there were persons among the refugees who were targeted. And the Government of B. [Burundi] solicited them in exchange for an enormous sum of money which they paid to certain local authorities.

"They obliged us," he [the witness] continues, "to take nothing from the house and to double-lock it. They drove us to a large hall where, in general, movies are shown. There, when we arrived there toward 7:30 [A.M.], there was already a large crowd of other captured." What surprised me mightily, Liisa, is that all the so-called irregulars were refugees who had come from Burundi fifteen years ago [i.e., in 1972]. So, today everyone poses the question of knowing the objective of this operation. At 8 o'clock in the morning, the news were spreading all over, to the effect that all the refugees were to be returned to their country of origin, willingly or by force. Many sought refuge for their belongings among the nationals, and hid themselves a little everywhere.

A further surprising thing, in Kigoma there are also refugees who have come from Zaire. But why did the operation target only the Hutu refugees? [. . .] Outside the town, it was one big terror. They collected all the fishermen who had just [gathered for a meeting that concerned them]. After the assembling, two lorries filled with police arrived, and the latter encircled the refugees. Then the agents of the police gave the order to everyone who knew himself to be a "Murundi" to be so kind as to board the lorries. They were driven to the same destination as the first (to the hall generally known as COMMUNITY CENTER in Mwanga). Why such a decision on the part of the Tanzanian authorities who had reserved such a warm reception for us 15 years ago, certain refugees asked themselves. In the hall where the refugees were concentrated, the immigration agents proceeded to the sorting,[9] as there were doubtful nationals who, they also, had been captured. After the sorting, the nationals were set free, the women of Tanzanian nationality married by refugees, as well as a good number of other refugees who had everything necessary following long negotiations, and after having spilled much money.

After the complete sorting, they were made to board the lorries that were there, specially for the transport. (This was at 16 hours.) Certain parents left their children of a tender age (3 to 6 years). And one asks oneself what will become of these children who have become orphans.

Elsewhere, like at Kasulu and Kibondo (these are districts) the operation was effected in a catastrophic and alarming manner. The people boarded the lorries by force, and those who resisted received blows of the hand or the fist by the police. Worse still, certain houses were burned by the nationals and all their belongings were pillaged by the police in connivance with the authorities. *NB.* In Kasulu and Kibondo, the operation began on the night of 31 March 1987, and the first refugees were handed over to the authorities of Burundi on 1 April 1987. The Burundi radio announced that by 6 April, they had already received 2,700 persons.

Meanwhile, the Burundi daily, *Le Renouveau du Burundi* on 14 April 1987 (p. 3) reported from the other side of the Burundi-Tanzania border:

They disembark every day by the hundreds since 2 April, the date of the arrival of the first contingent of Burundians refouled from Tanzania. [. . .] At Gisuru, *more than half of those who arrived declared themselves Tanzanians.* According to their declarations, almost all the young people were born in Tanzania, while the old persons had arrived [in Tanzania] in different periods, and [in the case of] some of the oldest, around 1940, in search of land and jobs. They had stayed in this country [Tanzania] up until their hosts decided to expulse them for reasons of which, they say, they are completely ignorant.[10]

The sheer number of letters I received about the roundup from the refugees in Tanzania prompted me to make further inquiries with the offices of the international organizations that were involved in refugee administration in the region. One representative (a nonrefugee) wrote this 3 June 1987 account:

According to the government, the objective of the operation was only to get rid of "illegal immigrants," not to touch refugees. Furthermore, it was only directed toward Burundians, not Zaireans. However, as you know well, the situation in the Kigoma region is quite complicated with different nationalities, people with different status, etc. What complicates everything [. . .] is that never a proper registration and issuance of ID-papers took place. [. . .] [The regional authorities] indicated each time that the refugees would not be touched, that a proper screening took place, etc., but in the meantime we received contrary information. Burundi gvt, made démarches as well, indicating that they could not accommodate 45,000 people (the number of TZ. authorities indicated would be expelled). Finally, because of pressure from the Burundi gvt., UNHCR—in DSM and Kigoma/, several Embassies, Tz. authorities suspended the operation on the 7th (April). In these few days appr. 5,000 people were sent across the border, and we had many reports that whole Barundi communities were indiscriminately rounded up, put on lorries and dumped at the border. Many who were informed in time, fled into the bush. Kasulu District, where most refugees [who are not in camps] are staying, was affected most. Kitanga village, the refugee area, was burnt down completely after the people had been taken out (probably by village authorities and mgambo's [*wanamugambo*, paramilitaries]. Other places were looted, refugees/immigrants started to sell their assets at ridiculously low prices. Families were separated, even in Kigoma township refugees with ID-cards were rounded up. Several people from Mishamo, who were in Kigoma were taken as well. In short, panic all over. When I visited Rusaba, all Barundi were already in the Churches for days, praying not to be sent back. So, a very serious situation; a quite unexpected breach of int. law by Tz. on such a scale. [. . .] The number of refugees refouled is difficult to establish, esp. because there was never a proper registration! Fortunately, quite many returned or are returning from Burundi—borders impossible to control. [. . .] Some are sent back by Bur. auth. because people claim to be Tanzanian. How to find out? Others, clever enough, indicated in Bur. that they were indeed illegal immigrants in TZ., and they were sent to their villages of origin [in Burundi]. Of course, after being released, they trickle back into TZ. Of those, who are really wanted by Bur. auth., we don't know their lot, or maybe better, fate. Refugees who returned indicated that they were put with hundreds in [warehouses] and schools, but that the treatment they received was okay. They were interviewed many times. In Makamba, I got information that all people had to stay in a godown [warehouse] till 20th. April. Many were released on that day, but reportedly, some 500–600 who had indicated that they entered TZ. during '72–'74 (the less clever ones) had to stay behind. HCR-Buja. is trying to find out what is going on there. In the meantime, TCRS has distributed emergency stuff in the most affected villages [. . .]. [L]et's hope the best for the people who were refouled and are still in Burundi.[11]

Shortly after the suspension of the roundup operation, then, the expellees began to return to Tanzania in large numbers finding in many cases that their homes had been broken into and pillaged, and sometimes even burned down. I expected that many people might not return to Kigoma under these circumstances. Certainly, my correspondents (none of whom had been expelled on this occasion[12]) agreed that the atmosphere was strained; but it appears that there was practically no resettlement by town refugees in the three already existing Hutu refugee camps in the aftermath of the *refoulement*.[13]

In reviewing the town refugees' accounts of the *refoulement*, I was once again struck by the variety of opinion among them. Some were left deeply embittered by the experience, while others took a more philosophical view. After the situation calmed down in Kigoma and most people had returned from Burundi, there was no further mention of the whole operation in people's letters.

While the short-lived *refoulement* apparently did not materially affect the Hutu refugee camps, the events were closely followed from Mishamo. As was mentioned in chapter 5, many there saw it as retribution for all the worldly, commercial wheeling and dealing in which the "merchant refugees" had been engaging. But there was also another, quite different side to the matter, and other concerns with which the roundup was linked by the camp refugees.

THE "NOCTURNAL VOYAGE"

The short-lived roundup of the refugees and "irregulars" occurred in the same month (April of 1987) as another event that received a great deal of attention in Mishamo: a tour of the camp by the Consul of Burundi to Kigoma. The coincidence in the timing of these events may or may not have been unplanned, but they created among my correspondents the impression—indeed, the certainty—that they were causally interconnected. The refugee residents of Mishamo were apparently informed neither of the Consul's presence nor of his intentions, with the result that the tour was taken as a sign of a conspiracy between the governments of Burundi and Tanzania. People quite reasonably assumed that their futures were somehow at stake in the visit. At least six letters mentioned the Consul's "nocturnal voyage" there. A 20 April 1987 letter from an old farmer in Mishamo exclaimed:

[P]ray for us refugees of Burundian provenance. With a multitude of moneys given by Batutsi as a purchase of our blood!! Do you know? [. . .] [T]he Ambassador [*sic* Consul] of Burundi passed an entire day in a house, the old house of Father Ferao [in Mishamo]. Then during the night, the master of the present place with his visitor began to make nocturnal voyages in all the villages of Mishamo. The sixteen villages were gone through in a single night. After some days, the authority of here began to load the unfortunate Bahutu on to lorries, and drove them to the abattoirs of Burundi. The first tours have arrived there. Our turn remains. Those from Kigoma, Kasulu, Kibondo, and other neighbouring regions, it is there that they started.

This old man's letter refers to the roundup of people from Mishamo. There were no other reports like his, and I am therefore unable to explain it. It appears, however, that the majority of people sent back were from Kigoma and Kasulu. The point I wish to make is simply that the *refoulement* of the town refugees was connected with two different themes by the camp refugees: on the one hand, it was understood as retribution for the illicit activities of the town refugees; but, on the other, it was a frightening sign of a presumed invisible alliance between the Governments of Burundi and Tanzania. One person—an ordinarily mild-mannered, middle-aged man living in Mishamo—clearly saw the second link as vital, and wrote on 12 April 1987: "The situation has been completely violated, and we who are in the camp, we simply await seizure, involuntary repatriation, and an ironic death."

## THE COUP D'ÉTAT IN BURUNDI

On 3 September 1987, a coup d'état ousted President Jean-Baptiste Bagaza from office, and Major Pierre Boyoya, a relative of the former, came to power.[14] On balance, there was remarkably little mention of this political change in the correspondence of the Hutu refugees. One 6 January 1988 letter captures the markedly jaded tone of many letters of the period:

The Colonel Jean-Baptiste Bagaza [has been replaced] by his cousin, the "Tutsi Hima Major Pierre Buyoya," from the southern province of Bururi. Bagaza had succeeded his cousin, the General Michel Micombero; as in the age of monarchy, Burundi is led by the cousins of the Tutsi minority.

As time was to show, it was under Buyoya's regime that the government of Burundi began to take steps toward the end of single-party rule and other forms of democratization.[15]

## THE 1988 MASSACRES IN NTEGA AND MARANGARA COMMUNES, BURUNDI

In August 1988, I began to receive numerous letters from Mishamo and Kigoma explaining that new mass violence was under way in Burundi.[16]

Liisa, in Burundi the Tutsi (minority) have one more time massacred the Hutu (majority) [. . .] resuscitating again all that which had [. . .] ceased to be the primary preoccupation of the Hutu, that is to say, the massacres of 1972. It is sure that your press speaks of it, and if you should come across one or another document or journal that speaks of it, do not hesitate to read it and share it with me. (Kigoma, 15 September 1988)

I think you have listened to the news and in the newspapers what has happened in the north of Burundi, the massacres of the crushed Hutu masses which took place from 14/8/88 above all in the two communes of Ntega in the province of Kirundo and Marangara in the province of Ngozi. The soldiers, the helicopters, attacked the Hutu and more than 100,000 have been killed and more than 65,000 have taken flight toward Rwanda.[17] For precise information, I myself, I went to Rwanda, Kigali, to see the refugees, to ask them good reports. I found that among them 1/4 are not physically complete. [. . .] Liisa, I hope to see you here in Mishamo at the end of this year before returning home [to Burundi]. (Mishamo, 10 October 1988)

One person described the social effects of the massacres, as seen from Kigoma:

we just received more than 200 refugees mixed of secondary school and university students and women who had just lost their husbands, accompanied by their children. [. . .] As for the origin of these troubles, certain refugees mention the lynching on the 4th of August of an old Tutsi soldier who had just killed two Hutu. Others affirm that it is the arrest, on the 13th or the 14th of August, of several Hutu [who were educated[18]] which set in motion the assassination of Tutsi by Hutu who dreaded a new massacre by the army like 1972. [. . .] The report given by the Party for the Liberation of the Hutu People has thus accused the military, "camouflaged as civilians," of having killed with guns, bayonets, and machetes the Hutu who had survived the bombardments of their villages. The Movement for Peace and Democracy in Burundi [Le Mouvement pour la Paix et la Démocratie au Burundi] cites the testimony of refugees telling that the Burundi army utilized armored trains, military lorries, and trains to transport soldiers who fired on the population. (Kigoma, 11 October 1988)

Two letters, both from Kigoma, claimed the use of napalm in the course of the Ntega and Marangara massacres. The pursuit of fleeing civilians by helicopters was also mentioned in several letters. One of them, dated 8 December 1988, says:

[T]he Tutsi have used nuclear arms to kill our brothers in the zone [of] the massacres, and [have burned] the land or the cultivated soil with these nuclear arms, which carry the name of NAPALM. With these nuclear arms they burned everything, the trees of the villages, the fruit trees, the stems [tiges] of the manioc, without forgetting the potato fields. [. . .] We have had many people from there, mixed of pupils, university students, peasant women and the children, all are new refugees. They were taken to the reception center of KIGWA. Up until now, they still have not had any aid, they only suffer from hunger because each refugee receives 40 gm of beans, like that, you see that this little, with 40 gm, man cannot live.

As in the case of the other mass killings that have taken place in Burundi, before and after 1988, the official and scholarly memory of the

Ntega and Marangara massacres has been subject to intense struggle. Different versions of these 1988 killings doubtless still circulate in oral form in Burundi and in the neighboring countries to which its citizens have fled; what is easier to follow is how parallel struggles over truth are being waged in scholarly publications in Europe and North America. On the one hand, there are texts that tend to mirror and support official positions of the government of Burundi,[19] such the short book produced by Jean-Pierre Chrétien, André Guichaoua, and Gabriel LeJeune, *La crise d'août 1988 au Burundi* (1989).

This work has since received devastating critiques of its politics and of its scholarship. Filip Reyntjens (1990), for example, traces troubling tendencies in Jean-Pierre Chrétien's historical accounts of the abortive coup of 1965 and the repression that followed, as well as the 1972 and 1988 mass killings. He sees a tendency for Chrétien and his academic collaborators to fall into using two main explanatory formulas; the older one is: "it is the fault of the coloniser," and the postcolonial one is: "it is the fault of the Hutu" (1990:109). Reyntjens also notes that Chrétien stresses aggression against the Tutsi in 1988 without any real attempt to explain the antecedents of the political violence: "selective arrests," discrimination in schools, "ambiguous declarations by certain officials," "provocations on the part of certain Tutsi, officials and others. . . . All this serves to prop up *the old thesis of a Hutu attack, always coming from abroad,* against which the Tutsi have done nothing but to defend themselves" (Reyntjens 1990:111–12; emphasis added).

The most salient aspect of this particular struggle over history is that it addresses the long-established historical pattern of blaming political opposition inside Burundi on external forces—foreign or criminal invaders from without.[20] This well-worn claim has seen many uses (for example, in the Government of Burundi *White Paper* of 1972); in the present case it is significant because of its potential connections to ongoing movements of refugees in the region. That is, if political challenges or threats are routinely, and officially, constructed as external to Burundi, then the repatriation of Hutu refugees (victims of state violence in Burundi) can reasonably be expected to become a contentious, even explosive, issue.

Certainly, many questions remain concerning the fates of the approximately sixty thousand persons who fled the 1988 killings into Rwanda.[21] It was reported in 1989 that

since Rwanda and Burundi have now agreed on "the swift and efficient repatriation of the refugees" and since Burundi officially assures that there are no more
problems [in Burundi], the [refugee] camps [in Rwanda] are being emptied at
this moment. The step of the human stream plodding back along mud paths
during these hot, humid December days is heavy. The possibilities of the Red
Cross and UNHCR representatives to observe the repatriation on the Rwanda
side appear to stop at the banks of the Akanyaru River. Nobody knows what
awaits the returnees on the Burundi side—or at least nobody wants to talk
about it. The situation is "very sensitive," the representatives of these organizations say. The government of Burundi has promised that not revenge but assistance in rebuilding awaits the returnees, but fear and suspicions have not let
up in the camps. Those who have secretly visited their homes [in Burundi]
speak of destroyed fields and houses, as well as interrogations and arrests that
the returnees have had, as a first order of business, to experience.[22]

THE REPORT OF THE NATIONAL COMMISSION TO STUDY THE QUESTION
OF NATIONAL UNITY IN BURUNDI

The violence of August 1988 in Ntega and Marangara (Amnesty International 1990a:54–6) was followed in October 1988 by President Pierre
Buyoya's appointment of a National Commission to Study the Question of National Unity in Burundi. The report of the Commission, issued in May 1989, proclaims every citizen's right to security, fundamental rights, and equality; it defines national unity as a "union within
the nation, a union of elements which, although different in nature,
merge with each other to live together in a single national entity."[23]
Remarkably, in the report of the National Commission, "no mention
whatsoever is made of ethnic labels" (Lemarchand 1989b:686).

A key aspect of the Commission's work was to address the questions of the existence of hundreds of thousands of Burundians outside the country (Government of Burundi 1990). Indeed, already in July
1988, my correspondents began to write about a call to the refugees to
return home:

Yes, Buyoya invites the refugees to return to Burundi. But [. . .] the refugees
refuse his invitation because they know that Buyoya's motivations are not generous. He wants quite simply to neutralize us. You know that in April 1987,
the Tutsi of Burundi succeeded in getting more than 3,000 Hutu refugees expelled from Tanzania! Certain of these ex-refugees were killed in Burundi. Many
others have returned to Tanzania.[24]

Having inquired about the program of national reconciliation and
the call for the repatriation of the refugees by the Burundi government,

I received a rather incredulous response dated 17 July 1988 from a young man in Mwanga, Kigoma:

According to the question about the invitation to the refugees to return to Burundi, this, I do not know anything about it and, besides, it is something which to me sounds very astonishing; nothing has changed in Burundi after the formation of the government of the Third Republic, and how does it happen that there can be an invitation to refugees very easily like that?

In November of 1988, the same critical distance prevailed in correspondents' letters. The following is from Kigoma:

Most recently a certain number of Hutu have been named to different ministries, of these the Prime Minister [is one], but all this changes nothing of the profound reality because the army remains monoethnic. We hope that with international aid the problem will be resolved soon. According to other sources of information, and especially on the part of the opposition, after the massacres of the month of August, the Tutsi power wants at all costs to show itself gallant[ly] in favor of national reconciliation, but, alas, it (the Tutsi power) is known now by the world.

That the Hutu refugees should have been skeptical of changes of government and of national policy in the absence of any change in the composition of the military forces in Burundi was, of course, very realistic. For, as will become evident shortly, the army has since taken center stage in blocking real political change in Burundi, and in authoring the most recent atrocities committed there.

THE ARREST OF PALIPEHUTU POLITICAL ACTIVISTS IN KATUMBA

In March of 1989, fifteen Hutu refugees from Burundi who had lived in refugee camps in Tanzania for many years were arrested for nonviolent political activities. According to Amnesty International (1990a:233), the arrests took place in Mishamo. But my correspondents indicated that they happened in Katumba, the largest of the three Hutu refugee camps. In letters from Tanzania, people wrote that the political activities had included displaying the flag of the PALIPEHUTU in public. Among those arrested by Tanzanian authorities was Gahutu Rémi, President of PALIPEHUTU (Parti pour la libération du peuple Hutu). Amnesty International reports:

The Tanzanian authorities accused the 15 of political activity which could be detrimental to Tanzania's relations with Burundi. The detainees were released shortly after arrest and ordered to leave the country. When they failed to depart they were rearrested and held in Keko Prison in Dar es Salaam, pending deportation to a third country. (Amnesty International 1990a:233)[25]

A 21 March 1989 letter from a fellow member of the PALIPEHUTU states:

It was the 22-2-89, international day of scouting, 14 leaders of the party [in] Katumba were arrested by the police [who were] accompanied by the [. . .] traitors. From that day up until the present, they remain in prison [. . .]. On 12-3-89 exactly, the police went to Mishamo to arrest Mr. Rémi [taking him] to Mpanda, directly in the dungeon [cachot]. Their intention was to expedite information to the enemies. In 7 days he is still in the shit or the dungeon, swollen [. . .]. He begins to swell, all the parts of his body [. . .] and he eats about 100 grams per day in comparison to the ordinary regime, a thing that even South Africa has never done among the police detainees. In his moment [à son moment], the chief of the province of Rukwa ordered the police to invade his private house and took so many items to expedite them to the authorities of Burundi. To date they have taken three refugee cards, from Belgium, Rwanda, and the United Nations, a pass [laissez-passer] for Zaire, a passport for Rwanda, a certificate of karate, an attestation of the receipt of a passport to go to Belgium in 1961, a card of the PALIPEHUTU party, etc.—

Throughout 1989, I received letters which confirmed that Gahutu Rémi and fourteen others were still in jail. Three different letters stated that the Government of Tanzania was trying to identify another asylum country for Gahutu Rémi. An 18 September 1989 letter said that "the Tanzanian government is negotiating with Belgium so that she would give political asylum to Rémi." Canada was the other country mentioned.

Then, on 23 August 1990, a nonrefugee correspondent wrote:

Liisa, there is a bad news, that Mr. Gahutu Rémi has died—on 17th August 90 in Dar. This is a radio news. As well as there was the problem in Burundi on the 14th August 90 because people from here went there to fight. The situation is very bad here at present. People are very much scared with all these problems. Some of them are inside the custody.[26]

According to Amnesty International, Gahutu Rémi "died as a result of illness possibly exacerbated by harsh prison conditions and poor medical facilities" (Amnesty International 1991:223). A heart attack has also been suspected as the cause of death.[27] The letters from the Hutu refugees in Tanzania were in universal agreement that he had died of unnatural causes; there were frequent mentions of a lethal injection. A 7 November 1990 letter notes: "the H.C.R. of Dar asked the government if it could bring expert doctors from outside the country, the government refused since he was killed by a government doctor." This letter identifies the place of death as Ukonga Prison in Dar-es-Salaam (opposed to Keko Prison, as reported by Amnesty International).

There were reports circulating (as in the above letter) that Hutu refugees had crossed the border into Burundi and attacked a military base. A 7 November 1990 letter from Mishamo offers this account of the alleged attack:

Buyoya has managed to [get] a little group in the refugee camps led by a coward, [name], situated in Katumba. This group appears to be supported by the Tutsi government. This is why, on 13 August [1990] this group sent youths to attack a military camp [located] at 20 kilometers from the border in the south of Burundi. At that point, the government declared that the soldiers of our party had attacked the country.[28]

Three persons mentioned in the letters from Tanzania were identified as traitors and sellouts. One reportedly lived in Katumba, the second in Kigoma, and the third was a former member of the PALIPEH-UTU and a former resident of Mishamo. Their role in the alleged attack on the military camp in Burundi, as well as other crucial details of this period, are unlikely to be definitively confirmed or challenged through other sources.

It is perhaps sufficient to note that 1990—a year that brought Gahutu Rémi's death and the alleged attack on the military camp—was a period that saw many in Mishamo, political activists as well as people who wanted no part of political activism, disheartened and sad:

In brief, Mishamo remains as you saw it and left it, except for the social and cultural (intellectual) life which is, in general, changed. The spirit of hedonism [l'eudomonisme], for the refugees, has been annihilated [anéanti]. The current state of a refugee is considered, in Africa, as an act of wickedness and criminality. (Mishamo, 15 November 1990)

You wish that we are all in good health here. On the contrary, death has exaggerated itself among us, on the question of problems of life. Without a doubt you know well the Tanzanian soil because you have lived in this country. By way of comparison, read one time the Old Testament, the Jews in Babylon. Alas, you have completed your thesis; when will we complete ours? God knows everything. Doubtless we will attain, we also, our desire. You know well that the dog is always loyal to its master. Hope and duties give a big V. (Mishamo, 13 May 1990)

1990: THE CIVIL WAR IN RWANDA

"In October 1990," reported Amnesty International (1993:1), "rebels belonging to the *Front patriotique rwandais* (FPR), Rwandese Patriotic Front (RPF), attacked Rwanda from neighboring Uganda. Most FPR fighters are Tutsi. Following the attack, some 7,000 people were arrested, most of them Tutsi; virtually all were subjected to severe beatings and some were killed or died before most were released uncharged six months later. Since the rebel attack, about 2,000 people, most of them Tutsi regarded as possible supporters of the FPR, and Hutu members of opposition parties, have been killed by Hutu gangs and members of the security forces. The authorities have so far not brought anyone responsible for the killings to justice. Fighting has been continuing in some parts of northern Rwanda, and cease fires have regularly broken down."

The RPF forces are reported to have been well supplied with arms. The government of Rwanda apparently suffered no lack of them, either. Rwanda's defense minister has been quoted as saying: "I think in this type of market everybody wants to get in" (Smyth 1994:585). Recognizing how very profitable arms dealing had become, the minister noted that suppliers were less interested in the outcome of the war than in the money that they made.

The fighting that was to last from 1990 to 1993 saw thousands (combatants and civilians) die, and 1 million people were displaced from their homes (Smyth 1994:585).

There was little evidence of this Rwanda conflict in the letters of the refugees in Tanzania. One of the few that arrived gave a brief descriptive account without much commentary.

[I]n Rwanda there is a tribal war [. . .]. Since 1 October 1990 the refugees who lived in Uganda, they attacked Rwanda coming from Uganda. They were well trained and well prepared, equipped with portable arms and heavy arms with a rocket launcher [*lance roquette*]; like this, in the first three days, [the government] almost lost their country *sans procès*. Luckily, the assailants killed each other because of political perturbation. Like this the Rwandan military got the chance to make them leave from the captured region. For the moment, there are [battles] but not that much. (Kigoma, 28 April 1991)

One might have expected that the invasion of Rwanda by its Tutsi refugees would inspire comparisons and contrasts to the situation of the Hutu refugees from Burundi, but such connections were pursued neither in people's letters nor during fieldwork in either Mishamo or Kigoma. And yet there are at least formal parallels: a Hutu-led revolution overthrew the Tutsi monarchical system in Rwanda in 1961. Violence surrounding the revolution resulted in the deaths of some twenty thousand people of Tutsi background. The UNHCR estimated in 1964 that one hundred and fifty thousand people (Rwandan Tutsi) had become refugees in Burundi, Tanzania, Zaire, and Uganda (Smyth 1994: 585). A quarter of a century later, descendants of these earlier refugees appear to make up a sizable part of the RPF.

### 1991: CALLS FOR REPATRIATION

In 1991, the first of a markedly large cluster of letters about repatriation to Burundi began to arrive from Tanzania.[29] By this time refugee repatriation had been a prominent part of the program of national reconciliation in Burundi for a few years.[30] In a telephone interview with me in June of 1991, Charles Neary, Desk Officer for Burundi at the United States Department of State, gave a synopsis of developments in the region. He said that the repatriation has been initiated at the instigation of Burundi. "Burundi is publicizing [this as a] durable solution to the refugee problem, and is seeking assistance from UNHCR." The number of people repatriated at the time of this conversation was four to five thousand. This was, Neary continued, part of the policy of national reconciliation. It was recognized that national reconciliation would not be complete without the resolution of the refugee problem. "The Rwanda conflict that started Oct.1.90 is cited as a lesson" in Burundi, noted Neary."Thirty years of refusal by the Rwandans to accept their Tutsi refugees back" was seen as the cause of the conflict presently going on there.[31]

A 7 November 1991 letter from Mishamo stated: "[T]his repatriation sung by the two governments that it is voluntary, this is not true. It was an accord of two countries," an accord, said the letter, about which there was already a prior understanding between the two governments. This was evident because "during the accord, there was not a single delegation of the concerned [. . .] on the ground." That is, as I understand it, this person considered that the refugees themselves had not been adequately consulted.

On 27 August 1991, a tripartite agreement concerning the repatriation of refugees to Burundi was signed by the Tanzanian Minister for Home Affairs, Hon. Augustine Mrema; the Minister of the Interior and of the Development of Local Collectives, Mr. Libère Bararunyeretse; and the UNHCR Representative in Tanzania, William Young. This accord followed the 23 January 1991 nomination, in Burundi, of the fifteen-member National Commission Charged with the Return, the Reception, and the Reinsertion of the Burundian Refugees (*Commission Nationale Chargée du Retour, de l'Acceuil et de la Réinsertion des Réfugiés Burundais*).

NOVEMBER 1991 KILLINGS IN BURUNDI

On 23 November 1991, an armed conflict was reported to have taken place between members of the PALIPEHUTU (*Parti pour la libération du peuple Hutu*) and the Burundi military forces. Other sources state that a series of executions of members of the PALIPEHUTU was at issue (Communauté des Réfugiés Burundais de Dakar 1991). Lemarchand has suggested that this violence should be seen in the larger political context of the fragile political reforms pursued by the Government of Burundi in this period: "[E]very effort was made by Buyoya to insulate the transition process from the incitements and pressures of ethnic extremists, Hutu and Tutsi, and this even at the cost of a bloody repression—as happened in 1991 when the provincial cadres of the Palipehutu were either killed or driven into exile (Lemarchand, n.d. [c]).

While a number of letters from the refugees in Tanzania mentioned the repatriation program and the 1991 violence in brief, only one letter—written on 9 December 1991 by a university student who used to live in Kigoma—discussed them at length.

REPATRIATION OR NATURALIZATION?: AN "ULTIMATUM"

In the course of 1992, people increasingly wrote about the prospect of repatriation in their letters. They explained that the Government of Tanzania had given all Hutu refugees residing in the country a period of three months in which to make known their wishes regarding their future.[32] The choice was phrased in the letters as repatriation to Burundi or naturalization in Tanzania. The third choice that the letters of the previous year had mentioned—to remain refugees in Tanzania indefinitely—seems not to have been offered by the government.[33] Yet, that is the choice to which most people had apparently clung up to this point in 1992.

The refugees' letters, as well as the few other available sources on the "ultimatum," give evidence that this period was one of flux and confusion, as well as wide variance of opinion. While everyone considered the prospect of a return to Burundi with caution, and while misgivings were many, some people had evidently decided that the proper time to return had come, and that it was necessary to try to look at things in a hopeful light. Others, like the man who wrote the following from Kigoma on 24 April 1992, were quite pessimistic and mistrustful:

Now one lives in a climate of generalized fear because the Minister of the Interior of Tanzania obliges us to choose between two things, both presenting serious inconveniences. *Primo* (1), repatriate oneself voluntarily, *secondo* (2) naturalize oneself voluntarily. Return to the native country, but up until now there are ethnic battles. One asks oneself why the asylum country forces us to return or to repatriate without having studied the problem that is going on in the country?

On 26 May 1992, the same person wrote another letter about the repatriation/naturalization choice:

At the level of humanitarian principles, the repatriation or the naturalization of the refugees are ideal measures for putting an end to the state of refugees. But for our case, the people are being forced to repatriate at a moment when the country is experiencing a [renewal] of repression (massive arrests, execution); massacres (November–December 1991), and a wave of exiles. In November–December 1991, 45,000 Hutu sought refuge in Zaire and ten thousand in Rwanda. Even today, they continue to come one by one. How do you expect to put at ease these refugees if they are called upon to return to the country? Those who repatriated themselves in 1989 have been pursued; those of Tanzania, what security are they being offered?

While some took a very cautious view of repatriation, then, it was clear that others thought about the prospect of returning to Burundi with hope and anticipation. One pastor from Mishamo wrote on 27 April 1992:

Do not count that [this tardy reply to your letter] is negligence or a diminution of sympathy, but it is caused by many preoccupations. Succinctly, all the Burundi refugees living in Tanzania have received the order of the Ministry of the Interior to make a decision during three months, to regain their country or else to ask to be naturalized a Tanzanian, otherwise to leave Tanzania without another process. Currently, the enrollment has already been put into motion and will finish up next June. It seems therefore that 90% of the people of Mishamo will prefer to regain their native country, included in that myself and my family. As soon as the registration has been completed, we will stay quite simply in anticipation of the displacement toward our native country. But this task will take a long period to be accomplished. Please pray for us so that God may reinstall peace in this blood-covered country and that we might be able to insert ourselves there with tranquility, without hindrance.

On 20 July of the same year, the pastor wrote another letter about going home. In the meantime, he had received my letter filled with queries, and with the observation that many people seemed worried about the return (and I was not an exception). He replied:

Do not be in bewilderment about our repatriation. Our repatriation will take place in accordance with international regulations. It is not a personal or national pact, but a bilateral accord between Tanzania and Burundi done with the [. . .] assistance of the competent representatives of the UN. During the past year, two times a Burundian and a Tanzanian delegation came to give us information on the basis of the politics of the current government of Burundi (Unity, peace, and justice.) In the beginning of June 1992, a delegation of refugees living in Tanzania went to Burundi to discern or examine from the point of view of politics, peace, security, and justice as this [is practiced] on a simple citizen, the reception of the repatriated [. . .]. [The delegation] spent days in traversing, here and there, all of Burundi. [. . .] If the atmosphere continues to be good [. . .], that peace, security, justice, and national unity reign currently in Burundi, I can move in September 1993. I still have enough time to live in Tanzania. Every day, ceaselessly, the returnees are displacing themselves toward Burundi. But the repatriation of [many] refugees will depend on the result of multipartyism in Burundi as in Tanzania. In case of repatriation, we will keep you *au courant*, and we will try to communicate to you every eventuality. I will leave you in peace now wishing you happiness and good health [. . .].

This letter is remarkable in many ways—first, perhaps, because it is a document to hopefulness and to a willingness to believe that radical historical transformations for the better are to be expected. It is also striking because, after decades of witnessing total breakdowns of ordinary civil life, extreme violence, and fear, this person had confidence that his family's repatriation would take place properly, "in accordance with international regulations."

At about this time, *Le Renouveau du Burundi* ran a front-page story on the repatriation process and on the official delegation of refugees and Burundian and Tanzanian officials who had come to explore the prospects for repatriation: "The Burundi politics of the voluntary repatriation of refugees bears more and more fruit. The repatriated do not cease coming, and national and international opinion are visibly interested in this question" (Ndikunkiko 1992:1). The journalist who wrote this story accompanied the refugee delegation's exploratory tour of the country and gave the following (to me) dreamlike account of it:

Our brothers [confrères] are astonished by everything. By the tarred roads, by the splendor of Bujumbura as by the other agglomerations on the interior that we traversed, by the reforestation on all the crests, by the cultivation on the side of the road, etc. . . . It is 10:30, we arrive at Kirundo, the Governor of the Province greets us, and briefly retraces the Burundi politics concerning the repatriation of refugees [. . .]. He declared himself very happy to receive our compatriots in this province: "We heard that there exist Barundi in Tanzania, but we did not know how they live and what they think of us. Be welcome, you are at home. (Ndikunkiko 1992:21)

The refugees who had been in the delegation that traveled in Burundi on 1–8 June 1992 were notably concerned with the unresolved question of the restoration of the land and property that had been lost in 1972. They observed that those repatriated by 1992 had not, in general, "recovered their property or their belongings," and that security "remained precarious" because the military were accused of intimidating the returnees (Government of Burundi 1992a:13).[34]

Meanwhile, the month of February 1993 found the pastor (quoted above) still in Mishamo, but in continued preparations for his family's return to Burundi. His letter, excerpted below, was (quite untypically)[35] dictated to an English speaker:

I suppose that you think that we have voluntarily regained [repatriated]. I should like to make you sure that we are yet here and we have not made our arrangements, but we have taken a decision to repatriate. We thought that we should repatriate next month of September 1993 [. . .]. We have decided voluntarily. In Mishamo settlement, four thousands six hundreds and twenty one humen [people] have decided to take voluntary repatriation this year; three thousands and sixteen humen have decided to be naturalized and twenty eight thousands seven hundreds and twenty humen decided to continue temporary as refugees. But they wait the result of multi-parties of Burundi which the election will be next [. . .] June 1993. It remembers [should be remembered] that some people were repatriated in 1990. We supplicate to pray for us in order [that] our repatriation will make the most of sth [sic], amenity, success and good process with good protection. We hope that our regain will procure us a great joy, a prosperity and an all importance or development needed for the life, not defame our honour or our life. (Mishamo, 15 February 1993)

The pastor's estimate of the proportions of people who had decided to repatriate, become naturalized, and remain refugees corresponded with another similar estimate I received from Mishamo. In the early part of 1993, many still appeared to be undecided in Mishamo. I received no reports of this from Kigoma.

A 27 November 1992 letter from a local observer of these processes said:

[T]he repatriation of Bur. refugees continues apace—most from Kigoma will return (2–3000 so far) & many from Katumba hop on a train & go back. Mishamo, not so many due to logistical problems—transporting possessions to Kigoma, etc. All in all, a logistical nightmare as returnees have accumulated possessions and want to bring all with them, so [therefore] only ± 20 per truck is possible.

On the Burundi side of the border, the National Commission charged with managing the return of the refugees reported, for its part, that between 1990 and 1992, more than twenty thousand Burundians had already repatriated (but it did not specify whether these returnees were coming from Tanzania, Rwanda, or Zaire) (Government of Burundi 1992b:5).

THE ELECTION OF PRESIDENT MELCHIOR NDADAYE

On 1 June 1993, to the surprise and (apparently) even shock of many, the first popular elections in the history of independent Burundi brought Melchior Ndadaye to office as the first Hutu President of the country. He received 65 percent of the popular vote, while the incumbent President, Pierre Buyoya, received only 33 percent. One foreign election monitor told a reporter: "The government is in a state of total shock. The Tutsis are very upset. They just did not expect this to happen.[36] On 29 June 1993, FRODEBU (Front pour la démocratie au Burundi), Ndadaye's party, won sixty-five of eighty-one seats in the National Assembly. This raised fears in the ranks of UPRONA (Union pour le progrès national), the party of all the previous Presidents of Burundi, the party that had been in power for thirty years. Lemarchand describes the aftermath of the elections thus:

What happened next brought into sharp focus the fears raised in the minds of Tutsi extremists by the victory of the opposition: no sooner were the results of the presidential poll officially known than thousands of Tutsi students and hardcore Upronistes took to the streets to protest against what some referred to as an "ethnic census"; then, on July 2, some 40 Tutsi troops of the Second Command Battalion led by a handful of officers—including Lt. Sylvestre Ningaba, Buyoya's directeur de cabinet—tried unsuccessfully to seize power by force. Undaunted, Ndadaye went ahead with the formation of a government consisting of seven Tutsi and fifteen Hutu, with the Prime Ministership going to a woman of Tutsi origins (Sylvie Kinigi). On July 10 the Frodebu leader was formally invested President of the Republic in a ceremony attended by the Presidents of Tanzania, Rwanda, and Zaire; in a gesture of conciliation that raised not a few eyebrows and gave an unexpected emotional touch to the proceedings, he and the outgoing President embraced each other in a mutual accolade. On this auspicious note ended a transition that began four and half years earlier, thus bringing to a close nearly three decades of Tutsi hegemony. (Lemarchand, n.d. [c])

Lemarchand's interpretations and readings of recent political processes in Burundi are a particularly valuable source of information because of his long study not only of Burundi but of the wider region. In what follows, I therefore rely heavily on his insight.

Writing in the aftermath of the elections, Lemarchand outlined areas of danger and uncertainty in Burundi's political life that might prove to be the undoing of the new political order ushered in by the popular vote. He turned first to Tutsi "extremists," noting that their

position is remarkably straightforward: to speak of a successful democratic transition to describe the 1993 elections is to confuse ethnic census and democratic consensus; the victory of the Frodebu is not a democratic victory but a Hutu victory; what is now emerging is the institutionalization of the tyranny of an ethnic majority, in short a Jacobine state under Hutu control. (Lemarchand, n.d.[c])

This assessment by the "extremists" fails, as Lemarchand notes, to reflect Ndadaye's platform of multiparty democracy and constitutionalism, and the consistent absence in his speeches of themes of "ethnic exclusivism" (Lemarchand n.d.[c]:2–3). Ndadaye also questioned the charge that it was simply "an ethnic vote" that put him in office. "If that was the case," he said, "I should have got 85 percent of the votes" (Hélène 1993:13).

So, while the "extremist" vision did not reflect the actual power-sharing arrangement that was worked out by Buyoya and the new government, it constituted "a fairly accurate yardstick of the perceptions of the 'activist' fringe among the Tutsi intellectuals and army men, those very same elements that took to the streets to protest against Ndadaye's victory" (Lemarchand, n.d.[c]:2–3).

Lemarchand identifies three other areas of danger to the new democracy, giving an outline of possibilities and fault lines that, sadly, has proven to be all too clearsighted:

1. access to land and the redistribution of resources and employment opportunities, and the relationship between these and the return of Burundi's tens of thousands of refugees;

2. plans to restructure key aspects of the military and its involvement in civilian public affairs;

3. the mutual reflections between political conflict and ethnic tension in Rwanda and Burundi.

Regarding the first point, Lemarchand writes: "Access to land remains a critical issue in many rural areas; competition for jobs in the urban sectors is fierce, and is likely to take on increasingly ethnic overtones; the exigencies of structural adjustment, meanwhile, can only benefit the well-to-do at the expense of the poor, with the Tutsi maintaining themselves as a dominant force in the private sector."[37]

The new President had also promised to initiate changes in the role and composition of the military, and here was another fault line, as Lemarchand observes:

When one considers the extent to which in the past the army has been involved in civilian politics, this reduction of military prerogatives may prove far more difficult to implement than some had anticipated. All the more so if one takes into account projected shifts in recruitment patterns. How the officer corps, an all-Tutsi preserve, may react to a major influx of Hutu recruits is anybody's guess. (Lemarchand, n.d.[c]:8)

As was mentioned earlier, as part of the policy of national reconciliation, a formal call had been issued to refugees from Burundi to repatriate, and following the election of a Hutu President, thousands of refugees apparently did, at last, start returning. This brought out in sharp relief an issue that had long been implicit, namely "the compensation of the returnees for the losses they suffered in the wake of the 1972 killings. Since most of the landed property passed into Tutsi hands, the resulting litigations are bound to create enormous social tension—and endless recriminations" (Lemarchand, n.d.[c]:8).

POSTELECTION REPATRIATION

In the summer of 1993, the unexpected outcome of Burundi's first democratic elections encouraged—according to representatives of international agencies in Tanzania and Hutu exiles in North America—much greater numbers of refugees to cross into Burundi. The repatriation was not a haphazard process; it was coordinated by the Government of Tanzania, the UNHCR, and TCRS. But there have also been reports of some people undertaking to return to Burundi on their own.[38]

It has been impossible to obtain official figures on the postelection repatriation process thus far. The rate of repatriation from Kigoma and environs was not known, according to the UNCHR, because the refugees were not registered and were thus difficult to monitor.[39] But a UNHCR official in Tanzania recently said that no figures for the numbers repatriated from Mishamo are available, either.[40] While the UNHCR has declined to estimate the numbers of returnees, there have been tentative estimates from other sources.

A relief worker from another organization reported that more than one hundred thousand people from the Hutu refugee camps applied for repatriation after the presidential elections in Burundi.[41] His unofficial estimate of the rate of repatriation was four hundred persons per week at the peak of the movement in that direction. Most of the repatriating refugees appear to have left from Ulyankulu and Katumba camps, with Mishamo's population being slower to take this step.[42] It is possible that continued transportation and other logistical problems contributed to the slow pace of the process in Mishamo in specific, since it is not near railway lines.

According to one UNHCR representative in Tanzania, land in Burundi had been the main problem in repatriation. It was, he said, "not easy to reallocate land anew, or to give people back the land they had lost in 1972."[43] Especially the people who had left Tanzania on their own, circumventing the organized repatriation procedures, had in many cases simply made their way back to the homes they left twenty-two years before, and asked that the current occupants leave. The Burundi government ministry in charge of overseeing the repatriation had to set up an arbitration program to deal with all the conflicts over land and homesteads.[44]

But there were other considerations, as well. In an interview with a man who was a Hutu refugee of 1972, the *Tanzanian Daily News* (November 1993) wrote:

[D]uring and after the run-up for the July elections, Tanzania's Prime Minister and First Vice President, Ndugu John Malecela and the Minister for Home Affairs and Deputy Prime Minister, Ndugu Augustine Mrema, had called on the Burundi refugees to return home now that things appeared to have normalised. "However, many of us refused on the ground that the political situation in that country was not as normal as the picture one saw from outside. We knew that something wrong was going to happen," says Jean. Mr. Jean says some members of the late Ndadaye's opposition party, FRODEBU, did come to Tanzania and urged them to go back home and help them (the party) in the electoral process. "We told them that we did not think all was well in that country." (Tagalile 1993:11)

It was in the spring of 1993 that I received the last letters I was to read from my correspondents in Tanzania. As of this writing (late April 1994), I have not had any word from any person living there as a refugee. It is reasonable to suppose that many of them went back to Burundi, although an unknown number may have remained in Mishamo and Kigoma.

## THE OCTOBER 1993 MASS KILLINGS IN BURUNDI
President Melchior Ndadaye was in office for approximately three months. On 21 October 1993, he was murdered in a military coup attempt orchestrated by high officials of the Burundi army (allegedly in collaboration with former President Bagaza and according to some, also with the knowledge or collaboration of former President Buyoya).[45] The coup ultimately failed to displace the new government, although many members of President Ndadaye's government were also killed by members of the military. When news of the assassination became public, people took to violence, apparently in grief and rage.[46] Members of the civilian Hutu population caught and killed people whom they knew or believed to be Tutsi. How many Tutsi lost their lives at the hands of the angry crowds in these days is not now known. The army quickly moved in to "restore order," just as it has done in the past. Systematic killing ensued, with the victims now overwhelmingly Hutu and the killers—military men—mostly Tutsi. But civilians reportedly also participated in the killing, on both sides.

Owing in part to the fact that there was remarkably little news coverage of the coup or its aftermath, it has proved difficult to provide information on the casualties. One widespread estimate of the deathtoll is one hundred thousand.[47] Another, much higher estimate of half a million was circulating after the heaviest killing among the international organizations in Dar-es-Salaam, but this figure has not been found in print.[48] Most of the dead were people who belonged to the Hutu category, but there was also an untold number of deaths in the Tutsi category.[49]

It is not only the astonishing scale of the 1993 massacres that resembles those of 1972; accounts and rumors of almost unthinkable atrocity have reappeared once more (Lorch 1993:3). Refugees from Burundi were quoted as saying that "Tutsi soldiers killed Hutu students and teachers at the school and patients in the hospital, including children in the nursery" (Stearns 1993:2). In connection with the Kirundo massacre of December 1993, *The Economist* (8 January 1994, p. 43) reported that "the bodies of mothers with dead children strapped to their backs, and toddlers slashed in half, still litter the fields." The same report (p. 43) also gives an odd and eerie account that is reminiscent of the techniques of killing that were so prominent in the mythico-history of the 1972 massacres: "A secret document, prepared by Tutsi extremists and circulated on both sides of the border, lays out '17 ways to treat a Hutu.' It includes advice to Tutsis to carry a bamboo stick to identify them as such, and a warning that a child born to a Tutsi mother and Hutu father should be killed by its mother and her neighbors." The historical memory and renarration of similar atrocities was, of course, very important in Mishamo. Whether these acts were being committed once again because they were part of a ghoulish repertory of violence that was already widely known, or for some other reason, must remain an important but unanswered question here.

AUTUMN 1993: REFUGEES, AGAIN

The killings that began in October 1993 produced hundreds of thousands of refugees. These new refugees outside of Burundi's borders are nearly all Hutu. As of January 1994, there were also reportedly 150,000 refugees within Burundi (Hélène 1994:13); it is reasonable to assume that these latter are predominantly Tutsi, as the army is reportedly giving them protection in "internal refugee camps."[50] At least 800,000 and, by other estimates, even one million people are now new refugees outside of Burundi's borders; half of them are in Rwanda and the rest are in Tanzania and, in smaller numbers, in Zaire.[51] The United Nations High Commissioner for Refugees (UNHCR) has set up camps for them, but these are extremely crowded. Dysentery, measles, malaria, and malnutrition plague them, and 8 to 9 out of every 1,000 persons were still dying each week in January of 1994.[52] Numerous international relief and refugee agencies, in addition to UNHCR, are presently working to help: Tanganyika Christian Refugee Service (TCRS); International Rescue Committtee; Médecins Sans Frontières (Doctors Without Borders); World Food Programme (WFP); Concern (an Irish organization); Oxfam; Tanzania Red Cross; Caritas (the Catholic relief organization); and local missions.[53] A representative of one of these organizations who had been involved in the relief efforts commented: "I have to say I have a very high opinion of the Tanzanian Government, HCR and the local population in the border area, especially the local population. [Without their help], there would have been mass starvation."

In the past months, there has been a great deal of movement across the Tanzania-Burundi border, in both directions. According to the UNHCR, the peak of the refugee influx was around Christmastime, 1993; at that time the UNHCR worked with an estimate of 245,000 refugees. In the same period, the Government of Tanzania was reporting in excess of 500,000 new refugees.[54] (Another estimate of the Hutu refugees in Tanzania was 250,000 (MacBride 1994:1). Clearly, there is wide variation in these figures.

Indeed, all of these numbers can be expected to remain in continual motion for the foreseeable future because there is so much movement in response to new political developments. The schedule of cultivation in Burundi has also affected these processes. Thus, in early January 1994, 10,000 Hutu refugees had decided to return to Burundi (many of them to care for their land); three weeks later, they were coming back into Tanzania.[55] The UNCHR in Dar-es-Salaam estimated the total refugee population to have dwindled down to 40,000 persons by February 1994; the rest, it was thought, had gone back to Burundi.[56] According to one relief worker, there were two distinct waves of early refugees:

[T]he army generals [in southeastern Burundi] refused to give out guns to their troops when the rioting began. So, people who lived just across the border in southeastern Burundi fled in anticipation of the violence, and did not actually witness a lot of the killing. This was the first wave of refugees. The second wave was from central Burundi, and there people saw actual killings. The army went for doctors, lawyers, teachers, students.[57]

The relief worker described at length social features of the groups of refugees to whom his organization had been attending. There had been one group of 180 secondary-school girls who had fled together.

Soldiers had locked them in a school and set it on fire. The girls escaped and ran about forty to sixty miles until they reached the Tanzanian border. The relief worker also observed:

There are [also] 600 secondary school children right now in Kigoma in TCRS godowns [warehouses]. They don't know what has happened to their families, whether they're still alive. [We are having] a big problem of tracing family and relatives. [. . .] There are no old people; [perhaps they] could not run fast enough. [. . .] Two weeks after the coup, lots of people started to go gack to harvest crops in Burundi—beans especially, it was time to harvest. A lot of them didn't come back.

There have apparently been few serious problems with disruption of civil order or violence among the refugees. But, as the relief worker quoted above explained,

one of the biggest problems right now is to separate the mixed marriages from the other ones. [They are] not tolerated by either side. [The "mixed" families/couples] are being protected by the H.C.R. and the local authorities, [and] housed in other institutional buildings separately from the rest of the refugees who are not in mixed marriages.

A UNHCR official also noted that the refugees' average family size had been unexpected.[58] The size was three, whereas five to six was considered more normal. The largest portion of the refugees consisted of women and children. Unaccompanied children and orphans also came in numbers much larger than expected; they are apparently being cared for by the International Committee of the Red Cross.[59] Relief workers seem to have harrowing memories of the injured children that they have treated.

In the midst of these recent movements is an unknown number of people who were refugees in Tanzania for two decades, were repatriated to Burundi, and now find themselves once again in exile in Tanzania. Repatriation was still in progress when the coup took place.[60] The *Sunday News* (Tanzania) on 31 October 1993 quoted Mustapha Nyang'anyi, Tanzania's Minister of State in the Office of the Prime Minister and First Vice-President, as saying that the coup in Burundi "was staged at a time when the [Tanzanian] government was in the process of repatriating the last batch of Burundi refugees" (Abdallah 1993:1). One person who has worked with the Hutu refugees for many years said that "the repatriators and new refugees met each other on the border."[61] Yet, there are also (non-eyewitness, unofficial) reports that many of Mishamo's old residents are still there. These reports do not mention the situation in Kigoma.

Terrible to contemplate are the unknown fates of those who were refugees in Tanzania for twenty years and then, at long last, decided to return to Burundi. There being no letters from the people whose words appear in this book, it is impossible to know what has happened to them. Are they still in Mishamo and Kigoma and, for some reason, unable or unwilling to write letters? If they went to settle in Burundi, did they perish in October–November 1993? If they are alive and displaced once more, which border did they cross? If they are in Tanzania, how likely are they to be given back their old houses or their five-hectare plots of mostly cleared, cultivated land in Mishamo? Who, if anyone, is living in the refugees' old dwellings in Mishamo and Kigoma now? Who is harvesting the crops that must still be growing in the fields there?

The relief worker quoted above said that the policy of the refugee agencies has been to "try to settle as many refugees in their own settlements as possible." This would seem to suggest that the number of the older, 1972 refugees repatriated was not negligible. The same person added that there are also·plans for new settlements. Kasulu, Kibondo, and Ngara are projected sites for the settlements that are being planned. The "plan is to make new settlements—not of the scale of Mishamo; that was a bit over the top."[62]

The crucial lacuna, then, is a tally of how many of the 1972 refugees returned to Burundi, when, and from which settlement areas. But the alchemy of numbers in conditions of extreme communal violence is sometimes capable of generating strange illusions. There appears, almost automatically, a need to know the numbers, and also an ill-defined expectation that 1 is, in some moral or ethical sense, less significant than 1,000. Yet it is too easy to forget that, at close range, these fluctuating numbers are actually persons.

One of the saddest cases to emerge from this repatriation movement must be the story of a man, a 1972 Hutu refugee, who had lived in Tanzania with his family for many years, and who was employed by an international agency in Dar-es-Salaam. He advised his whole family to return to Burundi in July 1993. They—there were eighteen of them—went back to Burundi in early October, 1993. Only two survived. This man considers himself responsible for his family's fate.[63]

THE DEATHS OF THE PRESIDENTS OF BURUNDI AND RWANDA

On 6 April 1994 (three weeks ago, as of this writing), news came that a plane carrying President Cyprien Ntaryamira of Burundi and President Juvénal Habyarimana of Rwanda had crashed at 8:00 P.M. local time as it was making its approach to Kigali, the capital city of Rwanda. The two presidents were returning from a meeting of heads of state in Dar-es-Salaam, a peace summit that had been called in order that some resolution to the political conflicts in Rwanda and Burundi might be found. Heavy-weapons fire had been heard near the airport at the time of the crash, and it is widely believed that an assassination plot existed. No one has claimed responsibility, but there has, not surprisingly, been much speculation. At least three different theories have been mentioned: (1) "The Rwandan Patriotic Front is interested in the death of President Juvénal Habyarimana. The Front has been in close connection with Museveni and the Burundi military. Now Burundi's army will say, 'we didn't do it; it happened in Rwanda!' Nobody will ever know who did what."[64] (2) Hutu political opponents of President Habyarimana who thought he had been too soft in negotiating with the RPF (usually specified as elements of the Presidential Guard) have also been suspected of engineering the crash. (3) Finally, it has been reported that residents of Kigali widely believe Belgian forces to have shot down the plane. Heavy-weapons fire was heard around the airport at the time of the crash, and the only people guarding the airport, it has been claimed, were Belgian troops.[65]

When the presidents' plane went down, both countries were already in fragile, tense political states. The Rwandan government, of course, had been involved from October 1990 until August 1993 in armed struggle against the Rwandan Patriotic Front.[66] In Burundi, the mass killings that had followed the October 1993 death of President Ndadaye had gone on for several months. Many thousands of Hutu refugees from Burundi had also fled to Rwanda, further polarizing Hutu-Tutsi relations there. Thus, both countries had seen a great deal of violence, instability, and ethnic hatred in the period immediately preceding the plane crash. Yet its aftermath seems thus far to have developed differently in the two countries.

In the case of Burundi, it has been claimed that since the assassination of President Ndadaye in October 1993, the fighting never completely stopped.[67] Nevertheless, it seems that no new radical escalation of violence began in response to the death of President Ntaryamira—the second head of state to die there in six months. Burundi has been re-markably quiet since the crash. The Belgian daily *Le Soir* (8 April 1994, p. 1) reported that news of President Ntaryamira's death "has been received with calm by a population that some describe as *petrified with horror.*"[68] It is also to be expected that the army would promptly move to quash any protest.

It is in Rwanda that life has gone to pieces. Within hours of the crash, President Habyarimana's Presidential Guard "began targeting po-litical opponents and critics irrespective of ethnicity. They included the interim Hutu Prime Minister, ten Belgian peace keepers who tried to save her, many priests and nuns, and journalists and human rights monitors. While these victims, running into the thousands, were pri-marily Hutu like the regime itself, the ruling-party militia along with bands of soldiers and drunken armed Hutu men killed tens of thousands of Tutsi" (Smyth 1994:587–88). In the nightmarish weeks since the crash, tens of thousands more have met their deaths, often in horrifying ways.

It continues, at this point, to be difficult to determine exactly what kinds of fighting are going on, who all the parties to the conflict really are, and where the political alliances might be now. Broadly, there would seem to be several different levels of violence. On the one hand, the Hutu-dominated Rwandan national army is fighting the Tutsi-dominated guerilla force, the Rwandan Patriotic Front (RPF), that formed itself in exile in Uganda over many years and then invaded Rwanda.[69] It should be remembered, however, that there are differences and cleavages within the categories "Hutu" and "Tutsi," "Govern-ment" and "RPF," splits which complicate the landscape of political violence considerably.[70] That said, it is also evident that the violence between the two principal fighting forces has caused countless people of both Tutsi and Hutu categories to die.

On another level of violence, it appears that there is also wide-spread, extremely brutal, ethnically defined killing being carried out by paramilitary forces, gangs of drunken young men, and other civilians. Here, the great majority of the victims of atrocity, by all accounts, have been people belonging to the Tutsi category.[71]

The death toll rose rapidly from 10,000 to 20,000, and by 20 April, much higher estimates had appeared."We will never know how many died, but I believe it must be 100,000 already," said the Rev. Pedro Sala of the Society of Missionaries of Africa (Montalbano 1994:A14).[72] This figure was widely cited for a time.[73] Most recently, with the radical escalation of fighting between the government forces and the RPF, it has been thought that the number of deaths (military and civilian) has now begun to approach 200,000 (Mann 1994:A1, A10).

ACCOUNTS AND ENACTMENTS OF ATROCITY

Depictions of a total chaos dominate press coverage as of late April. Piles of bodies in the streets of the capital city, rivers choked with bodies, constant echoes of automatic-weapons fire, blood, and screams fill the reports from the wire services.

These accounts bespeak an almost unimaginable horror. And yet they are not unique, and not the first such accounts to emerge from this region of central Africa. People in Burundi suffered in frighteningly similar ways just last October, in 1993. To suggest that connections and comparisons can (and should) be drawn between aspects of these different cases of mass killing is not to try to draw up (or redraw) geographies of blame; and it is not to make light of the tragedies of the people whose lives and human relationships are right now being ripped apart. What is important is to document that there is, once again, a "fearful symmetry" between older and newer enactments, older and newer narrative accounts, of massive violence.

Just as in the accounts of the Hutu refugees in Mishamo, there are now reports (through the medium of the press) of the violation of the most holy and valued places, places to which people are fleeing in hopes of finding sanctuary: schools, hospitals, and churches. In the words of a priest belonging to the Marian Fathers:

Always before, frightened people sheltered safely at churches and in the compounds and residences of the religious. This time there is no asylum. We don't understand why they will not respect the holy places. Women and children have been wantonly slaughtered, sick children murdered in their hospital beds. It surpasses understanding.[74]

The eerie, frightening symmetries between accounts from the violence of 1972, 1988, 1993, and 1994, in Burundi and Rwanda, are striking. One Roman Catholic nun described how "hospital patients paid their executioners for swift death. [. . .] The patients, who died by the hundreds, paid the assassins to kill them quickly and not with machetes" (Montalbano 1994:A14–A15). A nurse with Médecins Sans Frontières (MSF) said: "People tell me you can identify Tutsis because they have longer fingers than Hutus. So they are cutting off the fingers of the children" (Hilsum 1994:1). In another incident, MSF doctors found that patients they had treated and left in a tent hospital for the night had been killed in their beds (Gerstenzang and Marshall 1994:A9). There are accounts of brutal rapes, beheadings with machetes, severing of limbs, grenade attacks, and many other acts of cruelty. It seems clear that the social imagination of violence in the region—both in the perpetration and in the telling—forms larger thematic patterns. And these are patterns that will tragically reconfigure social memory for generations, withering, in the process, people's hopes for a better future.

THE NEWEST REFUGEES IN TANZANIA

The *New York Times* reported on 15 April 1994 that "[a]ccording to the United Nations, 17,600 people have fled Rwanda since the fighting began. These include 8,000 Burundi refugees who returned to Burundi from Rwanda and 8,000 Rwandans who have sought sanctuary in Zaire" (Lorch 1994:A3). Ten days later, the number of displaced people was put at 2 million by the *Los Angeles Times*, 25 April 1994 (p. A4).

According to a UNHCR representative in Dar-es-Salaam, both Hutu and Tutsi refugees have fled from Rwanda into northern Tanzania. As of 17 April, there were "a few hundred Tutsi and about 5,000 Hutu" there.[75] Now, in the last days of April 1994, the exodus from Rwanda has very radically escalated. United Nations officials estimated that before the Rwanda-Tanzania border was sealed by the RPF on Friday evening (Lewis 1994:1, 13), "250,000 people had fled from Rwanda into Tanzania in the last 24 hours—the biggest, fastest exodus that refugee officials said they had seen. Lines at the border stretched for miles." (Meisler 1994:A12). Sylvana Foa, a UNHCR spokeswoman, said that most of these newest refugees appear to be Hutu (Lewis 1994:1).

Brief news reports have also recorded new violence in Burundi, with the army apparently threatening people and "killing Hutus in revenge" (Meisler 1994:A12). Sounds of heavy shelling and gunfire in Bujumbura were reported on evening news broadcasts in Los Angeles on 29 April 1994.

THE ARCHITECTURE OF SILENCE

Eventually, Rwanda will disappear from world news, as Burundi already largely has, and a thick curtain of silence will once more come down on these two central African countries. It will seem to most of us who have followed the recent news that history has simply stopped there.

Soon not even even muffled sounds may be audible from Burundi and Rwanda. But if only the silence were as simple a presence as a curtain. Then it could be pulled aside. It is, of course, much more complex and multidimensional—at once micropolitical and politico-economic, local and transnational, planned and unwitting, sometimes a direct result of specific practices and at other times an accidental by-product. Many dimensions and surfaces compose this daunting architecture of silence.

On a micropolitical level, people from Burundi (and, presumably, Rwanda) have developed elaborate habits of caution, silence, and discretion. In Mishamo as in Kigoma, these habits had come to characterize everyday social conduct; and they are understandable as a vital dimension of the wider architecture of silence. This dimension was often discernible in the letters I received:

I apologize for taking such a long time without writing to you and in reality this is caused by events that have happened to us here in Mishamo, and, for this, I was afraid that the letters going abroad were very surveilled. (Mishamo, 23 January 1990)

You know, at the post office they keep certain of your letters because you are known by the Consul [of Burundi]. (Kigoma, 10 May 1987)

The architecture of silence, it seems, is not just a structure inhabited by those it represses; it also inhabits them, creating in them its own structures of feeling, habits of thought, routines of the body.[76] As the philosopher Melchior Mbonimpa has written of the (pre-1993) political order in Burundi,

when the watch dogs of the reigning order invade a house in search of pretexts for inculpation [*prétextes d'inculpation*], the victims, condemned in advance, are generally accused of possessing two types of object: arms and texts [. . .]. [I]n teaching African literature to children in Burundi, one always comes up against this innocent question: Why isn't there a single Burundian writer? The answer is simple, but no teacher will reveal it to the students without exposing him- or herself to the reprisals of the power in place. No one writes because the written text has become a mortal boomerang. The repression condemns to sterility even those who, objectively, would have nothing to fear [. . .].[77]

But the architecture of silence is not simply a matter of a local politics "internal" to Burundi. What makes it so incontestable is that it is shored up in countless ways externally. As Chomsky and Herman have observed, this region of the world can safely be left invisible and *incomprehensible* by the press; it is a location of "strategic invisibility" (Chomsky and Herman 1979; Sciolino 1994:A3). It has little political or economic significance to the rest of the world. Indeed, it has been argued that it has value only as a market for arms.[78] And the world press seems perfectly content with its explanation of the recent, massive violence as "ancient tribal warfare," a matter of "primordial tribal hatreds," between the "tall" Tutsi and the "stocky" Hutu. These opaque, fanciful, distorting terms allow for systematic misunderstandings of the tragic complexities of regional political history, misunderstandings that can be found in virtually the same form in colonial texts.

Other dimensions of the silence can be located by asking: If the people and their histories are not known, what is this region known for, if anything? It is safe to say that, if these areas were known to the reading or television-viewing public at all (prior to the present news coverage), they were probably visible as the wild green home of the imperiled mountain gorillas made famous by researchers like Dian Fossey and the popular film *Gorillas in the Mist*—just as western Tanzania is known for Stanley and Livingstone and, in more recent times, for Jane Goodall and the Gombe Stream Research Centre, and not for any human communities that live there now. Incredibly, as the recent news coverage has been coming in, an electronic mail debate has been going on about the possibility of an "emergency airlift"—not for the men, women, and children being slaughtered by the thousands, but for the mountain gorillas, to save them from the violence and possible extinction. They, after all, are a "world treasure" and "a flagship species."[79]

Another aspect of the silence is this startling phenomenon: the evacuation of European and American nationals from the bloodsoaked landscape of Rwanda has received the thrust of the coverage on Rwanda right up until the last group of evacuees had left the country, at which point television and front-page news coverage was also radically reduced. One is invited to draw the conclusion that this human drama— a convoy of frightened expatriates—is more compelling and newsworthy than the human drama of the horrifying, almost unimaginably frightening circumstances of the black citizens of these two countries, persons who (we think to ourselves) "belong" in the landscape,[80] persons who (some still imagine) are used to this kind of "periodic tribal warfare," persons who cannot put their children on any helicopters that will fly them to safety. When these black citizens of Burundi and Rwanda exercise their exit option, most of them will do so on foot. And as they cross the international border, they will undergo a transformation: they will emerge knowable again, on the other side, to international wire services and international relief organizations and development agencies and scholars as "African refugees," objects of a special, philanthropic mode of power. They will become not only a "problem"; they will also become an object of humanitarian relief and, eventually, recipients of innumerable benevolent interventions. It is to be hoped that they will receive more medical care, more food, more clothing, more social services (such as tracing missing family members), more money, more books, magazines, and radios that would help inform, orient, and pass the time, more than they are receiving now. But it is still worthwhile for us to ask: *What else* is entailed in becoming an object of "humanitarian assistance"?

The people who woke up in their own beds one morning, not so long ago, brushed their teeth, walked to the toilet, woke up their lovers and children and siblings, and went to begin the day's work, the people who listened worriedly to the radio in hopes of getting clarity about this or that political trouble, the people who argued over rights to this or that fruit tree, the people who got softly drunk together at twilight as they talked about memories and plans, all these people will become knowable to most of us, the global reading public, as "African refugees," promising objects of academic specialization, worthy objects of humanitarian attention. In becoming objects of the philanthropic mode of power,[81] the political, historical, and biographical specificity of their life worlds vanishes into a vast register labeled "unknowable, irrelevant, unconfirmed, unusable." Here, then, is one more dimension of the architecture of silence that has for so many years had the effect of dehumanizing and making disappear this small, worldly, complicated region of the world—a place where, ironically, people's eyes and dreams are so often turned toward a world community. I thought of this good-faith, optimistic worldliness again as I reread this passage from a letter written by Gahutu Rémi in the spring of 1987 in Mishamo:

How do the American people view our problem? Once Father Simon told me that the Americans completely ignore this affair. . . . I think that he was not *sensibilisé* [aware]. And then, after the Vietnam affair, the USA hesitates. . . . Nevertheless, our cause is very just; the Vietnam affair and our affair are as different as night and day. Perhaps in helping us, the Americans would efface a little bit the affair of Uncle Ho. I just cannot understand why the world seems to turn a deaf ear to our appeals. [. . .] Even the missionaries who know the problem very well, and have suffered almost the same as we, seem to ignore us. But this does not discourage us. Besides, my motto is "AD AUGUSTA PER ANGUSTA: it is through narrow paths that one arrives at grandiose results." (Mishamo, 2 March 1987)

A just peace for the people trapped within these bloodstained categories, "Hutu" and "Tutsi"—whether in Rwanda or Burundi—may now appear an impossibly grandiose result to emerge from the present moment, into which ever more blood, more terror, more racial, categorical hatred, more nightmares, more tears, and more death are being daily pumped. But in the middle of all this, might there not be "narrow paths" to be found after all? Those paths, if they exist, will be found somewhere in the thick of local histories, profoundly embedded in the crooked timber of social relationships in this long-suffering region. The pathways may be local, but that does not mean that a wider world can in conscience refuse to acknowledge its responsibility to participate in the process of disassembling structures of fear there, of giving names to silences, and of working toward justice and peace.

INTRODUCTION

1. Cf. Arendt (1973); Appadurai (1990, 1991); Anderson (1991); Renan (1990); Wright (1985).
2. Cf. Appadurai (1991:197ff.) on imagination and ethnography.
3. The term "refugeeness" is used here in preference to "refugee status," which suggests legally documented status, and "refugeeism," which seems to imply that being a refugee is a psychological condition or an ideology. Cf. Anderson (1991) on nationalism vs. nationness.
4. Cf. Turner's term "cultural topography" (1967:97).
5. Cf. also van Gennep (1922).
6. See also van Gennep (1960:11).
7. The term *limen* appears in Turner (1967:94).
8. Van Gennep has written about "territorial passage" as one example of rites of passage (1960:15–25), and this aspect might at first appear most directly applicable to the passages undergone by refugees. However, his classic formulation of the general principle of rites of passage remains more illuminating in this context.
9. See Proudfoot (1957); Stoessinger (1956); Arendt (1973). Cf. also Borneman (1986) on immigration as penetration, and Martin (1990) on the body as nation-state.
10. See also a critique of Douglas' work on classification in Tambiah (1986: 213ff.).
11. Cf. Malkki (1992:33–34).
12. Slavenka Drakulić (1992:68), writing about a friend who had fled Sarajevo and become a refugee, observed her own reactions: "Studying her I try to detect a trace of any changes in her face. It strikes me as odd that I am unable to see any, as if only by seeing pain painted all over her face I could believe her story. [. . .] I still am looking for traces of war on her face. [. . .] I notice that she is wearing makeup. This is what is confusing about her. [. . .] This is what doesn't fit the picture of a refugee." Drakulić also found herself angry that her friend who had lost everything and become a refugee wore black patent leather, high-heeled shoes. It was inappropriate. Her friend did not "fit into the refugee category at all. The truth is that every time I hear the word refugee, my mind recalls pictures of poorly dressed women covered with black scarves [. . .], their ankles swollen, with dirt under their nails."

    I would like to thank Deborah Mindry for bringing this article to my attention.

13. See, e.g., Adepoju (1982:31–32); UNHCR (n.d.; 1979); Forbes Martin (1992:5). More general portraits of men and women and children from all over the world are to be found in UNHCR, *Images of Exile, 1951–1991* (1991).
14. I would like to thank Jim Ferguson for bringing this review to my attention. The photos, by Edward Steichen, were published as *The Family of Man* (New York: Simon & Schuster, 1955).
15. Cf. Gilroy (1990a, 1990b); Anderson (1992).
16. Cf. Gilroy (1990b); and cf. Mazzini, who long ago declared: "Without the nation there can be no humanity, even as without organization and division there can be no expeditious and fruitful labour. *Nations are the citizens of humanity, as individuals are the citizens of the nation.* [. . .] Nationality and humanity are therefore equally sacred." Cited in Black (1964:84).
17. Cf. Malkki 1990b.
18. This passage is startlingly relevant to the debates that have begun to circle a central figure in the discipline of anthropology: Claude Lévi-Strauss. In 1952, he wrote the UNESCO lecture, "Race and History," that has been celebrated as a classic antiracist document. Almost two decades later, he wrote another lecture at the invitation of UNESCO, "Race and Culture" (1971). The later essay has created widespread astonishment and criticism. Its relevance here derives from the vision of "cultures" and cultural differences that Lévi-Strauss erects: "It is not at all invidious to place one way of life or thought above all others or to feel little drawn to other values. [. . .] Cultures are not unaware of one another, they even borrow from one another on occasion; but, in order not to perish, they must in other connections remain somewhat impermeable toward one another" (Lévi-Strauss 1985:xii–xiii, cited in Geertz 1994). One is invited to draw the conclusion that ethnocentrism is a natural aspect of the human condition. The political significance of Lévi-Strauss's argument (in the context of Gilroy's discussion) is that it vividly illuminates the formidable connection between visions of "cultural diversity" is bourgeois liberalism, on the one hand, and visions of difference in racist logics, on the other. These connections are traced in detail by Geertz (1994). Cf. also Balibar on racism as a kind of humanism (1990), and Lévi-Strauss's own recent account (1994).
19. Cf. Lévi-Strauss on immigration, racism, and deaths of Arab immigrants in France (1994:424).
20. Shawcross (1989:29) echoes this sense of the loss of culture: "the poignant voices of refugees recall their lost homes, their precious rituals forcibly abandoned [. . .]."
21. Cf. Appadurai (1988) on the spatial incarceration of the native.
22. It is not illogical in this cultural context that one of the first therapies routinely directed at refugees is a spatial one. The refugee camp is a technology of "care and control" (Proudfoot 1957; Malkki 1985:51)—a technology of power (Foucault 1979) entailing the management of space and movement—for "peoples out of place."
23. E.g., "floodtides" in Oxfam America (1984:8); "waves" in David (1969:73).
24. Cf. Hannerz (1987).

CHAPTER ONE

1. In the early 1970s, the figures were as follows: 75.44 inhabitants per square kilometer (and 185 per square mile in 1955) (Lemarchand and Martin 1974:5; Vansina 1972:3–4).
2. The 1972 estimate is from Kay (1987:3). Vansina's estimate is over 2 million (1972:3–4). The 1991 UN population estimate is cited in *The Economist Intelligence Unit Country Profile 1992–93* (1993:58). See also d'Hertefelt, Trouwborst, and Scherer (1962:120).
3. See also *Economist Intelligence Unit* (1993:63).
4. See also Richards (1960) on clientship.
5. See also Université du Burundi (1983).
6. However, the government has tried to implement a villagization program. See *Economist Intelligence Unit* (1993:62).
7. See a review of hypotheses in Richards (1960:28ff.). See also Nenquin (1967); d'Hertefelt, Trouwborst, and Scherer (1962); Berger (1981); Lemarchand (1970); Weinstein (1976); and Gahama (1983).
8. See also Vansina (1966:34,91) and Vansina (1972); Philippart de Foy (1984).
9. For Twa people in Rwanda, see Maquet (1961:11).
10. Cf. Ramirez and Rolot (1985:197ff.); Schrire (1984).
11. See extracts from colonial texts (Ménard, Jamoulle, Hiernaux) in Gahama (1983:275ff).
12. See the debate between Lemarchand (1990a, 1990b, 1991) and Chrétien (1990, 1991). See also Reyntjens (1990:107–12).
13. See also Richards (1960); Vansina (1966).
14. See Lemarchand (1970:23–4). His hypothesis linking lack of centralization of political power with a lack of ethnic division and conflict now seems less certain.
15. Lamb's journalistic exposé, *The Africans* (1985:12), also makes reference to this. See also Maquet (1961); Beattie (1964); Goody (1963); Berger (1981); Codere (1962); de Heusch (1964); Mair (1977:29); Newbury (1988).
16. See Richards (1960:378–93); Mafeje (1991:66ff.); and Taylor (1969) for a discussion of feudalism in the interlacustrine kingdoms. See also Goody (1963, 1971).
17. Coquery-Vidrovitch and Moniot (1974:145); Trouwborst (1962:120); Maquet (1961); Lemarchand (1970); Lemarchand and Martin (1974:5). See also Vansina (1972) (where Hutu, Tutsi, and Twa are referred to almost exclusively as castes); and Weinstein (1976). Richards (1960:30) points out some of the difficulties in using the term "caste" in reference to the interlacustrine kingdoms, but concludes that "we have found it difficult to think of a more useful term than caste." Cf. Codere (1962); Newbury (1988:3–13).
18. Lemarchand, in "The Burundi Genocide" (1992:3–4) traces these social transformations as follows: "Under the impact of colonial rule a new pattern of colonial stratification began to emerge, in which class-based cleavages tended increasingly to mirror Hutu-Tutsi differences. By withdrawing recognition from those Hutu notables who held influential positions at the Court and at the king's estates, the colonial state significantly altered

patterns of recruitment (mostly to the advantage of Tutsi elements). By imposing upon the Hutu masses a wide range of obligations, it added immeasurably to their traditional burdens; and by the selective allocation of educational opportunities to Tutsi children, it further reduced the life chances of the Hutu as a group. Even so, *on the eve of independence ethnic polarization was still at an incipient stage;* princely factionalism, rather than ethnic conflict, was the central characteristic of Burundi society. [. . .] Thus in contrast to what happened in Rwanda, where the sharpness of the Hutu-Tutsi cleavage led to a major revolutionary upheaval in the years immediately preceding independence, eventuating in the birth of a Hutu-dominated republic, in Burundi the Hutu-Tutsi split did not become politically significant until well after independence (1962), and then largely as a consequence of the demonstration effect of the revolution in Rwanda" (emph. added).

19. See also Trouwborst (1961).
20. Cf. Newbury (1988:260, n. 1).
21. A different, denaturalizing interpretation is given by Codere (1962).
22. See also Trouwborst (1961).
23. Translated from the French by the author.
24. Cf. Wagner (1991:10–14, 489–91, 499–506). The contemporary Hutu refugees in the environs of Kigoma distinguished themselves from Burundian immigrants of the colonial era. The latter are discussed in chapter 5. For further discussion of the effects of taxation and labour policies in the region, see Iliffe (1979:306ff.); Northrup (1988:37–80).
25. Here Lemarchand and Martin are citing A.F. Duke of Mecklemburg, *In the Heart of Africa* (1910).
26. Cf. also Ramirez and Rolot (1985:232): "[. . .] les Tutsi sont comparés aux Blancs [. . .] les Hutu sont donnés comme les véritables *nègres* du Ruanda, ce qui, par voie de conséquence, rend leur inféodation si légitime qu'il n'est même pas nécessaire de la justifier".
27. Seligman (1934).
28. A 1925 report of the colonial administration, cited in Gahama (1983:276). Translated from the French by the author.
29. See also Lemarchand's own assessment of the "passive obedience" and the "tremendous psychological insecurities among the Hutu peasantry" in (1970:43). The Hutu have also been portrayed as the embodiment of "Bantu naiveté, greediness, and ignorance", in *Plan de la colonisation Tutsi au Kivu et la region centrale de l'Afrique,* 1962, cited in: Lemarchand (n.d.:3). The same document proclaims, "un Hutu est crée pour servir" (Lemarchand n.d.:3).
30. See Boateng (1978:152–3); Lamb (1985:12).
31. The vote was introduced in 1956, six years before independence. According to Lemarchand and Martin (1974:9), "majority rule for many Tutsi was seen as synonymous with Hutu rule" and "was viewed with the greatest suspicion by the Tutsi minority.
32. Several informants in Mishamo insisted that Buyoya was the nephew of Bagaza, and Bagaza, the cousin of Micombero.
33. See Weinstein (1976); Lemarchand (1970); Kabera (1987).

34. Much higher estimates of these refugee populations are given by Watson (1992:53).

35. Sayinzoga (1982:51) estimates that between 1959 and 1973, political upheaval in Rwanda cost the lives of 50,000 persons. In addition some 350,000 fled as refugees and another 12,000 were internally displaced.

36. Violence and ethnicity in Rwanda and the circumstances of the Rwandese Tutsi refugees have been discussed in Lemarchand (n.d.); Gasarasi (1988: 220–7); Watson (1991); Clay (1984); Chrétien (1985); Vidal (1985); cf. also Newbury (1988). Sayinzoga's (1982:54) and Lemarchand's (n.d.) works suggest that in the narratives of the Rwandese refugees we might find a mythico-history that often mirrors and inverts that of the Hutu refugees in Tanzania.

37. See also Vail (1989); Ranger (1983).

38. Cf. Tambiah (1986:6–7); and Anderson (1991). See also Lemarchand and Martin (1974:7–9).

39. See Lemarchand and Martin (1974:8); Weinstein (1976:x).

40. Melady was United States Ambassador to Burundi from November 1969 to June 1972 and published his own account of the 1972 events (1974).

41. Estimate derives from Du Bois (1972). Other estimates in Lemarchand and Martin (1974:5); Kay (1987); Kuper (1982:164).

42. The quote derives from Bowen et al. (n.d., p. 6), cited in Chomsky and Herman (1979:106). The Bowen et al. report also states (p. 5) that the minority government attempted to "kill every possible Hutu male of distinction over the age of fourteen."

43. See appendices in Melady (1974) for announcements by the government of Burundi.

44. Melady in the *New York Times*, Oct. 27, 1974, cited in Chomsky and Herman (1979:108). See also longer discussion as to the implications of the "internal affairs" argument, with reference to Burundi, in Kuper (1982: 161ff., esp. 163). Weinstein (1976:xi) has suggested that the discovery of nickel deposits in Burundi may have served to subdue the response of the international community.

45. See also Kuper (1982:165).

46. See Perlez (1988:1) as an illustration of the terms used to define the most recent mass killings in Burundi in August of 1988.

47. See also Chrétien (1990:38–40) and Lemarchand (1990a). See further Reyntjens (1990).

48. See also Weinstein (1976:53).

49. The events leading up to 1972 and the massacres themselves have been covered in detail here because these were the historical processes that directly produced the refugees who were to become my informants. The important political transformations and upheavals that have occurred since 1972 will be taken up in the Postscript.

50. Kibirizi camp on Lake Tanganyika was one such reception and transit camp. Another was Pangale "holding camp" 500 kilometers inland in Tabora Region.

51. Daley (n.d.:16ff.) has discussed the establishment of the three large Hutu

refugee settlements, Mishamo, Ulyankulu, and Katumba, in the wider context of settlement schemes for refugees, village settlement schemes for nationals, and the role of Tanzanian refugee law in the management of agricultural production in settlements.

52. A more extensive study of Ulyankulu has been done by Christensen (1985).

53. Malkki (1989) gives comparative statistical information on the three main Hutu settlements in Tanzania.

54. The use of the terms *camp* and *settlement* requires a brief explanation. In the language of the agencies administering, settling, and studying refugees, a camp denotes a temporary or an emergency accommodation, while a settlement refers to a more permanently settled group of refugees. Insofar as the Hutu refugees in Mishamo have lived there continuously since 1979, they comprise a settlement. However, the usage of these terms by the refugees themselves was different from that of the organizations. For reasons that become apparent in the following chapter, the refugees insisted on the term *camp*. Here, the terms are used interchangeably.

55. Cf. Daley (n.d.) for a description of Katumba's comparable layout.

56. Census data used by Armstrong also show that only 1.3 percent of Mishamo's households reported ownership of more than one bicycle; he adds that the number of requests for more bicycles by refugees was extremely high (1988:63). Cf. Ogbru (1983).

57. No precise figures on motor vehicles owned by refugees in Mishamo have been located.

58. *Mishamo: A Guide Book of the Refugee Settlement* (TCRS n.d. [b]) was originally printed in Kiswahili and distributed to each household in Mishamo. See also, TCRS, *Village Handbook* (n.d. [b]). Daley (n.d.:24) has noted that "[t]oo often refugee participation refers to their willingness to provide unremunerated labour, euphemistically termed 'self-help.'"

59. U.S. $1 = 16.75 Tsh. (Tanzanian shillings) was the approximate official rate in 1986.

60. Cf. also Armstrong (1988:61–2).

61. According to Daley (n.d.:29), the Rukwa Region "refugee settlements together account for 88 percent of the district's maize, sold to Rukwa Regional Cooperative Union (RURECU), and 99 percent of its beans and cassava sales."

62. See also various TCRS Annual Reports.

63. Coulson (1982) provides an authoritative review of the relevant literature on villagization and broader issues in the political economy of Tanzania. See also Hyden (1980).

64. Armstrong also notes (1987:67) that the Village Chairman and Secretary are not salaried; they are paid a nominal honorarium of 200–300 Tsh. per month.

65. Daley (n.d.:22) has also described the administration of Katumba Refugee Settlement as "authoritarian", and notes that refugees are "arrested and fined for minor offences" and that their "personal property, like bicycles and radios, may be confiscated." Daley reports that in "July 1987 a

sixteen-year-old boy was sentenced to six months imprisonment after being caught in Mpanda town without a permit" (n.d.:37).

66. Translated from the French by the author.
67. Sixty-seven percent of the total was contributed by UNHCR and 33 percent by TCRS/LWF. See Armstrong (1987).
68. See also Roberts (1969:79–80).
69. The 1978 Government and Tanzania census, cited in TCRS (1984b:n.p.); Nindi and Mbago (1983:37) give different statistics.
70. An estimate of 23,000 Hutu refugees is given in TCRS (1984b:n.p.). Bifuko (1980:3) gives a figure of 36,444. Armstrong asserts that the number is over 30,000 (1986e:41).
71. See Nindi and Mbago (1983:3).
72. Cf. Lugusha (1981:49).
73. For a number of reasons, he had lived in Kigoma Region for several years, and was therefore fluent in Kiha.
74. Some work with refugee women in Mishamo has been done by Southey (1984a,b).
75. My thoughts on the distinctions between doing fieldwork and conducting an investigation have been largely formed in conversations with Robert Kant de Lima.

CHAPTER TWO

1. The term, charter, of course, recalls Malinowki's famed functionalist approach to myth. I deliberately invoke this tradition while seeking to go beyond it, toward a more dynamic idea of a charter as a site of struggle, of ongoing contestation over the moral and cosmological framework of social action. Cf. usage by Feldman (1991).
2. Cf. Vansina (1972:20–1ff.) on the "juridical style" of oral narratives; Rodegem and Bapfutwabo (1961); Rodegem (1973); Lemarchand (1970); and cf. Ndoricimpa and Guillet (1984). Studies of oral forms in Rwanda have been done, among others, by Pierre Smith (1975); Crepeau (1985); and de Heusch (1982).
3. Cf. Wagner (1991).
4. Oxford English Dictionary, 1971 ed., s.v. "morality."
5. Cf. Comaroff and Comaroff (1987:193). See also Schoffeleers (1987, 1988); Comaroff (1982); Ranger and Murray (1981); Herzfeld (1987); Hobsbawm and Ranger (1983).
6. Cf. Foucault (1973).
7. Cf. Vansina's (1972:9) reference to an "epoch of chaos" preceding dynastic history. Cf. also Isaiah Berlin (1991:20–1): "The main characteristic of most, perhaps all, Utopias is the fact that they are static. Nothing in them alters, for they have reached perfection. [. . .] Most Utopias are cast back into a remote past: once upon a time there was a golden age."
8. Cf. Wilson (1964). Cf. also Vansina (1972:9) on chaos in the pre-mwami epoch.
9. Cf. Vansina (1972:69ff.) on "les contes d'origine"; and (1972:197) on the origin of the name "Burundi." Cf. also Zuure (1932); and Richards (1960:33 n.1).

10. Cf. Vansina (1972:197) where the origin of the name Burundi is thought to have been a place name.

11. Cf. Malkki (1989:16). For a veritable obstetrics of nationhood, see Jessup (1974). Turning around the nation-as-body relation, Martin (1991) critically examines the body as nation-state.

12. Cf. Vansina (1972:113) on Rufuku, father of Ntare I; also Mair (1977:22) on the connection between the story of Kigwa and divine kingship; and Richards (1960:32) on the comparable "Ganda 'Kintu' legend" in which "the first kings described are God-like creatures who descend from heaven." Further, Richards notes in this connection (1960:33): "The legend of direct succession acts as a charter for the exercise of power by the present line of kings, and tales of the common origin of different tribes, however mythical they may be, express the belief of the Interlacustrine Bantu that they are closely akin [. . .]." The legends above, as well as arguments for the common origin of the peoples of Burundi, Buha, and Rwanda, were seen as Tutsi stories by informants in Mishamo.

13. Cf. Lan (1985:14).

14. *Webster's New Collegiate Dictionary*, 1980 ed., s.v. "autochthon."

15. Jean Comaroff, personal communication.

16. Vansina (1961:193): the Twa are "regarded as clowns." See also Philippart de Foy (1984).

17. Cf. Kapferer (1988:142) for the Noble Savage idea. For "indigenous people," cf. Appadurai (1988); Malkki (1992a); Torgovnick (1990).

18. According to F. Rodegem (personal communication), there has never been a real census of the population in Burundi, and these are eternal figures. Cf. Sayinzoga (1982:52) on the census in Rwanda.

19. Single narrative. Cf. Taylor (1992:30). Taylor has remarked on a comparable earth/sky opposition in Rwanda: "This difference between autochthonous and celestial origin should also be interpreted as the difference between cultivating Hutu and cattle-herding Tutsi."

20. Kigwa derives from the verb *kugwa*, "to fall from the sky." See Vansina (1985:65); Vansina (1961:25); Lemarchand (1970:33): "The Story of the Origins," a dynastic poem from Rwanda. See also Richards (1960:32).

21. A fascinating comparison is to be found in Taylor (1992:39) who cites this legend as explaining why the sociopolitical hierarchies in Rwanda operated in the manner that they did: "According to Rwandan legend, this state of affairs was justified by the different behaviors of the three brothers Gatutsi, Gahutu, and Gatwa, sons of the mythical Rwandan king, Gihanga (P. Smith 1975, 39). Gihanga gave each of the brothers a pot of milk and told them to guard it during the night. But Gatwa became thirsty and drank his pot of milk. Gahutu became drowsy and in dozing off, spilled some of the contents of his pot. Only Gatutsi succeeded in keeping a full pot of milk until the next morning. For this reason, Gihanga decreed that Gatutsi should possess cattle and enjoy the right to rule. Gahutu would only be able to procure cattle by the work and services he performed for his brother Gatutsi. As for Gatwa, he would never possess cattle; alternate periods of gluttony and starvation were to be his lot. Presumably, it was

only Tutsi who could be entrusted to keep the milk pot, which was
Rwanda, filled to its brim."
22. Single narrative by one person.
23. See Greenland (1973); Curtin (1978:121,167–71); Chrétien (1984) for critiques of the "Hamitic hypothesis."
24. Cf. Taylor (1992:38–9); Lan (1985:84). Lan mentions "accounts of 'tricks'
played by the conqueror to defeat the autochthons, the original owners of
the land." This strikes an interesting parallel with the Hutu mythico-
history. Cf. Beidelman (1980).
25. Cf. Vansina on *ubugabire* (1972:195); Lemarchand (1973:416–36) on *buhake* in Rwanda.
26. Composite panel extracted from a single conversation with one person.
27. A detailed examination of Maquet's flawed model is given by C. Newbury
(1988:3ff.).
28. See Vansina (1972:111–2) for a different version—perhaps one dissemi-
nated by the chiefly or princely strata?
29. See Vansina (1972:112ff.) for other, different versions of the "origin of the
castes."
30. Cf. Vansina's (1972:112) reference to a story of how the Twa first commanded Hutu and Tutsi. Vansina describes this as "*une situation chao-
tique typique pour un Rundi.*"
    One recalls, too, Lévi-Strauss's observation that "most of the peoples
that we term 'primitive' give themselves a name that signifies 'The True
Ones,' 'The Good Ones,' 'The Excellent Ones,' or even, quite simply, 'The
Human Beings,' and apply to other peoples a name that denies their humanity—for example, 'earth monkeys' or 'louse eggs'."
31. The actual relations of dependency between Hutu and Tutsi in Burundi
were, of course, complex; relations of patronage and quasi-kinship make
any simple designation of "slavery" or "servitude" questionable. (Cf. Lemarchand 1970, 1994:20; Rodegem, personal communication of 23 Oct.,
1990; Vansina 1972:194–5). But the point here is not that Hutu in Burundi before 1972 *actually were* "slaves" of the Tutsi; only that the refugees' narratives of the past constructed the relationship in this way.
32. Composite panel from several persons' narratives.
33. For the sake of brevity, substantial sections of the mythico-history concerning the relationship between people of the Hutu and Tutsi categories
in the precolonial era have been omitted. Omitted themes include the installation of the monarchy, the art of administration, and many others.
Some of these will appear in the course of later panels. Entirely left out
are narratives that represent particular, partial aspects of the major
themes already discussed here. At the thematic level, they would be repetitive.
34. Vansina (1961:118) describes "a traditional technique for discouraging the
enemy and for rallying faithful followers, which consists of spreading false
rumours for this purpose." Cf. Lemarchand (1970:9).
35. Wagner (1991:498, 505) gives testimony from elders in Buragane, on the
Burundi side of the Burundi-Tanzania border, showing that the Belgians
are still remembered there as harsh rulers. See also Newbury (1988:152–

199) on Belgian rule in Rwanda. The definitive work on the horrors of Belgian colonialism in King Leopold's Congo remains Morel (1904).

36. The views on the Kigoma township Hutu refugees on this issue throw light on the dark underbelly of colonial rule much more readily, and this will be discussed in Chapter Four.

37. Composite panel of two different narratives by one person.

38. See also Vansina (1961:102–7).

39. Single, continuous narrative by one person.

40. Lemarchand (1970:9) refers to "a cultural environment in which concealing or distorting the truth are traditionally regarded as both a virtue and an art."

41. Panel composed of two different conversations (four days apart) with one informant, and a smaller fragment from a second person.

42. One thirty-year-old clerical worker who was a Hutu refugee explained how, at sixteen, he had escaped with his life in 1972 when Burundi government soldiers came to round up Hutu students at his school: "I look like a Tutsi in the face." I asked: "Why did the Tutsi soldiers want sixteen-year-old boys?" He tried to explain this to me: "They did. They were Hutu. They just said: 'You! You! You!—and you also!' You should come with us to talk at the District . . . the Area Commissioner or something. Then they just never came back. They went to heaven. [. . .] The things started in 1965 when people started disappearing. They were just taken away with excuses. The Tutsi wanted to clean up—. So, they started to kill the intellectuals so they would not create problems in the future. [. . .] And in the 1960s, from '65, they used to ask people: 'Are you students or intellectuals? We have scholarships for people to study in Nigeria—this place, that place. Do you want to go?' The people, they said yes. So they took them to Bujumbura and finished. They didn't go to Nigeria. They went to heaven. Even sometimes they wrote letters to the family, saying: 'Oh, your son, he died in the air, the aeroplane never reached the place.' So they sent a condolence." (This conversation conducted in English)

43. Cf. Newbury 1988. My translation from the French.

44. See Gahama (1983:275). My translation from the French.

45. See Gahama (1983:279).

46. Composite panel consisting of passages from two different conversations (a month apart) with a single person.

47. Composite panel, drawn from conversations with two persons. The "insects" were often inyenzi, translated by one Hutu refugee living outside Tanzania as: "cafard, cancrelat, blatte, cockroach"; "an insect that flees light"; "Tutsi guerilleros who attack by night, clandestinely, without allowing themselves to be seen." Personal communication, 7 August 1992. In his essay on Rwandese Tutsi refugees, Sayinzoga (1982:51) also makes reference to this: "Inyenzi: nickname given to groups of guerilleros descended from refugees, who harassed Rwanda from 1960 to 1967." (Author's translation from the French)

48. Lemarchand gives a record of some colonial visions of "Tutsi laziness" (1970:42).

49. Cf. Comaroff (1985); Taussig (1980). This section was enriched through a discussion of power with Jean Comaroff.
50. Cf. Ferguson (1993).
51. Panel composed of thematically interrelated narratives told on several occasions by one person.
52. Cf. Lan 1985:84. Interestingly, Lan's work in Dande, Zimbabwe, shows a parallel theme of "marriages as deceitful tricks which end in the death of the husbands" (1985:84).
53. Panel composed of accounts by one person, given on different occasions.
54. Cf. Lemarchand (forthcoming); Lemarchand and Martin (1974); Chomsky and Herman (1979).
55. Colonial lists of "traits" as described by Lemarchand (1970:41,42ff.) are comparable to the body maps in the mythico-history. See also Gahama (1983).
56. Single narrative.
57. Cf. Adorno, as cited by Feldman (1991:64).
58. The entire panel is a composite of several different conversations with the same person.
59. Cf. Lash (1984:3) on Foucault, spectacles of power, the body, and the "mnemonics of pain."
60. Cf. Kiraranganya (1985:77). In this account, the pregnant woman is Mututsi.
61. Composite panel. Accounts by numerous persons are sequentially strung together without editing of fragments.
62. I would like to thank one of the anonymous reviewers of this manuscript for drawing attention to this point.
63. This recalls the point Hobsbawm makes about nations: that the nation relies for its self-definition on enemies, extenal and internal (1983:279). See also Nietzsche ([1889] 1968:44).
64. Cf. Chomsky and Herman (1979).
65. Cf. Feldman 1991; Coronil and Skurski 1991; Taussig 1987; Daniel 1990; Peters 1985.
66. The same claim was noted by Lemarchand and Martin (1974:18). See also Morel (1904:111ff.).
67. Cf. Anderson ([1983] 1991) on the centrality of census practices to the modern state.
68. For a parallel theme in the history of Rwanda, along with an account of the dubious origins of these widely cited demographic statistics, see Sayinzoga (1982:54). See also Chrétien, Guichaoua, and Le Jeune (1989:50) on the "Plan Simbananiye".
69. Cf. Leclercq (1973).
70. Composite panel. Passages arranged from three persons' descriptions. In the case of one person, excerpts from two different conversations with him (three weeks apart) were included.
71. See also Leclercq (1973).
72. See chapter 1, "Historical Contexts, Social Locations: A Road Map."
73. A single person's continuous narrative.
74. Cf. Marrus (1985:176) on the Kristallnacht.

75. An analogous observation of the colonization of thought is to be found in Steve Biko's writings on the Black Consciousness movement (1978).
76. Cf. Bisharat 1989.
77. See Goodman 1978:1–22.

CHAPTER THREE

1. Cf. Feldman 1991.
2. Emphasis added.
3. Emphasis in the original.
4. The phrase is from William Blake; cited in Northrop Frye (1969).
5. Panel consists of a single narrative from one person, with the second-to-last sentence inserted from another person's account of the same historical period. This panel was mistakenly identified in Malkki (1989:211,279 n. 4) as both a single *and* a composite narrative.
6. Some people (especially women) also mentioned these memories as a frequent source of nightmares.
7. Among these narratives there was not one account of a returnee who had remained alive, although there were several about individual Tutsi persons who had saved the lives of Hutu who were within the borders of Burundi.
8. While regionalism did not appear to be a salient feature of social life in Mishamo during fieldwork, in 1987 numerous people wrote to me at length about a flare-up of regionalism in Katumba, the largest of the Hutu refugee camps, to the south of Mishamo.
9. See also "The Hutu in Tanzania: Two Fieldwork Sites," in chapter 1 above.
10. Several informants had also stayed for some six months in Pangale camp.
11. Single narrative.
12. Similar accounts by refugees are reported in a study of Ulyankulu itself by Christensen (1985:83–4).
13. Emphasis added. In other narratives, Mishamo was also often referred to as "our camp" with ironic intent.
14. See, for example, Lamb's (1985) patronizing, neocolonial account of "the Africans." See also Appadurai's excellent discussion of the "spatial incarceration of the native" (1988).
15. Cited in Frye (1969:224).
16. Cf. Jean Comaroff on wilderness (1985); and Malkki (1992a).
17. The death rate among the elderly and young children in the first years of exile was high. See Christensen 1985. This was also affirmed by a senior staff member of the TCRS Dar-es-Salaam office.
18. Cf. *ubugabire* "clientage" with regard to tribute in Vansina (1965); Chrétien (1983).
19. Composite panel. The first half is transcribed from a conversation between two informants; the second half presents the recollections of a single informant.
20. Fruitlessness in this instance may be seen to refer not only to crops left unharvested by their cultivators, but also as a loss of other forms of property, houses, domestic animals, and other possessions.

21. Single quotation from one person.
22. Continuous narrative by a single person.
23. See, for example, Armstrong (1985); TCRS *Annual Reports* (1984–86).
24. Information on black marketing was, of course, not readily accessible. Accounts were collected, when possible, from TCRS and UNHCR representatives, the refugees, and representatives of the Ministry of Home Affairs in Mishamo. The issue of black marketing and its place in the mythico-history appears again in chapter 4.
25. Composite panel excerpted from three persons' narratives, each recorded individually on separate occasions.
26. I am indebted to Jean Comaroff for this reference.
27. Taussig's (1980) conception of the "power of the oppressed" becomes less persuasive in this context. Cf. also Kapferer (1989) on Taussig.
28. See "The Hutu in Tanzania: Two Fieldwork Sites" in chapter 1.
29. The caste issue has been much discussed in the literature on Burundi and Rwanda. See Vansina (1972); Maquet (1961); Trouwborst (1962); Leclercq (1973); Weinstein (1976); Richards (1960); Lemarchand (1970, 1973). See also the outline of Burundian history in chapter 1.

    The heroization of cultivator status raises two apparent puzzles: first, the essentializing of the Hutu as the cultivating category seemed to stand in opposition to the Hutu assertion of entitlement to higher education and highly skilled professions or posts. This, however, was not seen as a contradiction in the mythico-history, though it might be so defined by others. Second, it might be suggested that, if cultivating created a fund of power upon which the parasitical" governing "other" was dependent, then simply ceasing to feed the "other" would have made it possible for the Hutu to transform their own encapturement in a revolutionary way. When queried about this theoretical possibility, people's most common reply was, in the words of one person: "We cannot help it; we are cultivators." Other informants also noted, reasonably, that the only way to feed themselves was'to cultivate and hope that the NMC (National Milling Corporation) and TAT (Tobacco Authority of Tanzania) would buy up what was produced.
30. UNHCR Legal Protection Officer in Kigoma, personal communication.
31. Single, continuous narrative.
32. Tsh. 150–200 per household for new buses which would run between Katumba and Mishamo, buses which, reportedly, nobody wanted because lorries would have been more practical; Tsh. 1 per head for something the purpose of which the people did not know or could not remember; Tsh. 160 per person eighteen or older for building the new party offices in Sumbawanga and Dodoma.
33. In the *ubugabire* system in Burundi, Hutu "clients" paid tribute to obtain protection and in token of loyalty to the Tutsi chiefs, or *shebuja*. See Vansina (1962); Trouwborst (1962). Cf. Rwanda's *buhake* system as discussed by Maquet (1961); D'Hertefelt (1962); and Lemarchand (1970, 1973).
34. Daley (n.d.:28) notes that the refugees in Tanzania "contribute some six million shillings in annual taxation to the local coffers."
35. Single, continuous narrative.

36. Composite of three persons' narratives, recorded on separate occasions.
37. Composite panel: excerpts from separate conversations with two people.
38. Cf. TCRS, *Handbook for Motivation Workers* (n.d.[c]). There was, however, at least one person among my informants who spoke very highly of the training in the English language that he had received at Ulyankulu Refugee Settlement.
39. *Apathy* is a term that often appears in the literature on refugees, especially the policy-oriented literature. It is not surprising for it to have appeared among TCRS, UNHCR, or MHA staff in Mishamo as well, and, in this way, to have worked itself into the vocabulary of the mythico-history.
40. According to one primary school headmaster in Mishamo, the figures on secondary school places allocated to Mishamo have been as follows: "Zero in 1982; not more than ten in 1983; not more than twenty in 1984; thirty-five (eleven girls and twenty-four boys) in 1985; and twenty-seven (nine girls, eighteen boys) in 1986." For comparative figures for another region of Tanzania, see Moore (1986).
41. The same was said of the German period in Burundi. One young teacher in Mishamo, a refugee, explained: "The first German colonizers were deceived that the Hutu are not able to govern. The Tutsi said that the Hutu are t-r-u-e cultivators—and so, then: they are not accustomed to governing. They said this to the Germans. The Germans had to accept this lie. They wanted to give education to the two groups, but the Tutsi did not accept this because they did not want the Hutu to be able to govern, since they knew that the great mass [were] Hutu and Batwa. And they knew that if the Hutu took power, they would eliminate them [from] the earth. That is to say that the Tutsi feared the Hutu because of the crimes they had done to the Hutu—that if the Hutu gained power, they would have to exact vengeance. And the Germans accepted without knowing what the Tutsi had done."
42. English was valued as an international language that would enable people to reach beyond their local circumstances, and to try to capture the ear of the international community that they imagined to be "out there." Hardly surprisingly, an even greater value was placed on French as a world language.
43. Composite panel: sections of two persons' narratives were strung together sequentially. (In the case of one person, two separate conversations with him were excerpted). The tendency to channel people from the Hutu refugee camps in Tanzania into vocational training has also been noted by Patricia Daley (1991:261).
44. This question is linked to a host of others, as Mbonimpa (1993:10) has poignantly noted: "Ainsi, en enseignant la littérature africaine à des enfants du Burundi, on se heurte toujours à cette question innocente: pourquoi n'y a-t-il aucun écrivain burundais? La réponse est simple, mais aucun enseignant ne la révélera aux élèves sans s'exposer aux représailles du pouvoir en place. Personne n'écrit, car le texte écrit est un boomerang mortel. La répression condamne à la stérilité même ceux qui, objectivement n'au-

raeint rien à craindre en écrivant. Ceux qui exercent la violence et ceux qui la subissent souffront de la même maladie, incurablement!"

45. It should be noted, however, that the camp refugees' children were more likely to speak Kirundi than were the town refugees' children.

46. Cf. Malkki (1994).

47. *Daily News* (Dar-es-Salaam). This was also mentioned in conversation with the staff of UNHCR and TCRS.

48. Cf. *Sunday News* (Tanzania), "Burundi trouble is internal, says Malecela," Sunday, 15 July 1973, 1; *Daily News* (Tanzania), "Tanzania will not tolerate more raids by Burundi—PM," Friday, 13 July 1973, 5; *Daily News* (Tanzania), "Government fully backs dockers over Burundi," Friday, 13 July 1973, 3; *Sunday News* (Tanzania), "Burundi troops kill seven Tanzanians," 1 July 1973, 1. Cf. also Melander and Nobel (1979).

49. Cf. Malkki (1985).

50. Cf. Ritvo (1987).

51. Composite panel of two persons' narratives.

52. Composite of two persons' narratives.

53. Cf. Armstrong 1988.

54. Cf. Armstrong (1988:67).

55. The term in the original was *une confidence*; it might also have been translated as "a secret," or, perhaps, "an understanding."

56. UPRONA (Parti de l'Unité et du Progrès National) was confirmed by the 1981 constitution as the only recognized political party in Burundi. See Kay (1987:7). See also the Postscript for more recent political changes.

57. A single, continuous narrative.

58. Composite of two persons' narratives.

59. Armstrong's observations (1988:67) in Mishamo also point to the uneven success of UN protection work: "[A] recent survey undertaken among [Mishamo's] village leaders discovered the considerable concern which they feel at what they see as victimization, powerlessness and exploitation (Armstrong 1987). They allege apparently disturbing harassment and infringements of their rights including suppression, maltreatment and wrongful arrest, and even violations of and fears for their security and physical safety. Treatment perceived as discriminatory also gave rise to concern and included limited educational opportunities and access to essential commodities and extended to alleged exploitation in terms of having to pay too many arbitrary financial levies." Armstrong (1988:67) goes on to add that "similar dissatisfactions" have been "expressed by village leaders in non-refugee communities elsewhere in Tanzania."

60. Composite panel: to an excerpt from a conversation with an informant in Mishamo a passage from an informant's 5 September 1985 letter (posted from Mishamo to the author in Kigoma) has been appended.

61. Cf. placards held by demonstrators on dust jacket of C. Newbury's (1988) book: "Vive le Ruanda! Vive la Belgique! Veve [*sic*] l'ONU!"; "A bas le colonialisme Tutsi. Démocratie d'abord, indépendence viendra. A bas indépendance immedite [*sic*]"; "Nos champs s.v.p.!".

62. The internationalism of the refugees in Mishamo is discussed in Malkki (1994).

CHAPTER FOUR

1. See Mafeje (1991); Scherer (1960a, 1960b, 1962); and cf. Taylor (1969) and Wagner (1991).
2. Cf. Said (1986a:4, 6) on icons of "Palestinian-ness" and "refugee-ness."
3. For a critical examination of the classical concept of "situational ethnicity," see John Comaroff (1987).
4. Cf. Donzelot (1979); Fox-Piven and Cloward (1971).
5. Scherer (1960a, 1960b); Vansina (1966); d'Hertefelt, Trouwborst, and Scherer (1962).
6. Cf. Van Binsbergen (1981:60); Tambiah (1986:6–7). Cf. also Abner Cohen (1969:2) on "retribalization."
7. Cf. Anderson ([1983]1991:184–5). Anderson's work on the role of the census, the map, and the museum in the colonial construction of ethnic categories fits well with Foucault's vision of documentation as a technique of power.
8. The speaker meant that undocumented workers would be returned to their villages, as has been the practice of the Tanzanian government.
9. All five of the young men lived in Ujiji, a town widely regarded as a "wild" place, less accessible than most towns or villages to official interventions, such as levy collection or the apprehension of lawbreakers.
10. Cf. Malkki (1992a:39, n. 20).
11. Lemarchand (1994) offers more precise historical and demographic information on the victims of the 1972 mass killings in Burundi.
12. Indeed, reliable information on income levels and sources would have been singularly difficult, if not practically impossible, to obtain in this setting.
13. According to some accounts, citizens also wanted refugees to be moved into camps. One town refugee casually encountered in a bar said to my research assistant: "Sometimes we were chased from their villages, it being said to us that it is dangerous to receive refugees. One said: 'The refugees have their places chosen by the government. For this, they will make you leave for the camps.'"
14. *Mjanja:* cheat, impostor, knave, rogue, sharper; pl. *wajanja* (Johnson 1939).
15. Cf. Cooper (1980) on fruit theft.
16. At first glance, it seemed that the remarkably high valuation of education or schooling was an axis of commonality between the camp refugees and the town refugees. In both settings, schooling was unquestionably seen as a desirable, valorized thing from which the Hutu had long been blocked. Indeed, this was one domain in which the town refugees, too, made reference to Burundi. Upon closer reflection, however, a difference did emerge between camp and town. In Mishamo, education was valorized as a source of benign knowledge or illumination and as the kind of knowledge that would ultimately empower the Hutu to overcome the domination of the Tutsi minority in Burundi and to create a revolutionary new nation. At this level, education and knowledge were conceived in mythico-historical terms. In Kigoma, education appeared to be valued as a source of empow-

erment also, but here the rewards of education were not directly rooted in the "homeland." The reward was simply the possibility of bettering one's life, as the following comment from a refugee teacher in Kigoma suggests: "In life, in general, there is no difference between a citizen and a noncitizen. For example, I am a teacher and a citizen is a teacher. I think we live in the same way. But for us as refugees it is important to get education to get a good life—a little bit—because it is difficult. You could get posts so you can get a good life. But also we have only 2 percent [of the refugees] who go to secondary school. [. . .] We are not allowed to join universities or colleges outside Africa. We do not know why. We always ask this question." This teacher's comments were similar to other informants' views on education in Kigoma insofar as the rewards of education were not automatically linked to a future in Burundi. Rather, the rewards tended to be seen as a personal resource for the amelioration of one's life in the present, wherever one might be living. It seems that the contrast between camp and town in the domain of education may best be understood in reference to the existence of the mythico-history in Mishamo, and its absence in Kigoma.

17. Emphasis added.
18. After research was completed, President Bagaza was ousted by Major Pierre Buyoya; and in 1993, Melchior Ndadaye was elected president. (See Postscript.)
19. See also Malkki (1992a:39n. 22).
20. Cf. Appadurai (1981:202).
21. That informants were found was thanks, in no small measure, to my research assistant. He met, or knew, people that I never would have met, as I met others that he would not have come across. He was also able to interview people in Ujiji where my official authorization to work was revoked by local party officials some weeks into this part of the project.
22. Surprisingly, these differences between camp and town seemed to hold even for those among the town refugees who were more politicized than most.

CHAPTER FIVE

1. Stories on this ran in the *Tanzania Daily News* in 1986. See, for example, "Machunda warns refugees," *Daily News* (Tanzania), 30 September 1986, 1: "The Kigoma Regional Commissioner, Professor John Machunda, told refugees along Lake Tanganyika that it was against the law for them to earn their living through illegal means or to threaten the peace and security of Tanzania. [. . .] Professor Machunda said the region had launched an exercise under which all residents, refugees and immigrants on the shores of Lake Tanganyika would be registered so as to enable the Government to find suitable areas for them to settle."
2. Cf. Chapter 2.
3. A single narrative.
4. I have explored at greater length elsewhere (Malkki 1992b, 1994) how important the international community or the outside world was as an imagined global community in the mythico-history.

5. Interestingly, the fact that the local employees of the international organizations, like the government staff, casually monitored the Hutu for signs of a decreasing refugeeness and for levels at which the Hutu no longer "acted" or "looked" like "real refugees" was not elaborated mythico-historically.

6. This was brought up by informants in connection with the visits of levy collectors in Mishamo.

7. A single narrative.

8. A single narrative.

9. Translated by my research assistant into Kirundi as *umwana w'ikinege* or simply *ikinege*. He noted that people seized by greedy fishermen were "not usually women since women do not usually fish." The other term he used in this connection was *ikimara*.

10. A boat like a canoe; a dugout.

11. Johnson and Madan (1939) translate *dagaa* as "very small fish, fish in an early stage, like whitebait."

12. A single narrative. Narratives on the danger of water as a habitat for *ibisigo* (bad spirits, ghosts) were common.

    When asked for a definition of *ikimara*, one person wrote in a 7 August 1992 letter that he did not know what the term meant, but mentioned another term, *ikimazi*, which, he said, "means *victim of substitution*. Example: I offer or sacrifice my children (to the spirits) to obtain magical powers. The child replaces me as victim because my commerce with the spirits necessarily demands a human sacrifice."

13. Composite of two persons' narratives. Nocturnal slaves were frequently discussed by people in Mishamo. They were also known to many informants in town, but the explicit moral connection traced in the camp was not made there.

    The terms used were *mwangaji* (Swahili) or *musambizi* (Kirundi) for "owner of the nocturnal slave"; and *kabwitunge* for "the noctural slave."

14. A 7 August 1992 letter from a Hutu refugee living outside Tanzania recognized the phenomenon of nocturnal slaves, but called them "*umuzuka* (sing.), *abazuka* (plur.). The letter notes: "Literally, the word means 'resuscitated' because the slaves are first asleep (in a coma). They are buried in the belief that they are dead. Then the slavers (who know that these dead are not dead) go to the cemetery and steal the pseudo-cadavres, reanimate them, and use them as slaves."

15. The foregoing beings were distinguished from "ghosts", that is, *ibisigo* (pl.), *igisigo* (sing.). The 7 August 1992 informant letter cited above translated *igisigo* as *revenant, fantôme* in French and *mzimu* in Swahili, and explained: "This is not exactly a 'spirit' because the *igisigo* can be visible. It is a bad spirit that can reincarnate itself in order to do evil, for example, to avenge itself on a family that has forgotten to offer [him/her] sacrifices. *Igisigo* = a dead person [male or female] who comes to life, who 'returns' to trouble the happiness of the living. No happiness in the land of the dead → our dead are jealous of our happiness."

16. Composite of two narrative fragments from one person.

17. These lorries were the main link between Mishamo and Dar-es-Salaam.

They ferried building supplies, spare parts, mail, food, medicine, and other basic goods.

18. Cf. Taussig (1980). His work on the Devil and commodity fetishism examines the question of how unequal wealth is glossed, but his interpretation is not illuminating in the present context. See also Ferguson (1993).

19. A single narrative.

20. Several people in Mishamo made a distinction between their own visions of other-worldliness as the future life to come in the homeland, and some too-passive camp pastors' views of it as the heavenly home. In some cases, Pentecostal pastors were singled out for criticism for promoting the latter view.

21. Accounts by Hutu refugees as well as conversations and written correspondence with representatives of UNHCR and TCRS agreed that such a camp was being planned, but it appears that nothing was implemented in the end. Of course, when new groups of refugees from Burundi began to move massively into Tanzania from October 1993 onwards, the international agencies and the government of Tanzania had to set up a whole new regional apparatus for emergency care, shelter, and feeding. Presumably these resources will now also be directed to the newest refugees from Rwanda (see Postscript).

22. Excerpted from a 3 June 1987 letter from a UNHCR staff member who preferred to remain unidentified.

23. Excerpted from a 3 June 1987 letter to the author from a UNHCR staff member who requested anonymity.

24. Some of these letters have been excerpted in the Postscript.

25. A single narrative.

26. A single narrative.

27. Hers was one of three foreign households remaining in Mishamo since the handover of Mishamo to the government of Tanzania in 1985.

28. Thus, the perceived absence of "material culture" became a symptom of a more profound pathology.

29. See, for example, Ndoricimpa and Guillet (1983:4–5).

30. On neoracism, cf. Balibar, in Balibar and Wallerstein (1991:17–28).

31. Palestinian refugees sometimes carry keys and deeds to homes they have lost (George Bisharat, personal communication).

32. A single narrative.

33. See Tanzania Refugee Control Act of 1965; Melander and Nobel (1979).

CHAPTER SIX

1. It was Jean Comaroff (personal communication) who first pointed out to me that the town refugees' denials of history were not the same thing as having no relationship with history at all.

2. Cf. Spencer (1990).

3. Sahlins's (1981, 1985) dichotomy between history and structure becomes problematic here.

4. Cf. Feldman (1991).

5. Cf. Anderson (1991).

6. George Bisharat, personal communication.

7. Cf. Malkki (1994).
8. Cf. Vail (1989); Hobsbawm (1983).
9. This conflict is discussed by Leclercq (1973).
10. Cf. Guy and Thabane (1988:258–9).
11. I would like to acknowledge the editorial assistance of Jacques Mourrain in my translation of Mauss from the French. (Cf. Malkki 1994).
12. Ronald Cohen, cited in Handler (1988:7).
13. See Balibar (1990); Donham (1990).
14. Cf. Anderson (1991:184) on serialization.
15. Cf. Malkki (1990b).
16. Cf. Borneman (1988).
17. Cf. Douglas (1996) and Tambiah (1985) on cosmologies.

POSTSCRIPT

1. Lemarchand (1994:126) estimates that 50,000 Hutu peasants fled to Rwanda, but that some 45,000 have since returned. Many of the returnees apparently faced political harassment and arbitrary arrest.
2. "Estimates of the death toll far exceed those of the 1972 military rampage that left 150,000 civilians dead in two weeks and made close to a million people refugees," reported Jeff Sharlet in "Burundi Bleeds," The Nation, 17 January 1994, p. 41. See also "Burundi Toll May Top That of '72 Massacre," Los Angeles Times, 27 November 1993, A16.
3. Frank Prial, "1,000 Feared Slain as New Strife Hits Burundi," New York Times, 14 March 1994, A5. Prial also reported: "At one point after the coup, when the new Government appeared to have restored a semblance of order and Hutu refugees began to return to their farms, renegade army units renewed the killings."
4. Lemarchand (personal communication, 31 May 1994) has noted that "it is essentially the Presidential Guard (recruited from the north and led by Bashiru elements from Habyalimana's home region) that organized the killings, eventually causing the army to be sucked into it."
5. Daley (n.d.) has written about this operation in the wider context of the uses of refugee law in Tanzania.
6. In connection with the roundup, people wrote a great deal about the issuance of refugee identity cards to Hutu refugees in towns and camps. Most in Mishamo wished to be registered as refugees, but objected to the fact that they were overcharged for the four passport-sized photographs that were required for an identity card. The charge consistently reported was Tsh.100,- meaning that a family of ten would have to spend Tsh.1000, - to be photographed. The camp refugees were convinced that the procedure should have been free, as it surely had been paid for by the United Nations. In Kigoma, of course, refugee registration had occurred in a most partial and piecemeal manner.
7. Daley (n.d.:12) notes that the roundup also extended to Morogoro, Mwanza, and Tabora.
8. The term in the original was ressortissants.
9. The original term herein translated as "sorting" was trillage. I believe the intended term was triage.

10. Translated from the French by the author. Emphasis added.
11. Anonymity was requested.
12. As I have not been in correspondence with all my informants, I do not know if any of those who were not in the habit of writing were returned.
13. I inquired about this point one year later, in 1988, and was told that "there are still not any who have gone to a camp."
14. See ten Horn and van der Velden (1987:34) for an analysis of some of the catalysts for the coup. This source, as well as Vanderdonckt (1987), mentions conflicts over the role of religion as key. Informants from Mishamo and Kigoma wrote about the state repression of the Roman Catholic church in Burundi in late 1986. (Anne Vanderdonckt, "Ce n'est qu'un putsch, mon Colonel!", Pourquoi pas?, 10 September 1987, p. 46.)
15. In 1988, I received the first tentative mentions (in three different persons' letters) of a possible voluntary return to Burundi by the Hutu refugees. One of these letters, dated March 1988, talked about the ways in which, in the author's view, the Hutu refugees were being worked harder than ever by the camp administrators in Mishamo. The author took that as a reflection of their imminent departure: "In comparison between the Hutu and the Jews, it is logical since when the Egyptians learned that the Jews proposed to return home, the work was augmented many times. For example, the quantity of bricks, the construction of the pyramids, etc. . . . Same as when, at the moment, we are obliged to manufacture bricks for the construction of the tribunal and the houses for the judge and his [staff]."
16. See also Amnesty International 1990:54–6.
17. Estimates of the 1988 death toll generally vary between 15,000 and 30,000, as Lemarchand has observed (personal communication, 31 May 1994).
18. The words bracketed were almost illegible in the original; the translation is a best guess.
19. Cf. Reyntjens (1990:111) on "scientific support."
20. See Reyntjens (1990:111ff.); Leclercq (1973:13); and the Government of Burundi White Paper (1972).
21. The estimate of sixty thousand refugees is from Pesonen (1989:100) who also gives an estimate of the death toll as fifteen thousand to twenty-four thousand. (Hannu Pesonen, "Vaikea kotiinpaluu", Suomen Kuvalehti, 6 January 1989, 100–101.) Cf. also Lemarchand (1989a, 1994:118ff.).
22. Pesonen (1989:100–101). Translated from the Finnish by the author.
23. Cited in Lemarchand (1989b:686). See also Government of Burundi (1991).
24. Excerpt from a 16 July 1988 letter by a Hutu refugee living outside of Africa.
25. This same country report also documents: "In April [1989] at least 21 other Burundi refugees were reportedly arrested in Ulyankulu refugee camp, also for alleged political activities, and detailed in Urambo Prison. It was not clear if they remained in detention at the end of the year. The arrests coincided with improved relations between Tanzania and Burundi" (Amnesty International 1990:233).
26. "Amnesty International is concerned about the continuing detention in

Tanzania of 14 refugees from Burundi who were originally taken into custody in March 1989, and is investigating whether they are prisoners of conscience detained solely for their nonviolent activities. The organization is also concerned that Rémi Gahutu, President of a Burundi opposition movement, the *Parti pour la libération du peuple Hutu* (PALIPEHUTU), Party for the Liberation of the Hutu people, who was detained along with the other 14 Burundi nationals, is reported to have died in detention on 17 August 1990." In: Amnesty International (1990b:1).

27. According to a 16 November 1990 letter from a longtime resident of Tanzania (a nonrefugee).

28. Amnesty International reports: "At least four people were reported to have been severely beaten at the time of their arrest, during a violent assault in August on Mabanda military camp by an armed group which had apparently infiltrated the country from Tanzania. At least seven people died in the attack. The four were still held without charge or trial in Rumonge prison at the end of 1990" (Amnesty International 1991:53).

29. There were mentions of individual cases of repatriation prior to 1991.

30. See Comité de la Solidarité pour la paix au Burundi (1990).

31. Charles Neary, Burundi Desk Officer, United States Department of State, personal communication, June 1991.

32. Cf. "Agreement on the Establishment of a Technical Working Group for the Promotion of Durable Solutions for Burundi Refugees between the Government of the Republic of Burundi, the Government of the United Republic of Tanzania, and the United Nations High Commissioner for Refugees," signed on 27 August 1991 by Hon. Augustine L. Mrema (M.P.), Minister for Home Affairs; Libère Bararunyeretse, Ministre de l'Intérieur et du Développement des Collectivités Locales; and William C.E. Young, Representative in Tanzania, the United Nations High Commissioner for Refugees.

33. See "Agreement . . ." (note 32 above), p. 5.

34. See also Government of Burundi (1992b).

35. The pastor usually wrote in French. I do not know to whom, or why, this letter may have been dictated.

36. "Challenger Wins Burundi Election," *Los Angeles Times,* 3 June 1993.

37. Cf. Gray (1994:4).

38. A Hutu refugee in North America, personal communication, 30 April 1994; accounts by relief workers in Tanzania.

39. A UNHCR official in Dar-es-Salaam, personal communication, 17 April 1994.

40. Personal communication, April 1994.

41. Personal communication, February 1994. Anonymity requested.

42. A UNHCR official, personal communication, April 1994.

43. UNCHR official in Dar-es-Salaam, personal communication, 17 April 1994.

44. A Hutu refugee living outside Africa who had discussed the land issue with the minister overseeing repatriation told me about it on 30 April 1994.

45. Melchior Mbonimpa, personal communication, 30 April 1994.

46. As Lemarchand (personal communication, 31 May 1994) has noted, violence did not erupt in the same manner everywhere: "few people came out in the streets in Bujumbura, they were scared stiff, Hutu and [Tutsi]; it is on the hills that FRODEBU anger exploded [. . .]."

47. Estimate in "Coup in Burundi," *Los Angeles Times*, 4 January 1994, H3. See also "Burundi: Still Bleeding," *The Economist*, 8 January 1994, p. 43, which has the astonishing range of estimates from 25,000 to 150,000.

48. A relief worker who requested anonymity, personal communication, February 1994.

49. "Burundi: Still Bleeding," *The Economist*, 8 January 1994, p. 43.

50. The number of Tutsi refugees from Burundi was at this time estimated at 934 by a relief worker; most Tutsi displaced by the fighting apparently remained in Burundi, and were reportedly being protected in "internal refugee camps" by the Burundi army. Personal communication, 7 February 1994.

51. "UN says 100 Burundians Dying Daily in Rwanda Camps," *Daily News* (Tanzania) 27 November 1994, p. 1, quotes UNHCR as saying that 375,000 fled to Rwanda, 245,000 to Tanzania, and 50,000 to Zaire. Monica Luwondo, "International Red Cross Pledges Relief for Burundi Refugees," *Daily News* (Tanzania) 6 November 1993, p. 1, gives the total number of Burundian refugees in Kigoma and Ngara, Tanzania, as 294,488.

52. "Burundi: Still Bleeding," *The Economist*, 8 January 1994, p. 43. Cf. Hélène (1994:13): "For Burundian refugees in Tanzania and Rwanda, conditions are appalling. According to [. . .] Médecins Sans Frontières (MSF), the 230,000 refugees in Tanzania are receiving only a quarter of the rations recommended by the [UNHCR] [. . .]. Already the daily death rate hovers between two and five per 10,000 and full-scale epidemics are threatened."

53. The White Fathers, the Swedish Free Mission, and the diocese in Kigoma and Kagera were reportedly among these missions.

54. UNHCR official, personal communication, 17 April 1994. The same figure of 500,000 is cited in: Zephania Musendo, "Tired of Being a Refugee All Her Life," *Daily News* (Tanzania), 15 November 1994, p. 11.

55. A relief worker who requested anonymity, personal communication, 7 February 1994.

56. But, according to the UNHCR official cited earlier, there were still hundreds of people traveling to Tanzania as new refugees in February 1994. Personal communication, April 1994.

57. Personal communication, 7 February 1994.

58. Personal communication, 17 April 1994.

59. These children were reportedly in the care of the International Committee of the Red Cross (ICRC).

60. A relief worker who requested anonymity, personal communication, 7 February 1994.

61. Relief worker who requested anonymity, 7 February 1994.

62. Relief worker who requested anonymity, personal communication, 7 February 1994.

63. This story was told to me by a representative of an international organization in Dar-es-Salaam who requested anonymity.

64. Melchior Mbonimpa, personal communication.
65. These theories were all outlined by Melchior Mbonimpa. Personal communication, April 1994.
66. See, for example, Watson (1992); Lemarchand (n.d. [a]); Kabera (1987).
67. Melchior Mbonimpa, personal communication, April 1994.
68. Emphasis in the original. Translated from the French by the author.
69. With the exception of a brief peace signed at Arusha last autumn, these two armies have been at war since October of 1990. The RPF has accused Rwanda's slain President Habyarimana of not even intending to honor the peace accords, of intentionally delaying the formation of a new, broad-based government, and France of cynically bolstering Habyarimana's government throughout. Source: "Kapinalliset syyttävät YK:ta ja länttä kaaoksesta", *Helsingin Sanomat*, 11 April 1994, p. C2. See also: "Bloodletting Sweeps Rwanda capital", *International Herald Tribune*, 8 April 1994, pp. 1, 4.
70. For example, there appears to be a division between northern Hutu and southern Hutu that complicates the Hutu-Tutsi opposition in Rwanda. This is discussed in: "Burundi-Rwanda: Que réserve l'avenir?", *La Libre Belgique*, 8 April 1994, p. 2.
    Similar oppositions have existed in Burundi between the southern "lake people" (*lacustres*) and the more northern "mountain people" (*montagnards*). As noted earlier, this regionalist opposition did not appear to be salient during fieldwork, but did flare up briefly in Katumba one year later.
71. Cf. Hilsum (1994:1).
72. The figure of 100,000 deaths was also reported in "Rwanda Death Toll Put at 100,000," *Los Angeles Times*, 25 April 1994, p. A17.
73. "Burundi Coup Fails as Rwanda Killing Goes On," *Manchester Guardian Weekly*, 1 May 1994, p. 1; "Rwanda Fighting Rages; Burundi Coup Aborted," *Los Angeles Times*, 26 April 1994, p. A10; "170 Massacred in Rwanda Hospital as Talks Fail, Fighting Continues," *Los Angeles Times*, 25 April 1994, p. A4.
74. The Rev. Franiszek Filipiec, a Marian Father, as quoted in Montalbano (1994:A14). As of last year, there were about seventy Catholic missionary orders, mainly European, working in Rwanda (Montalbano 1994:A15).
75. UNHCR official in Dar-es-Salaam, personal communication, 17 April 1994.
76. Mauss's essay on "techniques of the body" (1973 [1934]) could very usefully be read in relation to the study of techniques of silencing and censorship.
77. Mbonimpa (1993:10). Author's translation from the French.
78. The account of the foreign presence in Rwanda would not be accurate without at least a mention of the fact that the international arms trade has found a profitable market here. Smyth (1994) makes a compelling case for the central role of France, South Africa, Uganda, and Egypt in supplying the Rwandan army, noting also that eastern European states in need of hard currency are all too ready to export weapons that are becoming cheaper by the day. A recent report by the Human Rights Watch Arms

Project, based in Washington, D.C., claims that during the war, the Rwandan military "built up a mighty armoury for such a small country," and that it was supplied by France, Egypt, and South Africa. Source: "Joined in Death," *The Economist,* 9 April 1994, 45, 47 (page cited: 47).

The following assessment by a Hutu refugee in North America was made in reference to Burundi, but it might equally have referred to Rwanda: "I do not think that the nations are really interested in the problems of Burundi: there is no oil, no gold, no diamonds. . . . The single thing that could be interesting in Rwanda and Burundi: war as an opportunity to sell arms = a market for guns, grenades, missiles. . . . It is very good for business. No, I am not cynical. I simply state coldly what is happening."

It has also been reported that the Rwandan rebels "hold the international community partly responsible for Rwanda's current bloodletting. According to the rebels, there have been naive efforts to force Rwanda into a western multiparty system, without there being in place in the country mechanisms needed for democracy." Source: "Kapinalliset syyttävät YK:ta ja länttä kaaoksesta", *Helsingin Sanomat* 11 April 1994, C2. Translated from the Finnish by the author.

79. This issue has been debated during April 1994 in an open electronic mail forum called "primate-talk." See also Richter 1994, p. A13: "'There are some groups terribly concerned about the gorillas,' says Rep. Patricia Schroeder (D-Colo.), whose state is home to a gorillas research organization. 'But—it sounds terrible—people just don't know what can be done about the people.'"

80. Cf. Appadurai (1988) on the "spatial incarceration of the native."

81. This term emerged in conversation with Deborah Mindry.

# References

Abdallah, Tuma. 1993. "Nyang'anyi Urges Help for Refugees." *Sunday News* (Tanzania), 31 October, p. 1.

Abu-Lughod, Ibrahim (ed.). 1971. *The Transformation of Palestine: Essays on the Origin and Development of the Arab-Israeli Conflict*. Evanston: Northwestern University Press.

Acquier, Jean-Louis. 1986. *Le Burundi*. Marseilles: Éditions Parenthèses.

Adepoju, Aderanti. 1982. "The Dimension of the Refugee Problem in Africa." *African Affairs* 81: 21–35.

Africa. 1985. "We Want the Falashas Back." *Africa* 164 (April): 25–27.

Agrar- und Hydrotechnik GMBH. 1978. *Mishamo: Settlement and Water Development Planning*. Essen, Germany: Agrar- und Hydrotechnik GMBH for UNHCR.

Alho, Olli. 1987. "Culture and National Identity." In B. Almqvist, S. O Cathain, and P. O Healai (eds.), *The Heroic Process: Form, Function and Fantasy in Folk Epic*. Dublin: The Glendale Press.

Amnesty International. 1990a. *Amnesty International Report 1990*. New York: Amnesty International.

———. 1990b. "Tanzania: Burundi Nationals Detained in Tanzania." AI Index: AFR 56/07/90. New York: Amnesty International.

———. 1991. *Amnesty International Report 1991*. New York: Amnesty International.

———. 1993. "Extrajudicial Execution/Fear of Extrajudicial Execution/Fear of Torture/Incommunicado Detention." AI Index: AFR 47/03/93, 18 February. Mimeographed, 2 pp., marked for general distribution.

Anderson, Benedict. [1983] 1991. *Imagined Communities: Reflections on the Origin and Spread of Nationalism*. London: Verso.

———. 1992. "The New World Disorder." *New Left Review* 193: 3–13.

Anzaldua, Gloria. 1987. *Borderlands/La Frontera: The New Mestiza*. San Francisco: Spinsters/Aunt Lute.

Appadurai, Arjun. 1981. "The Past as a Scarce Resource." *Man* (n.s.) 16: 201–19.

———. 1986. "Introduction: Commodities and the Politics of Value." In Arjun Appadurai (ed.), *The Social Life of Things: Commodities in Cultural Perspective*, 3–63. Cambridge: Cambridge University Press.

———. 1988. "Putting Hierarchy in Its Place." *Cultural Anthropology* 3(1): 36–49.

———. 1990. "Disjuncture and Difference in the Global Cultural Economy." *Public Culture* 2(2): 1–24.

———. 1991. "Global Ethnoscapes: Notes and Queries for a Transnational

Anthropology." In Richard G. Fox (ed.), *Recapturing Anthropology: Workingin the Present*, 191–210. Santa Fe, NM: School of American Research Press.

Appadurai, Arjun, and Carol Breckenridge. 1988. "Why Public Culture?" *Public Culture. Bulletin of the Project for Transnational Cultural Studies* 1(1): 5–9.

Arendt, Hannah. [1951] 1973. *The Origins of Totalitarianism*. New York and London: Harcourt Brace Jovanovich.

Armstrong, Allen. 1985. *Study of Population and Land Occupancy at Mishamo Settlement, Rukwa*. Dar-es-Salaam: Report for the Tri-Partite Commission, Ministry of Home Affairs, UNHCR, TCRS.

———. 1986a. "Mishamo ou la nature domptée." *Réfugiés* (UNHCR) 25: 33–4.

———. 1986b. "Mishamo: Few Post-handover Blues." *Refugees* (UNHCR). (September): 13–4.

———. 1986c. "Mishamo: Taming the Wilderness." *Refugees* (UNHCR) 25: 33–4.

———. 1986d. "Mishamo: Transition." *Refugees* (UNHCR). (September): 13–14.

———. 1986e. "Tanganyika Christian Refugee Service (TCRS)." *Refugees* (UNHCR) 32, 41.

———. 1987. "Developing New Refugee Settlements: An Evaluation of Mishamo's Establishment and Operation." Dar-es-Salaam: LWF/TCRS. Mimeographed.

———. 1988. "Aspects of Refugee Wellbeing in Settlement Schemes: An Examination of the Tanzanian Case." *Journal of Refugee Studies* 1(1): 57–73.

Asad, Talal (ed.). 1973. *Anthropology and the Colonial Encounter*. Atlantic Highlands, NJ: Humanities Press.

Ayok, Chol. 1983. "Refugee Rights and Obligations in Tanzania." UNHCR Research Report. Dar-es-Salaam: UNHCR.

Balibar, Étienne. 1990. "Paradoxes of Universality." In David Theo Goldberg (ed.), *Anatomy of Racism*, 283–94. Minneapolis: University of Minnesota Press.

Balibar, Étienne, and Immanuel Wallerstein. 1991. *Race, Nation, Class: Ambiguous Identities*. New York: Verso.

Barkan, Joel, and John Okumu (eds.). 1979. *Politics and Public Policy in Kenya and Tanzania*. New York: Praeger.

Barthes, Roland. [1957] 1992. *Mythologies*. New York: Noonday Press.

Beattie, John. 1964. "Bunyoro: An African Feudality." *Journal of African History* 5(1): 25–36.

Beidelman, Thomas. 1980. "The Moral Imagination of the Kaguru: Some Thoughts on Tricksters, Translation, and Comparative Analysis." *American Ethnologist* 7: 27–42.

Benard, Cheryl. 1986. "Politics and the Refugee Experience." *Political Science Quarterly* 101(4): 617–36.

Benthall, Jonathan. 1980. "The Refugee Experience." *RAIN: Royal Anthropological Institute News* 37: 1–3.

Berger, Iris. 1981. *Religion and Resistance: East African Kingdoms in the Precolonial Period*. Tervuren, Belgium: Musée Royal de l'Afrique Centrale.

Berlin, Isaiah. 1991. *The Crooked Timber of Humanity: Chapters in the History of Ideas*. New York: Alfred A. Knopf.

Betts, T.F. 1969. "Zonal Rural Development in Africa." *Journal of Modern African Studies* 7(11): 149–54.

———. 1981. "Rural Refugees in Africa." *International Migration Review* 15(1): 213–8.

———. 1984. "Evolution and Promotion of the Integrated Rural Development Approach to Refugee Policy in Africa." *Africa Today* 31(1), 7–24.

Bhabha, Homi (ed.). 1990. *Nation and Narration.* New York: Routledge.

Bifuko, Baharanyi. 1980. "Post-Independence Rural Development: The Kigoma District in Western Tanzania." *Les cahiers du CEDAF* 8: 1–67. Brussels: Centre d'étude et de documentation africaines.

Biko, Steve. 1978. *I Write What I Like.* San Francisco: Harper & Row.

Bisharat, George. 1989. *Palestinian Lawyers and Israeli Rule: Law and Disorder in the West Bank.* Austin: University of Texas Press.

———. 1992. "Displacement and Social Identity: Palestinian Refugees in the West Bank." Unpublished manuscript.

Black, Eugene (ed.). 1964. *Posture of Europe, 1815–1940: Readings in European Intellectual History.* Homewood, IL: Dorsey Press.

Blake, William. [1826] 1984. *Songs of Experience.* New York: Dover.

Bloch, Maurice. 1977. "The Past and the Present in the Present." *Man* (n.s.) 12(2): 278–92.

Boas, Franz. 1962. *Anthropology and Modern Life.* New York: Norton.

Boateng, E.A. 1978. *A Political Geography of Africa.* Cambridge: Cambridge University Press.

Borneman, John. 1986. "Emigres as Bullets/Immigration as Penetration: Perceptions of the Marielitos." *Journal of Popular Culture* 20(3): 73–92.

———. 1988. "Race, Ethnicity, Species, Breed: Totemism and Horse-Breed Classification in America." *Comparative Studies in Society and History* 30(1): 25–51.

Bourdieu, Pierre. 1984. *Distinction: A Social Critique of the Judgment of Taste.* Translated by Richard Nice. Cambridge: Harvard University Press.

Bowen, Michael, Gary Freedman, Kay Miller, and Roger Morris. N.d. *Passing By: The United States and Genocide in Burundi 1972.* New York: Carnegie Endowment for International Peace.

Brooks, Hugh, and Yassin El-Ayouty (eds.). *Refugees South of the Sahara: An African Dilemma.* Westport, CT: Negro Universities Press.

Bujra, Janet. 1975. "Women 'Entrepreneurs' of Early Nairobi." *Canadian Journal of African Studies* 9(2): 213–34.

———. 1978–79. "Proletarianization and the 'Informal Economy': A Case Study from Nairobi." *African Urban Studies* 3 (Winter): 47–66.

Bulcha, Mekuria, Gaim Kibreab, Peter Nobel, and Michael Stahl. 1983. *Refugees and Development in Africa: Notes from an On-going Research Project.* Uppsala: Scandinavian Institute of African Studies.

Burke, Fred G. 1964. *Africa's Quest for Order.* Englewood Cliffs, NJ: Prentice-Hall.

Burundi, Government of. 1972. *The White Paper on the Real Causes and Consequences of the Attempted Genocide against the Tutsi Ethny in Burundi.* New York: The Permanent Mission of the Republic of Burundi to the United Nations.

———. 1991. *Rapport sur la démocratisation des institutions et la vie politique au Burundi.* Bujumbura: Commission Constitutionnelle.

———. 1992a. *Rapport de mission effectuée au Burundi du 1er au 8 juin 1992 par*

*un groupe de réfugiés burundais vivant en République Unie de Tanzanie,
accompagné d'officiels tanzaniens.* Bujumbura: Commission Nationale Chargée
du Retour, de l'Accueil et de la Réinsertion des Réfugiés Burundais.

———. 1992b. *La politique de rapatriement volontaire des réfugiés burundais:
réalisations et perspectives d'avenir.* Bujumbura: Commission Nationale
Chargée du Retour, de l'Accueil et de la Réinsertion des Réfugiés Burundais.

Chambers, Robert. 1969. *Settlement Schemes in Tropical Africa: A Study of
Organizations and Development.* London: Routledge & Kegan Paul.

———. 1979. "Rural Refugees in Africa: What the Eye Does Not See." *Disasters*
3(4): 381–92.

———. 1982. "Rural Refugees in Africa: Past Experience and Future Pointers."
*Disasters* 6(1): 21–30.

Chatterjee, Partha. 1986. *Nationalist Thought and the Colonial World: A
Derivative Discourse.* London: Zed.

Chomsky, Noam, and Edward S. Herman. 1979. *The Washington Connection and
Third World Fascism.* Boston: South End Press.

Chrétien, Jean-Pierre. 1984. "Nouvelles hypothèses sur les origines du Burundi:
Les traditions du Nord." In L. Ndoricimpa and C. Guillet (eds.), *L'arbre-
mémoire: Traditions orales du Burundi.* Paris: Karthala.

———. 1985. "Hutu et Tutsi au Rwanda et au Burundi." In Jean-Loup Amselle and
Elikia M'Bokolo (eds.), *Au coeur de l'ethnie: Ethnies, tribalisme et état en
Afrique,* 129–65. Paris: Éditions La Découverte.

———. 1990. "Social Sciences Facing Ethnic Violence." *Issue: A Journal of
Opinion* (Magazine of the African Studies Association) 19(1): 38–40.

———. 1991. "Burundi: Le métier d'historien: Querelle d'école?" *Revue
Canadienne des Études Africaines* 25(3): 450–67.

———, ed. 1983. *Histoire rurale de l'Afrique des Grands Lacs.* Paris: Karthala.

Chrétien, Jean-Pierre, André Guichaoua, and Gabriel Le Jeune. *La crise d'août
1988 au Burundi:* Paris: Karthala, 1989.

Christensen, Hanne. 1985. *Refugees and Pioneers: History and Field Study of a
Burundian Settlement in Tanzania.* Geneva: UNRISD.

Cirtautas, Claudius Kazys. 1957. *The Refugee: A Psychological Study.* Boston:
Meador.

Clay, Jason. 1984. *The Eviction of Banyarwanda: The Story behind the Refugee
Crisis in Southwest Uganda.* Cambridge, MA: Cultural Survival.

Clifford, James. 1988. *The Predicament of Culture: Twentieth-Century
Ethnography, Literature, and Art.* Cambridge: Harvard University Press.

Codere, Helen. 1962. "Power in Rwanda." *Anthropologica* 4(1): 45–85.

Cohen, Abner. 1969. *Custom and Politics in Urban Africa: A Study of Hausa
Migrants in Yoruba Towns.* Berkeley and Los Angeles: University of California
Press.

Cohen, David William. 1989. "The Undefining of Oral Tradition." *Ethnohistory*
36(1): 9–17.

Cohen, Ronald. 1978. "Ethnicity: Problem and Focus in Anthropology." *Annual
Review of Anthropology* 7: 379–403.

Colson, Elizabeth. 1971. *The Social Consequences of Resettlement: The Impact of
the Kariba Resettlement upon the Gwembe Tonga.* Manchester, England:
Manchester University Press.

Comaroff, Jean. 1985. *Body of Power, Spirit of Resistance: The Culture and History of a South African People*. Chicago: University of Chicago Press.

Comaroff, John L. 1982. "Dialectical Systems, History and Anthropology." *Journal of Southern African Studies* 8: 143–72.

———. 1987. "Of Totemism and Ethnicity: Consciousness, Practice, and the Signs of Inequality." *Ethnos* 52: 301–23.

Comaroff, John, and Jean Comaroff. 1967. "The Madman and the Migrant: Work and Labor in the Historical Consciousness of a South African People." *American Ethnologist* 14(2): 191–209.

Comité de la solidarité pour la paix au Burundi. 1990. *Charte de retour au pays natal*. Geneva: Actes du colloque sur le problème des réfugiés burundais (24 November).

Communauté des Refugiés Burundais de Dakar. 1991. "Appel en faveur d'une paix durable au Burundi." Mimeographed.

Coquery-Vidrovitch, Catherine, and Henri Moniot. 1974. *L'Afrique noire de 1800 à nos jours*. Paris: Presses Universitaires France.

Cooper, Frederick. 1980. *From Slaves to Squatters: Plantation Labor and Agriculture in Zanzibar and Coastal Kenya*. New Haven: Yale University Press.

Coronil, Fernando, and Julie Skurski. 1991. "Dismembering and Remembering the Nation: The Semantics of Political Violence in Venezuela." *Comparative Studies in Society and History* 33(2): 288–337.

Corrigan, Philip, and Derek Sayer. 1985. *The Great Arch: English State Formation as Cultural Revolution*. Oxford: Basil Blackwell.

Coulson, Andrew. 1975. "Peasants and Bureaucrats." *Review of African Political Economy* 3: 51–5.

———. 1982. *Tanzania: A Political Economy*. Oxford: Clarendon Press.

Crapanzano, Vincent. 1980. *Tuhami: Portrait of a Moroccan*. Chicago: University of Chicago Press.

———. 1985. *Waiting: The Whites of South Africa*. New York: Random House.

Crepeau, Pierre. 1985. *Parole et sagesse: Valeurs sociales dans les proverbes du Rwanda*. Tervuren, Belgium: Musée Royal de l'Afrique Centrale.

Curtin, Philip, Steven Feierman, Leonard Thompson, and Jan Vansina. 1978. *African History*. Essex: Longman.

Daley, Patricia. 1991. "Gender, Displacement and Social Reproduction: Settling Burundi Refugees in Western Tanzania." *Journal of Refugee Studies* 4(3): 248–66.

———. n.d. "The Politics of the Refugee Crisis in Tanzania." Unpublished manuscript.

Daniel, E. Valentine. 1990. "The Individual in Terror." Paper presented at the annual meeting of the American Ethnological Society, 28 April, Atlanta, Georgia.

David, Henry. 1969. "Involuntary International Migration." *International Migration Review* 7(3/4), 67–105.

De Barrin, Jacques. 1986. "Kigoma, capitale de tous les trafics." *Le Monde*, 9 June, n.p. Mimeographed.

De Heusch, Luc. 1964. "Mythe et société féodale: Le culte kubandwa dans le Rwanda traditionnel." *Archives de Sociologie des Réligions* 18: 133–46.

———. 1966. *Le Rwanda et la civilisation interlacustre*. Brussels: Université libre de Bruxelles, Institut de Sociologie.

———. 1982. *Rois nés d'un coeur de vache*. Paris: Gallimard.

Deleuze, Gilles, and Felix Guattari. 1987. *A Thousand Plateaus: Capitalism and Schizophrenia*. Minneapolis: University of Minnesota Press.

D'Hertefelt, Marcel. 1962. "Le Rwanda." In Marcel D'Hertefelt, Albert Trouwborst, and J.H. Scherer, *Les anciens royaumes de la zone interlacustre méridionale: Rwanda, Burundi, Buha*. Tervuren, Belgium: Musée Royal de l'Afrique Centrale.

D'Hertefelt, Marcel, Albert Trouwborst, and Johan Herman Scherer. 1962. *Les anciens royaumes de la zone interlacustre méridionale: Rwanda, Burundi, Buha*. Tervuren, Belgium: Musée Royal de l'Afrique Centrale.

Dirks, Nicholas. 1992. Introduction to *Colonialism and Culture*, edited by Nicholas Dirks, 1–25. Ann Arbor: University of Michigan Press.

Doheny, Kevin, Fr. 1982. *Mishamo Refugee Settlement, Tanzania*. Unpublished manuscript.

Donham, Donald L. 1990. *History, Power, Ideology: Central Issues in Marxism and Anthropology*. New York: Cambridge University Press.

Donzelot, Jacques. 1979. *The Policing of Families*. New York: Pantheon.

Doob, L. 1964. *Patriotism and Nationalism*. New Haven: Yale University Press.

Douglas, Mary. 1966. *Purity and Danger: An Analysis of the Concepts of Pollution and Taboo*. London: Routledge and Kegan Paul.

Drakulić, Slavenka. 1992. "You Are Balkans, the World Tells Us, Mythological, Wild, Dangerous." *New York Times Magazine* 13 (September): 36–37, 68, 70.

Dreyfus, Hubert, and Paul Rabinow. 1983. *Michel Foucault: Beyond Structuralism and Hermeneutics*. Chicago: University of Chicago Press.

Du Bois, Victor. 1972. *To Die in Burundi*. American Universities Field Staff Reports, Central and Southern African Series 16(4). New York: American Universities Field Staff.

Economist Intelligence Unit. 1993. *EIU Country Profile, 1992–93: Burundi*, 56–76. London: The Economist Intelligence Unit.

Eisenstadt, S.N., and S. Rokkan. 1973. *Building States and Nations*. Beverly Hills, CA: Sage.

Eriksson, Lars-Gunnar, Goran Melander, and Peter Nobel (eds.). 1981. *An Analysing Account of the Conference on the African Refugee Problem: Arusha, May 1979*. Uppsala: Scandinavian Institute of African Studies.

Evans-Pritchard, Edward. 1940. *The Nuer*. Oxford: Oxford University Press.

———. 1976. *Witchcraft, Oracles, and Magic among the Azande*. Oxford: Oxford University Press.

Fabian, Johannes. 1983. *Time and the Other: How Anthropology Makes Its Object*. New York: Columbia University Press.

Fallers, Lloyd A. 1974. *The Social Anthropology of the Nation-State*. Chicago: Aldine.

Fanon, Franz. 1965. *The Wretched of the Earth*. New York: Grove.

Feldman, Allen. 1991. *Formations of Violence: The Narrative of the Body and Political Terror in Northern Ireland*. Chicago: University of Chicago Press.

Ferguson, James. 1993. "De-moralizing Economies: African Socialism, Scientific Capitalism, and the Moral Politics of Structural Adjustment." In Sally Falk

Moore (ed.), *Moralizing States and the Ethnography of the Present.* Washington, DC: American Ethnological Society.

Fishman, J. 1972. *Language and Nationalism: Two Integrative Essays.* Rowley, MA: Newbury House.

Forbes Martin, Susan. 1992. *Refugee Women.* London: Zed.

Foucault, Michel. 1972a. *The Archaeology of Knowledge and the Discourse on Language.* New York: Pantheon.

———. 1972b. *Power/Knowledge.* New York: Harper and Row.

———. 1973. *The Order of Things: An Archaeology of the Human Sciences.* New York: Vintage.

———. 1977. *Language, Counter-Memory, Practice.* Ithaca, NY: Cornell University Press.

———. 1979. *Discipline and Punish: The Birth of the Prison.* New York: Vintage.

———. 1980. *Power/Knowledge: Selected Interviews and Other Writings 1972–1977.* New York: Pantheon.

Fox-Piven, Frances, and Richard Cloward. 1971. *Regulating the Poor: The Functions of Public Welfare.* New York: Vintage.

Frankenberg, Ruth. 1993. *White Women, Race Matters: The Social Construction of Whiteness.* Minneapolis: University of Minnesota Press.

Freyhold, Michaela von. 1979. *Ujamaa Villages in Tanzania: Analysis of a Social Experiment.* New York and London: Monthly Review Press.

Frye, Northrop. 1969. *Fearful Symmetry: A Study of William Blake.* Princeton, NJ: Princeton University Press.

Gahama, Joseph. 1983. *Le Burundi sous administration belge.* Paris: C.R.A., Karthala, A.C.C.T.

Gasarasi, Charles. 1984. *The Tripartite Approach to the Resettlement and Integration of Rural Refugees in Tanzania.* Research Report No. 71. Uppsala: Scandinavian Institute of African Studies.

———. 1988. "The Effect of Africa's Exiles/Refugees upon Inter-African State Relations: Conflict and Cooperation, 1958–1988." Ph.D. diss., Tulane University.

Geertz, Clifford. 1973. *The Interpretation of Cultures.* New York: Basic Books.

———. 1994. "The Uses of Diversity." In Robert Borofsky (ed.), *Assessing Cultural Anthropology,* 454–65. New York: McGraw-Hill.

Gellner, Ernest. 1964. *Thought and Change.* London: Weidenfeld.

———. 1983. *Nations and Nationalism.* Ithaca, NY: Cornell University Press.

Gerstenzang, James, and Tyler Marshall. 1994. "10,000 Die in Rwanda; Many Foreigners Escape." *Los Angeles Times,* 11 April, pp. A1, A9.

Geschiere, Peter. 1988. "Sorcery and the State: Popular Modes of Action among the Maka of Southeast Cameroon," *Critique of Anthropology* 8(1): 35–63.

Ghosh, Amitav. 1989. *The Shadowlines.* New York: Viking.

Giddens, Anthony. 1987. *The Nation-State and Violence.* Berkeley and Los Angeles: University of California Press.

Gilroy, Paul. 1990a. "Nationalism, History, and Ethnic Absolutism." *History Workshop Journal* 30: 114–20.

———. 1990b. "One Nation under a Groove: The Cultural Politics of 'Race' and Racism in Britain." In David Theo Goldberg (ed.), *Anatomy of Racism.* Minneapolis: University of Minnesota Press, 263–82.

————. 1991. *There Ain't No Black in the Union Jack: The Cultural Politics of Race and Nation.* Chicago: University of Chicago Press.

Goffman, Erving. 1961a. "On the Characteristics of Total Institutions: The Inmate World." In D. Cressey (ed.), *The Prison,* 15–67. New York: Holt, Rinehart, and Winston.

————. 1961b. *Asylums.* New York: Anchor.

————. 1963. *Stigma.* Englewood Cliffs, NJ: Prentice-Hall.

Goodman, Nelson. 1978. *Ways of Worldmaking.* Indianapolis and Cambridge: Hackett.

Goody, Jack. 1963. "Feudalism in Africa." *Journal of African History* 4(1): 1–18.

————. 1971. *Technology, Tradition, and the State in Africa.* Oxford: Oxford University Press.

Gordimer, Nadine. 1984. *Something Out There.* Harmondsworth, England: Penguin.

Grahl-Madsen, Atle. 1983. "Identifying the World's Refugees." In Gilburt Loescher and John Scanlan (eds.), *The Global Refugee Problem,* special issue, *The Annals of the American Academy of Political and Social Science,* 11–23. Beverly Hills, CA: Sage.

Gray, Jerry. 1994. "Land Struggle Fuels Bloody Slaughter." *Manchester Guardian Weekly,* 17 April, p. 4.

Greenland, Jeremy. 1973. "Black Racism in Burundi." *New Black Friars* (Oxford), 443–51.

————. 1974. "African Bloodbath That Most of the World Ignored." *The Times* (London), 4 January.

————. 1976. "Ethnic Discrimination in Rwanda and Burundi." In Willem A. Veenhoven (ed.), *Case Studies in Human Rights and Fundamental Freedoms: A World Survey,* vol. 4, 95–134. The Hague: Martinus Nijhoff.

Greenland, Jeremy. 1980. "Western Education in Burundi 1916–1973: The Consequences of Instrumentalism." *Les Cahiers du CEDAF* no. 2/3, pp. 1–126.

Grillo, R.D. 1980. *"Nation" and "State" in Europe: Anthropological Perspectives.* London and New York: Academic Press.

Guy, Jeff, and Motlatsi Thabane. 1988. "Technology, Ethnicity and Ideology: Basotho Miners and Shaft Sinking on the South African Gold Mines." *Journal of Southern African Studies* 14(2): 257–78.

Hakizimana, G. 1987. "Des irréguliers refoulés de Tanzanie." *Le Renouveau du Burundi,* 14 April, 1.

Hamrell, Sven. 1967. "The Problem of African Refugees." In Sven Hamrell (ed.), *Refugee Problems in Africa.* Uppsala: Scandinavian Institute of African Studies.

Handler, Richard. 1985. "On Having a Culture: Nationalism and the Preservation of Quebec's *patrimoine.*" In George Stocking (ed.), *Objects and Others, History of Anthropology,* vol. 3, 192–217. Madison: University of Wisconsin Press.

————. 1988. *Nationalism and the Politics of Culture in Quebec.* Madison: University of Wisconsin Press.

Hannerz, Ulf. 1987. "The World in Creolisation." *Africa* 57(4): 546–59.

Haraway, Donna J. 1991. "Situated Knowledges: The Science Question in Feminism and the Privilege of Partial Perspective." In *Simians, Cyborgs, and Women: The Reinvention of Nature.* New York: Routledge.

Harland, David. 1988. "The Ivory Chase Moves On." *New Scientist*, 7 January, pp. 30–31.

Harrell-Bond, Barbara. 1986. *Imposing Aid: Emergency Assistance to Refugees.* Oxford: Oxford University Press.

Hebdige, Dick. 1979. *Subculture: The Meaning of Style.* London: Methuen.

———. 1987. *Cut'n'Mix: Culture, Identity and Caribbean Music.* London: Methuen.

Hélène, Jean. 1993. "Fear of the Unknown as President Is Ousted." *Manchester Guardian Weekly*, 13 June, p. 13.

———. 1994. "A Political Vacuum Waiting to Be Filled." *Manchester Guardian Weekly*, 9 January, p. 13.

Herzfeld, Michael. 1987. *Anthropology through the Looking-glass: Critical Ethnography in the Margins of Europe.* Cambridge: Cambridge University Press.

Heyer, Judith, Pepe Roberts, and Gavin Williams (eds.). 1981. *Rural Development in Tropical Africa.* London: Macmillan.

Hilsum, Lindsey. 1994. "Burundi Coup Fails as Rwanda Killing Goes On." *Manchester Guardian Weekly* (week ending 1 May 1994): 1.

Hobsbawm, Eric. 1983. "Introduction: Inventing Traditions." In Eric Hobsbawm and Terence Ranger (eds.), *The Invention of Tradition.* Cambridge: Cambridge University Press.

Hobsbawm, Eric, and Terence Ranger (eds.). 1983. *The Invention of Tradition.* New York: Columbia University Press.

Honko, Lauri. 1980. "Upptäckten av folkdiktning och nationell identitet i Finland." *Tradisjon* 10.

Hyden, Goran. 1980. *Beyond Ujamaa in Tanzania: Underdevelopment and an Uncaptured Peasantry.* Berkeley and Los Angeles: University of California Press.

———. 1983. *No Shortcuts to Progress: African Development Management in Perspective.* Berkeley and Los Angeles: University of California Press.

Iliffe, John. 1979. *A Modern History of Tanganyika.* Cambridge: Cambridge University Press.

Jessup, Philip C. 1974. *The Birth of Nations.* New York: Columbia University Press.

Johnson, Frederick, and Madan. 1939. *A Standard Swahili-English Dictionary.* Oxford: Oxford University Press.

Joseph, Bernard. 1929. *Nationality: Its Nature and Problems.* London: George Allen & Unwin.

Kabera, John. 1987. "The Refugee Problem in Uganda." In John R. Rogge (ed.), *Refugees: A Third World Dilemma*, 72–79. Totowa, NJ: Rowman and Littlefield.

Kapferer, Bruce. 1988. *Legends of People, Myths of State: Violence, Intolerance, and Political Culture in Sri Lanka and Australia.* Washington, DC: Smithsonian Institution Press.

———. 1989. "The Anthropologist as Hero: Three Exponents of Post-Modernist Anthropology." *Critique of Anthropology* 8(2): 77–104.

Kay, Reginald. 1987. *Burundi Since the Genocide.* Report no. 20. London: The Minority Rights Group.

Kedourie, Elie. 1960. *Nationalism*. London: Hutchinson.

Kemiläinen, Aira. 1964. *Nationalism: Problems Concerning the Word, the Concept, and Classification*. Jyväskylä, Finland: Jyväskylän kasvatusopillinen korkeakoulu.

Kibreab, Gaim. 1983. *Reflections on the African Refugee Problem: A Critical Analysis of Some Basic Assumptions*. Research report no. 67. Uppsala: Scandinavian Institute of African Studies.

Kimambo, Isaria, and Arnold Temu (eds.). 1969. *A History of Tanzania*. Nairobi: East African Publishing House.

Kiraranganya, Boniface. 1985. *La vérité sur le Burundi*. Sherbrooke, Quebec: Éditions Naaman.

Kismaric, Carole. 1989. *Forced Out: The Agony of the Refugee in Our Time*. New York: Random House.

Kohn, Hans. 1955. *Nationalism: Its Meaning and History*. Princeton, NJ: Van Nostrand.

———. 1962. *The Age of Nationalism*. New York: Harper.

Kopytoff, Igor. 1988. "Public Culture: A Durkheimian Genealogy." *Public Culture: Bulletin of the Project for Transnational Cultural Studies* 1(1): 11–16.

Kritz, Mary, Charles Keely, and Silvano Tomasi (eds.). 1983. *Global Trends in Migration: Theory and Research on International Population Movements*. New York: Center for Migration Studies.

Kuper, Leo. 1982. *Genocide: Its Political Use in the Twentieth Century*. New Haven: Yale University Press.

Lamb, David. 1985. *The Africans*. New York: Vintage.

Lan, David. 1985. *Guns and Rain: Guerillas and Spirit Mediums in Zimbabwe*. London: James Currey.

Lash, Scott. 1984. "Genealogy and the Body: Foucault/Deleuze/Nietzsche." *Theory, Culture, and Society* 2(2): 1–17.

Leclercq, C. 1973. "Les racines du mal . . . ou la triple mystification." *La relève* 29(28): 11–5.

Lemarchand, René. 1970. *Rwanda and Burundi*. New York: Praeger.

———. 1973. "Power and Stratification in Rwanda: A Reconsideration." In Elliott P. Skinner (ed.), *Peoples and Cultures of Africa*. Garden City, NY: Doubleday.

———. 1989a. "The Killing Fields Revisited." *Issue: A Journal of Opinion* 18(1): 22–28.

———. 1989b. "The Report of the National Commission to Study the Question of National Unity in Burundi: A Critical Comment." *Journal of Modern African Studies* 27(4): 685–90.

———. 1990a. "L'école historique burundo-française: Une école pas comme les autres." *Revue Canadienne des Études Africaines* 24(2): 235–48.

———. 1990b. "Response to Jean-Pierre Chrétien." *Issue: A Journal of Opinion* 19(1): 41.

———. 1991. "Réponse à Jean-Pierre Chrétien." *Revue Canadienne des Études Africaines* 25(3): 468–70.

———. 1992. "The Burundi Genocide." Unpublished manuscript.

———. 1994. *Burundi: Ethnocide as Discourse and Practice*. New York: Woodrow Wilson Center Press and Cambridge University Press.

———. n.d. (a) "The Rwanda Refugees: Exile and Eternal Return." Unpublished manuscript.

———. n.d. (b) "Rwanda Politics since the RPF Invasion." Mimeographed.

———. n.d. (c) "Postscript" to *Burundi: Ethnocide as Discourse and Practice.* Forthcoming.

Lemarchand, René, and David Martin. 1974. *Selective Genocide in Burundi.* Report no. 20. London: The Minority Rights Group.

Leslie, J. A. K. 1963. *A Social Survey of Dar es Salaam.* Oxford: Oxford University Press.

Lévi-Strauss, Claude. 1966. *The Savage Mind.* Chicago: University of Chicago Press.

———. 1976. *Structural Anthropology.* Vol. 2, translated by Monique Layton. New York: Basic Books.

———. 1985. *The View from Afar.* Translated by Joachim Neogroschel and Phoebe Hoss. New York: Basic Books.

———. 1994. "Anthropology, Race, and Politics: A Conversation with Didier Eribon." In Robert Borofsky (ed.), *Assessing Cultural Anthropology,* 420–29. New York: McGraw-Hill.

Lewis, Paul. 1994. "'U.S.' Examines Way to Assist Rwanda without Troops." *New York Times,* 1 May, pp. 1, 13.

Loescher, Gilbert, and John Scanlan. 1983. "Preface." In G. Loescher and J. Scanlan (eds.), *The Global Refugee Problem,* special issue, *The Annals of the American Academy of Political and Social Science,* 9–10. Beverly Hills, CA: Sage.

Lomoy, Jon. 1981. "Planning Spatial Change: The Use of Settlement Pattern as a Variable in Kigoma, Tanzania." *Papers from the Department of Geography* (University of Trondheim) 19: 1–35. Reprinted in *Choros* 1982: 2, 162–78.

Lorch, Donatella. 1993. "Burundi after Mutiny: Horror Stories Everywhere." *New York Times,* 21 November, p. 3.

———. 1994. "UN in Rwanda Says It Is Powerless to Halt the Violence." *New York Times,* 15 April, p. A3.

Lugusha, E.A. 1981. "Final Report of a Socio-Economic Survey of Barundi Refugees in Kigoma Region." Dar-es-Salaam: Economic Research Bureau, Univ. of Dar-es-Salaam. Unpublished manuscript.

Lyotard, Jean François. 1973. *Des dispositifs pulsionnels.* Paris: Union Générale d'Éditions.

MacBride, Oistin. 1994. "First Aid for Burundi Refugees." Unpublished manuscript, p. 1.

Mafeje, Archie. 1991. *The Theory and Ethnography of African Social Formations: The Case of the Interlacustrine Kingdoms.* London: CODESRIA.

Mair, Lucy. 1977. *African Kingdoms.* Oxford: Clarendon Press.

Malinowski, Bronislaw. 1944. *Freedom and Civilization.* New York: Roy.

Malkki, Liisa. 1985. "The Origin of a Device of Power: The Refugee Camp in Post-War Europe." Unpublished manuscript submitted as the "Specials Paper," Department of Anthropology, Harvard University.

———. 1989. "Purity and Exile: Transformations in Historical-National Consciousness among Hutu Refugees in Tanzania." Ph.D. diss., Harvard University.

———. 1990a. "Context and Consciousness: Local Conditions for the Production of Historical and National Thought among Hutu Refugees in Tanzania." In Richard G. Fox (ed.), *Nationalist Ideologies and the Production of National Cultures*. American Ethnological Society Monograph Series, no. 2. Washington, DC: American Anthropological Association.

———. 1990b. "Violence and Ethnography: Problems of Representation and Dehumanization." Paper presented at the annual meeting of the American Anthropological Association, New Orleans.

———. 1992a. "National Geographic: Rooting of Peoples and the Territorialization of National Identity among Scholars and Refugees." *Cultural Anthropology* 7(1): 24–44.

———. 1992b. "A Global Affair: Nationalism and Internationalism as Cultural and Moral Practices." Paper presented at the annual meeting of the American Ethnological Society, Memphis, TN, March 1992.

———. 1994. "Citizens of Humanity: Internationalism and the Imagined Community of Nations." *Diaspora* 3(1): 41–68.

Mann, Jim. 1994. "Clinton Calls on Rwanda Rivals to End Warfare." *Los Angeles Times*, 1 May, pp. A1, A10.

Mankekar, Purnima. Forthcoming. "Reflections on Travel, Bifocality, and Diasporic Identities." *Diaspora*.

Maquet, Jacques. 1961. *The Premise of Inequality in Ruanda: A Study of Political Relations in a Central African Kingdom*. London: Oxford University Press.

Marrus, Michael. 1985. *The Unwanted: European Refugees in the Twentieth Century*. New York: Oxford University Press.

Martin, Emily. 1991. "Toward an Anthropology of Immunology: The Body as Nation-State." *Medical Anthropology Quarterly* 5: 410–26.

Marx, Karl, and Friedrich Engels. [1846] 1970. *The German Ideology*. New York: International Publishers.

Mauss, Marcel. 1954. *The Gift: Forms and Functions of Exchange in Archaic Societies*, translated by Ian Cunnison. London: Cohen and West.

———. [1920?] 1969. "La nation et l'internationalisme." In Marcel Mauss, *Oeuvres*, ed. V. Karady, vol. 3: *Cohésion sociale et divisions de la sociologie*, 573–639. Paris: Minuit.

———. [1934] 1973. "Techniques of the Body." *Economy and Society* 2(1): 70–88.

Mazzini, Giuseppe. [1849] 1891. "The Holy Alliance of the Peoples." In *Life and Writings of Joseph Mazzini*. Vol. 5, *Autobiographical and Political*, 265–82. London: Smith, Elder.

Mbonimpa, Melchior. 1993. *Hutu, Tutsi, Twa: Pour une société sans castes au Burundi*. Paris: L'Harmattan.

McHenry, Dean. 1979. *Tanzania's Ujamaa Villages: The Implementation of a Rural Development Strategy*. Berkeley: Institute of International Studies, University of California.

McNeill, William H. 1986. *Polyethnicity and National Unity in World History*. Toronto: University of Toronto Press.

Meisler, Stanley. 1994. "UN Leader Asks for Troops for Rwanda." *Los Angeles Times*, 30 April, pp. A1, A2.

Melady, Thomas. 1974. *Burundi: The Tragic Years*. New York: Orbis Books.

Melander, Göran, and Peter Nobel (eds.). 1978. *African Refugees and the Law*. Uppsala: Scandinavian Institute of African Studies.

———. 1979. *International Legal Instruments on Refugees in Africa.* Uppsala: Scandinavian Institute of African Studies.

Meyer, Hans. 1916. *Die Barundi: Eine völkerkundliche Studie aus Deutsch-Ostafrika.* Leipzig: O. Spamer.

Ménard, François. 1918. *Barundi: Moeurs et coutumes.* Rome: Archives des Pères Blancs. Doc. 803.12.

Miserez, Diana (ed.). 1988. *Refugees—The Trauma of Exile: The Humanitarian Role of Red Cross and Red Crescent.* Dordrecht and London: Martinus Nijhoff.

Mitchell, Timothy. 1988. *Colonising Egypt.* Cambridge: Cambridge University Press.

———. 1992. "Orientalism and the Exhibitionary Order." In Nicholas Dirks (ed.), *Colonialism and Culture.* Ann Arbor: University of Michigan Press.

Montalbano, William. 1994. "Rwanda Offers No Sanctuary from Chaos." *Los Angeles Times,* 20 April, pp. A14–A15.

Moore, Sally Falk. 1986. *Social Fact and Fabrication: "Customary" Law on Kilimanjaro, 1880–1980.* Cambridge: Cambridge University Press.

Morel, Edmund D. 1904. *King Leopold's Rule in Africa.* London: Heinemann.

———. [1906] 1969. *Red Rubber: The Story of the Rubber Slave Trade Flourishing on the Congo in the Year of Grace 1906.* New York: Negro Universities Press.

Mwansasu, Bismarck, and Cranford Pratt (eds.). 1979. *Towards Socialism in Tanzania.* Toronto: University of Toronto Press.

Mworoha, Émile (ed.). 1987. *Histoire du Burundi: Des origines à la fin du XIXe siècle.* Paris: Hatier.

Nairn, Tom. 1977. *The Break-Up of Britain: Crisis and Neo-Nationalism.* London: Verso.

———. 1982. "Nationalism and 'Development.'" In Hamza Alavi and Theodor Shanin (eds.), *Introduction to the Sociology of "Developing Societies."* New York: Monthly Review Press.

Ndikunkiko, Léonidas. 1992. "Les réfugiés burundais vivant en Tanzanie visitent les villages de Gatete et de Nyakazi." *Le Renouveau du Burundi,* 5 June, pp. 1, 2.

Ndoricimpa, Léonidas, and Claude Guillet. 1983. *Les tambours du Burundi.* Bujumbura: Centre de la Civilisation Burundaise, Ministère de la Jeunesse, des Sports et de la Culture.

———, (eds.). 1984. *L'arbre-mémoire: Traditions orales du Burundi.* Paris: Karthala; Bujumbura: Centre de la Civilisation Burundaise.

Nenquin, Jacques. 1967. *Contributions to the Study of the Prehistoric Cultures of Rwanda and Burundi.* Tervuren, Belgium: Musée Royal de l'Afrique Centrale.

Newbury, Catharine. 1988. *The Cohesion of Oppression: Clientship and Ethnicity in Rwanda, 1860–1960.* New York: Columbia University Press.

Nietzsche, Friedrich. [1889] 1968. *Twilight of the Idols.* Translated by R.J. Hollingdale. Harmondsworth, England: Penguin.

———. [1873–1876] 1983. *Untimely Meditations.* Translated by R.J. Hollingdale. Cambridge: Cambridge University Press.

Nindi, B.C., and M.C.Y. Mbago. 1983. "A Final Report of a Survey of Zaireans Living along Lake Tanganyika." Dar-es-Salaam: Departments of Sociology and Statistics, University of Dar-es-Salaam. Mimeographed.

Nobel, Peter (ed.). 1983. *Meeting of the OAU-Secretariat and Voluntary Agencies* on *African Refugees: Arusha, March 1983*. Uppsala: Scandinavian Institute of African Studies.

———. 1987. *Refugees and Development in Africa*. Uppsala: Scandinavian Institute of African Studies.

Norconsult/NORAD. 1982. "Kigoma Water Master Plan, United Republic of Tanzania, Ministry of Water and Energy." Sandvika, Norway: Norconsult; Oslo, Norway: NORAD.

Northrup, David. 1988. *Beyond the Bend in the River: African Labor in Eastern Zaire, 1865–1940*. Athens: Ohio University Center for International Studies.

Norwood, Frederick. 1969. *Strangers and Exiles: A History of Religious Refugees*. Vols. 1 and 2. New York: Abingdon Press.

Ogbru, Benjamin. 1983. *Tanzania Refugee Caseload Survey*. Dar-es-Salaam: UNHCR.

Orwell, George. 1968. *As I Please 1943–1945*, edited by Sonia Orwell and Ian Angus. New York: Harcourt Brace Jovanovich.

Oxfam America. 1984. *Facts for Action: World Refugee Crisis, Winning the Game* 6: 1–8.

Parkin, David (ed.). 1975. *Town and Country in Central and Eastern Africa*. London: Oxford University Press.

Parmentier, Richard J. 1987. *The Sacred Remains: Myth, History, and Polity in Belau*. Chicago: University of Chicago Press.

Perlez, Jane. 1988. "Burundi Reports 5,000 Are Dead in Resurgence of Tribal Warfare." *New York Times*, 23 August, 1.

Pesonen, Hannu. 1989. "Vaikea Kotiinpaluu." *Suomen Kuvalehti*, 6 January, 100–1.

Peters, Edward. 1985. *Torture*. Oxford: Basil Blackwell.

Philippart de Foy, Guy. 1984. *Les Pygmées de l'Afrique centrale*. Roquevaire: Éditions Parenthèses.

Piscatori, James. 1986. *Islam in a World of Nation-States*. Cambridge: Cambridge University Press and the Royal Institute of International Affairs.

Pitterman, Shelly. 1984. "A Comparative Survey of Two Decades of International Assistance to Refugees in Africa." *Africa Today* 31(1): 25–54.

Pratt, Jeff. 1980. "A Sense of Place." In R.D. Grillo (ed.), *"Nation" and "State" in Europe: Anthropological Perspectives*. London and New York: Academic Press.

Proudfoot, Malcolm J. 1957. *European Refugees: 1939–1952*. London: Faber and Faber.

Ramirez, Francis, and Christian Rolot. 1985. *Histoire du cinéma colonial au Zaïre, au Rwanda et au Burundi*. Tervuren, Belgium: Musée Royal de l'Afrique Centrale.

Ranger, Terence. 1983. "The Invention of Tradition in Colonial Africa." In Eric Hobsbawm and Terence Ranger (eds.), *The Invention of Tradition*, 211–62. Cambridge: Cambridge University Press.

Ranger, Terence, and Colin Murray. 1981. Introduction to *Journal of Southern African Studies*, special issue on history and anthropology, 8(1): 1–15.

Renan, Ernest. 1990. "What Is a Nation?" In Homi Bhabha (ed.), *Nation and Narration*, 8–22. New York: Routledge.

Reyntjens, Filip. 1985. *Pouvoir et droit au Rwanda: Droit public et évolution*

*politique, 1916–1973.* Tervuren, Belgium: Musée Royal de l'Afrique
Centrale.

Reyntjens, Filip. 1990. "Du bon usage de la science: L'école historique
Burundo-Française." *Politique Africaine* 37: 107–12.

Richards, Audrey (ed.). 1960. *East African Chiefs: A Study of Political
Development in Some Uganda and Tanganyika Tribes.* London: Faber and
Faber.

Richter, Paul. 1994. "Rwanda Violence Stumps World Leaders." *Los Angeles
Times,* 30 April, p. A13.

Ritvo, Harriet. 1987. *The Animal Estate: The English and Other Creatures in
Victorian England.* Cambridge: Harvard University Press.

Roberts, Andrew (ed.). 1969. *Tanzania before 1900.* Nairobi: East African
Publishing House.

Robertson, Jennifer. 1988. "Furusato Japan: The Culture and Politics of Nostalgia."
*Politics, Culture, and Society* 1(4): 494–518.

Rodegem, F.M. 1960. "Le style oral au Burundi." *Congo-Tervuren* 4: 119–27.

———. 1973. "Burundi: La face cachée de la rébellion." *Intermédiaire,* 12–15 June,
15–19.

———. 1975. "Une forme d'humour contestataire au Burundi: Les wellerismes."
*Cahiers d'études Africaines* 14(3), 521–42.

———. 1976. "Quinze ans de vie politique au Burundi (1960–1975)." *Cultures et
développement: Revue internationale des sciences du développement*
(Université Catholique de Louvain) 8(4), 666–725.

———. 1978. *Documentation bibliographique sur le Burundi.* Bologna: EMI.

———. 1986. "Bibliographie du Burundi." Brussels: Editions Rundi.
Mimeographed.

———, (ed.). 1973. *Anthologie rundi.* Paris: Armand Colin.

Rodegem, F.M., and Jean Babfutwabo. 1961. *Sagesse Kirundi: Proverbes, dictons,
locutions usités au Burundi.* Tervuren, Belgium: Musée Royal du Congo
Belge.

Rosaldo, Renato. 1980. *Ilongot Headhunting 1883–1974: A Study in Society and
History.* Stanford, CA: Stanford University Press.

Rowlands, Michael. 1988. "Repetition and Exteriorisation in Narratives of
Historical Origins." *Critique of Anthropology* 8(2), 43–62.

Rubin, Neville. 1974. "Africa and Refugees." *African Affairs* 73, 290–311.

Ruhumbika, Gabriel (ed.). 1974. *Towards Ujamaa: Twenty Years of TANU
Leadership.* Kampala, Nairobi, Dar-es-Salaam: East African Literature Bureau.

Rushdie, Salman. 1991. *Imaginary Homelands: Essays and Criticism, 1981–1991.*
London: Granta Books.

Sahlins, Marshall. 1981. *Historical Metaphors and Mythical Realities: Structure in
the Early History of the Sandwich Islands Kingdom.* Ann Arbor: University of
Michigan Press.

———. 1985. *Islands of History.* Chicago: University of Chicago Press.

Said, Edward. 1978. *Orientalism.* New York: Pantheon.

———. 1986a. *After the Last Sky: Palestinian Lives.* New York: Pantheon.

———. 1986b. "On Palestinian Identity: A Conversation with Salman Rushdie."
*New Left Review* 160, 63–80.

Sartre, Jean-Paul. 1960. *Critique de la raison dialectique.* Paris: Gallimard.

————. 1963. *Search for a Method.* Translated by Hazel E. Barnes. New York: Vintage.

Saul, John. 1979. *The State and Revolution in Eastern Africa.* New York and London: Monthly Review Press.

Sayinzoga, Jean. 1982. "Les réfugiés rwandais—quelques repères historiques et réflexions socio-politiques." *Genève-Afrique* 20(1), 49–72.

Scandinavian Institute of African Studies. 1981. *The Recommendations from the Arusha Conference on the African Refugee Problem.* Uppsala: Scandinavian Institute of African Studies.

Scherer, J.H. 1960a. "The Ha." In Audrey Richards (ed.), *East African Chiefs*, 212–28. London: Faber and Faber.

————. 1960b. "The Ha of Tanganyika." *Anthropos* (Vienna) 54, 841–904.

————. 1962. "Le Buha." In Marcel D'Hertefelt, Albert Trouwborst, and J.H. Scherer, *Les anciens royaumes de la zone interlacustre: Rwanda, Burundi, Buha.* Tervuren, Belgium: Musée Royal de l'Afrique Centrale.

Schoffeleers, Matthew. 1985. "Oral History and the Retrieval of the Distant Past." In Wim van Binsbergen and Matthew Schoffeleers (eds.), *Theoretical Explorations in African Religion*, 164–88. London: Routledge and Kegan Paul.

————. 1987. "Ideological Confrontation and the Manipulation of Oral History: A Zambesian Case." *History in Africa: A Journal of Method* 14, 257–73.

————. 1988. "Jan Vansina: Oral Tradition as History [Review]." *Journal of Southern African Studies* 14(3), 487–8.

Schrire, Carmel. 1984. "Wild Surmises on Savage Thoughts." In Carmel Schrire (ed.), *Past and Present in Hunter-Gatherer Studies.* Orlando, FL: Academic Press.

Sciolino, Elaine. 1994. "For West, Rwanda Is Not Worth the Political Candles." *New York Times*, 15 April, p. A3.

Seligman, C.G. 1934. *Egypt and Negro Africa: A Study in Divine Kingship.* London: George Routledge and Sons.

————. [1939] 1979. *The Races of Africa.* London: Oxford University Press.

Seton-Watson, Hugh. 1977. *Nations and States: An Enquiry into the Origins of Nations and the Politics of Nationalism.* London: Methuen.

Shawcross, William. 1984. *The Quality of Mercy.* London: Andre Deutsch.

————. 1989. "A Tourist in the Refugee World." In Carole Kismaric, *Forced Out: The Agony of the Refugee in Our Time*, 28–30. New York: Random House.

Sheriff, Abdul. 1987. *Slaves, Spices, and Ivory in Zanzibar.* London: James Currey.

Shils, Edward. 1957. "Primordial, Personal, Sacred, and Civil Ties." *British Journal of Sociology* 7, 113–45.

Shivji, Issa. 1976. *Class Struggles in Tanzania.* Dar-es-Salaam: Tanzania Publishing House.

————, (ed.). 1985. *The State and the Working People in Tanzania.* Dakar, Senegal: Codesria.

Simpson, John. 1939. *The Refugee Problem: Report of a Survey.* London: Oxford University Press.

Skinner, Elliott (ed.). 1973. *Peoples and Cultures of Africa.* Garden City, NY: Doubleday, Natural History Press.

Smith, Anthony. 1986. *The Ethnic Origins of Nations.* New York: Basil Blackwell.

Smith, Pierre (ed.). 1975. *Le récit populaire au Rwanda.* Paris: Armand Colin.

Smyth, Frank. 1994. "Blood Money and Geopolitics." *The Nation*, 2 May 1994, pp. 585–8.

Southey, Sara. 1984a. "Life in Mishamo." *Africa News*, 4 June, 3–4.

Southey, Sara. 1984b. "The Women of Mishamo." *Refugees* (UNHCR) 2: 11–2.

Spencer, Jonathan. 1990. "Writing Within: Anthropology, Nationalism, and Culture in Sri Lanka." *Current Anthropology* 31(3): 283–300.

Stearns, Scott. 1993. "Refugees Continue to Flee as UN Condemns Coup." *Christian Science Monitor*, n.d., p. 2.

Steichen, Edward. *The Family of Man: The Photographic Exhibition Created by Edward Steichen for the Museum of Modern Art.* New York: Simon and Schuster, 1955.

Stein, Barry. 1981a. "Understanding the Refugee Experience: Foundations of a Better Resettlement System." *Journal of Refugee Resettlement* 1(4): 62–71.

———. 1981b. "The Refugee Experience: Defining the Parameters of a Field of Study." *International Migration Review* 15(1): 320–30.

———. 1981c. "Documentary Note: Bibliography." *International Migration Review* 15(1/2): 331–93.

———. 1983. "The Commitment to Refugee Resettlement." In G. Loescher and J. Scanlan (eds.), *The Global Refugee Problem*, special issue, *Annals of the American Academy of Political and Social Science*, 187–201. Beverly Hills, CA: Sage.

Stepputat, Finn. 1993. *National Conflict and Repatriation: An Analysis of Relief, Power, and Reconciliation.* Centre for Development Research Project Proposal 93.4. Copenhagen: Centre for Development Research.

Stoessinger, John. 1956. *The Refugee and the World Community.* Minneapolis: University of Minnesota Press.

Tabori, Paul. 1972. *The Anatomy of Exile: A Semantic and Historical Study.* London: Harrap.

Tagalile, Attilio. 1993. "Taking the Lid off Burundi Power Game." *Daily News* (Tanzania). 12 November, p. 11.

Tambiah, Stanley J. 1985. *Culture, Thought, and Social Action: An Anthropological Perspective.* Cambridge: Harvard University Press.

———. 1986. *Sri Lanka: Ethnic Fratricide and the Dismantling of Democracy.* Chicago: University of Chicago Press.

Taussig, Michael. 1980. *The Devil and Commodity Fetishism in South America.* Chapel Hill: University of North Carolina Press.

———. 1987. *Shamanism, Colonialism, and the Wild Man.* Chicago: University of Chicago Press.

Taylor, Brian. 1969. *The Western Lacustrine Bantu.* London: International African Institute.

Taylor, Christopher. 1992. *Milk, Honey, and Money: Changing Concepts in Rwandan Healing.* Washington, DC: Smithsonian Institution Press.

TCRS (Tanganyika Christian Refugee Service). 1972. *Annual Report 1972.* Dar-es-Salaam: TCRS.

———. 1975. *Annual Report 1975.* Dar-es-Salaam: TCRS.

———. 1981. *Annual Report 1981.* Dar-es-Salaam: TCRS.

———. 1982. *Comments on Mid-Term Review for Mishamo, Rural Settlement for Burundi Refugees, Rukwa Region, Tanzania.* Dar-es-Salaam: TCRS.

———. 1983. *Annual Report 1983.* Dar-es-Salaam: TCRS.

———. 1984a. *Annual Report 1984.* Dar-es-Salaam: TCRS.

———. 1984b. *TCRS Twenty Years.* Dar-es-Salaam: TCRS.

———. 1985. *Annual Report 1985.* Dar-es-Salaam: TCRS.

———. n.d. (a). "Mishamo: A Guide Book of the Refugee Settlement." Dar-es-Salaam: TCRS. Mimeographed.

———. n.d. (b). "Village Handbook." Dar-es-Salaam: TCRS. Mimeographed.

———. n.d. (c). "Handbook for Motivation Workers." Dar-es-Salaam: TCRS. Mimeographed.

ten Horn, Joost, and René van der Velden. 1987. "Burundi: The Inside Story." *New African,* November, 34.

Thompson, Dorothy. 1938. *Refugees: Anarchy or Organization?* New York: Random House.

Tilly, Charles (ed.). 1975. *The Formation of National States in Western Europe.* Princeton, NJ: Princeton University Press.

Torgovnick, Marianna. 1990. *Gone Primitive: Savage Intellects, Modern Lives.* Chicago: University of Chicago Press.

Trevor-Roper, Hugh. 1983. "The Invention of Tradition: The Highland Tradition of Scotland." In Eric Hobsbawm and Terence Ranger (eds.), *The Invention of Tradition,* 15–41. Cambridge: Cambridge University Press.

Trouwborst, Albert. 1961. "L'organisation politique en tant que système d'échange au Burundi." *Anthropologica* (n.s.) 3(1): 1–17.

———. 1962. "Le Burundi." In Marcel D'Hertefelt, Albert Trouwborst, and J.H. Scherer, *Les anciens royaumes de la zone interlacustre méridionale: Rwanda, Burundi, Buha,* 113–69. Tervuren, Belgium Musée Royal de l'Afrique Centrale.

Turner, Victor. 1967. *The Forest of Symbols: Aspects of Ndembu Ritual.* Ithaca, NY: Cornell University Press.

UNHCR. 1977a. *Potential Sites Survey Report on Proposed New Refugee Settlements.* Dar-es-Salaam: UNHCR.

———. 1977b. *Settlement Planning and Development: Some Considerations.* Dar-es-Salaam: UNHCR.

———. 1979. *The Refugee Child.* UNHCR Projects for Refugee Children, International Year of the Child. Geneva: UNHCR.

———. 1981. *Managing Rural Settlements for Refugees in Africa: Proceedings of a Workshop on the Follow-Up to Arusha Recommendations on Rural Refugees in Africa.* Dar-es-Salaam: UNHCR.

———. 1982. *Mishamo, Rural Settlement for Barundi Refugees, Rukwa Region, Tanzania: Mid-Term Review.* Dar-es-Salaam: UNHCR.

———. 1991. *Images of Exile, 1951–1991.* Washington: UNHCR.

———. n.d. "The Majority of Refugees Are Women and Girls." Mimeographed.

UNHCR/TCRS. 1985. *Handover Documents for Mishamo Refugee Settlement, Mpanda District, Rukwa Region.* Dar-es-Salaam: UNHCR.

Université du Burundi, Faculté des Sciences Économiques et Administratives. 1983. *Enclavement et sous-développement au Burundi.* Bujumbura: F.S.E.A., Université du Burundi.

Vail, Leroy. 1989. *The Creation of Tribalism in Southern Africa.* London: James Currey.

Van Binsbergen, Wim. 1981. "The Unit of Study and the Interpretation of Ethnicity." *Journal of Southern African Studies* 8(1): 51–81.

Van Binsbergen, Wim, and Matthew Schoffeleers (eds.). 1985. *Theoretical Explorations in African Religion*. London: Routledge and Kegan Paul.

Van Gennep, Arnold. 1922. *Traité comparatif des nationalités*. Paris: Payot.

———. 1960. *The Rites of Passage*. Chicago: University of Chicago Press.

Van Onselen, Charles. 1976. *Chibaro: African Mine Labour in Southern Rhodesia 1900–1933*. London: Pluto Press.

Vanderdonckt, Anne. 1987. "Ce n'est qu'un putsch, mon Colonel!" *Pourquoi Pas?* 10 September, p. 46.

Vansina, Jan. 1961. *De la tradition orale: Essai de méthode historique*. Tervuren, Belgium: Musée royal de l'Afrique centrale.

———. 1962. "Introduction générale." In Marcel d'Hertefelt, Albert Trouwborst, and Johan H. Scherer, *Les anciens royaumes de la zone interlacustre méridionale: Rwanda, Burundi, Buha*, 1–7. Tervuren, Belgium: Musée Royal de l'Afrique Centrale.

———. 1965. *Oral Tradition: A Study in Historical Methodology*. Translated by H.M. Wright. Chicago: Aldine.

———. 1966. *Kingdoms of the Savanna*. Madison: University of Wisconsin Press.

———. 1972. *La légende du passé: Traditions orales du Burundi*. Tervuren, Belgium: Musée Royal de l'Afrique Centrale.

———. 1985. *Oral Tradition as History*. Madison: University of Wisconsin Press.

———. 1990. *Paths in the Rainforests: Toward a History of Political Tradition in Equatorial Africa*. Madison: University of Wisconsin Press.

Vidal, Claudine. 1985. "Situations ethniques au Rwanda." In Jean-Loup Amselle and Elikia M'bokolo (eds.), *Au coeur de l'ethnie: Ethnies, tribalisme et état en Afrique*, 11–48. Paris: Éditions La Découverte.

Vincent, Joan. 1971. *African Elite: The Big Men of a Small Town*. New York: Columbia University Press.

———. 1982. *Teso in Transformation: The Political Economy of Peasant and Class in Eastern Africa*. Berkeley and Los Angeles: University of California Press.

Wagner, Michelle. 1991. "Whose History Is History?" A History of the Baragane People of Buragane, Southern Burundi, 1850–1932." Ph.D. diss., University of Wisconsin.

Wagner, Roy. 1975. *The Invention of Culture*. Chicago: University of Chicago Press.

Walzer, Michael. 1970. *Obligations: Essays on Disobedience, War, and Citizenship*. Cambridge: Harvard University Press.

Waters, Tony. 1988. "Practical Problems Associated with Refugee Protection in Western Tanzania." *Disasters* 12(3): 189–95.

Watson, Catherine. 1991. "Exile from Rwanda: Background to an Invasion." Issue paper. Washington, DC: The United States Committee for Refugees.

———. 1992. "War and Waiting." *Africa Report*, November/December, 51–5.

Watts, Michael. 1992. "Space for Everything (A Commentary)." *Cultural Anthropology* 7(1): 115–29.

Weber, Max. 1978. Economy and Society: An Outline of Interpretive Sociology.

Vol. 2, edited by Guenther Roth and Claus Wittig. Berkeley and Los Angeles: University of California Press.

Weinstein, Warren. 1976. *Historical Dictionary of Burundi.* Metuchen, NJ: Scarecrow Press.

White, Luise. 1990. *The Comforts of Home: Prostitution in Colonial Nairobi.* Chicago: University of Chicago Press.

White, Robert. 1985. "Communicative and Educative—A Bible Study on Refugees and the Uprooted." Dar-es-Salaam: unpublished manuscript.

Williams, Gavin. 1986. "Rural Development: Partners and Adversaries." *Rural Africana* 25(26): 11–23.

Wilson, Monica. 1959. *Communal Rituals of the Nyakyusa.* London: Oxford University Press.

———. 1964. "Myths of Precedence." Mimeographed, n.d., received at Peabody Museum Library, Harvard University, 24 July 1964.

Wilson, William. 1976. *Folklore and Nationalism in Modern Finland.* Bloomington: Indiana University Press.

Wolf, Eric. 1982. *Europe and the People without History.* Berkeley and Los Angeles: University of California Press.

Wright, Patrick. 1985. *On Living in an Old Country: The National Past in Contemporary Britain.* London: Verso.

Zolberg, Aristide. 1983. "The Formation of New States as a Refugee-Generating Process." In G. Loescher and J. Scanlan (eds.), *The Global Refugee Problem,* special issue, *Annals of The American Academy of Political and Social Science,* 24–38. Beverly Hills, CA: Sage.

Zuure, Bernard, 1932a. "Poésie chez les Barundi." *Africa* 5(3): 344–54.

———. 1932b. *L'âme du Murundi: Études sur l'histoire des réligions.* Paris: Beauchesne.

———. 1949. "Les croyances des Barundi révélées par leurs contes." *Grands lacs* (Namur) 64(7): 11–14.

Comaroff, Jean. 1985. *Body of Power, Spirit of Resistance: The Culture and History of a South African People.* Chicago: University of Chicago Press.

Comaroff, John L. 1982. "Dialectical Systems, History and Anthropology." *Journal of Southern African Studies* 8: 143–72.

———. 1987. "Of Totemism and Ethnicity: Consciousness, Practice, and the Signs of Inequality." *Ethnos* 52: 301–23.

Comaroff, John, and Jean Comaroff. 1967. "The Madman and the Migrant: Work and Labor in the Historical Consciousness of a South African People." *American Ethnologist* 14(2): 191–209.

Comité de la solidarité pour la paix au Burundi. 1990. *Charte de retour au pays natal.* Geneva: Actes du colloque sur le problème des réfugiés burundais (24 November).

Communauté des Refugiés Burundais de Dakar. 1991. "Appel en faveur d'une paix durable au Burundi." Mimeographed.

Coquery-Vidrovitch, Catherine, and Henri Moniot. 1974. *L'Afrique noire de 1800 à nos jours.* Paris: Presses Universitaires France.

Cooper, Frederick. 1980. *From Slaves to Squatters: Plantation Labor and Agriculture in Zanzibar and Coastal Kenya.* New Haven: Yale University Press.

Coronil, Fernando, and Julie Skurski. 1991. "Dismembering and Remembering the Nation: The Semantics of Political Violence in Venezuela." *Comparative Studies in Society and History* 33(2): 288–337.

Corrigan, Philip, and Derek Sayer. 1985. *The Great Arch: English State Formation as Cultural Revolution.* Oxford: Basil Blackwell.

Coulson, Andrew. 1975. "Peasants and Bureaucrats." *Review of African Political Economy* 3: 51–5.

———. 1982. *Tanzania: A Political Economy.* Oxford: Clarendon Press.

Crapanzano, Vincent. 1980. *Tuhami: Portrait of a Moroccan.* Chicago: University of Chicago Press.

———. 1985. *Waiting: The Whites of South Africa.* New York: Random House.

Crepeau, Pierre. 1985. *Parole et sagesse: Valeurs sociales dans les proverbes du Rwanda.* Tervuren, Belgium: Musée Royal de l'Afrique Centrale.

Curtin, Philip, Steven Feierman, Leonard Thompson, and Jan Vansina. 1978. *African History.* Essex: Longman.

Daley, Patricia. 1991. "Gender, Displacement and Social Reproduction: Settling Burundi Refugees in Western Tanzania." *Journal of Refugee Studies* 4(3): 248–66.

———. n.d. "The Politics of the Refugee Crisis in Tanzania." Unpublished manuscript.

Daniel, E. Valentine. 1990. "The Individual in Terror." Paper presented at the annual meeting of the American Ethnological Society, 28 April, Atlanta, Georgia.

David, Henry. 1969. "Involuntary International Migration." *International Migration Review* 7(3/4), 67–105.

De Barrin, Jacques. 1986. "Kigoma, capitale de tous les trafics." *Le Monde,* 9 June, n.p. Mimeographed.

De Heusch, Luc. 1964. "Mythe et société féodale: Le culte kubandwa dans le Rwanda traditionnel." *Archives de Sociologie des Réligions* 18: 133–46.

———. 1966. *Le Rwanda et la civilisation interlacustre*. Brussels: Université libre de Bruxelles, Institut de Sociologie.

———. 1982. *Rois nés d'un coeur de vache*. Paris: Gallimard.

Deleuze, Gilles, and Felix Guattari. 1987. *A Thousand Plateaus: Capitalism and Schizophrenia*. Minneapolis: University of Minnesota Press.

D'Hertefelt, Marcel. 1962. "Le Rwanda." In Marcel D'Hertefelt, Albert Trouwborst, and J.H. Scherer, *Les anciens royaumes de la zone interlacustre méridionale: Rwanda, Burundi, Buha*. Tervuren, Belgium: Musée Royal de l'Afrique Centrale.

D'Hertefelt, Marcel, Albert Trouwborst, and Johan Herman Scherer. 1962. *Les anciens royaumes de la zone interlacustre méridionale: Rwanda, Burundi, Buha*. Tervuren, Belgium: Musée Royal de l'Afrique Centrale.

Dirks, Nicholas. 1992. Introduction to *Colonialism and Culture*, edited by Nicholas Dirks, 1–25. Ann Arbor: University of Michigan Press.

Doheny, Kevin, Fr. 1982. *Mishamo Refugee Settlement, Tanzania*. Unpublished manuscript.

Donham, Donald L. 1990. *History, Power, Ideology: Central Issues in Marxism and Anthropology*. New York: Cambridge University Press.

Donzelot, Jacques. 1979. *The Policing of Families*. New York: Pantheon.

Doob, L. 1964. *Patriotism and Nationalism*. New Haven: Yale University Press.

Douglas, Mary. 1966. *Purity and Danger: An Analysis of the Concepts of Pollution and Taboo*. London: Routledge and Kegan Paul.

Drakulić, Slavenka. 1992. "You Are Balkans, the World Tells Us, Mythological, Wild, Dangerous." *New York Times Magazine* 13 (September): 36–37, 68, 70.

Dreyfus, Hubert, and Paul Rabinow. 1983. *Michel Foucault: Beyond Structuralism and Hermeneutics*. Chicago: University of Chicago Press.

Du Bois, Victor. 1972. *To Die in Burundi*. American Universities Field Staff Reports, Central and Southern African Series 16(4). New York: American Universities Field Staff.

Economist Intelligence Unit. 1993. *EIU Country Profile, 1992–93: Burundi*, 56–76. London: The Economist Intelligence Unit.

Eisenstadt, S.N., and S. Rokkan. 1973. *Building States and Nations*. Beverly Hills, CA: Sage.

Eriksson, Lars-Gunnar, Goran Melander, and Peter Nobel (eds.). 1981. *An Analysing Account of the Conference on the African Refugee Problem: Arusha, May 1979*. Uppsala: Scandinavian Institute of African Studies.

Evans-Pritchard, Edward. 1940. *The Nuer*. Oxford: Oxford University Press.

———. 1976. *Witchcraft, Oracles, and Magic among the Azande*. Oxford: Oxford University Press.

Fabian, Johannes. 1983. *Time and the Other: How Anthropology Makes Its Object*. New York: Columbia University Press.

Fallers, Lloyd A. 1974. *The Social Anthropology of the Nation-State*. Chicago: Aldine.

Fanon, Franz. 1965. *The Wretched of the Earth*. New York: Grove.

Feldman, Allen. 1991. *Formations of Violence: The Narrative of the Body and Political Terror in Northern Ireland*. Chicago: University of Chicago Press.

Ferguson, James. 1993. "De-moralizing Economies: African Socialism, Scientific Capitalism, and the Moral Politics of Structural Adjustment." In Sally Falk

Lightning Source UK Ltd.
Milton Keynes UK
UKOW04f2322050116

265850UK00002B/121/P